CELEBRATING
the NEW MOON

Woman at Rosh Chodesh

CELEBRATING
the NEW MOON

A Rosh Chodesh Anthology

edited by

SUSAN BERRIN

JASON ARONSON INC.
Northvale, New Jersey
Jerusalem

First Jason Aronson Inc. softcover edition—1998

For credits, see page 323.

This book was set in 10 pt. Times Roman.

Library of Congress Cataloging-in-Publication Data

Celebrating the new moon : a Rosh Chodesh anthology / edited by Susan
  Berrin.
      p. cm.
  Includes bibliographical references and index.
  ISBN 1-56821-459-6 (hardcover)
  ISBN 0-7657-6022-3 (softcover)
  1. Rosh Hodesh. 2. Rosh Hodesh—Literary collections. 3. Jewish
women—Religious life. I. Berrin, Susan.
  BM695.N4C45 1996
  296.4'39—dc20
                                                                      95-15808

Manufactured in the United States of America. Jason Aronson Inc. offers books and cassettes. For information and catalog write to Jason Aronson Inc., 230 Livingston Street, Northvale, New Jersey 07647.

To
Noa Chana, Yosef Chaim, and Tzvia Raizel
Three bright stars in a new moon sky

Contents

II APPROACHES TO ROSH CHODESH

III THE CYCLE OF THE MONTH

IV POETRY, PRAYERS, SONGS, AND MEDITATIONS

Foreword

Blu Greenberg

"Life," a friend of mine was wont to say, "is like an Isaac Bashevis Singer novel. Those who were on top are now down, those who were down are now on top." If my friend had reached a bit deeper into her Jewish consciousness, she might have drawn an analogy to the minor Jewish holiday of Rosh Chodesh. For indeed, its anchor, the moon, is a symbol of the ebb and flow of life: death and disappearance, life and reemergence; peak periods and low ones: light overtaking darkness overtaking light: the cycles of nature paralleling the rhythms of human emotion, the sway in human fortune.

Had my friend further compared life to Rosh Chodesh rather than to a Singer novel, she would have benefited more so. For embedded in the former is a theme not found in the latter, a central idea about optimism. We find this most prominently in the curious timing of the ritual that marks Rosh Chodesh.

Logic would suggest that the ritual be timed to the full moon. Why not name each moon cycle at its richest showing, its most exuberant, most romantic moment? Why not celebrate in the beauty of a round moon and the safety of its glowing light?

Moreover, tradition confirms what logic suggests: the festivals of joy and deliverance, Sukkot and Pesach; the jubilant feast of Purim; the planting of tree saplings—all coincide with the fullness of the moon. It was not simply to light the pilgrims' way on their night journeys to the Temple in Jerusalem but rather that a bright and beaming moon seemed to fit the spirit of happiness and well-being, a feeling that *should*, in fact, accompany the celebration of the new month.

Nevertheless, the ritualization of the Rosh Chodesh was tied to the peak of night darkness rather than to the peak of its light, for the central message was—is—that each new month is a time again for optimism. Light follows darkness, hope returns; here's another chance, an opportunity for renewal. We don't even wait for the first sliver of light to appear;* we announce the new month in a state of total eclipse and celebrate it at the first glimmer of light—because we have faith. Rosh Chodesh says to us, "It's coming, it's coming, even though you can't see it." We have absolute trust that a force will light the darkness, that we shall not be abandoned. At life's darkest moment . . .

These are themes that not only Jews should carry in their hearts throughout their lives. These are universal messages. They suit the human condition in all of its varied forms. We Jews are good at getting across these kinds of messages to the world. In fact, we enjoy such a role. With gusto we tell the story of the Exodus, for ourselves and for all downtrodden people and all oppressors. Passover is the most widely celebrated holiday among Jews today, not because of the good food or intense preparation, but rather because of its core message—that God loves us and redeems us, lifts us up even from abject slavery. Even in the most horrible conditions, a savior will come to take us out. That message has served us well; it has also become the central theological underpinning of other monotheistic religions. The message of Rosh Chodesh, too, is one that we should be telling to all the world.

And yet, modern Jews, except those tied to the liturgy with regularity, have all but forgotten this holiday, have all but ignored its message. They search in other places for a whiff of optimism. Randomly ask one hundred Jews about this special day that comes eleven times a year, and ninety of them will offer a blank stare. There are far more Jewish bird-watchers than there are moon-watchers. Even those who mark the day liturgically (and those who bless the new moon on the Sabbath preceding its appearance) limit their celebration to exactly that—recitation of special prayers. No foods, no special rituals, no prohibitions that serve to define parameters, nothing that imparts a feeling of sacredness to the whole day.

This unceremoniousness is even more remarkable when one considers the extent of Rosh Chodesh celebration and meaning in ancient times. The sight-

---

*We don't wait, but in those months when Rosh Chodesh is celebrated two days, we do spot a glimmer of moonlight.

ing of the first sliver of moon from the mountaintop, the resounding signals from one mountain to another, the runners making haste to the court to give testimony, the system of relaying the news to distant communities. What excitement, what anticipation, what joy! Now all would know when to celebrate the holidays, when to take the firstfruits, when to begin the fast days! Now individuals would set aside work and bring special sacrifices in gratitude, marking the renewal of night's light.

Why did Rosh Chodesh awareness/appreciation lapse? Perhaps it had to do with the destruction of the Temple and end of the sacrificial cult; perhaps it was a natural fallout of the loss of a homeland and the need to calculate the Jewish calendar well in advance so that diaspora communities flung far and wide would know when to celebrate the holidays. Perhaps Jews of the diaspora simply found it easier to adopt the solar/ Christian calendar to which the lunar calendar had already been intercalated. (In fact, so well integrated have Jews become to a calendar not their own that if you were to ask again one hundred Jews the dates of their Hebrew birthday, ninety would not know.)

Perhaps Rosh Chodesh ran afoul of the ideology of modernity. The twin themes of vulnerability and faith were replaced by ideas of human resourcefulness, initiative, steadily up the ladder, independent of nature rather than being controlled by its vicissitudes.

But here we are with Rosh Chodesh being reclaimed in our times as a day to be known and a day to be celebrated: spread to greater numbers beyond traditional Jews who mark its occurrence in the formal prayers; and marked by more than the recitation of those prayers. It is a remarkable phenomenon, fully recorded in the very pages of this book. Like the internal meaning of the day itself, Rosh Chodesh is being renewed. It is flowing back into the collective Jewish consciousness to a place of meaning and spirit from which it has been absent for the past few centuries.

And just as we asked why it lapsed, we are bidden to ask why it is now coming out of obscurity. One cannot help but wonder, poised as we are at the lip of reemergence of a sacred day, why this is happening particularly in our times.

I believe there are two explanations. One has to do with living as a Jew after the Holocaust. With the dawn of modernity, Jews everywhere were lulled into thinking that we were no longer as vulnerable as we had been during the long diaspora. We had begun to believe that the messages of enlightenment regarding equality and dignity of humankind would offer us protection. We thought that an end to victimization was in sight and that we would find a secure place among the nations of the world.

But the cataclysm that was the Shoah flung us back into a different reality, a return to the state where vulnerability quietly rumbles beneath a surface of calm and well-being. Fifty years later—and forever after—we all carry within ourselves a lingering, terrifying memory of something that was worse than anything that went before it.

But we have also experienced in our flesh the miracle that light can follow total darkness. I speak, of course, of the miracle of the rebirth of Israel, the recreation of a homeland after centuries of longing. *The beginning of the flowering of our redemption*—that is the Rosh Chodesh of our collective lives.

Perhaps more than at any other moment in our history since the Exile, we feel the powerful sweep of the tides of history and the great swings of darkness and light in our national sensibility. So a day whose themes are about the vicissitudes of life and the hope and optimism for better times finds great resonance in present Jewish consciousness.

The second impetus for resurgence of this minor holiday comes from without — from the broad social movement that is feminism. In one sense, feminism can be seen as the waxing of women in the context of human history.

One consequence of a new self-perception of women is their relationship to spirituality. Women everywhere are engaged in the search for ritual—women of all faiths. In the past, women of traditional religions were one step removed from large parts of the ritual and liturgical enterprise. Men were right up close, in charge of the construction of sacred space and the organization of sacred time. In Judaism, women were not often seen or heard in the performance of communal rituals. Rather, they functioned as enablers or observers.

But women's sights have risen, their spiritual aspirations enlarged. In the process undertaken by Jewish women, it was only natural to connect the search to an existing holiday, to a day that already enjoyed a special association with women in traditional lore, one that was linked to women's unique biological cycle, the menses. The fact that it was a minor holiday in need of resuscitation made the match perfect.

Thus, when in 1973, the now classic article by Arlene Agus appeared, reclaiming Rosh Chodesh as a woman's holiday, it was both revolutionary and natural at the same time. The article was published in the first major anthology of Jewish feminism and the process was underway. Little by little, groups of women began to take a look at Rosh Chodesh, not a new look but in fact a first look by women of this generation. They began to gather to celebrate, to study, to feast, to pray, to talk. The numbers were small, but the momentum kept growing.

This remarkable book is the next milestone in the process. It records not only the history and halacha of Rosh Chodesh but also its unfolding during the past two decades; it offers a blueprint for ways to celebrate Rosh Chodesh. In that sense, this work is a Rosh Chodesh siddur and anthology all in one. And a measure of how the climate of community has changed—less suspicion and more receptiveness to women's new celebration and ritual—is the fact that this volume of ritual is edited by a woman, among the first of its kind in Jewish history.

And yet, were we to close on this note, we would be ignoring a significant dilemma, one raised by the very breakthrough. Reclaiming Rosh Chodesh as a woman's holiday begets its own question: is it right and proper for women to arrogate to themselves a special holy day? Especially after the Shoah, where no distinction was made between male and female, young and old, traditional and secular, should the day whose implicit message is about swings in nature and history be specially inclined toward women? And if the reverse were true, if Jewish men now placed a special lien on a Jewish holiday, would it sit well with contemporary women?

Somehow the answer lies in the dialectical tension. True, there is something special about the association of women with Rosh Chodesh. One cannot deny it. But that fact does not at all diminish the sense of Rosh Chodesh as a holiday for everyone. Happily, Susan Berrin, the editor of this volume, has managed to maintain the perfect balance here. What comes through these pages is the joy of a recreated holiday, one that is special in many ways to women, yet does not make men feel pushed aside, neither those who are potential newcomers to it nor those who have marked the day faithfully for generations. The contributions of both women and men in these pages, the perceptions of women and men, and the celebrations all add up to a wonderful paradigm for past and future religious creativity. Women will not be seen as "taking the day"; rather, their special overlay will enlarge and carry along the whole community in its acts of sacred celebration.

We who live in this generation have been privileged to witness a renewal in many areas of Jewish life. The observance of Rosh Chodesh is but one of them. Reading these pages confirms what we often feel in our hearts: that the possibilities are endless, the flowering contagious, the elements interconnected, and the witnesses blessed to be part of this whole process of Jewish rebirth.

Rabbi Joseph B. Soloveitchik takes the lesson of the new moon further and onto a much larger canvas. In *Halachic Man*, Soloveitchik reflects on the inner meaning of the ceremony of *kiddush levanna* (the sanctification of the moon), the essence of which is a prayer for the cosmos. The lawful waning and waxing of the moon, says Soloveitchik, is a symbol of the defectiveness and replenishment of creation. Thus, in this prayer over the sliver of new moon, human beings express their hope for the perfection of creation and repair of the defects in the world, an enterprise in which human beings are partners with God.

The pages that follow, which confirm the renewal of Rosh Chodesh, should be read then as a symbol of something larger: not only as part of a movement to replenish Jewish spirituality, or merely as a symbol of restoration of women to their rightful place as coequal partners in Jewish life and faith, but also as part of a universal movement for *tikkun olam*—perfection of the cosmos and redemption of human history. In this way, Jews continue to witness that we are all part of a cosmic plan in which life will someday reach its fullest realization.

This book is both a small *tikkun* and part of that larger *tikkun*. May we all learn from it the lesson of Rosh Chodesh, of a never-tiring, never-ending renewal that illuminates the world with light and hope.

Acknowledgments

I began to think about collecting material for a Rosh Chodesh anthology during the summer of 1992. I was attracted to the holiday because of its deep symbolism: the recurring moon, hope drawn from its waning and waxing, the illumination of its light. While I felt drawn to the holiday when I began this project, studying and understanding its subtlety and the connections between the moon, women, and Rosh Chodesh have given me an entirely new awareness and appreciation for it, now honoring it as a most meaningful moment in the calendar cycle.

As I sought out secondary sources on Rosh Chodesh, I found little written material available. There were so many strands to this holiday—if only they could be woven as a text into a beautiful tapestry. And so, I offer this book as that tapestry. I hope it does justice to the sentiment, the nuance, the depth of Rosh Chodesh. I would like to thank many people who have helped to weave the tapestry, some with threads visible to the eye and others with threads visible only to the heart:

Rick Kool for making endless computer house calls and bringing the world of technology to my study.

Lindy Shortt for delivering to me endless faxes and worrying for me when they didn't arrive.

Rabbi Daniel Siegel for his generous help with the Hebrew texts in the appendix.

Hanna Tiferet Siegel, the sweetest spirit-soul, for introducing me many years ago to Jewish feminist spirituality.

Rabbi Vicki Hollander, Suzanne Kort, Martin Levin, Rabbi Debra Robbins, Deena Roskies, and Louis Sutker for their critical readings of various parts of the manuscript.

Janet Warner, my editor at Jason Aronson Inc., whose editorial insights bless this book.

Vera Berrin, my mother, whose support and encouragement have been a life-long gift.

My husband, Victor Reinstein, who creates with me a home filled with books and a deep respect for learning. We have shared hundreds of hours mulling over ideas and mining sources concerning Rosh Chodesh. Victor has also read and critiqued much of this manuscript. His insight has been extraordinarily helpful.

The untold many women who have encouraged me with letters and telephone calls and provided me with wonderful sources of insight and information. From here in charming Victoria, never before the hub of Jewish life, I felt connected with Jewish women around the globe.

And to all of the contributors to this book, without whom this would be a very slim volume, *thank you*.

Introduction

Rosh Chodesh is a holiday marking each month's new moon. This anthology was conceived as a means to offer writings about Rosh Chodesh that are educational, inspirational, scholarly, programmatic, entertaining, and insightful; writings that teach tradition while inspiring innovation; writings from a variety of women and men, representing many writing styles, relationships to Judaism, and levels of observance. It is my hope that this "sourcebook," which waxed without waning over the months of two years, will reflect the diversity and richness of its contributors.

Rosh Chodesh raises many themes, some particular to women. This collection addresses each nuance of Rosh Chodesh, from the historical to the contemporary; from the traditional to the feminist and deconstructionist. I have attempted to understand Rosh Chodesh in a variety of ways: as a symbol of renewal, as a women's covenant, as a marking of time, and as a reminder of cyclical development and focus. Rosh Chodesh is a forever-returning opportunity for spiritual development and healing, a time to look inward and skyward, an occasion to contemplate the reflection of oneself in the moon's crescent light.

The commandment to observe the new moon as a holiday came on the eve of the departure from Egypt. It was given to the Israelites as they were preparing for freedom:

הַחֹדֶשׁ הַזֶּה לָכֶם רֹאשׁ חֳדָשִׁים רִאשׁוֹן הוּא לָכֶם לְחָדְשֵׁי הַשָּׁנָה׃

"This renewal of the moon shall be for you a beginning of new moons; it shall be for you the first among the months of the year." (Exodus 12:2)

This verse includes two specific commandments: first, that each month will be marked by the physical viewing of the moon, and second, that the months of the year will be counted from Nisan, the month of our liberation from Egypt.[1] Emphasizing the word *lahem*, "to you," Samson Raphael Hirsch points out that the renewal is for the people, newly liberated from slavery, that they should see "the sickle of the moon struggling to emerge from darkness into renewed light" as a way of understanding their own lives: "This is to be the model for your own conduct! Even as the moon renews itself by the law of nature, so you, too, should renew yourselves, but of your own free will."[2] What we are asked to establish is not an astronomical cycle of months, but a monthly cycle of personal and community renewal.

The renewing moon is a sign to the desert wanderers that God will renew the People. Are we not all, in some way, desert wanderers? Are we not asked at the Pesach seder to see ourselves as if we personally were leaving Egypt? Like the rainbow after the Flood, the crescent moon is a sign of God's presence and renewing powers. Both events were crystallizing moments of faith and demanded a powerful, covenantal sign. The moon became that covenant of hope.

In any covenant, a genuine commitment to partnership is essential. Observing the new moon, the miracles of the seasons, and the richness inherent in our holidays reminds us that it is only within partnership with the Creator that the gifts and cycles of nature are sustained.

Maimonides, the medieval Jewish scholar, sees the returning moon as renewing moments of the year.[3]

"Chodshei haShanah *hem* Chodshei halevana"

חדשי השנה הם חדשי הלבנה

The renewing moments of the year, *they* are the renewals of the moon.

This quality of renewal implied in the cyclical nature of the moon is not limited to Judaism. Mircea Eliade, the French philosopher and scholar of comparative religion, wrote:

> The sun is always the same, always itself, never in any sense "becoming." The moon, on the other hand, is a body which waxes, wanes and disappears, a body whose existence is subject to the universal law of becoming, of birth and death. . . . For three nights the starry sky is without a moon. But this "death" is followed by a rebirth: the "new moon." . . . This perpetual return to its beginning, and this ever-recurring cycle makes the moon the heavenly body above all others concerned with the rhythms

of life. . . . It might be said that the moon shows us our human condition; that in a sense we look at ourselves, and find ourselves anew in the life of the moon.[4]

There is a wisdom to be found in the changing form of the moon. The moon, of course, does not change. Only its appearance to us on earth changes. In fact, we do not actually see the moon, but rather the light of the sun reflecting on the moon. Because of this phenomenon, the moon represents light within darkness, hope within despair, knowing within the unknown.

Rosh Chodesh occurs at the moment of the *molad* or birth of the moon. At this moment, the moon is directly between the sun and the earth[5] and is invisible to us. Six hours after the *molad*, when a fraction of light reflects off of the moon, it begins to become visible.

As is so often the case in Jewish life, this moment of beginning is signaled with precision and fanfare. The Torah provides several clues to the importance of the holiday and the manner of its observance. Rosh Chodesh was declared a festive day, a day to include sacrifices similar to those offered on other festivals. "And in your new moons ye shall present a burnt-offering unto the Lord: two young bullocks, and one ram, seven he-lambs of the first year without blemish."[6] The legacy of these sacrifices is the Rosh Chodesh musaf, which also serves as a way of offering thanksgiving for the return of the moon. Preparing a festive meal, wearing new clothes, and eating new seasonal fruit were other parts of the observance of Rosh Chodesh. While it was deemed a festive day, there were no general prohibitions, although some restrictions on work may have been levied.

The festive nature of Rosh Chodesh in biblical times was also marked by the blowing of the *shofar*. "Also in the day of your gladness, and in your appointed seasons, and in your new moons, ye shall blow with the trumpets over your burnt-offerings, and over the sacrifices of your peace-offerings; and they shall be to you for a memorial before your God: I am the Lord your God."[7] Today, the *shofar* is only blown on Rosh Chodesh Elul and onward through the month, to signal the process of preparation for the Days of Awe.

In ancient times, the new month began with the actual sighting of the new moon. Visually observing the new moon, therefore, was crucial, for it was incumbent on all Jewish communities to observe holidays at the same time, and the holidays were based on the date of the new moon. An ingenious system of sighting the crescent and giving testimony of the sighting before a court developed during the Mishnaic period. Two witnesses to the sighting were required, who had to be known and reputable. They were called before the *Bet Din* (a rabbinic court of three judges), and each witness was separately questioned (with the older witness interrogated first) about the exact location and details of the moon's appearance. "Relate how thou sawest the moon: in front of the sun? To the north of it or to the south of it? How high was it? And in what direction was it leaning? And how wide was it?"[8] If the testimonies were identical, then it was declared to be Rosh Chodesh. The remaining testimonies of witnesses were also heard so that they would not leave the *Bet Din* unheard and disappointed. They were always encouraged to return the next month.

The beginning of the month was then communicated to more distant communities by setting flares on the hilltops around Jerusalem. From mountaintop to mountaintop, the flares would spread word of the holiday. This method was later changed because of problems with the Samaritans, who deliberately set fires at incorrect times to mislead the people. An alternate system of runners to spread the word was then introduced.[9]

The talmudic period saw a greater codification of laws surrounding the observance of Rosh Chodesh. It is in the Talmud that we see for the first time reference to Rosh Chodesh as a special holiday for women. "The Talmud rules that work is permitted on the new moon but describes a tradition that women abstain from work on the day. Later sources explain that on this semi-festival, partial abstention from labor was a reward to the righteous women who refused to surrender their jewelry for the creation of the Golden Calf."[10]

There are many sources in our vast compendia of *Sifrei Kodesh*, holy books, that address Rosh Chodesh and the moon. Following are two examples: "Queen Esther, who brought light to Israel, is likened to the Moon which enables people to walk and rejoice when it illuminates darkness."[11] "Whoever pronounces the benediction over the new moon in its due time, welcomes, as it were, the presence of the *Shechinah* [female aspect of the Divine]."[12]

The blessing of the new moon was seen as a way of bringing oneself closer to God. Food also played an important role in the observance of Rosh Chodesh. In the haftarah for *Machar HaChodesh* (chanted when Rosh Chodesh begins on Saturday evening), we get a glimpse of the festive meal. Jonathan warns David of the king's anger toward him and bids him not to come to the new moon meal.[13]

During the Babylonian period, the Rosh Chodesh meal also marked the festive atmosphere of the holiday: "The type of food to be eaten is specified. The meal would take place at night. Fasting was prohibited on Rosh Chodesh."[14] Manuscripts found in the Cairo Genizah reveal that a special *kiddush* was also included during the meal.[15] Today, the additions to the *Birkat HaMazon* (blessings after a meal) honor Rosh Chodesh while marking its ancient roots as a festive holiday.

The eighteen chapters in this book, as well as the poems, songs, and prayers, constitute a compendium of writings by a very diverse group of people. The subject matter often defines the style: some are scholarly, while others are straightforward and practical.

Arlene Agus offers her classic piece from 1976, "This Month Is for You," which outlines the traditional sources for understanding Rosh Chodesh as a women's holiday ("Examining Rosh Chodesh"). Leah Novick's chapter ("The History of Rosh Chodesh and Its Evolution as a Women's Holiday") provides a detailed accounting of the development of Rosh Chodesh as a women's holiday. She traces the observance of Rosh Chodesh from its most ancient sources through to the nineteenth century, always with an eye to the spiritually unusual and interesting.

A visual diagram or guide to the texts associated with Rosh Chodesh can be found in Appendix A. This chart provides a visual outline to many, but certainly not all, of the textual sources mentioned in this anthology. It is provided as an aid to understanding the nature of Jewish text; its depth and breadth.

Rosh Chodesh as a Mapping of Time

Time, and its marking, form an essential cornerstone of observing holiness. The importance of time and its cycles within Jewish life has been the subject of many scholarly and inspirational works. We have daily cycles and cycles of the week, month, and year; cycles of every seven years and every forty-nine years. While contributing to the sense of continuity in Jewish life, these cycles also provide an ongoing way of observing and participating in the richness of Jewish living.

The wealth of blessings and the thematic patterns around each of these cycles centers us within our lives. Daily *davening* sets a mood for the day, a tone, for keeping life in perspective by thanking God for the miracles even when life looks bleak.

The weekly cycle culminates in Shabbat. On our home bulletin board is posted a bumper sticker reading, "Hang in There, Shabbat Is Coming," which reminds us that before long, we will arrive at the "sanctuary in time." Even Shabbat itself has a mood-cycle: beginning with *Kabbalat Shabbat,* which is expansive in its welcoming of the extra Shabbat soul, followed by Shabbat morning, which is festive and celebratory, and Shabbat afternoon, which brings us wistfully to *Havdalah* and departure.

The monthly cycle parallels the moon's waxing and waning; its blessings are many. A section of this book is devoted to the cycle of the month: in "Anticipating the New Moon," Victor Hillel Reinstein writes with scholarly depth about the development of traditions associated with *Birkat HaChodesh,* the announcing of the new moon on *Shabbat Mevorchim* (the Shabbat prior to

Rosh Chodesh); Shefa Gold introduces her sond, "Dark Rays of the Moon,"
with a fascinating description of *Yom Kippur Katan*, which is a mini holiday
falling on the day before Rosh Chodesh and serves as a spiritual preparation
for the new month ("The Dark Rays of the Moon—Yom Kippur Katan as
Preparation for Rosh Chodesh"); and Geela-Rayzel Raphael explores the traditional *Kiddush Levana* and then creates a new ceremony to sanctify the
moon "Kiddush HaLevana").

One of my favorite local storytellers, Jack Gardner, who is originally from
the town of Stary Sambor in Poland, recounts that *Mechoidesh Levona* (Kiddush Levana), the sanctifying of the moon, occurred when the

> moon was full out and not cloudy. A hundred people would gather out-
> side the shul with the prayers written on cardboard signs. After the *dav-
> ening*, we would all turn to each other saying, "Shoilem Aleichum,
> Aleichum Shoilem." If it was cloudy and the *levona* disappeared behind
> a cloud, we would have to stop. One of the men, we called him Yudel
> Chsvak because Chsvak means nail, always joked that we should nail
> the *levona* in place so we wouldn't have to disrupt our *davening*!

There is also a cycle of months, in which Nisan is the first of the months,
while Tishrei, the seventh month, becomes the first month of the new year.

Our yearly cycle is lunar-solar based. The months follow the moon, while
the seasons and festivals follow the sun. In a brilliantly formulated intercalation, the secret of which was purportedly given to Moshe,[16] the Jewish year
comprises twelve months, except for a leap year. During a leap year, which
occurs seven times within nineteen years, an extra month—Adar Sheini or
Adar II—is added to the calendar. The system of intercalation, in which the
lunar and solar cycles are balanced, is a cycle of nineteen years. It is by the
adjusting of these cycles that the holidays remain in their seasons (according
to Israeli seasons, Pesach in the spring, Sukkot in the fall). If the lunar and
solar cycles were not adjusted, the holidays would continuously "float."

Beyond the yearly cycle, the Torah declares each seventh year as a sabbatical year, when the earth rests and replenishes itself. And every forty-ninth
year, beginning on Yom Kippur, is a Jubilee Year, during which loans are forgiven, land reverts to its original owner, and slaves are freed.

Each new moon brings the promise of a full moon. While Rosh Chodesh is
observed as the covenant of the moon's reappearance, the full moon is noted
for several holidays, including Tu B'Shvat, Purim, and two of the three pilgrimage festivals: both Sukkot and Pesach fall on the full moon. Only Shavuot
falls neither on the new or full moon. Shavuot arrives when we are focused on

counting days—the forty-nine days of the Omer—rather than observing the phases of the moon.

As each cycle ends, it immediately begins anew. Just as we celebrate the finishing and beginning of reading the Torah at Simchat Torah, never to be out of the cycle, so, too, in all cycles of Jewish life. We are never outside of the cyclical framework: we are always within an ongoing frame of time. "The Rabbis saw in the letters of the words <u>Roshei</u> <u>Chodshim</u>, heads of the months, the word <u>rechem</u>, womb. The circle of the year is a womb in which the seasons, the earth, the festivals, the sacred stories are born anew, again and again."[17]

Within the year are many months. Appendix C includes a brief look at each month as a way of understanding its gifts, the qualities inherent to that particular cycle of the moon, and the spiritual focus of that Rosh Chodesh observance ("Focal Points for Each Month"). These monthly foci are included as a way of connecting the particular months of the year with the rhythm of the moon. They may be used as a resource for the Rosh Chodesh Ceremony also found in the appendices. The ceremony is created as a skeleton of observance, waiting to be dressed by the women and men who use it. Rosh Chodesh, as a holiday marking both constancy and variability, demands a ritual that is both fluid and solid. The ceremony, therefore, remains open to the creative and elaborative processes of its participants. It provides constancy of form, while allowing for variability in content.

The cycle of the moon mirrors women's body cycles. Menstruation, which means "moon change,"[18] is women's reflection of the moon. It is a way to connect our experiences of change with the cycles of all women who have come before us. In the course of one menstrual cycle, which corresponds to the twenty-nine and a half day revolution of the moon, a woman may experience her own personal waxing and waning of energy and desire.[19] Robin Zeigler ("My Body, My Self and Rosh Chodesh") has written an account of the lessons we learn about change and continuity from women's cycles. She explores the relationship between women's cycles and transformations and the cycle of the moon. Among the Ditidadxht, a Native Canadian nation not far from my home, a girl's first menstrual cycle generally occurs on the full moon. For her first menstrual period, the young girl is taken by several of the elder women into seclusion, only to be returned to her village at the next new moon. During this time, she is coached and taught about her body and the physical changes that are beginning to take place. Many Native Peoples adhere to the belief that a menstruating woman has "supreme strength," and she is therefore discouraged from ritual performance, lest in her strength she damage any sacred objects. Penina Adelman's *midrash* (illuminating story), "The Origins of Rosh Chodesh," recounts the first menstrual cycle of the desert-wandering women. At the new moon, when the entire party of women began to menstruate, they secluded themselves in the "Wadi of the Moon." For a week they sang and told stories, refreshed themselves with fragrant spices, and bathed in the moon's light.

The Rosh Chodesh moon, as a symbol of covenant—a symbol of transition and change—lends itself as a time to mark rites of passage. Rosh Chodesh gatherings have become celebrations of life's transitions: celebrating babies entering the covenant, bat mitzvah, and aging. Shonna Husbands-Hankin shares with us the ritual she created to honor her daughter's "first moon-cycle," in which friends gathered at Rosh Chodesh with flowers and blessings to welcome the young girl-woman with womanly wisdom ("New Moon–First Moon Celebration"). The new moon, as a metaphor for rebirth, suggests that each of life's stages be approached as a sacred time.

Teachings of Rosh Chodesh

Sh'mot 12:2 has inspired a great deal of commentary and analysis. Why does the commandment to observe the new moon, Rosh Chodesh, come when we are being redeemed from slavery? We learn that only as a free people are we able to reckon the months: God wanted the months to be counted from Nisan in order to count the months from liberation, in order that we count as a free people. Rabbi Meir commented, "The redemption will be Mine and yours, as if to say: 'I will be redeemed with you.'"[20] After the experience of slavery, God, too, was in need of redemption. In the Shabbat Rosh Chodesh Musaf Amidah, we find the line, "In love God, You have given us Shabbat for rest and New Moon Festivals for atonement." Rosh Chodesh offers us a chance each month to contemplate and review our behavior and our relationships with others and the community: to seek atonement in renewal and renewal in atonement.

This anthology includes several chapters that offer new teachings on Rosh Chodesh. Hillel Goelman's piece on the B'nai Yissasschar opens a window into the teachings of the Dynover Rebbe ("Kiddush HaChodesh"). The rebbe's insights into the flow of time and its connection with Divine presence are deeply revealing. The chapter gives us a taste of the chasidic/kabbalistic tradition of mining a text for its deepest, most remote and hidden meanings.

Roselyn Bell writes about Hallel, the Praises of God sung on Rosh Chodesh. Her ruminations on the psalms that comprise Hallel and the relationship of these psalms to women's lives is illuminating. Jane Litman, Judith Glass, and Simone Wallace analyze the midrashim (illuminating stories) upon which Rosh Chodesh has been connected to women and offer us critical, thought-provoking insights into this women's holiday ("Rosh Chodesh: A Feminist Critique and Reconstruction"). They have created a new ritual based on the text of Marge Piercy's poem, "At the new moon: Rosh Hodesh," emphasizing a nonlinear model of

understanding women's lives that reflects the cyclical nature of (even postmenopausal) woman's being.

A Window into Women's Lives

"The symbol which above all others has stood throughout the ages for woman,
not in her likeness to man . . . but in her difference from man, distinctively
feminine in contrast to his masculinity, is the moon. In poetry, both modern
and classical, from time immemorial in myth and legend, the moon has represented the woman's deity, the feminine principle."[21] It is fitting, therefore, that
Rosh Chodesh be a window into the lives of women.

Tkhines, women's devotional prayers, were a sixteenth- to early nineteenth-
century liturgical form of prayer. Tracy Guren Klirs's chapter "Tkhines for Rosh
Chodesh" portrays the varied nature of women's religious lives. The chapter
guides us through an understanding of the society in which women lived, the
precious desires of their homes, and their dreams and fears. We are treated to
the text and translation of several Yiddish *tkhines*, as well as a modern-day one
written by Geela-Rayzel Raphael. These Yiddish prayers of devotion address
the concerns of women by honoring the new moon in a language and demeanor
reflective of that era.

Susan Starr Sered introduces us to the new-moon customs of older Middle
Eastern Jewish women in Israel ("Rosh Chodesh among Older Sefardic Women").
She writes about the importance of simple rituals and the ways in which these
rituals help women to connect their deceased family members with luminous
Jewish ancestors. Of particular interest is the way in which the ordinary tasks
of a woman's life become holy.

Bonna Devora Haberman describes the courage and commitment of women
in Jerusalem (with an international network of support) who pray at the *Kotel*
(Western Wall of the Temple) on Rosh Chodesh mornings ("Nashot HaKotel").
I was honored to be part of this wonderful group for many Rosh Chodesh *tefillot*
(prayers) during a sabbatical in Jerusalem several years ago. The integrity and
perseverance with which this group approaches the legal framework and
halachic (Jewish law) issues is admirable. Bonna, one of the founding members of the group, writes clearly of its aim: to make the *Kotel* a place where
women can pray, sing, and read Torah freely and without fear.

Observing Rosh Chodesh takes many forms. As different as one woman is
to the next, so are the ways in which Rosh Chodesh is marked in our lives. The
"Annotated Directory of Rosh Chodesh Groups" is a listing of nearly a hundred groups around the globe (see appendices). Included for each listing is a
contact person and a brief description of the group. While some groups offer
similar programs, the diversity is also obvious. I am most gratified that the list-

ings include groups from such a wide variety of geographic areas and religious leanings. I envisioned the directory as a way of including the many women who observe Rosh Chodesh and I hope that it will serve as a clearinghouse for ideas and contacts between groups.

There are also three short chapters in the anthology that are reflections on observing Rosh Chodesh. The first, by Charlotte Atlung Sutker, describes simple ways of observing Rosh Chodesh through small, solitary acts ("Echad B'Yachad: Private Acts of Faith"). Norma Joseph describes Rosh Chodesh in her Orthodox *tefillah* group ("Reflections on Observing Rosh Chodesh with My Women's *Tefillah* Group"). Celia Szterenfeld shares some insight into observing Rosh Chodesh in the Southern Hemisphere, where Chanukah comes in the summer and Pesach in the fall. ("Bat Kol: Jewish Women in Brazil Observe Rosh Chodesh").

Ruth Berger Goldston and Merle Feld have contributed a chapter (after speaking with dozens of people in groups across the continent) detailing the joys, frustrations, and methods of creating and sustaining a Rosh Chodesh group ("Starting and Growing a Rosh Chodesh Group"). Both women have been involved in the evolution of several groups and provide some practical insight into growing and nurturing a home for Rosh Chodesh observance.

Ellen Brosbe suggests ways to teach children about the moon's cycles and the Jewish calendar. Her chapter, "Rosh Chodesh for Children," offers some very practical advice on how to use both formal curriculum materials and informal teaching experiences to enhance children's awareness of our lunar cycle.

Women's relationships with the moon, though varied in form, are a constant throughout time and place. The phases of the moon can be drawn metaphorically as the phases of our lives: the new moon as the young woman, the full moon as a woman in her middle years, and the waning moon as the aging woman. Each phase leads to another; even the waning moon moves toward a renewal.[22]

Rosh Chodesh and the Wells of Creativity

The inconstant nature of the moon bids us to look deeper. It teaches that all is not as it appears; it is neither static nor all-revealing. There are many ways of seeing, of reading, of being. Rosh Chodesh is a time to seek out these many ways. It is a time to reinvite women back into a Judaism that they left, being ignorant of its richness, disillusioned by its patriarchy, or disenfranchised by a rigid definition of community. For some women, participating in a Rosh Chodesh group is a first step, a first adult taste of the Jewish culinary feast: a step toward healing the wounds of disenfranchisement.

Rosh Chodesh has become a pivotal force in Jewish feminism. After campaigning first for "equal access" in Jewish religious and communal life and then working toward "the feminization of Judaism," many women are now trying to pursue and create Jewish rituals and observances that reflect a feminist gender base. Rosh Chodesh gatherings, whether focused on study or ritual, are becoming the creative wellsprings of such a feminist Judaism.

Rosh Chodesh is a moment to look toward messianic time, when the "light of the moon shall be as the light of the sun, and the light of the sun shall be sevenfold, as light of seven days."[23] The moon is our call to look deeper into the unknown parts of our lives, to contemplate the sense of awe and wonder within us and around us. And yet, contemplation in and of itself is not our goal: rather it is to connect our inner spiritual renewal with the world around us (so often in need of attention), to unite our act of prayer with an activism growing out of that prayer; it is to create a relationship between our observance of Rosh Chodesh and the concerns enumerated through our understanding of the month or season.[24]

The task of inward and outward transformation is part of the well of Rosh Chodesh creativity. Drawing on our ancestry, imparting our wisdom, experiencing new roles, developing new skills, mining new treasures; all are parts of the Rosh Chodesh experience. Because Rosh Chodesh is rooted in our history and yet a holiday without strictures for observance, it is an ideal holiday on which to experiment with creative ritual.[25]

Cultural Perspectives of the Moon

For many cultures, including our own, time is measured by the moon. In Sanskrit, the word *me* (moon) means to measure time.[26] The Koran notes that "God created the moon and appointed its houses in order that men might know the number of years and the measure of time."[27] In some cultures, the word for *moon* is feminine; in others, it is male. In Hebrew, there are three words for moon: *yare-ach* ירח is masculine; *levana* לבנה is feminine, and *sa-harah* סהרה (sharing a root with the word *zohar*, which means transcendent light) is also feminine.

The moon is a powerful symbol in many traditions: for the Buddhist, it represents peace, serenity, and beauty. Both the new and full moons are times of spiritual strength in Buddhist tradition. For the Hindu, the crescent moon is associated with a newborn baby who is eager to grow.[28] Over a thousand years ago, the Chinese viewed the "yin-yang" symbol as an expression of the phases of the moon, and because the dark lobe contains a spot of light and the light lobe contains a spot of dark, it had "female" traits in both light and dark periods.[29]

The moon also plays significantly in the festivities and mythologies of many cultures. The Chinese, since ancient times, have held a festival called "Yue-Ping" (Loaves of the Moon—now called Moon Festival). It is celebrated in the fall, and although it originated as a women's holiday, all participate in the festivities today. The African Pygmies celebrated the new moon just prior to the onset of the rainy season. It was also a women's celebration.[30] Because of women's connections to the cyclical nature of the moon and the role women played in making things grow—tending the children, crops, and fire—the moon festivities became times for women to celebrate.

The Kaushitaki Upanishad 1.2, an ancient Hindu text, offers this understanding of the role of the moon in life and death:

> "All who part from this world or this body go first to the moon, by their lives his waxing half is swelled and by virtue of his waning part he forwards their rebirth. But the moon is also the door to the heavenly world and who can answer his questions, him he sends beyond." In Persian, Hindu and Egyptian literature, the moon is represented as the place where the soul goes after death. On the moon the soul is judged and goes either to the upper world or back to the earth in a fresh incarnation.[31]

This Hindu text sees the moon as male, and although the moon is not responsible for its own rebirth, it is responsible for the rebirth of souls.

Islam, which follows exclusively a lunar cycle, uses the crescent as a primary symbol and often places the crescent on tombstones. Ramadan begins with the sighting of the new moon for the ninth month of the Islamic calendar and ends with the sighting of the new moon of the tenth month. It is a monthlong holy period of fasting from sunrise to sunset. The fasting teaches about, and creates, an awareness of "limitation," without which knowledge is impossible.[32]

The Mayan culture of 1,700 years ago was also very attuned to sky watching and developed many lunar myths. A "sophisticated lunar calendar [was] found among the Mayan hieroglyphic inscriptions. . . . Even to this day, the moon is valued as the regulator of important life events by the descendants of the Maya."[33]

It is important to note that among these cultures, as well as within Jewish tradition, the observation or regard for the moon is not viewed as moon worship. The rabbis warned about this danger, particularly in reference to Kiddush Levana, where the moon is physically observed. Much of the cultural folklore about the moon that is described here is historical. But for some, as in the Jewish tradition, the customs growing out of moon observance remain relevant and continue to be practiced in contemporary society.

The Kalderash Gypsies remove their clothes and recite an invocation to the moon, asking for health and prosperity: "The New Moon has Come Out—May She be Lucky for Us—She has found us Penniless—May She Leave us with Good Fortune—And with Good Health and More."[34] The stance of this incantation resembles the Kiddush Levana, while the folk-inspired request for good health and sustenance resembles the plea of the *tkhines*. And although we can only speculate as to why the Gypsies removed their clothing before saying these verses, what comes to mind is the nakedness of *mikvah*, of erasing any barriers between the self and the act.

Many Wiccan practices[35] are rooted in the moon's orientation. When the moon is not visible, which often includes the day before the new moon, the day of the new moon, and the day after, is a time of regeneration. It is considered the depth realm, and it is to this phase that imagination is attributed—the ability to hold in one's mind an image that is not visible. During this phase, rituals of regeneration, such as hair cutting, are performed, while as the moon begins to wax, rituals of increase are performed.

Moon symbolism is also prevalent among Native peoples in North America. Each Native band or tribe has its own reflections and understandings of the moon. Sioux Indians refer to the moon as "The Old Woman Who Never Dies," and Iroquois call the moon, "The Eternal One."[36] The Ditidadxht nation, one of several nations on Vancouver Island in Canada, schedules healing rituals and initiations into sacred societies at the new moon.[37] The word for moon, *daack*, is the same as the word for sun, reflecting that these two celestial bodies enjoy equal significance.

Among some peoples, the moon was revered more than the sun because, while the sun shone during the day, the moon provided light at night, when it was most needed. The moon mythologies and folklore are often an attempt to understand mystery and give honor to the unknown. The Babylonians, for example, created the zodiac (which means "circle of animals"), as a way of understanding and describing the moon's travels through the sky. Ancient synagogue floors depicting the zodiac have been excavated in Israel, reflecting the societal influence of the Babylonians. And the Assyro-Babylonians called the moon god Sinn, from which derived the name of "moon mountain," Mount Sinai.[38]

An old and poignant Guatemalan myth was recorded by Robert Briffault, a noted folklorist of the early 1900s. It recounts the story of a beautiful woman. Her father kept her hidden, especially from the sun, who wanted to marry her.

One day when the sun was not so bright (during a time of eclipse, perhaps) she stepped out into the shadow. Seeing how truly beautiful she was, the sun slid down on one of his rays and took her up to the sky, where the two were actually happy together. Her father was displeased. He was beside himself at the loss of his daughter, and decided to hire a man to build an enormous dart gun, the biggest one in the world, to shoot the sun. When the time came, however, the sun tricked the father by putting red pepper in the gun. This caused the father to sneeze so hard that his daughter fell out of the sun's arms and landed in the ocean, where she broke into a thousand pieces. The scattered pieces cried so pitifully to be reunited with the sun that the fish, hearing the pleas, obliged. They gathered up the pieces and then wove themselves together in a ladder that stretched up toward the sun. They became the Milky Way. The daughter became the moon. Even to this day, she follows the sun across the sky, and at times she almost catches up with him.[39]

One can't help but be aware of the parallels with two Jewish symbols in this story: the scattered shards and the ladder. Both the scattered shards of kabbalistic tradition and Jacob's ladder can be seen to bridge our own appreciation of the moon with the deep and valuable traditions of other peoples.

Moon Poetry and Spirituality

Poetry charged with moon metaphor describes a pendulum of emotion and image: from despair and pathos to hope and consolation. Sylvia Plath, in "The Moon and the Yew Tree," wrote of her despair, and Sara Teasdale, in "The New Moon," views the moon as a sign of hope. Out of a despairing day, a day that has bruised and beaten the poet, she looks to the moon for comfort. She sees the moon as a wisp of beauty in a hardened, gray world, its waxing crescent as an affirmation of life.[40] Walt Whitman, in "Look Down Fair Moon," describes the moon as a blanket of comfort to cover the dead and console the grief-stricken. The moon is a mother, bathing the child in womblike water.[41]

The moon is often a muse for poetry because of its mysterious and transforming qualities. To some poets, the moon is a female symbol, while it is male to others. The moon takes on the nature of the writer; it absorbs and reflects the emotion of the poet. The section in this anthology on poetry, songs, prayers, and meditations offers a wide range of verse. It reflects the soulful nature of the moon and the grandeur of the awe it inspires. Poetry has the capacity to nurture the soul by applying poetics to everyday life. It brings to the reader a vast world in small, digestable fragments.[42]

As grand and awesome as the moon is, it is also whimsical and playful. It inspired Vita Sackville West, a well-known Bloomsbury writer, to create an all-white garden, which is still flourishing and available to view at her former home in Sissinghurst Castle, Kent, England. This garden, where all the flowers are white, pale green, gray, or pale blue, has been replicated and is referred to as a "moon garden."

In either its whimsical mood or its more somber tone, the moon as symbol has much to offer. The word *chodesh* means month. Changing the letters slightly creates the word *chadash*, new, or *chidush*, insight. It is at Rosh Chodesh that the month is created anew, with insight and welcoming spirit. And it is in that spirit that I welcome you to the writings contained in these pages.

Notes

1. See the translation of Exodus 12:2 and Hirsch's comments on this verse in Samson Raphael Hirsch, *The Pentateuch* (New York: Judaica Press, 1986), p. 250.

2. Ibid.

3. Rambam, *Mishneh Torah*, Sefer Z'manim, Hilchot Kidush haChodesh.

4. Mircea Eliade, "The Moon and Its Mystique," in *Patterns in Comparative Religion,* ed. Mircea Eliade (London: Sheed and Ward, 1958).

5. This is called conjunction and is explained more fully in Appendix F.

6. Numbers 28:11–15.

7. Numbers 10:10.

8. Mishna Rosh HaShanah 2:6, Philip Blackman translation.

9. For a more in-depth discussion of the development of the announcement of, and liturgy for, Rosh Chodesh, see Barbara Goldman-Wartell's unpublished rabbinic thesis, "The Development of Rosh Chodesh Liturgy" (New York: Hebrew Union College, 1985).

10. Irving Greenberg, *The Jewish Way: Living the Holidays* (New York: Summit Books, 1988), p. 414.

11. Exodus Rabbah 15:6.

12. Sanhedrin 42a.

13. Samuel 1 20:18–42.

14. Goldman-Wartell, *Rosh Chodesh Liturgy*, p. 30.

15. Ibid., pp. 49–50.

16. See *Sod Ha-Ibur, Batei Midrashat* 2:43.

17. Penina Adelman, *Miriam's Well: Rituals for Jewish Women around the Year* (New York: Biblio Press, 1990), p. 94.

18. Janice Delaney, Mary Lupton, and Emily Toth, *The Curse: A Cultural History of Menstruation* (New York: Dutton and Co., 1976), p. 164.

19. See M. Esther Harding, *Woman's Mysteries: Ancient and Modern* (New York: Harper Colophon Books, 1976), p. 68, for a discussion of women's energy cycles. Harding states that she is not suggesting that women are incapacitated by the monthly changes in their bodies, but rather that they can become attuned to them.

20. Soncino English, Midrash Rabbah, 3: 174.

21. Harding, *Woman's Mysteries*, p. 20.

22. Older women, who are finally free to abandon the caretaking roles they played most of their lives, often become more adventurous in their older growing years. For

example, see the studies of anthropologist Barbara Myerhoff, especially "Bobbes and Zevdes: Old and New Roles for Elderly Jews," in *Remembered Lives: The Work of Ritual, Storytelling and Growing Older*, ed. Marc Kaminsky (Ann Arbor, MI: University of Michigan Press, 1992). The recent works of Gloria Steinem and Betty Friedan also speak about "age as adventure."

23. Isaiah 30:26.

24. Rebecca Alpert discusses using Jewish womenspirit to transform the ills of the world and Rosh Chodesh gatherings as a means of social activism, in "Our Lives Are the Text: Exploring Jewish Women's Rituals" *Bridges* 2:1 (Spring 1991): 66–80.

25. For a fuller discussion of this subject, see Sue Levi Elwell, "Reclaiming Jewish Women's Oral Tradition? An Analysis of Rosh Hodesh," in *Women at Worship: Interpretations of North American Diversity*, ed. Marjorie Procter-Smith and Janet R. Waltron (Louisville, KY: Westminister/John Knox Press, 1993).

26. J. C. Cooper, *Brewers Book of Myth and Legend* (Oxford: Helian Publishers, 1993), p. 189.

27. Kathleen Cain, *Luna Myth and Mystery* (Boulder: Johnson Books, 1991), p. 107.

28. See J. C. Cooper, *An Illustrated Encyclopedia of Traditional Symbols* (London: Thames and Hudson Publishing, 1978), pp. 106–107, for other listings of the moon as symbol.

29. Barbara Walker, *The Woman's Dictionary of Symbols and Sacred Objects* (San Francisco: Harper and Row, 1988), p. 18.

30. Cain, *Luna Myth*, p. 122.

31. Harding, *Woman's Mysteries*, p. 229.

32. Cyril Glass, *The Concise Encyclopedia of Islam* (San Francisco: Harper and Row, 1989), pp. 329–330.

33. Cain, *Luna Myth*, pp. 17–18.

34. Anne Kent Rush, *Moon Moon* (New York: Random House, 1976), p. 142.

35. Wicca is based on personal, rather than collective, belief and ritual. For an understanding of the relationship of the moon to wiccan practice, see Anne Baring and Jules Cashford's *The Myth of the Goddess* (New York: Viking/Penguin, 1992).

36. Barbara Walker, *The Woman's Encyclopedia of Myths and Secrets* (San Francisco: Harper and Row, 1983), p. 673.

37. This information was gathered during conversations between myself and Chief Randy Chipps, herideitary chief of his village, Cheanuwxe, in what is now Sooke, British Columbia.

38. Rush, *Moon Moon*, pp. 122, 172.

39. Cain, *Luna Myth*, pp. 23–24.

40. Sara Teasdale, "The New Moon," in Robert Phillips, *Moonstruck: An Anthology of Lunar Poetry* (New York: Vanguard, 1974).

41. Walt Whitman, "Look Down Fair Moon," in Phillips, *Moonstruck*.

42. Understanding soul as a "quality or dimension of experiencing life and ourselves" is addressed poetically and profoundly in Thomas Moore's *The Care of the Soul: A Guide for Cultivating Depth and Sacredness in Everyday Life* (New York: HarperCollins, 1992.)

God's crescent kiss renews us
again and again

I

Teachings of Rosh Chodesh

1
Examining Rosh Chodesh: An Analysis of the Holiday and Its Textual Sources

Arlene Agus

In 1972, after serious exploration of the nature of women's spirituality and the role of women in Jewish ritual, a small group of women discovered that the celebration of Rosh Chodesh—the Festival of the New Moon—had traditionally held unique significance for women, perhaps dating back as far as the biblical period.

We did not, at that time, comprehend how Rosh Chodesh would link us to all that was precious to us as Jews and how this hidden scroll would inscribe women into Jewish history. We did not understand how ultimately these lessons would sustain us, as Jewish feminists, during the lean years of struggle ahead.

Even with our initial, limited understanding of Rosh Chodesh, its significance as a Jewish women's holiday soon became apparent. First, Rosh Chodesh was already a Jewish holiday; there was no question of its special stature within the Jewish calendar. Second, because its special designation as a legal holiday for women was cited by undisputed, central rabbinic authorities, it provided a halachically permissible means of expanding the role of women in tradition.

In addition, the historical seriousness granted to women by the rabbinic employment of a proof text from the biblical period—namely, the righteous behavior of women in the Golden Calf episode—provided an unbroken spiritual link between contemporary women and their female forebears in the formative period of Jewish nationhood.

Politically, the indisputable authenticity of Rosh Chodesh served as valuable refutation of charges that feminism originated in non-Jewish, hence insidious, influences. This inscription of "herstory" into the corpus of halacha suddenly obviated the need to cobble it together from the sparse models and sources then available to Jewish women.

Finally, on a spiritual level, charting new paths in an old tradition and discovering new possibilities in Judaism and in our own lives seemed appropriately symbolized by this holiday of new beginnings.

For religious feminists seeking inclusion without revolution, celebrating Rosh Chodesh quickly became important. And, although it alone could not secure the goal of full equality within Judaism, it promised embattled feminists credibility and leverage in a conservative community skeptical of change.

On a practical level, Rosh Chodesh was a user-friendly holiday. Bearing only one halachic obligation specifically for women, namely, a modified work prohibition, it presented the opportunity but not the requirement to celebrate; it supplied a record of documented women's customs as a nucleus around which to experiment; and, unlike the three major festivals, it made no demands for cooking, cleaning, and clothing.

For many Jewish feminists, Rosh Chodesh became a "room of one's own," a room that did not require leaving our homes within Judaism. But one of the most potent lessons of Rosh Chodesh remained largely unrecognized at that time: the voice speaking to us from the past defined us as "special" rather than "other." We were defined within the norm rather than as outside it.

We began observing Rosh Chodesh with a special ceremony and feast, combining traditional practices associated with the holiday with additions from contemporary sources.

Much has transpired within the Jewish women's community since 1972. Rosh Chodesh has become a popular and frequently observed holiday. It offers unlimited opportunities for the exploration of feminine spiritual qualities and experimentation with ritual, all within the framework of an ancient tradition. The celebration of Rosh Chodesh is the celebration of ourselves, of our uniqueness as women, and of our relationship to nature and to God.

Historical Overview of Rosh Chodesh

The association of the moon and women began as early as the Creation story. Since that time, Jewish literature has portrayed the moon, in its relationship to the sun, as symbolic of women, the Community of Israel (Knesset Yisrael), and the Shechinah, the feminine aspect of the Godhead. The divine promise to the moon that she is destined to become an independent luminary like the sun[1] parallels the promise to women that in the world to come they will be renewed or rejuvenated like the New Moon and the promise to the Shechinah that when the world is redeemed, she will receive direct emanations of divine light.[2]

On the fourth day of Creation, "God made the two great luminaries" (Genesis 1:14–19). According to the Talmud (Hullin 60b), the two stars were originally of equivalent size, prompting the moon to ask God, "Sovereign of the Universe, can two kings share a single crown?" God answered, "Go and make yourself smaller." "Sovereign of the Universe!" the moon cried. "Because I presented a proper claim, must I make myself smaller?" And God, realizing the justice of her plea, compensated for her diminution by promising that the moon would rule by night, that Israel would calculate days and years by her, and that the righteous would be named after her. God also decreed that a sacrifice be instituted to atone for God's sin in making the moon smaller. And finally, that in the future, God would intensify the moon's light to equal that of the sun.[3]

It was a similar challenging of God's judgment in creation, in creating two equal human beings, that led to the diminution of woman's status. On the sixth day of Creation, "God created mortal in his image . . . male and female God created them." According to the *midrash*, Adam's first wife, Lilith, having been created equal to Adam, refused a role of subservience and was replaced by Eve.

Lurianic Kabbalah claims that, like the two lights and the first two humans, the male and female aspects of the Godhead were equal in the embryonic stage. But as a result of Eve's sin and the subsequent banishment from the Garden, the moon became smaller and the Shechinah went into exile. It is only when the world is redeemed that the two will be restored to their rightful places.[4] A similar destiny is promised to women.

The source for this promise—and the halachic basis for observance of Rosh Chodesh by women—is a passage in the Babylonian Talmud[5] discussing the laws of work on Rosh Chodesh. Rashi and Tosafot comment that while men are permitted to work on the New Moon women are not, as explained in Pirke DeRabbi Eliezer (Chapter 45):

The women heard about the construction of the Golden Calf and refused to submit their jewelry to their husbands. Instead they said to them: "You want to construct an idol and mask which is an abomination, and has no power of redemption? We won't listen to you." And the Holy One, Blessed be God, rewarded them in this world in that they would observe the New Moons more than men, and in the next world in that they are destined to be renewed like the New Moons . . . [shehen atidot lehithadesh kemotah].

This is later echoed in *Mekore Haminhagim*: "Women were enthusiastic about the *mishkan*, Sanctuary, and reluctant about the Calf, and were therefore rewarded with the observance of Rosh Chodesh as a minor festival."[6]

Why was Rosh Chodesh chosen? Because the three major festivals had already been assigned to the forefathers[7] and, according to the Or Zaruah, because Rosh Chodesh is an obvious reference to the monthly cycle after which women renew themselves, like the moon, through immersion.[8]

But what exactly does it mean that in the world to come, "women will be renewed like the New Moons"? Women already experience a physical renewal each month. What further renewal or rejuvenation will they experience in the world to come? The promise is rather unclear but can be understood as a parallel to the future renewal of the moon. Just as that star will be elevated in size and brilliance without becoming identical to the sun, so women will ascend in function and status without becoming identical to men.

Women and Work

In what way were Jewish women to observe the day? By refraining from work. Rashi says that women specifically refrained from spinning, weaving, and sewing on Rosh Chodesh,[9] which were the very skills women so enthusiastically contributed to the *mishkan*.

The authoritative source confirming the validity of the women's abstinence from work is the Jerusalem Talmud, which says: "It is an acceptable custom for women not to work on the New Moon."[10]

At one time, work may have been prohibited on Rosh Chodesh because of the Musaf sacrifice in the Temple on that day.[11] Some say that there was no real prohibition on work, but during the period in which the Sanhedrin would notify the people of the beginning of the new month through a system of torch relays, no work would be done while everyone awaited notification. After the Exile, the celebration of Rosh Chodesh more closely resembled *hol ha-mo-ed*, the intermediate days of a festival, and gradually fell only to the women.

It appears that the custom of abstaining from work was widely observed by Jewish women, although there was some disparity among the forms of work women permitted themselves on that day. The Tashbetz (thirteenth century) describes the differentiation between types of work; for instance, the women were strict regarding spinning but lenient with sewing, a simpler task.[12] A ban on gambling was declared in the Middle Ages, partly because "mischievous Jewish women" were squandering family money to engage in the practice during their free time on Rosh Chodesh.

The following lecture on *musar* (ethics) regarding Rosh Chodesh was written in the seventeenth century:

> Women should appreciate the glorious, majestic splendor of the day, in that they observe Rosh Chodesh more than men. Although it is proper for them to completely refrain from work because of their refusal to join the men in the sin of the Golden Calf, there is no actual prohibition of work, as on a holiday, so as not to embarrass the men. Women of every rank and status must observe the day.
>
> It is horrifying that there are women who do laundry on Rosh Chodesh. Moreover, some even save time on workdays by leaving the laundry for the holiday. These women are clearly misguided and should abstain from this wretched, depressing task. Hard work is prohibited even to men on Rosh Chodesh. Men should make their wives aware of the wisdom and value of the day so that they may glorify it and behave modestly and perform the most virtuous deed of the day—the collection of *tzedakah*, charity—from among the women. Rosh Chodesh is not for licentiousness and tempting others in sin. Modest, God-fearing women will act properly. If not, they will cause a "stain on high" and are not permitted to refrain from work.[13]

The *Shulchan Aruch* states that women's abstinence from work on Rosh Chodesh is a good custom. The Beur Halachah describes at length the rabbinic opinions regarding the binding nature of the custom. He points out that despite considerable feeling that Rosh Chodesh is simply a custom for those who adopt it or follow in their maternal tradition, it is in fact a tradition from our foremothers from ancient times and the *mitzvah* still applies to all Jewish women. A woman may not treat the day as if it were a regular weekday. However, depending on her family custom, she is permitted to perform light work.[14]

Heroines of Jewish history are linked with Rosh Chodesh as well. Queen Esther is compared with the moon in two ways. First, for "giving birth" to the redemption during her symbolic monthlong period wait for her meeting with the king. Second, for bringing to her Persian kin "light and joy, gladness and honor."

In addition, there exists an ancient custom in which women refrain from working while the Chanukah candles are burning. Among certain Sephardic communities girls would gather on the 7th night of Chanukah, which is Rosh Chodesh Tevet, for a special holiday known as "The Girls' Holiday" or "Women's Rosh Chodesh."

Some relate these customs to the heroine Judith, who is believed to have slain the Greek general Holofernes on that night, thereby creating favorable conditions for a Maccabean victory.

Still others attribute the double holiday of Chanukah and Rosh Chodesh not to Judith alone but to all three heroines of Chanukah: Judith, Hannah, who martyred her seven sons rather than submit them to idolatory, and the unnamed "Daughter of Matityahu, the High Priest," sister of Judah Maccabee.

According to legend, the Maccabean revolt was stalled by internecine disputes. Out of frustration, this woman stripped at her own wedding ceremony and successfully challenged her brothers to avenge the honor not just of one Jewish family but of the entire People, brought to shame by Hellenism.

Rosh Chodesh is introduced in Exodus 12:2 in the verse "This month is for you the first of months" and is the source of the *mitzvah* of observing Rosh Chodesh. In Numbers 10:10 and 28:11, Rosh Chodesh is described as a day on par with the other festivals, requiring the blowing of trumpets and special sacrifices. Several of the prophets equate Rosh Chodesh with the Sabbath or the three major festivals.

In the days of the Second Temple, when the declaration of the New Moon by the sages depended on its being sighted by two witnesses, a feast was held for these witnesses in order to encourage their coming.[15] From this and from King Saul's feast[16] we derive the *mitzvah* of holding such a meal on Rosh Chodesh.[17]

Rosh Chodesh Customs

The day preceding Rosh Chodesh is called Yom Kippur Katan [see Shefa Gold's chapter, "Dark Rays of the Moon: Yom Kippur Katan as preparation for Rosh Chodesh"], a minor Day of Atonement. It was traditionally a day of repentance and mourning over the destruction of the Temple and a day to spiritually prepare oneself for Rosh Chodesh. Rosh Chodesh itself is similar to Rosh Hashanah; on it we pray for blessings of renewal. We are judged for our sins and we are purified.

The theme of renewal recurs throughout the many customs of Rosh Chodesh. In fact, it is sometimes called the Day of Good Beginnings. As such, it was an appropriate day for holding housewarmings, dedications, and other "simchas," a day for wearing new clothes and shoes, for saying Sheheheyanu over a newly ripened fruit, and for beginning a new book in school. Joy and song are associated with the day and no fasts are permitted.[18]

After the torch relays were discontinued by Rabbi Yehudah Hanasi, the practice of lighting a special candle for Rosh Chodesh remained. In Yemen, candles would be lit in the synagogue and at home. In Algiers, gold coins or rings, possibly as reminders of the Golden Calf incident, were placed inside the burning lanterns for good luck. Different traditions vary on the number of candles to be lit on Rosh Chodesh: some require one more than Shabbat, some one less, but all agree that a differentiation should be made.

Today, Rosh Chodesh is observed by the recital of special holiday prayers,[19] partial Hallel, a *Musaf* service, and reading from the Torah. In addition, *Yaaleh v'Yavo* is included in both the *Amidah* (silent, standing prayer) and the *Birkat HaMazon* (Grace after Meals).[20] The Haftarah portion on Shabbat Rosh Chodesh (if Rosh Chodesh falls on Shabbat) is of particular interest here because, in this prophecy of redemption, Isaiah uses the imagery of fertility in describing God and Zion as life-bearers, providing nurturance to the people of Israel.[21]

The link between women and the moon is strong and far-reaching, touching Jewish law, custom, mysticism, and even superstition. Let us now turn to a ceremony of Rosh Chodesh.

The Rosh Chodesh Ceremony

Rosh Chodesh is celebrated only eleven times a year. Tishrei, the month Rosh Chodesh coincides with Rosh Hashanah, is omitted. If Rosh Chodesh falls on two days, the ceremony may be performed on either one or both days, though the second is the more important.

The ceremony is a celebration of Divine creation and of those characteristics women share with the moon—the life cycle, rebirth, and renewal. Just as the Jewish calendar sanctifies time annually through the holidays, weekly through Shabbat, and daily through prayers, so Rosh Chodesh sanctifies time monthly. And just as birth ceremonies, brit milah, bar and bat mitzvah, weddings and funerals mark each nexus point in the life cycle of members of the religious community, so Rosh Chodesh corresponds to and celebrates the life-giving monthly cycle of the community's women.

The symbols of water, spheres, and circles, representing monthly purification and rebirth in the *mikveh*, the shape of the moon, and the cyclical nature of life, as well as foods containing the seeds of life, will recur throughout the ceremony.

The following is not meant to be a standard text for the observance of the holiday. The creative process, exemplified in this ceremony, should be enhanced and developed by the creativity and imagination of individual women. Naturally, the traditional parts of the ceremony, for example, the giving of charity, the candle, the feast and the special Rosh Chodesh prayers, should be given special emphasis and lend some uniformity.

The Ceremony Itself

All are dressed in nice clothing, or, if possible, in new clothes saved for the occasion. A *pushke* (box for collecting monies for charity) can be available for the giving of charity before the ceremony begins.

A. Light a candle to burn for twenty-four hours.

A floating light closely resembles the moon floating in the sky.

B. Read a poem. One could choose "Create Me Anew" by Hillel Zeitlin.

C. Usher in the upcoming month.

This can be done in several ways: focus on the Jewish holiday occurring in that month, learn a text concerning the laws or customs pertaining to that holiday, observe the *yahrzeit* (anniversary of death) of a famous Jew due to occur that month, commemorate the anniversary of a historical event, and so on.

D. Kiddush.

A traditional holiday Kiddush is not appropriate, since the holiness of Rosh Chodesh more closely resembles the interim days of a holiday, when one is permitted to work, than the festivals, when one is not. The text used is the same one chanted at the blessing of the New Moon. Note its references to those who are carried in the womb and to the divine promise that they are destined to be renewed like the moon.

Blessed is God who created the heaven by his word and by the breath of God's mouth all of its hosts. God appointed for them a time and a limit so they might not alter their rounds [but rather be] happy and joyous doing the will of their Creator. Trustworthy Creator whose creation is trustworthy. And to the moon God said that she might always be renewed, as a glorious crown to those borne in the womb, who themselves are destined to be renewed like her and to praise their Creator for God's glorious rule.

ברוך אשר במשמרו ברא שחקים וברוח פיו כל־צבאם, חוק

וזמן נתן להם שלא ישנו את־תפקידם, ששים ושמחים לעשות

רצון קונם, פועל אמת, שפעולתו אמת, וללבנה אמר,

שתתחדש עטרת לעמוסי בטן, שהם עתידים להתחדש

כמותה, ולפאר ליוצרם על שם כבוד מלכותו

Raise a cup of wine and recite the following blessing:

Blessed are you, Adonai our God, Sovereign of the universe, creator of the fruit of the vine.

ברוך אתה יי אלהנו מלך העולם, בורא פרי הגפן:

The Feast

It is a *mitzvah* to eat in abundance on Rosh Chodesh. As is traditional with Jewish feasts, two rolls or challot are used. For Rosh Chodesh, it is appropriate to use round or crescent-shaped rolls. It is customary to buy a new fruit for Sheheheyanu. The first course may consist of a special Rosh Chodesh dish like the egg soup eaten often on Passover, the holiday that celebrates the birth of the Jewish people. (Again the seed of life is being immersed in liquid.) Sprout salad is another possibility. The main course should be festive, preferably containing two cooked dishes, as is customary on Sabbath and holidays. You may also wish to use nut loaf for the seeds and quiche for its circular shape.

During the meal, Rosh Chodesh songs, Hallel songs, or songs from the forthcoming holiday should be sung. *Birkat HaMazon* (Grace after the Meal) following the feast includes *Shir HaMa-alot* and *Yaaleh v'Yavo* for the New Moon. If Rosh Chodesh falls on Shabbat, it is customary either to add a special dish to the Sabbath meal in honor of the New Moon or to have a feast for Rosh Chodesh during the *Seudah Shlisheet* (third Sabbath meal), and extend it until after Shabbat.

Earlier we read that the biblical source for the *mitzvah* of Rosh Chodesh is "This month is for you," about which the *midrash* comments that God granted the Jewish people the authority to sanctify the New Moons—unlike the Sabbath, which is sanctified in heaven. As Israeli feminist Debbie Weissman points out, the acronym of *roshei chodoshim* (new moons) spells *rechem* (womb). The revival of Rosh Chodesh as a holiday for Jewish women is an opportunity for spiritual development, an occasion for speaking to the Creator and experimenting with the dialogue. It is offered here as a pause in which to thank God for creating us women.

Notes

1. Pirke DeRabbi Eliezer, chaps. 45 and 51; see also Midrash Konen, pp. 25–26.
2. Sefer Hemdat Yamim 1: 25. This and other mystical references courtesy of Rabbi Daniel Shevitz.
3. Isaiah 30:26.
4. Gershom Sholem, *Major Trends in Jewish Mysticism* (New York: Schocken Books, 1941), pp. 231–232.
5. Megillah 22b.
6. Mekore HaMinchagim, no. 38.
7. Sefer HaHasidim, no. 121.
8. J. D. Eisenstein, *Otzar Dinim U'Minchagim* (Tel Aviv, 1970), p. 377.
9. Megillah 22b.
10. Taanit 1:6.
11. Haggigah 18a; Tosefta and J. Taanit 1:6.

12. Tashbetz, sec. 3, no. 244.

13. Sefer Hemdat Yamim 1: 23b–24a.

14. *Shulchan Aruch*/Mishnah Berurah no. 417.

15. Rosh HaShanah 2:4.

16. 1 Samuel 20:5–6.

17. Rambam, Mishneh Torah, chap. 8.

18. Taanit 15b.

19. See additional Rosh Chodesh readings in the appendices for a complete listing of special prayers said on Rosh Chodesh.

20. *Shulchan Aruch*/Mishnah Berurah, nos. 421–424.

21. Isaiah 61.

2
The History of Rosh Chodesh and Its Evolution as a Woman's Holiday

Leah Novick

Virtually all ancient peoples, and particularly the cultures of the Middle East, had rituals for honoring the monthly reappearance of the moon. That revered crescent was invariably associated with the divine feminine, who was seen as the birth-giver to the sun, moon, stars, and planets. The moon was also linked to the menstrual cycle of the human female, whose birth-giving powers emulated the Divine Mother. The Jewish people, whose Sumerian and Chaldean origins would have exposed them to the various moon goddesses of that area,[1] then journeyed to Egypt where, again, they came in contact with temple practices that included the veneration of the moon.

The ancient Hebrews received the revelation of the Torah at Mount Sinai, a site some scholars associate with the moon-god Sinn in the Babylonian and

13

Sumerian tradition.[2] While some appear to be making the case linguistically, at least one Near Eastern mythologist[3] attempts to attribute Moses' knowledge of the mountain sanctuary to his contact with Jethro the Midianite priest, who was his mentor and father-in-law. Another source[4] points to similarities between early Near Eastern and Jewish prayer texts. We might then wonder if it is a coincidence that the women of Israel were, according to Jewish legends, given Rosh Chodesh as their own, unique holiday at the site of the holy mountain. The aggadic literature tells us that women were rewarded for their nonparticipation in the creation of the Golden Calf. They had, according to midrashic sources, refused to contribute their jewelry for the construction of the pagan idol, which was then crafted primarily of gold jewelry donated by the men.

We have no accounts describing exactly how women were to celebrate the Rosh Chodesh festival. Not working, lighting candles, and preparing a festive meal became customary, but the age of these customs is difficult to establish.[5] While there were no explicit directives about the mode of celebration for the day, there are references in the Tanach suggesting abstention from business (Amos 8:5), preparation of festive meals (1 Samuel 20:18), and visiting a prophet (2 Kings 4–23). And of course, the Torah gives specific instructions for the sacrifices to be brought on the New Moon (Numbers 28:11–15). These are similar to the Passover sacrifices. Other references to the new moon are in Isaiah 24:23 and 30:26 and also in Song of Songs 6:10 and Samuel 20:5 and 20:18. In Genesis, there are references to the moon as "the lesser luminary" (Genesis 1:14, 1:16), a subject that led to considerable speculation in the mystical texts about God's diminution of the moon and its connection to the sacrifices.

It seems reasonable to assume that the new moon festivities of the early Israelites might have followed patterns similar to those already in existence among the various groups living in the land of Canaan. Pagan moon celebrations of that time would possibly have included bonfires (which were common to many ancient cultures), music, dance, prayers of thanksgiving, sharing of festive food and drink, and, possibly, sacred sex. Despite turf conflicts between the Jews and their neighbors, the Torah reveals celebratory contact between the Israelites and their Canaanite neighbors during the period of the conquest of the land.[6]

One form of festive food were cakes baked in molds that emulated the pointed headdress of the Goddess Astarte. The descriptions of this practice, which would have taken place between 600 and 700 B.C.E. (during the last monarch), comes from the book of the Prophet Jeremiah. His disapproval includes the details of baking cakes for "the Queen of Heaven."[7] Discoveries of these molds through archaeological digs in Israel have confirmed Jeremiah's text. And from the research of Professor Raphael Patai and the Tanach itself, we know that many of these nature-oriented forms of worship were retained for hundreds of years.[8]

As the Jewish monarchy developed, new elements were added to the observance of the New Moon. Immediately recognized was the need to establish an agreed-upon calendar that would determine the setting of the dates for the religious holidays. This responsibility was delegated to the Sanhedrin, or religious parliament, which established the months for both spiritual and secular purposes (such as tax collecting). During the period when the Sanhedrin sat in Jerusalem on the 30th day of the month, their designation of Rosh Chodesh was actually connected to human sitings of the fresh lunar crescent. After the new moon had been seen, runners would be dispatched to Jerusalem to testify. When the parliamentary body was satisfied that two witnesses of upright character had brought the same evidence, they would announce the new month.[9]

In the Great Temple, sacrifices would be offered with the accompanying special prayers, incense offerings, and music. A most intriguing description of the ritual that the prince was to carry out for the whole people is provided for us in the Haftarah for Shabbat HaChodesh (from Ezekiel 45). In that amazing set of instructions—with its emphasis on the directions and the application of blood to various areas—there is the implication of a deep mystery within the New Moon ritual. The ceremony, conducted on behalf of all the people, is portrayed as having the power to cleanse the whole nation of its inappropriate actions.

While the great drama was being enacted in the Temple, the witness-runners would proceed back to their rural villages, stopping along the way to inform the residents of the communities through which they ran. This would make it possible for the populace within Israel to join in observance of Rosh Chodesh. As the news made its way across the country, groups of people would go up to the rural shrines or "high places" (possibly the same "bamoth" that had been used in the worship of the Canaanite mother-goddess, Asherah) and set bonfires[10] to alert the neighboring communities of the pronouncement of the new month. Some sources state that during the first exile of the Jews to Babylon, the fires extended from Jerusalem to Baghdad (a reverse route from the pattern of the missiles fired over that same 250 miles during the Gulf War). Even now, in contemporary Israel, it is still popular to set bonfires on certain holidays, notably Lag B'Omer and civil occasions like "Yom Yerushalayim" (Jerusalem Day), when there is no prohibition on work or building fires.

As the Jews became more urbanized and sophisticated, they no longer relied on personal witnesses for determining the months. With their exile to ancient Persia, they incorporated Babylonian knowledge into the emerging Jewish "luach" (calendar). As early as the second century, the months in the Jewish lunar calendar—which are still called by their Babylonian names—were already associated with the twelve tribes and the corresponding twelve houses of the zodiac. Two superb artistic examples of the connection of the tribes with the zodiac from that time period were set in the beautiful mosaic floors of the sixth-century synagogues at Beit Alpha and Hamat Tiberiah in northern Israel. In the Tiberias synagogue, the four seasons are represented by classic female faces. And at Beit Alpha, the sun-god Shamash occupies the center of the design along with his horses, indicating that the Jews of the north felt comfortable incorporating pagan symbolism and astrological knowledge into a Jewish place of worship.

The exile from Israel also led to a more serious and philosophical approach to observing the new moon, which became more closely connected to synagogue ritual. Some of the current prayers for blessing the moon and the recitation of Hallel (praises of God) date from the Babylonian exile. The progression toward synagogue new moon practice coincided with increased rabbinical authority over prayer and ritual life. As the Babylonian Talmud was developed, the sages spelled out the numerous laws for the observance of the new moon, which were focused on establishing an appropriate sacred atmosphere for the monthly event.

Over the next thousand years, rabbis and communities would take up this question: When, after the appearance of the crescent, would it be appropriate to bless the new moon? Different responses emerged to answer the query, ranging from three to fifteen days.[11] What was always agreed upon was the importance of doing Kiddush Levana (the blessing of the new moon upon physically seeing the crescent) outdoors , in a festive mood, and on a clear night when the moon was visible. For that reason the sages favored Motzei Shabbat (Saturday evening) as an optimal time if it was close enough to the first half of the moon's cycle.

Ironically, the concern over the "halachah" (religious law) surrounding Rosh Chodesh and the belief regarding women's legendary responsibility for the diminution of the moon strengthened the opinion that women were "exempt" from blessing the moon as a "time-bound mitzvah."[12]

Early legends, based on references to the Creation of the Greater and Lesser Luminaries in Genesis 1:14, taught that at the beginning of time, both sun and moon were equal and that the moon was reduced in size for being outspoken in her desire to be important. Other commentaries console us with the prospect of the male sun and the female moon becoming equal once again with the coming of the messianic era. The moon, representing the "Shechinah" (feminine Divine Presence) and "Knesset Yisrael" (the people Israel), now in exile and suffering, would be redeemed from exile in messianic time.

The developing talmudic perspective warned against any worship of the heavenly bodies during Kiddush Levana, which would be viewed as a remnant of pagan or foreign practice. The sages cautioned against looking at the moon for too long or giving the impression of worshiping it, although observant Jews jumped up toward the moon three times as part of their "prayer for protection." Along with the specific instructions for the timing and wording of the new moon rituals came an emphasis on the spiritual messages associated with each month. These were connected to the holidays, Jewish history, or the month's astrological aspects. This latter focus, which the Jews shared with their Persian neighbors, was undoubtedly in the mainstream at that time. Nonetheless, the presence of astrological implications in the mystical literature often comes as a surprise to contemporary Jews, who have been taught that Torah and Jewish law are opposed to any belief in the influences of astrology.

Meanwhile, outside the synagogue and the "Beit Midrash" (house of study), women living all over the Middle East were visiting each other on the new moon and taking a one-day holiday. In Europe, Rosh Chodesh became a "demi-" or half-holiday, with women doing no heavy work, such as sewing, on the new moon. What they actually did during their celebrations remains uncertain. We do know of the existence of female drummers who performed at women's gatherings in Sephardic countries. Conventional approaches suggest that women were just getting together and exchanging family news over coffee and sweets.

We are aware of the new moon practices of the "Mizrachi" (Eastern) Jewish families who observed home rituals such as candle lighting and a festive meal in which all family members probably participated. Recognized as a time of joy and special blessings, one does not fast on Rosh Chodesh, and weddings are allowed on the new moon during the Omer, when they are normally prohibited. Until modern times, there were special practices or ceremonies for particular months of the year, which were usually connected to a holiday or biblical event within that month. For example, Rosh Chodesh Adar among the Jews of Syria signals the start for collecting the half-shekel contribution; formerly the census, it later became the fund for charity in Jerusalem. Rosh Chodesh Nisan launched Passover preparations for the Jews of Tunis, where members of the family dipped a coin or ornament into the oil of the "kandil" (lantern), uttering good wishes for the next year. This fits with the idea that Nisan was the beginning of the year in ancient times. In Libya, on the eve of Rosh Chodesh Nisan (which was called the "night of the bassisa"), the entire family congregated in the home of the eldest member. A special dish of porridge was set on the table and the elder poured oil into the mixture, stirring it with a key and saying special prayers calling for abundance. The mistress of the house then dropped an ornament into the porridge, where it stayed overnight. The Libyan Jews also placed gold coins in the oil lanterns made of glass to commemorate the ancient Israelite's offerings for the construction of the tabernacle in the wilderness that was set up on Rosh Chodesh Nisan.[13]

Another custom from Libya (which was also practiced in other eastern countries) was "Ladies Day." The first day of Tevet was called the "New Moon of the Daughters." On that Rosh Chodesh, gifts were given to young women, especially those engaged to be married. There is a tradition in various Sephardic communities of reserving the seventh night of Chanukah as a time for celebrating the heroism of women and telling the stories of Judith and Holofernes and of the martyrdom of Chana and her seven sons.

In North Africa, the women and girls had a special night in the synagogue, with opportunities for handling and kissing the Torah scrolls and receiving benedictions from the rabbi. There was also a special prayer for the women at that time. In Salonica, arguments between girls were reconciled as they would be before Yom Kippur. Implied in many of these ceremonies is the belief that one could set the direction for the whole month by one's attitudes and practices at the beginning of its cycle.

Additionally, the sages taught that on Rosh Chodesh, one could tap into deeper levels of prayer and meditation than at other times. According to the mystical tradition, the various aspects of the soul ("nefesh," "ruach," and "neshamah") are in harmonious alignment with each other on Rosh Chodesh, when the earth, moon and sun are also in direct conjunction. These concepts were promoted by Eastern and Western scholars, ranging from Saadia Gaon to the Chatam Sofer, throughout Jewish history.

Perhaps one of the most profound contributions to Rosh Chodesh practice was the institution of "Yom Kippur Katan" within the sixteenth-century kabbalistic community of S'fad. (See Shefa Gold's chapter, "Dark Rays of the Moon.") Each month, on the day before the new moon, the entire community gathered to fast and pray. Discussion was focused on self-rectification, which involved confession and mutual criticism. The intent was to examine and clear the "klipot" (flaws) or sins of the entire community for the previous month and allow the most benign fresh energy to flow in for the new period. It seems very likely that both men and women would have participated in this activity. Although the kabbalist school of S'fad had enormous influence on the emergent chassidic movement in Eastern Europe, the confessional practices of Yom Kippur Katan did not continue. Chassidic new moon practices became less somber as the early masters, including the Baal Shem Tov and the Maggid of Mezerich, tried to limit self-mortification practices among their followers and emphasize joyful worship.

Perhaps the most serious and dramatic utilization of new moon as a time for spiritual transformation is the holiday of Siged observed by the Ethiopian Jews on the 29th of Cheshvan, one day before Rosh Chodesh Kislev.[14] At that time, the entire "Beta-Yisrael" (Jewish Ethiopian) community participates in a solemn day of fasting, meditation, and prayer focused on the principle of rededicating oneself to the Torah. Readings from the Prophets Ezra and Nehemiah are chanted and a long litany of prayers follow. According to author Kay Shulamay, the Beta Yisrael link Siged with Ezra's proclamations against the Babylonian wives (Ezra 10:10–12). The prayers in the ritual I attended in Jerusalem (Talpiot) a few years ago were accompanied by standing meditations and "ululuing" (Middle Eastern tongue-flapping sounds) by the women. After the "break-fast" there is singing and dancing to launch the new month joyously.

Siged is considered an older practice than Yom Kippur Katan. Its origin is attributed to the fifteenth century, when the "Beta-Yisrael" was seeking divine guidance on how to deal with persecution from their Ethiopian rulers. It is certainly interesting that two geographically separated Jewish communities developed somewhat similar spiritual practices connected to the lunar celebration. It should also be noted that the "Beta-Yisrael" hold other traditional Jewish beliefs—including the concept of Shechinah—despite the fact that the Ethiopian community did not have access to the posttalmudic literature shared by the rest of the Jewish world. The fact that the Siged has survived to our own time is a tribute to the tenacity and devotion of Ethiopian Jewish community, which still conducts the ceremonies in Jerusalem, with great dignity, each year.[15]

For the large numbers of Jews whose roots are European, there is also a tradition of women abstaining from heavy work and sewing on Rosh Chodesh. Like their Middle Eastern counterparts, Ashkenazi women went visiting as part of their Rosh Chodesh celebration. Although we do not know exactly what transpired during their monthly outings, there is some suggestion that they may have gambled![16] While it is difficult to find specific dates for the origins of folk customs, it should be noted that medieval Jews had practices connected with the cycles of the moon.[17]

The writings of the Jewish medieval mystics, including Rabbi Eliezer of Worms, indicate that people scheduled weddings during the waxing moon and moved into new homes during the first half of the lunar month. Rosh Chodesh was also considered a favorable time to have children begin classes at school. Moreover, Rabbi Eliezer mentions that cutting hair and finger nails on Rosh Chodesh was discouraged because growth should not be checked on the day most auspicious for it. The literature from that period suggests that the Jews of the Rhineland saw Rosh Chodesh as a time for enlisting the grace of the ancestors in their prayers.

Feminist Jewish scholars are currently studying European women's prayers for the new moon, as part of a whole genre of "tkhines" (women's prayers in Yiddish), which often focused on personal issues of birthing, illness, and family problems. (See Tracy G. Klirs' chapter, "Tkhines for Rosh Chodesh.") This genre of liturgy provides some clues to the intimate prayer life of European Jewish women.

What emerges is an interesting picture of a separate women's prayer tradition for various times of the year, including Rosh Chodesh. This may have provided women with a specialized feminine prayer practice that would include prayers for the home as well as the synagogue. In the synagogues of Eastern and Western Europe, there were foresayers or *firzogerin*, women who translated prayers into the vernacular for the less learned.[18]

While it is not clear whether the same leaders were involved in both synagogue women's prayer and Rosh Chodesh home gatherings, those who wrote tkhines seemed to be providing prayers for home as well as synagogue use. And if modern developments are indicative, we might expect that those who were learned and pious would be active in both settings. We can speculate that Rosh Chodesh traditions were transmitted through the authors of the tkhines and continued by the "tsadkaniot" (righteous women). This deserves to be the subject of more study and exploration, along with a more detailed review of Rosh Chodesh practices in the varying chasidic communities.

An important figure who emerged from the ecstatic and devotional consciousness of Eastern European Chasidism was the legendary "Maid of Ludomir," Hana Rachel Werbemacher.[19] Her life as rebbe and miracle worker was a challenge to nineteenth-century chasidic leaders. Toward the end of her luminous life, the "Betulah" (Maiden) led hundreds of people to the Tomb of Rachel on Rosh Chodesh to pray for redemption. While a more complete understanding of the prayers of the Betulah and others awaits additional scholarship and insight, what is clear is that contemporary Jewish women's groups celebrating Rosh Chodesh are reestablishing a connection to their ancestors' observances. Perhaps contemporary Jewish women are emulating the Maid of Ludomir when we pray for the redemption of the planet and a time of justice that will include our full participation in Jewish spiritual life. Because our predecessors were " written out of history," we are often in the position of inventing or reinventing ritual. However, there can be no doubt that we are anchored in generations of spiritual devotion that links us back to the very first matriarchs.

Notes

1. Merlin Stone, *Ancient Mirrors of Womanhood* (Boston: Beacon Press, 1979). This book provides descriptions of the various moon goddesses worshiped in the Middle East.

2. Hayden Paul, *Queen of the Night: Exploring the Astrological Moon* (Shaftesbury, Dorset: Element Books, 1990). Paul maintains that Mount Sinai derived its name from the Babylonian moon-god Sinn, a god representing the three aspects of the moon. Also see the section, "Sinai, Sinn" in Barbara G. Walker's *The Woman's Encyclopedia of Myths and Secrets* (San Francisco: Harper and Row, 1983).

3. John Gray, *Near Eastern Mythology* (London: Hamlyn Publishing Group, 1969), p. 21. Gray makes the case that Moses would have known of the location of the mountain sanctuary through his contact with the Midianites or Kenites who occupied the Kadesh oasis.

4. Walter Bayerlin, *Near Eastern Religious Texts Relating to the Old Testament* (London: SCM Press, n.d.), pp. 80, 83, 104, 112, 116, 130, 148, 258. Bayerlin refers to Sin as Suen and also describes the disc of the moon as being considered the crown of Sin. He explains the exalted status of the moon-god by attributing the Sumerian "raising of the Hands" prayer to the moon-god Nanna-Suen. This prayer may well be connected to the famous Steli unearthed at the Hazor excavation in northern Israel by Yigal Yadin. That unique stone drawing portrays the raised hands in prayer position. Yadin speculated that this was a mode of prayer to the moon goddess of the area.

5. Hayyim Schauss, *The Jewish Festivals* (New York: Schocken Books, 1938), pp. 272–276.

6. See, for example, Parshat Balak, Numbers, chapter 25, which makes reference to the participation in eating and licentious rites of the children of Israel. Specifically, Zimri a prince of the tribe of Shimon, brings his associate, Cuzbi, a Midianite woman (and daughter of a tribal leader), to the Hebrew encampment, where they are slain together by the priest Pinchas.

7. Jeremiah 7:18.

8. Raphael Patai, *The Hebrew Goddess* (Detroit: Wayne State University Press, 1967; repr., 1978). See also 2 Kings 21:3 regarding King Menasseh and 2 Kings 23:5 regarding King Josiah's abolition of the Asherah worship and the offerings to the sun and moon.

9. Mishna Rosh HaShanah 2:6.

10. See Mishnah 13 re. fires.

11. See the Kitzur *Shulchan Aruch* for a condensed version of the laws of Rosh Chodesh.

12. Chaim Lipschitz, *Kiddush Levano* (New York: Moznaim Press, 1987), p. 75. A responsa is presented discussing the question of whether Kiddush Levana is a time-bound mitzvah, which would make it exempt for women: "I wonder at this because a time-related mitzva is only one which one cannot perform every day of the year, and it is the time factor which prevents one from performing it at certain times. Here however, in the case of the moon, there is no time-related factor preventing one from reciting Kiddush Levono each day of the year. What prevents it is the physical absence of the moon, which is no longer renewing itself."

13. Dvora HaCohen and Menachem HaCohen, *One People: The Story of the Eastern Jews* (New York: Adama Books, 1986), pp. 91, 103.

14. The author was fortunate to interview and collect material about the Siged from Rabbi Yosef Hadani in Jerusalem. See also Kay Shelmay, *Music, Ritual and Falasha History* (Detroit: Michigan State University Press, 1989).

15. The author participated in such a Siged celebration in Jerusalem, 1991.

16. Judith R. Baskin, *Jewish Women in Historical Perspective* (Detroit: Wayne State University Press, 1991). In the chapter on Jewish women in the Middle Ages, the author

cites a reference to the will of Rabbi Eleazar ben Samuel of Mainz in which he indicates that his daughters may have amused themselves for trifling stakes on the new moon. Also see Israel Abrams, *Jewish Life in the Middle Ages* (Brooklyn, NY: Mazanaim Press, 1978), for a description of games played by Jewish women on festival days.

17. Joshua Trachtenberg, *Jewish Magic and Superstition: A Study in Folk Religion* (New York, Atheneum, 1974), pp. 114, 119. The author also indicates that certain incantations were best undertaken three days prior to the new moon.

18. See *Written Out of History*, by Sondra Henry and Emily Teitz (Fresh Meadows, NY: Biblio Press, 1983), for a description of the foresayers, *firzogerin.*

19. For a fuller description of the life of the Maid of Ludimir, see Gershon Winkler's *They Called Her Rebbe* (New York: Judaica Press, 1991).

3
Rosh Chodesh: A Feminist Critique and Reconstruction

Jane Litman, Judith Glass, and Simone Wallace

Introduction

We are three feminist Jews who have been involved in various Jewish spiritual, cultural, and intellectual activities for a number of years. Recently, we have been members of a feminist Shabbat group that emphasizes creating ritual. This led us to many deep and far-ranging discussions about the coming together of feminism and Judaism. In 1991 we shared with each other our discomfort with some elements of many contemporary Rosh Chodesh celebrations. By happy coincidence, at this time we were fortunate to be asked to lead a Rosh Chodesh service for the Los Angeles Jewish Feminist Center. We used this opportunity to explore our discomfort, focus our critique, and create a ritual authentic to tradition, yet genuinely feminist in philosophy.

What caused our discomfort? The contemporary women's observance of Rosh Chodesh is based on ideology from two aggadic texts and rabbinic commentaries on the *midrash*. The first[1] tells that women were given the holiday of Rosh Chodesh as a reward for not donating their jewelry to Aaron's construction of a golden calf at the base of Mount Sinai while Moses was up on the mountain receiving the ten commandments.

This is a strange story from a feminist perspective. Anthropology and archaeology teach us that women in many different cultures celebrated the cycles of the moon eons before the Exodus.[2] This *midrash*'s late dating of women's celebrations of Rosh Chodesh clouds the longevity of the association that ancient women made between their menstrual cycles and the phases of the moon.

Rosh Chodesh is not the appropriate reward for women's refusal to worship the golden calf. Justice would suggest that women's loyalty be rewarded with priestly power and leadership. Aaron should have been deposed and the righteous women ordained in his place. But no, the patriarchal story "gives" women what they already had!

The story also presupposes a hierarchy of power in which women are the passive recipients of the holiday, the feminine receptors of the largesse of the masculine God as formulated by his male priests and, later, rabbis.

Last, this *midrash* tells us that, like the new moon, women will be fully renewed in the *Olam Haba*, the world to come. We wonder why we have to wait so long.

The other aggadic rabbinic text[3] about the moon and its relation to women is equally strange from a feminist point of view. This *midrash* says that the moon and the sun were once of equal size but that God reduced the moon's size due to overly assertive female behavior. In later Jewish mysticism, this is explicitly linked to the garden of Eden story in Genesis as well as to the exile of the *Shechinah* (the feminine immanent aspect of God). This talmudic tale tells us that it is only in the world to come that the moon (and the *Shechinah*) will be restored to its proper size. In addition, this *midrash* teaches, as does the first one, that it will be only in the distant future that women will be restored to their proper place.

The division of symbolic inanimate objects into binary gender roles is unfortunate. The explicit association of men with the sun and women with the moon and the hierarchical positioning of the former over the latter are misogynistic. This division is part of a dualistic way of thinking that tends to value, among other things, the male over the female, the larger over the smaller, rich over poor, youth over age, and day over night.

If this weren't enough, the whole catastrophe is blamed on Eve, the archetype for woman. Eve's "sin," that is, the desire for moral enlightenment and the ability to think for oneself, is not generally viewed as a bad thing. It is only when women or other underclasses challenge authority by acquiring knowledge that dire consequences are invoked. As feminists, however, we view Eve as a heroine.

Eve, and consequently all women, are blamed for the *Shechinah*'s exile from the world.[4] But women are not to blame for any absence of spirituality, either in Judaism or the larger society. That, unfortunately, is something for which all of us must assume responsibility.

How could we use our discomfort and critique of these traditional interpretations to create an affirmation of the connection between women and the moon? The relationship between women and the moon is ancient. The most obvious connection is that between women's menstrual cycles and the lunar phases. This obvious connection leads into the more subtle and complex symbology of the phases of the moon as representative of the phases of women's lives.

These phases teach us two things. The first is that it is important to welcome periods of retreat and rest, from which we emerge renewed, refreshed, and with energy to meet the challenges of public and private life. Dark and light times intermingle and connect—neither is permanent; in fact, they are but different phases of a larger cycle.

The second metaphorical lesson is to value the full extent of phases in our lives, seeing in each the beauty and potential appropriate to it. The moon as a cyclical symbol is especially important in our culture, which devalues women in general, and in particular encourages us to doubt our self-worth and significance when we are either younger or older than our "prime." The nonlinear model of the moon can help us to overcome the linear thought and consequent ageism of our society. The phases of the moon validate and sanctify women at all stages of our spiritual, emotional, and physical lives. Women are strengthened and dignified by the celestial symbol of woman.

The ritual we created, which both challenges nonfeminist elements of Rosh Chodesh and affirms women's primal connection to the moon, is presented in this chapter. We initially led this ritual for a group of seventy women and a handful of men, most of whom were strangers to each other. Subsequent to this time, two of us have led this ritual on several other occasions, with groups of about twenty women. It has consistently been well received, engendering spiritual energy and enthusiasm as well as intense discussion. There were some differences in experience which, while foreseeable, are instructive. The levels of self-revelation, vulnerability, and trust achieved by the smaller groups of women were much deeper than those of the larger group, whose members exhibited some self-consciousness and nervousness about issues of menstruation, menopause, and life crises.

The ritual contains a mix of elements: liturgy, song, poetry, activity, and discussion. There is an emergent body of feminist art and literature on which we drew. We particularly want to acknowledge Debbie Friedman, Shefa Gold, and Faith Rogow for their extraordinary songs. The framework for much of the ritual is Marge Piercy's poem, "At the new moon: Rosh Hodesh." The Torah portion for the initial week during which we led this ritual included Exodus 35:25, the story of the women weaving for the sacred tabernacle in the desert. ("And all the women that were wise-hearted did spin with their hands, and brought that which they had spun, the blue, and the purple, the scarlet, and the fine linen.") We, therefore, wove this strand of Torah into the fabric of the ritual.

The Ritual

1. Opening Niggun

2. Introductions
"I am _____ bat (mother's name) bat (grandmother, etc.)."

3. Welcoming Song: "Bruchot Haba'ot" by Debbie Friedman

Bruchot Haba'ot tachat kanfay hashechinah
Bruchim Haba'im tachat kanfay hashechinah

May you be blessed beneath the wings of Shechinah
Be blessed with hope, be blessed with peace

4. Moon Theme

Rosh Chodesh, the new moon, is an ancient Jewish women's celebration. In modern times, this holiday has been popularized by Arlene Agus in her article "This Month Is for You."[5] In it she writes:

The association of the moon and women began as early as the Creation story. Since that time, Jewish literature has portrayed the moon, in its relationship to the sun, as symbolic of women, of the Community of Israel, and of the Shechinah, the feminine aspect of the Godhead. . . .

But as a result of Eve's sin and the subsequent banishment from the Garden, the moon became smaller and the Shechinah went into exile. It is only when the world is redeemed that the two will be restored to their rightful places. A similar destiny is promised to women.

The source for this promise—and the halachic basis for the observance of Rosh [C]hodesh by women—is a passage in the Babylonian Talmud. . . . As explained in Pirke De Rabbi Eliezer (chapter 45):

The women heard about the construction of the golden calf and refused to submit their jewelry to their husbands. Instead they said to them: "You want to construct an idol and mask which is an abomination, and has no power of redemption? We won't listen to you." And the Holy One, Blessed be He, rewarded them in this world in that they would observe the new moons more than men, and in the next world in that they are destined to be renewed like the New Moon.

(The group may choose to add an optional paragraph focusing on the particular Jewish month.)

The first Rosh Chodesh of the Jewish year, Rosh Chodesh Nisan, occurs this week. We appreciate Agus's efforts at reclaiming this holiday for contemporary Jewish women, and today, as we are about to enter a new cycle of moons, we wish to deepen our understanding of the connections between women and the moon.

5. Litany

They say: It was a result of Eve's sin.

We say: The desire for knowledge is no sin.

They say: The Shechinah went into exile.

We say: We refuse to be blamed for the absence of spirituality in the world.

They say: The moon is to the sun as women are to men.

We say: Both women and men have the potential to shine.

They say: The women refused to give their jewelry to build a golden calf.

We say: Of course we rejected an idolatrous male god created by an exclusively male priesthood.

They say: The women were rewarded by being given a holiday of exemption from work.

We say: Who are they, to reward us?

They say: Because of this *midrash*, Rosh Chodesh is now a women's holiday.

We say: Long before men told the story of building a golden calf, our grandmother's grandmothers saw the link between the cycles of

They say: Women will be restored   *We say*:   women and the cycles of
            to their rightful place in   the moon and passed this
            the next world.   celebration to us.
                                                     We are coming to fullness
                                                     in this world.

6. "Ancestors' Song" by Shefa Gold[6]

Chorus: yai dai dai lai dai dai dai . . .

Rejoice in the sliver of moon
whose voice announces a new-born light
Let the flowers of blood descend
From the womb of the fertile night.

Chorus:

May a time of awakening come to pass
When as wanderers we cease to roam
Tho we plant in tears may we reap in joy
When the Harvest brings us Home.

Chorus:

May the darkness send us deep inside
Where the hidden fire is burning strong
Let my soul be restored
In the power of this song

Chorus:

Rejoice in the moon's returning light
May her fullness find my faith renewed
Borchi nafshi sh'china
Halleluya!

7. At the New Moon

We have chosen Marge Piercy's poem "At the new moon: Rosh Hodesh" as
the framework for today's lunar exploration. We read it in lunar phases. The
first four stanzas, the waxing moon, are followed by a weaving ritual. The next

four stanzas, the waning moon, are followed by a sharing of the phases of our lives. The final stanza returns us to the new moon.

At the new moon: Rosh Hodesh
Marge Piercy

Once a two day holiday, the most sacred stretches
in the slow swing of the epicycling year;
then a remnant, a half holiday for women,
a little something to keep us less unsatisfied;
then abandoned at enlightenment along with herbals
and amulets, bobbe-mysehs, grandmothers' stories.

Now we fetch it up from the bottom of the harbor,
a bone on which the water has etched itself,
and from this bone we fashion a bird, extinct
and never yet born, evolving feathers
from our hair, blood from our salt, strength
from our backs, vision from our brains.

Fly out over the city, dove of the light,
owl of the moon, for we are weaving your wings
from our longings, diaphanous and bony.
Pilots and rabbis soared. The only females
to fly were witches and demons, the power
to endure and the power to destroy alone

granted us. But we too can invent,
can make, can do, undo. Here we stand
in a circle, the oldest meeting, the shape
women assume when we come together
that echoes ours, the flower, the mouth,
breast, opening, pool, the source.

7a. "We Are Weaving Our Wings"

"And all the skilled women spun with their own hands, and brought what they had spun, in blue, purple, and crimson yarns."[7] We now weave the blue, crimson, and purple balls of yarn that we have brought today into the symbolic web of our spiritual intuition. Make one of the following statements as we stand in a circle and pass the yarn to one another (logistical hint: pass across the circle at first and make sure you hold on to the yarn as you pass the ball to the next woman).

1. I long for _____:
2. I soar when I _____:
3. I am inventing, doing, or undoing _____:

We greet the moon that is not gone
but only hidden, unreflecting, inturned
and introspective, gathering strength to grow
as we greet the first slim nail paring
of her returning light. Don't we understand
the strength that wells out of retreat?

Can we not learn to turn in to our circle,
to sink into the caves of our silence,
to drink lingering by those deep cold wells,
to dive into the darkness of the heart's storm
until under the crashing surge of waves
it is still except for our slow roaring breath?

We need a large pattern of how things change
that shows us not a straight eight-lane tearing
through hills blasted into bedrock; not stairs
mounting to the sacrificial pyramid where hearts
are torn out to feed the gods of power, but the coil
of the moon, that epicycling wheel

that grows fat and skinny, advances and withers,
four steps forward and three back, and yet nothing
remains the same, for the mountains are piled up
and worn down, for the rivers eat into the stone
and the fields blow away and the sea makes sand
spits and islands and carries off the dune.

7b. "That Epicycling Wheel"

We come together now, "to turn in to our circle," to explore the cycles in our lives. We share the phases of our biological lives, knowing that the moon in all her phases calls on women to celebrate our "selves" at all times, contrary to the messages of our culture. The moon has always taught women the beauty and power of waxing, full, waning: anticipation, fullness, simplicity.

Now, come together in small groups according to the life phase/age cohort you are in. You may want to relate this to your menstrual cycle. For example, are you a person who menstruates? Are you pregnant? Are you experiencing menopause? Have you had a hysterectomy? Share the strengths that come with this phase of your life, and what challenges are raised by it. What do you need from others now?

In unison:

Let the half day festival of the new moon
remind us how to retreat and grow strong, how to
reflect and learn, how to push our bellies forward,
how to roll and turn and pull the tides up, up
when we need them, how to come back each time
we look dead, making a new season to shine.

8. Closing Song: "Woman I Am"[8]

Woman I am
Spirit I am
I am the Infinite within my Soul
I have no Beginning
And I have no End
All this I am

Isha ani
Ruach ani
Ani hanefesh b'toch nafshi
Ain li Sof
Ain li Chathalah
Kach ani

Celebrate Moon
Renewing Moon
The cyclical symbol
which guides our lives
The shapes that we see
Remind us to be
All that we are

Conclusion

We found the creation and celebration of this ritual at times challenging, at times frustrating, at times liberating. The excitement of incorporating new insights into our tradition is countered by the difficulty of accomplishing this objective. New ideas are often threatening, particularly if they carry a "feminist" label.

We believed that our critique would change the contemporary, midrashically based mythos of Rosh Chodesh. This has turned out to be surprisingly difficult, not only in traditional communities but in feminist communities as well. Rosh Chodesh ceremonies still incorporate the uncritical acceptance of the standard antifeminist *midrashim*. There still exists considerable resistance to analyzing in a critical vein the aggadic texts associated with Rosh Chodesh and creating new, feminist liturgy for Rosh Chodesh.

We find that as we continue to present this ritual to different groups, it stimulates discussion about the ways in which Judaism and "Western" civilization devalue women. We hope that this deconstructive critique and model for affirmation will encourage and illustrate the promise of what can be, if we can learn to take seriously a nonlinear understanding of the moon that teaches us the value of retreating, resting, and renewal while it helps us to affirm ourselves in all phases of the life cycle.

Notes

1. Pirke de Rabbi Eliezer, chap. 45.
2. Anne Kent Rush, *Moon Moon* (New York: Random House, 1976).
3. Hullin 62b.
4. This idea occurs repeatedly throughout Jewish mystical texts.
5. In Elizabeth Koltun, *The Jewish Woman* (New York: Schocken Books, 1976), pp. 85–86.
6. On the audiotape *Abundance*, available from P.O. Box 355, Las Vegas, New Mexico 87701.
7. Exodus 35:25.
8. This version of the folk song "Woman I Am" has been crafted by Judith Glass, who wrote the final verse.

4
My Body, My Self and Rosh Chodesh

Robin Zeigler

It is that time of the month again. My menstrual blood flows freely. Yet I am almost oblivious to the deeper meaning of this experience.

It is that time of month again. The moon is renewed throughout the celestial spheres. We hardly see it. Its meaning is all but lost.

It is that time of month again: Rosh Chodesh. Yet as a modern woman of faith, I feel lost within this cycle. Where is its spiritual focus? Where is its connection to the traditions of my past?

Many moons ago, the sanctity of Rosh Chodesh was entrusted to Jewish women. Sadly, the treasures of the past have become buried in the sands of today. The luminance of the moon is diminished by our modern lights. How does Rosh Chodesh speak to us today?

Puberty, menstruation, pregnancy, birthing, breast-feeding, menopause—a woman's body is characterized by cycles of change. Likewise, each month the moon waxes and wanes with a comforting predictability. Throughout history and across cultures, the moon has often been associated with the feminine. It is no accident. While modern-day women and men often appear oblivious to the message of the moon, societies of yesteryear guarded it as an important tradi-

33

tion. They recognized the feminine lunar connection. Judaism charges us to honor this connection. Rosh Chodesh can help show us how.

The Seeds of an Answer: Judaism and the New Moon

Jewish tradition has always had a special connection to the moon. Unbeknownst to many, the first *mitzvah* (commandment) given to the Jewish people after leaving Egypt was the sanctification of the new moon.[1] And the Jewish months are determined by the lunar cycle.

Up until the first century C.E., each month was announced by special messengers who went out into the fields to sight the new moon. They then traveled to Jerusalem to testify that they in fact saw the moon on a particular day. This important job was done amidst much fanfare and tradition. For example, the messengers, who were afforded great respect, received a special meal in the holy city of Jerusalem for their effort.

Around the seventh century, many customs and traditions came to be associated with Rosh Chodesh. Among them were holiday meals, the giving of charity, special recognition of teachers, and an association between the holiday and the opportunity for repentance and renewal.[2]

Rosh Chodesh has long been regarded as a special holiday for women. Tradition states that women were rewarded for their refusal to participate in the sin of the golden calf. As a result, the women's celebration of Rosh Chodesh was meant to be even more special than that of the men. In recognition of their merit, women traditionally refrained from certain types of work on Rosh Chodesh such as laundry, spinning, and sewing.[3]

Blood, Womanhood, and Renewal

Perhaps most important, tradition contains allusions to the unique spiritual connection between women's cycles and the cycle of the moon.

> You should know that each month the woman becomes renewed and immerses herself and returns to her husband, and she is beloved to him as on the wedding day. Similarly the moon becomes renewed every Rosh Chodesh and everybody desires to see it, just as the woman when she becomes renewed every month, her husband desires her, and she is endeared to him like a new woman.[4]

For much of their adult lives, women are faced with the reality of a monthly menstrual cycle. Symbolically the potential for life is followed by the blood of loss. Personal history, present life circumstances, and cultural and religious expectations all interact to color our reactions to menstruation. At times the blood is a welcome sight, reassuring the woman that she is not pregnant. At other times, the woman may be saddened and troubled, longing for the news of pregnancy and potential life. Finally, sometimes the woman is seemingly oblivious to the commonplace event.

A great deal has been written regarding the laws of the menstruant. Law and tradition assert that menstruation is an important aspect of women's lives. The Jewish woman is not to remain oblivious to this important monthly occurrence. Nor is she to look down on the period as mundane, dirty, or shameful. Rather, she is charged with the task of sanctification.

The potential for creation of another human is a miracle unprecedented by any other aspect of our lives. The monthly blood or lack thereof heralds an important message about creation. Loss of blood cries out about the loss of potential life. Likewise the absence of blood heralds hope of new birth and an addition to humankind. Woman and man have become united with God in the creation of a new life. Yet it is woman who has been blessed with the special opportunity to nurture the fetus and birth the new life. She is alone in her tasks, just as she is truly alone in her experience of blood loss.

Women are faced with a life of cycles and transitions. Our bodies are constantly facing changes through menstruation, pregnancy, birth, breast-feeding, and so on. As women, we must recognize and prepare for these transformations.

The traditional Jewish married woman is faced with a system of laws and customs (*taharat ha'mispacha*—family purity) to sanctify the changes. The menstruating woman withdraws from her husband physically for about twelve days during each menstrual cycle. At a time symbolic of a mini-death experience, she is charged with the task of withdrawing into herself. Paradoxically, this physical withdrawal is meant to strengthen the couple's connection.

> Because a man may become over-acquainted with [his wife] and thus repelled by her, therefore the Torah said she should be considered a *niddah* [separate from her husband] for seven days, i.e., after the end of her period, so that she might become beloved of her husband on the day of her purification even as she was on the day of her marriage.[5]

It is as if this withdrawal away from the other strengthens the self and thereby the relationship to the other. The Jewish woman is not allowed to lose herself in relationship to her spouse.

Other ancient cultures have their own behavior patterns and customs around menstruation. The symptoms of physical uneasiness or emotional moodiness leading up to and during menstruation can be viewed as a calling toward seclusion, similar to the period of *niddah*. "A period of introversion and seclusion of this kind is often very valuable, but it must be a real introversion, a *turning within*, more actively undertaken than a mere submission to physical necessity . . . instead of being pulled down and depleted by the monthly period, women have gained a contact with the deeper sources of their own feminine natures."[6]

At the end of the "menstrual period" (menstruation plus seven nonbleeding days), the woman immerses herself in the *mikvah*, a collection of natural waters. Symbolically, this immersion leaves the woman in a state of spiritual purity. It is no accident that this immersion requires natural waters. These waters, like the amniotic fluid, is a symbol par excellence of renewal and rebirth.

Other Traditions of Transformation

The laws of family purity and *mikvah* are the most obvious references to the sanctification of the woman's body. Yet if one looks further, there are other hints of transformation and sanctification.

In biblical texts, we find reference to the transformative qualities of weaning. We are told that Abraham held a weaning party for Isaac. "And she [Sarah] said, 'Who would have said to Abraham that Sarah would nurse sons, for I have given birth to a son in his old age.' And the child grew, and he was weaned, and Abraham made a great party in the day that Isaac was weaned."[7]

Based on the entire biblical account, one can speculate that this party was a very emotional moment for Sarah. Tradition tells us that only a few years earlier, Sarah, a postmenopausal woman, had lost all hope of ever parenting a biological child. As we see, not only was she able to birth a child but Sarah was also blessed with renewed capacity to nurse and nurture her infant in this special way.

The story of Chana, the prophetess, also alludes to the importance of nursing and weaning. The Book of Samuel opens with the story of Chana, an infertile woman, who prays for the birth of a child. She is eventually answered with the birth of Samuel, an important prophet. The Book of Samuel quotes Chana's terse prayer to god. However, the Talmud spends a good deal of time exploring the meaning of that prayer. The rabbis expound upon one aspect of the prayer with:

On "And Chana, she spoke in her heart" R. Eleazar said in the name of R. Jose b. Zimra: She spoke concerning her heart. She said before God, "Sovereign of the Universe, among all things that You have created in a woman, You have not created one without a purpose, eyes to see, ears to hear, a nose to smell, a mouth to speak, hands to do work, legs to walk with, breasts to give suck. These breasts that You have put on my heart, are they not to give suck? Give me a son, so that I may suckle with them."[8]

This colorful passage in the Talmud points to the poignant imagery of breasts and nursing for women over the ages.

Perhaps an even more obvious vehicle for transformation is the Jewish woman's use of prayer. Women throughout the ages have supplemented the codified daily prayers of the rabbis with personal supplications related to feminine concerns. There are several books available on the subject of *tkhines*, women's devotional prayers.[9] These collections of women's prayers identify special supplications for many different life stages, including immersing in the *mikvah*, engaging in marital relations, the different stages of pregnancy, breast-feeding, parenting, and so on. The prayers contain elements of hope, comfort, and thankfulness. But above all, they sanctify transformation and add meaning to the concerns of everyday life for women.

The Special Tasks of Womanhood

It seems that Jewish women are deemed a special task. Our bodies bear a special relationship to the cycles of nature and change. The waxing and waning of the moon must be connected in a special way to the waxing and waning of a woman's body and likewise, a woman's life. In fact, in several languages and cultures, the word for menstruation and the word for moon is identical.[10]

Women throughout the generations have worn the various hats of puberty, pregnancy, childbearing, and menopause. Each of these different life stages have required different skills. Womanhood demands flexibility and change. Puberty calls for excitement, energy, and a newfound creativity. Pregnancy begs for a slowing down and thoughtful contemplation of the newness of birth and life. The breast-feeding mother must change her pace to accommodate an infant with countless hours of nursing, holding, and soothing. Menopause brings a new freedom and redirection of energy.

All throughout the generations, women have experienced the same cycles of life. Like the familiar moon, the body gently speaks to us. The moon's cycles are reflected in our counting and deposited in our bodies. One can look at the moon to observe its phases, and likewise, a woman can observe her own internal body changes:

Every woman can look into herself and see the crescent moon shining there. If you use a speculum, such as is used for inspecting the cervix, a mirror and a torch [flashlight], you will see inside an appearance rather like a globe resting in a crescent, all of which shines and glistens. This is the cervix of the womb. . . . The exact appearance will depend on the time of the month when you look at it, since color, shape and size vary with the menstrual cycle.[11]

Some Personal Notes

I look in my closet, and I struggle. My closet is filled with so many different sizes and types of clothing. At one extreme are the prepregnancy clothes. I look at them and remember back to much thinner days at the height of my professional career. I can't bring myself to give them away, for I fantasize that I will once again fit into them. At the other extreme are my pregnancy clothes—the big comfortable blouses, the suit that attempts to reflect professionalism, and all of the jean skirts with the stretch material around the tummy. I am reminded of the ninth month of pregnancy, when nothing seemed quite right; I seemed to drag my body from place to place, waiting anxiously for the big day. Then there are the clothes for after the birth—the blouses to accommodate a much bigger bosom and the two-piece outfits to make breast-feeding that much easier. Finally, there are the jean skirts and practical blouses to accommodate spit-up, days in the park, art projects, and sitting on the floor. Gradually the bigger sizes and the more practical clothes are outnumbering my professional outfits.

I have struggled to become more comfortable with my closet—my many sizes and "hats." As an adult woman, I have continually struggled with my weight. Too often I have found myself wishing I were just a few pounds thinner. Too often, I have attempted a diet or a change in my eating habits.

I suspect my struggle for a more organized closet represents the difficulties of a modern woman. I grew up in a society that worships a beautiful, thin female figure. Thus, I am destined to struggle with my body and self-image. I, too, struggle with Rosh Chodesh—what we have lost over the generations. I must work to remind myself of the waxing and waning of the moon—of my body—of the changing seasons—and of life as a woman.

Rosh Chodesh, as the waxing and waning of the moon, speaks to my feminine tasks. I must remind myself that my life is filled with constant change. My body, whether pregnant, birthing, breast-feeding, or menstruating, is constantly changing. My reality is to learn to live with these changes—to ebb and flow with them—to live with all of the hats in my closet.

Notes

1. Exodus 12:2.
2. This material is summarized in A. Ben-Ezra, *Minchagai Chagim* (Jerusalem: Hostaat Sefarim 1962).

3. Ibid.

4. *Or Zarua*, The Laws of Rosh Chodesh, 454.

5. Niddah 31b.

6. M. Esther Harding, *Woman's Mysteries: Ancient and Modern* (New York: Harper and Colohon, 1976), pp. 74–75.

7. Genesis 21:7–8.

8. Babylonian Talmud Brachot 62b.

9. See Rivka Zakutinsky, *Techinas: A Voice from the Heart* (Brooklyn, NY: Aura Press, 1992), or Tracy Guren Klirs, *The Merit of Our Mothers* (Cincinnati: HUC Press, 1992). A chapter on *tkhines* appears in this anthology.

10. For a discussion of other cultural names for menstruation, see Katherine Cain, *Luna: Myth and Mystery* (Boulder: Johnson Books, 1991), p. 113.

11. Penelope Shuttle and Peter Redgrove, *The Wise Wound: Menstruation and Every Woman* (London: Paladin Grafton Books, 1986), p. 147.

5
"Kiddush HaChodesh": Teachings of the *B'nai Yissasschar* on Rosh Chodesh

Hillel Goelman

The *B'nai Yissasschar* was written by the Dynover Rebbe, Reb Tzvi Elimelech Shapira (1785–1841).[1] The *sefer* (book) is an exploration of time. Drawing on biblical, talmudic, and kabbalistic sources, the Dynover sensitizes the reader to the heartbeat of Divine presence in each moment that we as human beings experience as "time." As such, he brings together what we have come to label as the more legalistic and linear qualities of Judaism, which many have described as "masculine," with the qualitative and rhythmic flow of the experience of the presence of Shechinah across and throughout time, which have been described as "feminine."

The selection which follows is offered as a "thematic translation" and commentary on the chapter in *B'nai Yissasschar* concerning Rosh Chodesh. It is taken primarily from the first section of the *sefer* entitled, "Kiddush HaChodesh," blessing the new moon and includes the Dynover Rebbe's commentary on the biblical injunction found in Exodus 12:2 to keep Rosh Chodesh. Many codes and commentaries note that this was the first commandment given to our ancestors upon leaving Egypt. Keeping Rosh Chodesh, attuning ourselves to the "moonthly" flow of time, is seen as the first and major understanding a free people must have in relating to the Divine presence in the world.

A definitive and critical translation of this *sefer* has yet to be published, and the material I bring here is not intended to serve as a scholarly, literal translation of the text. The translations are loyal to the meaning and intent of the original text and are interwoven with my attempts to explain and contextualize it. When the *B'nai Yissasschar* is quoted directly and/or literally, the text is presented indented. My hope is that this chapter can make the content of this nineteenth-century *sefer* accessible and comprehensible to interested readers who may wish to pursue their own studies of this wonderful book.[2]

The first teaching: "Months" and "Months of the Year"

HaChodesh ha *ZEH* lachem rosh *chodashim*; rishon *HU* lachem l'*Chodeshay ha shanah* (Exodus 12:2).

החודש הזה לכם ראש חדשים ראשון הוא לכם לחדשי השנה

This month shall be the beginning of the *months*; it is for you the first of the *months for the year*.

The Dynover writes[3] that in order to understand this verse properly, we must consider two ideas therein. The first is the apparent redundancy in the reference to "months" in the first part of the verse and "months for the year" in the second part. The second point to look at is the use of *zeh* ("this"), implying something present or revealed, in the first part and the use of *hu* ("it"), implying something hidden, in the second part of the verse.

Citing the work of a text known to him as the "Revealer of the Depths" (*M'galeh Amukot*), which in turn cites the Zohar as well as the teachings of the AriZal (Rabbi Yitzchak Luria), the Dynover explains that this verse is referring to two manifestations of Divine energy in the world that are reflected in two different ways of experiencing time. When God's energy is thought of as "flowing" from a source more accessible to us, this translates into a notion of time described as "months." The term *zeh* also is seen as implying a more present and accessible source.

When God's energy is perceived as flowing from a source that is more remote, it is described as "months of the year." This is referred to by the Torah as *hu*, in the third person, making it less present and immediate. The most accessible time frame to which we can connect to the Divine is through the cycle of the months and the phases of the moon within each month. The seeming unchangingness of the sun renders the solar calendar as the more inscrutable and inaccessible map of time.

We can draw a parallel using the imagery of the sefirotic tree of life. In this metaphorical tree, God's manifestation in the world is perceived by human beings as ten distinct but mutually interactive *sefirot* or "aspects" of Divine energies. The *sefirah* of *malchut* is seen as the *sefirah* of closest and greatest accessibility to the source of Divine energy. The moon is the symbol of *malchut*, which is the symbol of the presence of God in a personal and meaningful way. While the other *sefirot*, we are taught, are included in *malchut*, they are also hidden and at times impossible to experience. This, the Dynover teaches, is the mystery of the diminishing and near disappearance of the moon. The manifestation of Divine energy ebbs and flows; it is more obvious at certain times and more subtle at other times. Even in its smallest, most diminished form, the moon remains as a "tiny light." The light from the other nine *sefirot* are barely perceptible within the secret of the diminishing of the moon, "the one point" of God's light that we can visually perceive.

The AriZal refers to this as "the mystery of the original point of light and the additional nine [*sefirot*]" and says there are two possible understandings of these mysteries. One understanding claims that the moon, on her own, is the point of light referred to in this mystery. The other way to understand it is that the sun, symbolizing the first *sefirah* of *keter*, is the revealed and explicit *sefirah*, while the other nine *sefirot* are hidden.

There are two ways to look at time: from the known and the accessible, on the one hand, and from the unknown and inaccessible on the other. The *sefirah* of *malchut*, representing the moon, is known and accessible. Its phases are more readily apparent, and through it we know where we are in time and how to attune ourselves to the Divine energy of that time. The Divine energy from *keter*, the highest, most remote of the *sefirot*, is much more difficult to know and access. Divine energy is hidden, difficult to know and to feel. In both *keter* (the first *sefirah*) and *malchut* (the last *sefirah*), the Divine energy is manifest and present.

On yearly cycles of the long journey earth takes around the sun, Divine energy is more difficult to read or to know: its nuances and gradations are not so apparent to human perception. On a monthly cycle, however, the phases and moods of the flow of time are more apparent to us. The *B'nai Yissasschar* provides a detailed analysis of each month's specific and unique characteristics, including which letter of the Hebrew alphabet and which of the twelve tribes of Jacob is aligned with each month. Such alphabetic, numeric, and mythic calibrations begin to help instruct us as to the beauty and mystery of each of the months in the lunar year.

The Second Teaching: The Word *Chodesh*

In "Maamar Daled" (Section 4), the Dynover explores aspects of the word *chadash*, or "new," as part of his discussion on Rosh Chodesh. What does the word itself teach us about relating to God in every moment, in every breath of being?

The Dynover begins by using gematria, the numerical value of each Hebrew letter in a given word. The word *chodesh* adds up to a value of 312 (300 = שׁ, 4 = ד, 8 = ח). He points out that the numerical value of God's name is 26 (5 = ה, 6 = ו, 5 = ה, 10 = י). If the value for God's name is multiplied by 12, the number of months in a year, the result is also 312, the same as the value of the word *chodesh*. The teaching it brings is that in each month, and in each renewing of each month, the Divine name is manifested.

The Dynover goes on to write that the specific quality or aspects of the Divine presence changes in each month. Just as kabbalists have explored the power and meaning of the changing permutations of the four-letter name of God, YHVH, each of these combinations and permutations reveals a different aspect of God: twelve months, twelve combinations of God's name.

The word *chodesh* derives from *chadash*, "new," and implies the "renewal" of time in each month. That is, the change in the combination/manifestation of God's name in each month brings into existence a new aspect of God's being. And, we are taught, "This month shall be for *you*" (Exodus 12:2), that we can interact with the flow of time through our actions in concert with the teachings of Torah. Each month has its own teaching, its underlying energies. It is our task to come to understand the uniquenesses, the possibilities and challenges of each beat of the Divine heart throughout the year. Only in so doing, the Dynover has taught, can we begin to discern the Godly presence in our lives, to embrace and to be embraced by that presence.

The Third Teaching: The Meaning of the Word *zot*, the Feminine Word for "This"

The Dynover cites one of the early teachers of Hasidut, Reb Dov Ber of Mezrich. In the first teaching discussed above the AriZal discussed two ways of relating to time: through the yearly cycle of the sun and the "moonthly" cycle of the moon. In this teaching, Reb Dov Ber discusses the weekly and "moonthly" cycles of time.

Zot olat chodesh b'chodsho

זאת עלת חדש בחדשו לחדשי השנה

This is the sacrifice/going up to God, in each and every month (Numbers 28:14)

This teaching is based upon the word *ZOT*, which in Hebrew is spelled *ZAYIN-ALEF-TAV* זאת. This verse teaches that there are really two ways of being in the world. The first way of being, aligned with the letter *Zayin*, whose numerical value is seven and is symbolic of the seven days of creation. Every week of seven days is emblematic of the original seven days of creation. The seven days of creation are the unchanging paradigm of what was brought into being by God on each day.

Above this weekly paradigm, however, there is a second way of being, and this is the way of being according to the Torah. That is, the people Israel will live according to the Torah and in this way can be proactive and renew time for goodness and life. And this way of being is called *Alef-Tav*—that is, the first and last letters of the Hebrew alphabet. The Torah, our reality map of life (as Reb Zalman Schachter-Shalomi has put it), is made up, at its core essence, of the twenty-two letters of the Hebrew alphabet. The renewal of the moon each month on Rosh Chodesh serves as our reality map through time and is also based on the secrets (*ZOT*—the *alef-bet*) that we lift up (*Olat*) each and every month (*Chodesh b'chodsho*).

The Dynover writes that the *Shechinah*, the feminine presence of God as well as that which is often symbolized through the phases of the moon, is often referred to as *ZOT*.

The Fourth Teaching: Why the *Sefer* Is Called *B'nai Yissasschar*

U'mi'b'nai Yissasschar, yodai binah l'itim, la daat mah yaaseh Yisrael; roshayhem matayim v'chol achayhem al pihem.

ומבני יששכר יוֹרעי בינה לעתים לרעת מה-יעשה ישראל ראשיהם
מאתים וכל-אחיהם על-פיהם

And the tribe of Yissasschar know how to understand time to determine how Israel should act; they had two hundred chiefs and all of their kinsmen followed their words. (1 Chronicles 12:33)

This verse is drawn from the description of how each of the twelve tribes came forward to participate in the anointing of King David. Each tribe, all of which were descended from the sons of Jacob, was seen as providing its own special and unique gift. The question is, why was it important that those "who know how to understand time" come to anoint the king? Further, what does it actually mean that the children of Yissasschar knew "how to understand time"? It means that they actually understood when one month changed into another and, therefore, the appropriate time to bless the month.

The children of Yissasschar understood the secrets and underlying structure of time through which it was determined that the hour is divided into 1,080 *halakim* (sections) of 3½ seconds each. This they derived from the gamatria of *itim* (time) and other secrets revealed to them from God. This is a difficult teaching, however, and the Dynover tells us that it is certain that the precise secret upon which this is based has been lost to us.

The Dynover cites a reference from the AriZal that after the middle of the month, when the moon begins to diminish, the severity of Divine judgment increases. For this reason, weddings are not held at this time of month. And when the moon is renewed, the severity of judgments is sweetened. How is the time to be sweetened? Through *binah*, which means "understanding."

But "understanding" what? If one understands the rhythm and flow of time, this is what can sweeten harsh decrees. And how does one use "understanding/ *binah*" to sweeten harsh decrees? When one uses his or her *binah* to accurately and precisely calculate the *molad*, the actual moment at which a new month begins. This allows us to bless the month and bring *kedusha* (holiness) to it by reciting Kiddush HaChodesh, blessings for the moon.

And so, when people can use their understanding of time to ascertain the birth of the new month, they can create holy impulse/arousal from this plane of reality, which rises to higher realms, bringing a sweetening to the severity of decrees in the 1,080 *halakim* of each hour. This is what is meant in Deuteronomy 4:6:

ki hi hochmatchem u' binatchem l'aynay ha-amim

כי הוא חכמתכם ובינתכם לעיני העמים

this is your wisdom and understanding among the nations

And this, really, is what the quote ("those who know how to understand time") about *B'nai Yissasschar* is really all about: the verb "to know" implies intimate knowledge, joining , conjoining, and union (as in Genesis 4:25, "And man knew woman"). That is, what the B'nai Yissasschar were capable of was not simply "knowing time," but joining, bringing together, TIME and UNDERSTANDING. In bringing an UNDERSTANDING to the flow of TIME, they could raise peoples' awareness of various aspects of time and guide their actions accordingly. Thus, at a time when the moon is almost completely diminished and the severity of judgment imbues almost every moment of existence, they can determine the precise moment when the *molad*, the birth of the new moon, is imminent, can bless that moment and, in so doing, can sweeten the judgments in all 1,080 moments of the hour.

And this is why there were two hundred leaders of Yissasschar and this is why their people followed the words of their mouths (*peh-pihem*) in matters related to the moon. The gamatria of mouth (*b'peh* = 87) and moon (*levanah* = 87) is the same. That is, the two hundred leaders of Yissasschar were teaching their kinsmen orally (*b'peh*) about the moon (*levanah*) through understanding its phases.

The Dynover concludes this section with a typically elusive, koan-like instruction: "I have given you hints in a very general way. The insightful person will walk in paths of righteousness."

The Fifth Teaching: Each Breath and between Each Breath

In this short section, the Dynover continues to explore the 1,080 *halakim* of each hour. Readers may find this portion somewhat puzzling, but are encouraged to "hold on for the ride" and to read the following two to three paragraphs more slowly, perhaps more than once. No, a calculator is not necessary, but if you wish to check the Dynover's math (as I have), go right ahead. The beauty of the basic ideas and the confluence of the Hebrew letters, their mystical values, and the growing awareness of God's presence in each breath makes this short teaching, I think, a beautiful jewel of Torah and one of the most exquisite examples of the *B'nai Yissasschar*'s light.

In a dazzling and sometimes confusing display of his mastery of the secrets of gamatria, the Dynover points out a number of striking features. For example, the number 1,080 is the sum total of the number of *halakim* in each hour and is also the result of the following bit of arithmetic: multiplying the numerical value of one of the first two letters of God's name, Yud Heh (=15) by the numerical value of *hesed* (graciousness = 72). This means that each moment of each hour is imbued with the Divine name of (Yah or Yud Heh) and the Divine attribute of *hesed*/loving-kindness and is referred to in Psalm 150, verse 6:

kol ha neshama tihallel YAH.

כל הנשמה תהלל יה

every breath shall praise GOD.

In every single breath, God's existence is renewed in graciousness, as the existence comes and returns with each breath (Psalm 115:17–18):

lo ha-maytim yihallelu-YAH . . . v'anachnu nevarech YAH may atah v'ad olam.

לא המתים יהללו יה ואנחנו נברך יה מעתה ועד עולם

the dead will not praise GOD . . . we shall bless GOD from this moment until the end of time.

While most hours in fact are made up of the 1,080 *halakim*, because of the rotation of the planet, there are from time to time an additional 793 "extra" *halakim*. As noted above, 1,080 is the value of Hesed multiplied by the value of the first two letters of God's name (Yud Heh). Now, when the value of *hesed* is multiplied by the value of the second two letters of God's name (*Vav Heh*), the result is 792. The value of one is added to create the number 793. The 793 "extra" *halakim* are obtained by adding one to God's *hesed* (72) multiplied by *Vav Heh*, the last two letters of God's name.

And what is the significance of this number of "extra" *halakim*? In the Dynover's words: "This teaches us that Vav and Heh are the secret of Time—in Hebrew, 'z'man.' The value of 'ha z'man,' the time, is 97, the same as for the phrase 'mah beyn' which means, 'that which is between.' The Vav and Heh are the letters which span the hours and bridge one time to the next, from one month to the next. And this is why there are 793 halakim between each month—Vav Heh times Hesed."

The Sixth Teaching: Toward an Understanding of Rosh Chodesh—Bridges in Time

The *B'nai Yissasschar* defies simple summarization, description, or categorization. In trying to capture some of the major themes of the Dynover's writings on Rosh Chodesh, the most we could hope to do would be to identify some of the more salient threads woven into this beautiful tapestry, to highlight the striking nuances within the intricacy of the text—the broad sweep of ideas throughout the book—and participate in the dance of images that illuminate each page.

The central image is of time in general and Rosh Chodesh in particular as essential components of the experience of *devekut*, adhering closely or clinging to God. The flow of time weaves us into an ongoing and intimate relationship with God. The sense of *devekut* is enriched and deepened specifically through the experience of Rosh Chodesh since each month reveals to us different manifestations of the Divine Presence, allowing us to participate in and know that Presence with our deepest spiritual selves.

The feminine attributes of this experience of *devekut* through Rosh Chodesh are spoken to directly in the B'nai Yissasschar: the structure of the language (*zot*) and the manifestations of *Shechinah* in this world through the changing phases of the moon and the rhythmic changes of our innermost beings. Rosh Chodesh, the birth of each new month, brings us back to an awareness of our connection to the Source of All Being, both in the larger planetary revolutions of celestial lights and in the immanence and immediacy of every breath we draw.

Notes

1. A fuller description of the life of the Dynover Rebbe and the *B'nai Yissasschar* can be found in a chapter entitled, "The B'nai Yissasschar: A Thematic Translation and Commentary," in *Worlds of Jewish Prayer: A Festschrift in Honor of Rabbi Zalman M. Schachter-Shalomi*, ed. Shoshana Harris Wiener and Jonathan Omer-Man (Northvale, NJ: Jason Aronson Publishers, 1994).

2. I would be most interested in hearing from others who are studying the *B'nai Yissasschar*.

3. Maamaray Rosh Chodesh, Maamar Alef, "Kidush HaChodesh."

6
Tkhines for Rosh Chodesh: Women's Prayers of Devotion

Tracy Guren Klirs

The current foment in women's studies and the arrival of feminist concerns into discussions of Jewish issues have brought a renewed interest in an old and hitherto virtually forgotten Yiddish liturgical genre—that known as *tkhines*. Taking its name from the Hebrew *techinnot*, or supplications, this uniquely feminine prayer literature was written in the vernacular (*mame loshn*), rather than the sacred language (*loshn koydesh*) so as to be immediately accessible to its predominantly female readership. Since their earliest appearance in the late sixteenth century, tkhines eventually developed into one of the most popular genres of Yiddish writings. Published originally in small pamphlets, tkhines later were produced in complete volumes (known as *shas tkhines*) or in the backs of *siddurim*. In the early decades of the twentieth century, some tkhine collections were published in the United States. But, owing to the decline of both traditional Jewish piety and of Yiddish, the genre soon disappeared from the American scene. At the same time, the Nazis' near destruction of the world's largest Yiddish-speaking population sounded the death knell of the tkhine literature in Europe.

The tkhines emerged out of the traditional piety of premodern Eastern European Jewry. They shared the same yearnings, hopes, and beliefs expressed in the classical Hebrew liturgy—the *siddur* (prayer book), *machzor* (High Holy Day prayer book), and *haggadah* (Passover liturgy). Yet the uniqueness of the tkhines lay in the fact that, in addition to prayers for weekdays, sabbaths, and holidays—the cycle of the Jewish year—they also contained prayers addressing the day-to-day needs and concerns of women, as well as the significant biological events of women's lives. These included earning a livelihood; the safety, health, and well-being of one's family; and the education and moral upbringing of one's children. They also included a woman's "life cycle": marriage, menstruation, conception, pregnancy, childbirth, brit milah, weaning, death, and mourning; as well as the three specific *mitzvot* (commandments) for women: making challah, candle lighting, and *niddah* (family purity).

Tkhines also diverged from the standard Hebrew liturgy in style, voice, and tone. The siddur speaks in the normative voice of the (male) collective, frequently in the first person plural, and tends towards the formal and formalistic. The tkhines, on the other hand, are intimately personal, speaking in the first-person singular, and tend to be informal, folksy, even conversational. The siddur's classic style, lofty and poetic, contrasts sharply with the prosaic, stream-of-consciousness feel of the tkhines. Yet both types of literature bear the undeniable mark of religious authenticity.

Finally, while the standard Hebrew liturgy was created by men primarily for men, the best known and most commonly imitated composers of tkhines were women, who wrote specifically for other women. This was, in fact, Judaism's first *religious* literature in whose shaping women played a significant role. Popular authors of the eighteenth and nineteenth centuries, such as Sore bas Toyvim, Seril bas Yankev Halevi Segal (the daughter of the famous Dubner Maggid), and Sore Rivke Rokhl Leye Horowitz, set the standard for generations to come and were frequently plagiarized. In fact, male authors—including poor Yeshiva students hoping to cash in on the genre's popularity and *maskilim* (free-thinkers of the Enlightenment period) seeking to discredit tkhines through overwrought parodies—sometimes composed and published tkhines pseudonymously under the names of the classic women authors. Even though many of these works appeared long after the death of their purported authors, they were eagerly snatched up by avid tkhine readers.

Not surprisingly, Rosh Chodesh presented one of the more common occasions for composing tkhines. Rosh Chodesh had long been associated with women, who had celebrated it as a semiholiday since antiquity, based primarily on the famous midrash in which God rewarded women with a monthly day of rest for their refusal to participate in the great idolatry of the golden calf. But the holiday's connection to women is, in fact, far deeper and more universal than the midrash would suggest. After all, Rosh Chodesh demarcates the cycles of the moon, providing the foundation for the entire lunar Hebrew calendar. In virtually every culture, the cycles of the moon are associated with women. This is attested to by the very word we use to describe a woman's monthly cycle: *menstruation*, from the Latin *menstrualis* or "monthly." In many languages, the word for "moon" is feminine. While these themes certainly played no conscious role in the writing of tkhines, the universally female and regenerative symbolism of the moon makes Rosh Chodesh a natural subject for women's prayers.

Several of the most famous authors of original tkhines wrote special prayers for Rosh Chodesh. Sore bas Toyvim's best known work, *Shloyshe Sh'orim* (Three gates) contains a lengthy section to be recited "when one blesses the New Moon" (i.e., on Rosh Chodesh). In this section, Sore strives to invoke God's compassion upon Israel through "zkhus oves"—the merit of our fathers (ancestors). In particular, she invokes the three patriarchs—Abraham, Isaac, and Jacob—as well as Moyshe Rabeynu ("Moses our teacher") to arise from their graves and plead for the children of Israel before the throne of the Almighty. Sore also invokes Meylekh Hamoshiakh—King Messiah—to plead Israel's case.

Sore's tkhine also includes language that closely parallels the Birkat HaChodesh, blessing of the new moon, recited in the synagogue on the Sabbath immediately preceding each new moon. This prayer asks that the new month bring God's blessings of life, livelihood, abundance, and health. Sore includes all of these blessings but also greatly expands upon them, weaving in *midrashim*, illuminating stories that extrapolate a text, and other embellishments. Sore also asks God to erase her sins and those of her people, to enable her and her husband to support Torah scholars and give generously to *tzedakah*, righteousness in the form of charity, and to rebuild the Holy Temple. These themes recur throughout the tkhine literature.

But Sore's most unusual addition to the section for Rosh Chodesh is her detailed description of *gan eydn* (paradise). In Sore's *gan eydn*, there are six chambers, each higher than the next, containing the souls of many thousands of her righteous ancestors, who spend their days praising the Almighty and studying the Torah. Some of the greatest biblical figures reside there. What makes Sore's vision of paradise so remarkable, however, is that it is populated entirely by women! Amongst the residents of this *gan eydn* are Pharaoh's daughter, Moses' mother (Yocheved), his sister Miriam the Prophetess, Deborah the

Judge, and, in the uppermost chamber where no one else may enter—the four matriarchs, Sarah, Rebecca, Rachel, and Leah.

Seril bas Yankev Halevi Segal wrote a "Tkhine of the Matriarchs for the New Moon of Elul." Tkhines in general include a great deal of penitential prayer. This one, for the month of Elul (which precedes the penitential season of Rosh Hashanah and Yom Kippur), contains both the traditional themes of the Hebrew liturgy for this season as well as more specifically "feminine" themes focused on domestic life. Seril pleads for God's mercy, not based on her own righteousness or merit, but based rather on God's ability to identify with the suffering of her ancestors (again, the power of *zkhus oves*) and memory of past divine mercy and forgiveness. Seril reminds God that the angels were moved to mercy at the sight of Isaac bound on the altar, and that their tears of compassion prevented Abraham from slaughtering his son. She offers her tears of contrition in the hopes that, in similar fashion, they will move *Eyl Moley Rakhamim* (God Full of Compassion) to forgive her sins.

Elsewhere in her tkhine, Seril invokes the memory of Joseph, and calls upon each of the matriarchs in turn—Sarah, Rebekah, Rachel, and Leah—to arise from their graves, intercede with God, and to plead for mercy and a good year for all of Yisroyel. Hence the name: "Tkhine of the Matriarchs." Not only does Seril ask that she and her people be forgiven of their sins, but that their families, and especially their young children, be kept safe and intact during the coming year, and that she and her husband be enabled to earn a livelihood with dignity and not (God forbid!) be forced to rely upon charity. This last sentiment, repeated frequently throughout the tkhine literature, is deeply embedded in Jewish tradition. One of the clearest expressions can be found in Birkat Hamazon, the grace after meals. ("We beseech You, O Lord our God, let us not be in need either of the gifts of flesh and blood or of their loans, but only of Your helping hand, which is full, open, holy and ample, so that we may not be ashamed or confounded forever and ever.") Seril asks for all of these things, not only through the merit of her pious biblical ancestors, but also through the merit of her own innocent children, who are worthy by virtue of their study of the Torah.

In her impassioned argument for a lenient sentence on the upcoming High Holy Days, Seril frequently quotes the Torah to the Judge of All the World, as if to say: Your own words compel You to behave with compassion towards your weak creatures. She compares herself to the righteous Chana (whose story is recounted in the Rosh HaShanah Haftarah), mother of the prophet Samuel, who went to the shrine at Shilo to pray for an end to her barrenness. Chana figures prominently in the tkhine literature, first, for her own sake as a model of great piety and as a sympathetic figure from whom barren women could draw encouragement, and second, because her name forms a Hebrew acronym for the three special women's *mitzvot*: "חנה," in which "ח" = *challah*, "נ" = *niddah*, and "ה" = *hadlakat nerot* (lighting of candles).

Seril's tkhine concludes with sections for the *Yizkor* (memorial) service, for Yom Kippur, and for the *shofar* service for Rosh Hashanah. This tkhine was to serve a twofold purpose: (1) to be used in private meditation at home in preparation for the High Holy Days, and (2) to be taken to the synagogue and used as a replacement for, or supplement to, the *Machzor*, during the High Holy Day services.

Another tkhine for Rosh Chodesh is simply entitled, "Tkhine for the Blessing of the New Moon." Again, the author asks for those things that are most immediate and essential to life: sustenance, food, livelihood with honor, success, and joy. She then goes on to ask for protection from troubles and sorrow for herself and all Yisroyel, for forgiveness of sins, and for protection against all kinds of evil (e.g., the evil inclination, the evil eye, thieves, malicious people, sickness, false accusations, evil spirits, hunger, and mishaps). Here the author simply reflects the very real fears and terrors that beset the typical inhabitant of the *shtetl* (village) in her day. Faced with the ever-present threat of war, pogrom, famine, infant death, disease, and impoverishment, East European Jews personified their fears in the form of a whole host of demons, imps, poisoned looks, and magical powers. Of course, some of their most feared demons—such as thieves, gossips, and hunger—still have not been vanquished to this day.

"Tkhine for the Blessing of the New Moon"[1] also mentions two of the "women's *mitzvot*"—*challah* and *niddah*—and asks that each part of the petitioner's body be used for a holy purpose: "You have opened my eyes to see Your Kingdom and my ears to hear of Your wonders . . . ; you have opened my mouth to tell of Your might and my hands to do Your mitsves. . . . May my feet walk to shul to praise You. . . . May my breasts nurse children who will be strong. . . ." This author, rather than feeling any shame about her body and its functioning, rejoices that God created each part of her for a specific purpose, which, if properly directed, can lead to a life of holiness and mitzvot.

The author also asks that her children devote themselves to the study of Torah and performance of mitzvot, and that they be protected from all harm. She ends with a quotation, in the original Hebrew, from Psalm 19, traditionally recited at the end of the silent amidah: "May the words of my mouth and the meditation of my heart be acceptable to You, O God, my Rock and my Redeemer." Here, too, the author follows the typical pattern for composing tkhines, which frequently either begin or end with a Hebrew quotation drawn from the *siddur* (prayer book) or the Bible.

Another of the classic tkhine composers, Sore Rivke Rokhl Leye Horowitz, also composed a Rosh Chodesh tkhine.[2] She named the tkhine after herself: "Tkhine of Sore, Rivke, Rokhl and Leye." As the title implies, her tkhine also invokes the four matriarchs. Like those already discussed, this tkhine was intended to be read on *Shabbes M'vorkhim*—the Sabbath preceding Rosh Chodesh. It asks for a return to Jerusalem (an aspect of the ancient messianic hope) and invokes the merit of each of the four matriarchs in turn, as well as the three patriarchs—Abraham, Isaac, and Jacob—and King David. Themes found elsewhere in tkhines for Rosh Chodesh are reiterated here: requests for a month of goodness, blessing, sustenance, and strength; for worthy and God-fearing children; and to be spared humiliation and shame.

Several collections of tkhines, which appear later than the works described above, contain a separate tkhine for each month of the Hebrew calendar. The Rosh Chodesh tkhines described below can be found in a particularly popular collection, published in 1916 in New York under the name, *Shas Tkhines Rav P'ninim*, (*Many Pearls Tkhine Collection*). These tkhines, published anonymously, share some themes and concerns with the (generally) longer works by the classic authors, yet each of the Rosh Chodesh tkhines in the *Rav Peninim* collection also reflects the unique quality of a particular Hebrew month. Each refers to an event traditionally believed to have occurred in a given month, as well as to particular holidays or customs observed in that month. Frequently, biblical personages associated with the month in question are invoked. For instance, in the month of Cheshvan, Rachel died giving birth to Benjamin, and King Solomon completed the first Temple. Hence the author invokes Rachel and Benjamin to arise from their graves and "beat on the doors of mercy" on Israel's behalf. The tkhine for Cheshvan also contains a plea for the rebuilding of the holy Temple.

The tkhine for Kislev recalls that the matriarch Leah's first son, Reuben, was born in Kislev. The petitioner pleads with Leah to beseech God on behalf of her own children, asking especially that they be enabled to marry "good and pious" husbands. It also reviews the story of Chanukah (which begins on the 25th of Kislev), including a conflation of the Chanukah story with the Apocryphal book of Judith. In the tkhine's rewriting of the Apocrypha, the heroine, Judith, cuts off the head of Antiochus rather than Holofernes. Through the merit of Judith—the savior of her people—the tkhine author pleads for the security of her own family.

The following passage from the tkhine for the month of Kislev is a dramatic reminder that Jewish parents' concerns for their children have changed very little over the centuries:

> Stand up, our Mother Leah, and present yourself before the Throne of
> Glory to plead for your children and also for me, your daughter [so and

so, the daughter of so and so], that I and my husband will merit to raise our children, and may our beloved daughters not—God forbid!—fall to the lot of evil husbands. And may we have luck in earning a livelihood so that we may be able to give them good and pious husbands, so that they may have good and pious children!

In similar fashion, Abraham is invoked for the month of Tevet, Moses for the month of Sh'vat, Mordechai and Esther for Adar, Miriam for Iyyar, Joseph for Tammuz, and Aaron for Av. Most of these tkhines close with a supplication that the author has carefully tied to the historical and religious associations developed earlier in the tkhine. The tkhine for Tevet, following a litany of various tragedies that befell the Israelites in that month, ends with a plea for redemption from all troubles. The tkhine for Sh'vat, the month in which the New Year of Trees is observed, asks God to bless the fruit of the trees and protect the Jews from cold and death. The tkhine for Adar asks God to forgive their sins through the merit of all the tzedakah the Jews give on the festival of Purim. On other months, petitioners plead for livelihood, protection of family, for children who engage in the study of Torah, for redemption, sustenance, and divine mercy. These themes are by no means limited to the tkhines for Rosh Chodesh. Indeed, they are typical of the entire corpus of tkhines.

Each of the Rosh Chodesh tkhines remains distinctive by virtue of mention of the specific holidays, customs, and observances of a given month; by invoking historical events or biblical forebears and heroes who have been associated, no matter how tangentially, with that month; and by offering petitions that are appropriate to the occasion.

The tkhines represent a remarkable and highly significant chapter in the story of Jewish women's prayer literature. Recently, a number of tkhines have been translated into English and published. The books and articles containing these new translations have begun to open the door into the private religious lives of our foremothers and, in so doing, have breathed new life into an old form. In their search for an authentic voice that affirms their identity as women yet remains anchored in Jewish tradition, some religious poets are composing new tkhines today. Geela Rayzel Raphael captures the rhythm and flavor of the original tkhines, while infusing her "Tkhine for Rosh Chodesh" with a late twentieth-century feminist consciousness.

Tkhine for Rosh Chodesh

Sacred Mother of the Moon, You have given us this time of Rosh Chodesh for enjoyment and renewal. As Your daughters gather in the darkness, we attune to Your sacred energy. Your crescent sign, a reminder of the waxing cycles of the Jewish people, is for us a symbol of Your ever-present ability to restore our souls. We light candles to honor Your presence and welcome You with warmth as our female ancestors did in the desert.

Shechinah, Feminine Divine Presence, You have remained with us through hard times. Observing Rosh Chodesh was almost a forgotten observance, yet You have again demonstrated Your steadfastness by helping us recover our sacred time. Be with us again as we enter this new month filling our life with bounty and blessing.

Tkhine for the Blessing of the New Moon

Please, I beseech You, blessed God, who generously provides food and clothing to all creatures, give me my sustenance and provide food for my household and a decent living for all *yisro'el*, with contentment of spirit and not with sorrow, with honor and not with indignity, so that I may not be ashamed. May all our endeavors bring good results, with blessing and success, and may there be benediction in our work. May You bring us joy and raise me up high. Have mercy upon us in all that we ask and strengthen our will and our hearts to do good. Shield us from darkness and give us light. Be a protector to me and to my household and to all *yisro'el,* and shield me from all kinds of trouble and sorrow this year and in all years to come and in all months and weeks and in all hours and in the time it takes to blink the eyes. Protect me from all confusion and from all the ominous fears of my heart. May we hear good tidings,[3] true and righteous. Forgive the sins and misdeeds that I have committed. I have sinned and wronged and offended. May there be no more sin or misdeed in me.

May the *yeytser hore* not lust within me and may You protect me from thieves and malicious people, from sickness and false accusations. May You save me from evil spirits such as *sheydim* and *mazikim* and from all evil encounters, and from hunger and from mishaps and sorrows, and may I be worthy of grace and mercy in Your eyes.

I turn toward Your Holy Name so that Your Holy Name will be identified with me, and my enemies will be in awe of me. May my face be illuminated, and may this awe envelop all creatures. May we be praised on high in all the heavens and upon all of the earth and may my good name be known throughout all the land. May my dreams be fulfilled and bring good results through the power of holiness that strengthens everything and by virtue of Your thirteen attributes, which, we have been assured through *moyshe*, Your servant, will never be reversed. May this merit stand me in good stead. These are the thirteen attributes:

The Lord, the Lord God is gracious and compassionate,
  patient, abounding in kindness and faithfulness,
assuring love for a thousand generations, forgiving iniquity,
  transgression, and sin, and granting pardon.[4]

Yehi rotsn, God, my God and God of my ancestors, that You grant me grace and compassion and joy and happiness and bring good luck to me in all my endeavors and may I merit grace in Your eyes.

Illumine my children's eyes[5] through the study of *toyre*, and may they not forget what they have learned. May You give clarity, beauty, felicity, and grace to my speech, and may everything that I request come to pass and bring good results.

Please, I beseech You, God of *yankev*, for the sake of Your Holy Name. You are known throughout the world. You heard the prayers of *yankev* and shielded him from evil. You gave him his garments of glory and with Your great power You performed wonders and signs for *yisro'el*. Thus, I also ask that You open Your hand and sustain and protect me forever from all evil encounters and from debilitating illness. Perform miracles for my benefit, always and in the blink of an eye. I beg of You, my Lord, listen to my plea, for You listen to everyone's prayers. You, who are compassionate and just, seated on the throne of mercy, open all the seven heavens[6] to my prayer and accept my requests.

Riboyne shel oylem, I beseech You to forgive my sins against You and against all people, so that I may come in purity to the other world and so that I may have rest in my grave. Be compassionate to me in my lifetime, and hear my prayer, just as You heard our ancestors' prayers, and as You heard the prayer of our pious mother *khane*.[7] For I, a poor woman, want to reveal to You all that is in my heart, just as a child confides to its father. Even as it is written, "like a father is compassionate to his children,"[8] so may You also be compassionate to me, as a father to his child.

Riboyne shel oylem, as You have helped me until now, continue to help me by sending good angels to lead me on the right path, so that I and my children may be nourished by Your hand and not—*khas vesholem*—by others. May I not be degraded, and may the *ayin hore* not have any power over me. Save us from all evil, and may I live in peace.

Riboyne shel oylem, You have not created human beings in vain. You have opened my eyes to see Your kingdom and my cars to hear of Your wonders throughout the world; You have opened my mouth to tell of Your might and my hands to do Your *mitsves*.

Dear God, You have commanded us to take *khale* and to light candles and to examine ourselves for menstrual blood so that our souls may remain pure. May my feet walk to *shul* to praise You and may I walk in Your path. May my breasts nurse children who will be strong. I beg of You, dear God, may violent death not overtake them. May You strengthen my children's hearts through the study of *toyre*, and may their hearts be as open as the gates of the entryway and the hall of *gan eydn*, and may we see them grow up to devote themselves to the study of Your *toyre* and *mitsves*. May there be no tears in my eyes because of worry, and may there be no sound of wailing or mourning in my household. May we not have to be fed by others, and may we merit to see salvation and consolation.

Riboyne shel oylem, I beseech You to give me good luck and if I—*khas vesholem*—have no good luck, shield me, Almighty Lord, and destroy my bad luck this year and every week and every day and every minute. Renew my weeks and my days, that they may be blessed with success, and may You heal all broken hearts. Grant me grace and favor in Your eyes and also in human eyes, so that no one will gossip about me. I raise my eyes to heaven, and with a broken heart I say to You as *dovid hamelekh, olev hasholem* wrote: "God will not despise a broken heart and a rejected heart."[9] Favorably fulfill all the requests of my heart,[10] for You are a God of mercy. May the words of my mouth and the meditations of my heart be acceptable to You, O God, my Rock and my Redeemer.[11]*Omeyn*.

תחנה פון ראש חודש בענטשין

אָנָא אִיךְ בֶּעט דִיךְ גָאט יִתְבָּרַךְ דֶר דָא בְּרֵייט אָן דִיא שְׁפֵּייז צו אַלֶע
בַּשֶׁעפֶענֶעש אוּן בְּרֵייט אָן מַלְבּוּשִׁים שִׁיק מִיר מַיין דֶר נֶערוּנג אוּן דוּ זָאלְשְׁט
מִיךְ שְׁפֵּייזִין אוּן מַיין הוֹיז גיזִינד אוּן כָּל יִשְׂרָאֵל אַיין פַּרְנָסָה טוֹבָה מִיט נַחַת
רוּחַ אוּן נִיט מִיט צַעַר מִיט כָּבוֹד אוּן נִיט מִיט בִּזָיוֹן דָשׁ אִיךְ זָאל נִיט פַּאר
שֶׁעמְט וֶוערִין אוּן צוּ גוּטִין זָאל זֵיין אוּנְזָר אַרֶבֶּט מִיט בְּרָכָה אוּן הַצְלָחָה
אוּן עֵשׂ זָאל זֵיין אַיין בֶּענְטשׁוּנג אִין אוּנְזָר וֶוערק אוּן זָאלְשְׁט אוּנְז בַּגְלִיקִין
אוּן אוֹיף צוּ בְּרֵיינְגֶען מִיךְ דֶר בַּאריִם דִיךְ אִיבֶּר אוּנְז אִין אַלֶעם וָואשׁ מִיר
פַר לַאנְגֶן אוּן דוּא זָאלְשְׁט בַּגיטִיגֶן אוּנְזֶר וֵוילן אוּן אוּנְזֶער הַארְץ צוּ גוּטִין
אוּן בַּאשִׁירֶעם אוּנְז צִיא אוּנְז אוֹישׁ פוּן דִיא פִּינְצְטֶערְנֶעשׁ אוּן דֶר לַייכְט אוּנְז
אוּן זַאיי אַיין בַּאשִׁיצֶער צוּ מִיר אוּן צוּ מַיין הוֹיז גיזִינד אוּן צוּא כָּל יִשְׂרָאֵל
אוּן בַּשִׁירֶעם מִיךְ פוּן אַלֶע מִינֵי צָרוֹת אוּן צַעַר אִין דֶעם יָאר אוּן אִין אַלֶע
נָאךְ קוּמֶענְדִיגֶע יָאר אוּן אִין אַלֶע חֲדָשִׁים אוּן וָואכִין אוּן אַלֶע שָׁעוֹת אוּן
אַלֶע אוֹגֶן בְּלִיק אוּן בַּאשִׁירֶעם מִיךְ פוּן אַלֶע פַּאר טוֹמלוּנג אוּן פוּן אַלֶע בַּייזֶע

דֶער שְׁרֶעקֶענֶשׁ פוּן מַיין הָאָרץ אוּן זָאלשְׁט מִיךְ לָאזִין הֶערִין בְּשׂוֹרוֹת טוֹבוֹת
וְאָרהָאפְטִיגֶע אוּן רֶעכְט פָּארטְגֶע אוּן זָאלשְׁט מִיר פַר גֶעבְּן מַיינֶע חֲטָאִים
וַעֲווֹנוֹת שֶׁחָטָאתִי וְשֶׁעָוִיתִי וְשֶׁפָשַׁעֻתִּי אִין מִיר זָאל נִיט זַיין אִין מִיר קֵיין חֵטְא
וְעָוֹן אוּן עֶשׁ זָאל נִיט גִּילוּסטִין אִין מִיר דֶער יֵצֶר הָרָע אוּן זָאלשְׁט מִיר
בַּשִׁירְמֶן פָּאר גַזְלָנִים אוּן פָּאר בֵּייזֶע לַייט פוּן קְרֵיינְק אוּן פוּן בִּלְבּוּלִים אוּן
פָּאר שֵׁדִים וּמַזִיקִים אוּן פָּאר בֵּייזֶע אַלֶע פַר בֵּייזֶע בַּאגֶעגֶענֶעשׁ אוּן פָּאר אוּן
פָּאר בֵּייזֶע צוּא קוּמֶענֶשׁ אוּן פָּאר טְרַוּיֶערְקֵייט אוּן זָאלשְׁט מִיר גֶעבְּין חֵן
וְחֶסֶד וְרַחֲמִים אִין דַיינֶע אוֹיגִין אוּן צוּא דִיר טוּא אִיךְ הָאפִין אוּן דוּא
זָאלשְׁט מִיר עֶנטְפֶערִין אוּן צוּ דַיינֶעם נָאמֶן טוּא אִיךְ מִיר קֶערִין דָאשׁ דַיין
הֵיילִיגֶער נָאמֶן זָאל גִירוּפִין זַיין אוֹיף מִיר זַייא זָאלִין זִיךְ פָארכְטִין פַר מִיר
מַיין פָּנִים זָאל דֶר לַייכְטִין מַיין פָארכְט זָאל זַיין גְנָוארְפְן אוֹיף אַלֶע אַלֶע בַּשְׁעפֶנֶשׁ
אוּן מִיר זָאלְן גִילוֹיבְּט זַיין אוֹיבִּין אִין אַלֶע הִימְלֶען אוּן אוּנטִין אוֹיף דֶער
עֶרד אוּן מַיין גוּטֶער נָאמֶען זָאל זַיין אִין אַלֶע לֶענדֶר אוּן מַיינֶע חֲלוֹמוֹת
זָאלִין מִיר זַיין צוּא גוּטִין מִיט דֶעם קְרָאפְט דָאשׁ הֵיילִיקֵייט דֶער זִיךְ אַלֶשׁ
שְׁטַּארְקְט אוּן דֶר זְכוּת פוּן דִיא דְרַייצֶעהֶן מִדוֹת דָאשׁ.דוּ הָאשְׁט פָאר זִיכֶערְט
דוּרךְ מֹשֶׁה דַיין קְנֶעכְט אַז דָאשׁ זָאל נִיט וֶוערִין לֵיידִיג וִוידֶער גִיקֶערְט דֶער
זְכוּת זָאל מִיר בַּייא שְׁטַיין דָאס זֶעלְבִּיגֶע זַיינֶען דִיא דְרַייצֶעהֶן מִדוֹת :

יְיָ יְיָ אֵל רַחוּם וְחַנּוּן אֶרֶךְ אַפַּיִם וְרַב חֶסֶד וֶאֱמֶת נוֹצֵר חֶסֶד לָאֲלָפִים
נוֹשֵׂא עָוֹן וָפֶשַׁע וְחַטָאָה וְנַקֵּה :

יְהִי רָצוֹן עֶשׁ זָאל עֶשׁ זַיין דֶער וִוילִין פַאר דִיר גָאט מַיין גָאט אוּן גָאט פוּן מַיינֶע
עֶלטֶערִין אַז דוּא זָאלשְׁט מִיר גֶעבִּין לַייבִּין זֶעלִיקֵייט אוּן דֶר בַּארִימְקֵייט אוּן
פְרֵייד אוּן דֶער פְּרֵייאוּנג אוּן מַאנ בַּגְלִיקִין מִיר אִין אַלֶע מַיינֶע וֶוערק אוּן
זָאלשְׁט מִיר גֶעבִּין לַייט זֶעלִיקֵייט אִין דַיינֶע אוֹיגִין אוּן דֶר לַייכְט מַיינֶע
קִינְדֶר זֵייעֶרֶע אוֹיגִין אִין דֶר תּוֹרָה אוּן מַיינֶע קִינְדֶר זָאלִין נִיט פָאר גֶעסִין
וְוָאשׁ זֵייא הָאבִּין גִילֶערִינְט אוּן אִין מַיינֶע רֵייד זָאלְשְׁטוּ גֶעבִּין לוֹיטֶרְקֵייט
אוּן שׁוֹנהַייט אוּן לַייט זֶעלִיקֵייט אוּן גִינָאד אוּן אַלֶץ וְוָאשׁ אִיךְ בֶּעט זָאלְשְׁטוּ
מִיר בַּעוֶוערִין צוּ גוּטִין :

אָנָא אִיךְ בֶּעט דִיךְ גָאט פוּן יַעֲקֹב וֶוענִין דַיין הֵיילִיגִין נָאמֶען דוּא וֶוערְשְׁט
דָאךְ דֶער קֶענְט אִין דֶער גַאנְצֶער וֶוֶועלְט דֶען דוּ בִּישְׁט דֶר דָא הָאט גֶהֶערְט
דֶשׁ גִיבֶּעט פוּן יַעֲקֹב אוּן הָאשְׁט אִים בַּהִיט פָאר אַלֶעם בֵּייזִין אוּן הָאשְׁט
אִים גִיגֶעבִּין זַיין מַלְבּוּשֵׁי כָּבוֹד מִיט דַיינֶע גוּטֶע מַאכְט אוּן הָאשְׁט גִטָאן
וְוָאוּנְדֶר אוּן צַייכֶן מִיט דִי יִשְׂרָאֵל דְרוֹם טוּא אִיךְ אוֹיךְ בַּגֶערִין פוּן דִיר אַז
דוּ זָאלְשְׁט עֶפֶנֶען דַיין הָאנְט אוּן זָאלְשְׁט מִיךְ זָאלְשְׁט מִיךְ בַּהִיטִין הַיינְט
אוּן אֵייבִּיג פוּן אַלֶע בֵּייזֶע בַּגֶעגְנֶשׁ אוּן בֵּייזֶע קְרַאנְקַייט אוּן זָאלְשְׁט מִיר
נִסִּים טָאן צוּ גוּטִין אַלֶע צַייט אוּן אַלֶע אוֹיגִן בְּלִיק בֶּעט אִיךְ דִיר דֶר הֶער

פֿון מיר מײַן גְבֶּעט דֶען דו דֶר הֶערְשְׁט דִי גְבֶּעט פֿון אַלֶע מײַלֶר רַחוּם וְצַדִיק
יוֹשֵׁב עַל כִּסֵא רַחֲמִים דֶער זָאל מִיךְ אוֹיף טָאן צו מײַנֶע תְּפִלָה אַלֶע זִיבְּן
הִימְלֶען אוּן מִיךְ פֿאַר נֶעמֶען וָואס אִיךְ וָויל הָאבִּין פֿון פֿאַר דִיר :

רִבּוֹנוֹ שֶׁל עוֹלָם אִיךְ טוּא דִיךְ בֶּעטִין דוּא זָאלְשְׁט מִיר פֿאַר גֶעבְּן מײַנֶע זִינְד
וָואס אִיךְ הָאבּ וָוידֶר גִיטָאן דִיר גִיטָאן אָדֶער וָואס אִיךְ הָאבּ וָוידֶר לײַטִין גִיטָאן
דֶר מִיט כְּדֵי אִיךְ זָאל קֶענֶן קוּמֶן אוֹיף יֶענֶר וֶועלְט לוֹיטֶר כְּדֵי אַז אִיךְ זָאל
מְנוּחָה הָאבִּין אִין קֶבֶּר אוּן בַּיא מײַן לֶעבְּן זָאלְסְטוּ מִיט מִיר טָאן לוֹיטֶר
דֶר בַּארִימְקַייט דוּ זָאלְשְׁט דֶר הֶערִין מײַן גֶבֶּעט גְלײַךְ אַז דוּ הָאשְׁט דֶר
הֶערְט אוּנְזֶערֶע עֶלְטֶרִין אוֹיךְ וִוי דוּא הָאשְׁט דֶר הֶערְט אוּנְזֶר פֿרוּמֶע מוּטֶר
חַנָה דֶען אִיךְ בֶּעט אָרוּם וֶוייבּ אִיךְ וָויל דִיר אוֹיש זָאגִין וָואס מִיר אוֹיף מײַנֶעם
הַארְצִין לִיגְט דֶען וָואס אִיךְ טוּא דִיר בֶּעטִין גְלײַךְ וִוי אַיין קִינְד טוּט בֶּעטִין
צוּ זײַנֶעם פֿאָטֶר וָוי עֶס שְׁטַייט גִישְׁרִיבִּין כְּרַחֵם אָבּ עַל בָּנִים זָאלְשְׁטוּ
מִיר אוֹיךְ טָאן וִוי וָוי אַיין פֿאָטֶר טוּט צוּ זײַן קִינְד :

רִבּוֹנוֹ שֶׁל עוֹלָם וִוי דוּ הָאשְׁט מִיר גִיהָאלְפִֿין בִּיז אַהֶער אַזוֹ זָאלְסְטוּ מִיר
וַוייטֶר הֶעלְפִֿין דוּא זָאלְשְׁט מִיר שִׁיקִין גוּטֶע מַלְאָכִים דִיא זָאלְן מִיךְ פֿירֶן
אִין רֶעכְטִין וֶועג כְּדֵי אַז אִיךְ אוּן מײַנֶע קִינְדֶר זָאלִין גִישְׁפֿײַזְט וֶוערִין פֿון
דײַן הַאנְט אוּן נִיט חַ״ו פֿוּן דִי לײַט דוּ זָאל נִיט קוּמֶן צו שְׁפֿלוּת עֶש

זָאל אִין זֵיי קַיין עַיִן הָרָע נִיט שׁוֹלֵט זַיין אוּן זֵייא אוּנְז מַצִיל פֿוּן אַלֶע
שְׁלֶעכְטִיגְקַייט אוּן אִיךְ זָאל לֶעבִּין אִין שָׁלוֹם :

רִבּוֹנוֹ שֶׁל עוֹלָם הֶער פֿוּן דֶר גַאנְצֶר וֶועלְט דוּא הָאשְׁט דוּא מֶענְטְשִׁין דֶעם מֶענְטְשִׁין
נִיט אוּם זוּנְשְׁט דוּא הָאשְׁט גִיעֶפִֿינְט גִיעֶפִֿינְט מײַנֶע אוֹיגֶן צו זֶעהֶן דײַן קִינִגְרַייךְ אוּן
מײַנֶע אוֹיעֶרִין צו הֶערִין דײַנֶע וָואוּנְדֶר פֿוּן דֶר גַאנְצֶר וֶועלְט אוּן מײַן מוֹיל
זָאל דֶר צֵיילֶן דײַנֶע גְבוּרוֹת אוּן מײַנֶע הֶענְט זָאלִין דײַנֶע מִצְות לִיבֶּר
גָאט דוּ הָאשְׁט אוּנְז גִיבָּאטִין חַלָה צוּ נֶעמֶן אוּן לִיכְט צוּא צִינְדִין אוּן בּוֹדֶק
צוּ זַיין פֿוּן נִדָה דִיא נְשָׁמָה זָאל רֵיין זַיין אִין דײַנֶעם בְּלַייבִּין אוּן מִיט מײַנֶע פֿיס צוּ גֵיין אִין
דֶר שׁוּל אוּן צוּ לוֹיבִּין דִיךְ אוּן צוּ גֵיין אִין דײַנֶעם וֶועג מײַנֶע בְּרִיסְט צוּ זַייגִין
קִינְדֶר דָאש זֵייא זָאלִין שְׁטַארְק זַיין דָרוּם בֶּעט אִיךְ דִיךְ לִיבֶּר גָאט עֶש
זָאל אִין זֵיי נִיט שׁוֹלֵט זַיין קַיין מִיתָה מְשׁוּנָה אוּן זָאלְשְׁט מײַנֶע קִינְדֶר
שְׁטַארְקֶן דָאש הֶערְץ אִין דֶער תּוֹרָה אוּן זֵייעֶר הַאָרֶץ זָאל אָפִֿין זַיין אַז דִיא
טוֹיעֶרִין פֿוּן אוֹלָם וְהֵיכָל אוּן מִיר זָאלִין זֶעהֶן פֿוּן זֵייא בָּנִים עוֹסְקִים בַּתּוֹרָה
וּבְמִצְות אוּן מײַנֶע אוֹיגֶן זָאל נִיט זַיין קַיין טְרוֹיעֶרְקַייט פֿוּן דַאגָה אוּן
נִיט צוּ הֶערִין קַיין יָאמֶער אוּן קְלָאג אִין גָאר מײַן הוֹיז גִיזִינְד אוּן נִיט צוּא
גִישְׁפֿײַזְט וֶוערִין דוּרְךְ דֶער הַאנְט פֿוּן אַיין בָּשָׂר וָדָם אוּן מִיר זָאלִין זוֹכֶה
זַיין צוּא זֶעהֶן יְשׁוּעוֹת וְנֶחָמוֹת :

רִבּוֹנוֹ שֶׁל עוֹלָם אִיךְ בֶּעט דִיךְ דוּא זָאלְשְׁט בַּאגִיטִיגְן מַיין מַזָל אוּן אוֹיב דָאשׁ
מַזָּל אִיז חַס וְשָׁלוֹם נִיט בַּאגְלִיקְט בַּאהִיט מִיךְ אַל שַׁדַּי אוּן צוּ בְּרֵעךְ דָאשׁ
שְׁוֶוערֶע מַזָל דָאשׁ יָאר אוּן אַלֶע אוּן אַלֶע טָאג אוּן אַלֶע רֶגַע אוּן זַייא
זַייא מְחַדֵּשׁ לְטוֹבָה וְלִבְרָכָה וְהַצְלָחָה אוּן הֵייל דִיא צוּא בְּרָאכֶנֶע הֶערְצֶר אוּן
גִיב מִיר חֵן וָחֶסֶד אִין דַיינֶע אוֹיגִין אוּן אִין לַייטִינֶשׁ אוֹיגְן דָאשׁ קַיינֶר זָאל
נִיט הָאבִּין אוֹיף מִיר צוּ רֵיידִין מַיינֶע אוֹיגִין הֵייב אִיךְ אוֹיף צוּם הִימֵל אוּן
גָאר מַיין צוּ בְּרָאכִין הַאַרֶץ טוּא אִיךְ צוּ דִיר זָאגִין אַזוֹ וְוִיא דָוִד הַמֶּלֶךְ ע"ה
הָאט אָן גִישְׁרִיבְּן אַיין צוּ בְּרָאכִין הַאַרֶץ אוּן אַיין פַאר שְׁטוֹיסֶן הַאַרֶץ טוּשְׁט
דוּ גָאט נִיט פַאר שְׁעמֶען אוּן זַייא מִיר מְמַלֵּא כָּל מִשְׁאֲלוֹת לִבִּי לְטוֹבָה כִּי
אֵל רַחוּם אָתָּה · יִהְיוּ לְרָצוֹן אִמְרֵי פִי וְהֶגְיוֹן לִבִּי לְפָנֶיךָ יְיָ צוּרִי וְגוֹאֲלִי אָמֵן :

Tkhine of Sore, Rivke, Rokhl, and Leye

Riboyne shel oylem, Almighty God, You created heaven and earth and all creatures with great compassion within six days and with only ten words.[12] And on the seventh day, which is *shabes koydesh*, You rested from Your work. And You also commanded Your beloved people, *yisro'el*, that they, too, should rest on *shabes koydesh* from all work, and also refrain from speaking words which are not words of *toyre*, which each person should study according to his ability. And women, too, should know how to perform their obligations that God has commanded.

You have also given us new moons which the *sanhedrin* used to consecrate.[13] And today, when we consecrate and bless *roshkhoydesh* on the *shabes* before the *roshkhoydesh*, it is a time to entreat God. Therefore we extend our hands to You, God, in supplication, and pray that You will return us to *yerusholayim* and renew our days as of old.[14] For we do not have a *beys hamikdesh* now, nor an altar, nor a *koyen godl* to absolve us, but only our prayer, which is a substitute for the sacrifices.[15] Therefore, may You accept and answer our prayer.

Answer us this month, through the merit of our mother *sore* for whose sake You commanded and said: "Do not dare to touch my anointed ones,"[16] which means: Do no evil to my anointed people, and do no harm to my prophets.

And may the merit of our mother *rivke*, who caused our father *yankev* to receive the blessings from his father *yitskhok*, cause the blessings to be fulfilled soon through her children *yisro'el*.

And may the merit of our faithful mother *rokhl*, to whom You promised that through her merit her children *yisro'el* would be delivered from exile,[17] cause the promises to be fulfilled. For when *yisro'el* was led into exile, they passed not far from the grave in which our mother *rokhl* lies. *Yisro'el* begged the enemy to allow them to go to *rokhl*'s grave, and there they began to weep and to cry out: "Our dear mother, how can you watch us being led into exile?"[18] Then *rokhl* went up to *hashem yisborekh* with a bitter cry and said, "*Riboyne shel oylem*, Your compassion is certainly much greater than the compassion of a human being. You, who are certainly a merciful and gracious God, surely have compassion." God answered her: "You are right. I will take your children out of their misery."[19] Thus we ask that this may come to pass for her merit and for the merit of our mother *leye* and that through her merit You may illumine our eyes so that we may overcome darkness.

Since we are called *bney avrom*, the children of *avrom ovinu*, how is it then that we are still so neglected? Wash me thoroughly; continue to wash me of my sins.[20] Therefore renew us and bring us a new and joyful month. May all be turned to good through the merit of our holy forefathers, *avrom, yitskhok*, and *yankev*. Source of our strength,[21] You are our great Lord: raise us up high and cause only good to come to us.

Yehi rotsn, God, our God and God of our ancestors, that You renew for us this month[22] and cause good and blessing to come to us, and that You give us a long life, a good life, and a blessed life, that we may be nourished by God—praised be He. Give us a life of ample sustenance, with pleasure and not with anxiety, a life of strong bodies, that our bones may become strong. Give us a life of *yires shomayim*, that our children may believe in God—praised be He—and walk in God's path, so that their own paths may be to good fortune. Give us a life without shame or dishonor, that I may not be ashamed, either in this world or in the world-to-come before the heavenly court. Give us a life of wealth and honor, that we may raise our children to *toyre*, to the *khupe*, and to *maysim toyvim*.[23] As *dovid hameylekh—olev hasholem—*prayed: "*Riboyne shel oylem*, let me die like a king and not like a pauper."[24] May we be granted a life filled with love of *toyre* and *yires shomayim*. May my children believe in God—praised be He—as did the children of *yankev ovinu—olev hasholem*. For when *yankev* was about to die, he wished to reveal the final redemption but lost the ability to prophesy and was afraid. He said to his children: "Perhaps there is among my children one who is evil." And they responded: "*Shma yisro'el*, the Lord our God, the Lord is One," which means, Listen, our father *yisro'el*, God who is Your God is also our God and is One.[25] Grant us our request and cause good to come to us by merit of the prayers of many generations. *Omeyn, selo.*

תחנה פון שרה רבקה רחל ולאה

רִבּוֹנוֹ שֶׁל עוֹלָם דוּא הֶער פוּן דֶער וֶועלְט דוּא אַלְמַאכְטִיגֶר גָאט דוּ הָאסְט
בַּאשַׁאפֶין מִיט דַיין גְרוֹיש דֶער בַּארִימְהַארְצִיקְיַיט הִימֶל אוּן עֶרְד אוּן אַלֶע
בַּשֶׁעפֶעניש אִין דִי זֶעקְס טֶעג נָאר מִיט צֶעהֶן וֶוערְטֶר אוּן אִין זִיבֶּעטֶן טָאג
דָאש אִיז דֶער שַׁבָּת קוֹדֶש דֶער הֵיילִיגֶר שַׁבָּת הָאסְטוּ גְרוּעֶט פוּן דַיין וֶוערק אוּן
אוֹיךְ הָאסְטוּ גִיבָּאטֶין צוּא דַיין לִיב פָאלְק יִשְׂרָאֵל אַז זֵיי זָאלֶן אוֹיךְ רוּעֶן
אוּם שַׁבָּת קוֹדֶש פוּן אַלֶע אַרְבֶּעט אוּן אוֹיךְ פוּן אַזֶעלְכֶע וֶוערְטֶר וָואש מֶען
דַארְף נִיט צוּ רֵיידֶין נֵייעֶרְט זֵייא זָאלֶין רֵיידִין דִבְרֵי תּוֹרָה אוּנ צוּא לֶערְנֶן
אִיטְלִיכֶר נָאךְ זַיין יְכוֹלֶת וָואש עֶר קָאן לֶערְנֶן אוּן אוֹיךְ דִי וַוייבֶּר זָאלֶן
וִוישֶׁין וִויא צוּ הַאלְטֶן זֵייעֶרֶע מִצְוֹת וָואש גָאט הָאט זֵיי גִיבָּאטֶין אוֹיךְ
הָאסְטוּ אוּנֹז גִיגֶעבֶּין חֲדָשִׁים וָואש דִי סַנְהֶדְרִין פלֶעגִין הֵיילִיגֶין דִי חֲדָשִׁים
אוּן הַיינְט וָואש מִיר זַיינֶן פַר חוֹדֶש הַחוֹדֶש אוּן מִיר בֶּעֶנְטְשִׁין רֹאש חוֹדֶש אִין
שַׁבָּת וָואש פַר רֹאש חוֹדֶש אִיז אוּן דֶענְסְט מָאל אִיז צַייט מֶען זָאל בֶּעטִין
דָרוֹם טוּעֶן מִיר פַר שְׁפְרֵייטֶין אוּנְזֶערֶע טֶענֶער פַר הַשֵׁם יִתְבָּרַךְ אוּן מִיר טוּעֶן
תְּפִלָה אַז דוּ זָאלְסְט אוּנְז וִוידֶער קֶערִין קַיין יְרוּשָׁלַיִם אוּן זָאלְסְט דֶער נֵייעֶן
אוּנְזֶערֶע טֶעג אַזוֹי וִויא צוּם עֶרְשְׁטִין דֶען מִיר הָאבִּין אִיצוּנְד נִיט קַיין בֵּית
הַמִקְדָש אוּן קַיין מִזְבֵּחַ אוּן קַיין כֹּהֵן גָדוֹל וָואש זָאל אוֹיף אוּנְז מְכַפֵּר זַיין
נָאר אוּנְזֶר תְּפִלָה אִיז אָן שְׁטָאט פוּן דִיא קָרְבָּנוֹת דָרוֹם פָאר נֶעם אוּנְזֶער
תְּפִלָה אוּן זָאלְסְט אוּנֹז עֶנְטְפֶערִין אִין דֶעם חוֹדֶש אִין דֶעם זְכוּת פוּן אוּנְזֶר
מוּטֶר שרה וָואש דוּא הָאסְט פוּן אִירְט וֶועגִין גִיבָּאטֶין אוּן הָאסְט גֶעזָאגְט
אַל תְּגֵעוּ בִּמְשִׁיחָי כו' דָש אִיז טַייטְש אִיר זָאלְט נִיט אָן רִירֶן צוּ בֵּייזֶן צוּ
מַיינֶע גֶעזַאלְבֶּטֶע אוּן אִין מַיינֶע נְבִיאִים זָאלְט אִיר נִיט טָאן קַיין שְׁלֶעכְטֶץ
אוּן אִין דֶעם זְכוּת פוּן אוּנְזֶער מוּטֶר רבקה וָואש זִיא הָאט גָורֶם גֶעוֶוען אַז
אוּנְזֶער פָאטֶער יַעֲקֹב זָאל מְקַבֵּל זַיין דִיא בְּרָכוֹת פוּן זַיין פָאטֶער יִצְחָק אוּן
אִין דֶעם זְכוּת פוּן אוּנְזֶער מוּטֶר רחל דִיא גִיטְרֵייעֶ גִיטְרֵייעֶ וָואש דוּ הָאסְט אִיר
צוּא גִיזָאגְט אַז אִין אִיר זְכוּת וֶועלִין אִירֶע קִינְדֶער יִשְׂרָאֵל פוּן דֶעם גָלות
בָּבֶל אַרוֹיש גֵיין דֶען אַז מֶען הָאט דִי יִשְׂרָאֵל אִין גָלות אַרַיין גִיפִירְט הָאט
מֶען זֵייא גִיפִירְט נִיט וַוייט פוּן דֶעם קֶבֶר וָואש אוּנְזֶער מוּטֶר רחל לִיגְט
דְרִינֶען הָאבִּין דִיא יִשְׂרָאֵל זִיךְ אוֹיש גִיבֶּעטִין בֵּייא דֶעם שׁוֹנֵא אַז זֵיי זָאלֶן
גֵיין אוֹיף דֶעם קֶבֶר אוּן וִויא דִי יִשְׂרָאֵל זַיינֶען גִיקוּמֶען אוֹיף דֶעם קֶבֶר פוּן
אוּנְזֶר מוּטֶר רחל הָאבִּין אָן גֶיהוֹבִּין צוּ וֵויינֶען אוּן צוּ שְׁרַייעֶן · אוּנְזֶר
גִיטְרֵייעֶ מוּטֶר וִויא קֶענְשְׁטוּ דָאש צוּ זֶעהֶן אַז מֶען זָאל אוּנֹז פִירִין אִין

גָּלוּת אַרַיין אִיז רָחֵל אִיז גִיגַאנְגֶען צוּ הַשֵּׁ"י מִיט אַיין בִּיטֶר גִישְׁרֵייא אוּן
הָאט גִישְׁפְּרָאכִין רִבּוֹנוֹ שֶׁל עוֹלָם דַיין רַחֲמָנוּת אִיז דָאךְ פִּיל גְרֶעשֶׁער ווִיא
דָאשׁ רַחֲמָנוּת פוּן דֶעם מֶענְטשִׁין דוּא גָאט בִּישְׁט דָאךְ גָאר רַחוּם וְחַנּוּן
גִיהֶערְשְׁטוּ פְּשִׁיטָא רַחֲמָנוּת צוּ הָאבִּין אַזוֹ הָאט גָאט אִיר גִיעֶנְטְפֶערְט דוּא
הָאשְׁט בַּייא מִיר רֶעכְט אִיךְ וֶועל דַיינֶע קִינְדֶער אוֹיש דִי צָרוֹת אוֹיש צִיהֶען ·
דָרוּם בֶּעטִין מִיר דִיךְ אַז דָאשׁ זָאל מְקוּיָם וֶוערִין וֶוערִין אִיר זְכוּת אוּן אִין
דֶעם זְכוּת פוּן אוּנְזֶער מוּטֶער לֵאָה אִין אִיר אִיר זְכוּת זָאלְשְׁטוּ אוּנְז דֶער לַייכְטִין
אוּנְזֶערֶע אוֹיגִין פוּן דֶעם פִינְצְטֶערְנֶעשׁ מִיר וֶוערִין דָאךְ גִירוּפִין בְּנֵי אַבְרָהָם
דִיא קִינְדֶער פוּן אַבְרָהָם אָבִינוּ ווִיא זָאלִין מִיר הַיינְט זַיין אַזוֹ פָאר לָאזִין
הָרֵב כַּבְּסֵנִי טוּא מֶערִין צוּא וַואשִׁין מִיר דִי זִינְד דָרוּם דֶער נַייא אוּן בְּרֵיינְג
אוֹיף אוּנְז דֶעם חוֹדֶשׁ צוּא פְרִיד אוּן עֶשׁ זָאל אוּנְז פָאר קֶערְט וֶוערִין אַלְץ
צוּא גוּטִין · גָאוֹן עוֹזֵנוּ דוּא בִּישְׁט דָאךְ אוּנְזֶער גְרוֹיסֶער הֶערְשַׁאפְט דוּא
זָאלְשְׁט דֶער הֵיבִּין אוּנְז אוּן זָאלְשְׁט פָאר קֶערִין צוּ גוּטִין פוּן וֶוערִין דֶעם
זְכוּת פוּן אוּנְזֶערֶע אָבוֹת הַקְּדוֹשִׁים אַבְרָהָם יִצְחָק וְיַעֲקֹב :

יְהִי רָצוֹן מִלְפָנֶיךָ יְיָ אֱלֹהֵינוּ וֵאלֹהֵי אֲבוֹתֵינוּ שֶׁתְּחַדֵּשׁ עָלֵינוּ אֶת הַחוֹדֶשׁ הַזֶּה
לְטוֹבָה וְלִבְרָכָה וְתִתֶּן אוּן דוּא זָאלְשְׁט גֶעבִּין צוּא אוּנְז חַיִּים אֲרוּכִים חַיִּים
שֶׁל טוֹבָה חַיִּים שֶׁל בְּרָכָה מִיר זָאלִין פוּן גָאט בָּרוּךְ הוּא גִישְׁפַּייזְט וֶוערִין
חַיִּים שֶׁל פַּרְנָסָה טוֹבָה מִיט נַחַת אוּן נִיט מִיט צַעַר חַיִּים שֶׁל חִלּוּף עֲצָמוֹת
אוּנְזֶערֶע בֵּיינֶער זָאלִין גִישְׁטַארְקְט וֶוערִין חַיִּים שֶׁיֵּשׁ בָּהֶם יִרְאַת שָׁמַיִם
אוּנְזֶערֶע קִינְדֶער זָאלִין גְלֵייבִּין אִין גָאט בָּרוּךְ הוּא זֵייא זָאלִין גֵיין אִין גָאטְשׁ
וֶועג כְּדֵי זֵייא זָאלְן בַּאגְלֵייקִין זֵייעֶר וֶועג חַיִּים שֶׁאֵין בָּהֶם בּוּשָׁה וּכְלִימָה אִיךְ
זָאל נִיט קוּמֶען צוּא אַיין פָאר שֶׁעמוּנְג אִיךְ זָאל נִיט פַר שֶׁעמְט וֶוערִין נִיט
בָּעוֹלָם הַזֶּה אוּן נִיט בָּעוֹלָם הַבָּא פָאר דֶעם בֵּית דִין שֶׁל מַעֲלָה חַיִּים שֶׁל עוֹשֶׁר
וְכָבוֹד מִיר זָאלִין אוּנְזֶערֶע קִינְדֶר מְגַדֵּל זַיין לַתּוֹרָה וּלְחוּפָּה וּלְמַעֲשִׂים טוֹבִים
ווִיא דָוִד הַמֶּלֶךְ עָלָיו הַשָּׁלוֹם הָאט גִיבֶּעטִין רִבְשֵׁ"ע לָאז מִיךְ שְׁטַארבֶּן ווִיא
אַיין מַלְכוּת אוּן נִיט ווִיא אַיין אֶבְיוֹן חַיִּים שֶׁתְּהֵא בָּנוּ אַהֲבַת תּוֹרָה וְיִרְאַת
שָׁמַיִם מַיינֶע קִינְדֶר זָאלִין גְלֵייבִּין אִין גָאט בָּרוּךְ הוּא ווִיא דִי קִינְדֶער פוּן
יַעֲקֹב אָבִינוּ עָלָיו הַשָּׁלוֹם וְוארוּם אַז יַעֲקֹב אָבִינוּ הָאט גִיזָאלְט שְׁטַארבִּין
הָאט עֶר גִיוָואלְט מְגַלֶּה זַיין דֶעם קֵץ פוּן דֶער גְאוּלָה הָאט זִיךְ דִיא נְבוּאָה
פוּן אִים אָפ גִיטָאן הָאט עֶר זִיךְ דֶער שְׁרָאקִין אוּן הָאט גִיזָאגְט צוּ זַיינֶע
קִינְדֶר אֶפְשָׁר אִיז צְווִישִׁין מַיינֶע קִינְדֶער דָא אַיין שְׁלֶעכְטֶר הָאבֶּן זֵיי
גִיעֶנְטְפֶערְט שְׁמַע יִשְׂרָאֵל יְיָ אֱלֹהֵינוּ יְיָ אֶחָד דָאשׁ אִיז טַייטשׁ הֶער צוּ אוּנְזֶער
פָאטֶער יִשְׂרָאֵל דֶער גָאט וָואשׁ אִיז דַיין גָאט דֶער אִיז אוּנְזֶער גָאט אוּן אִיז
אַיינֶער אוּן דוּא זָאלְשְׁט אוּנְז גֶעבִּין מְשַׁאֲלוֹתֵינוּ לְטוֹבָה בִּזְכוּת תְּפִלַּת רַבִּים
אָמֵן סֶלָה :

Notes

1. See pages 56–61 of this chapter for the complete text of "Tkhine for the Blessing of the New Moon" in English and Yiddish.

2. See pages 61–64 of this chapter for the complete text of "Tkhine of Sore, Rivke, Rokhl, and Leye" in English and Yiddish.

3. Isaiah 52:7.

4. Exodus 34:6–7.

5. Cf. Psalm 19:9.

6. Louis Ginzberg, *Legends of the Jews*, 5:9–12.

7. 1 Samuel 1:19–20.

8. Psalm 103:13.

9. Cf. Psalm 51:19.

10. From the liturgical Prayer for the New Moon.

11. Psalm 19:15.

12. Mishnah, Avot 5:1; this refers to the ten-fold "And God said"s in Genesis 1 and 2.

13. Mishnah, Rosh Hashanah 1–3.

14. Lamentations 5:21.

15. Cf. Hosea 14:3 and Psalm 141:2.

16. Cf. Psalm 105:15 and 1 Chronicles 16:22.

17. Cf. Jeremiah 31:15–17.

18. Louis Ginzberg, *Legends of the Jews*, 2:21.

19. *Legends*, 2:135 and 7:396.

20. Cf. Ezekiel 36:25 and Psalm 51:4.

21. Cf. Ezekiel 24:21.

22. Paraphrase of the liturgical Prayer for the New Moon.

23. From the circumcision ceremony.

24. Cf. 1 Samuel 21:11–16 and Psalm 34:7.

25. *Legends*, 2:131, 140.

7
Nashot HaKotel: Women in Jerusalem Celebrate Rosh Chodesh

Bonna Devora Haberman

On the day that the moon is hiding, we make our appearance. Women gather together at the side of the large expanse in front of the old Wall, the Kotel, remnant of the protecting wall surrounding the Holy Temple. Each massive stone is a dear friend; we acknowledge one another. Cool dew is damp and fresh in the early hour of Jerusalem morning. Strong sun will soon burn off the softness that envelops us. More women trickle into our pond, which gently ripples with songs of praise. *Halleluyahs* from all places and generations meet and ascend toward the One. Doves gurgle and circle above, messengers of prayer.

Women are scattered around the plaza adjoining the Kotel; some huddle next to the partition straining to hear the men's words. Our group, gathering to *daven*, pray, on Rosh Chodesh, assembles as knowledgeable, independent, whole, and proud of our celebration. Sometimes women threaten and storm against our calm. Insults. We then leave the plaza to sing Hallel with full voice, reading from the Torah scroll overlooking rather than at the Kotel. Here, in the archeological garden overlooking the Kotel, we are free to dance and share words of Torah. We feel uplifted by the honor of taking part in this Rosh Chodesh women's prayer community. Tonight, a fresh young crescent moon will rise at dusk.

Since December 1988, a group of women has been gathering at the Kotel to pray on Rosh Chodesh and on Friday mornings. On several occasions we have been violently attacked, verbally and physically; we have been cursed, slandered, and incited against. We have been refused adequate protection, our assailants have not been reprimanded. Tales of these events have been told far and wide. There is controversy and disagreement. The violence has been unconscionable, yet few have unconditionally condemned it. By a miracle no one has been gravely injured. We have lodged our complaints against the police and filed an appeal to the Supreme Court. Deeper issues that arise, both at a practical and a symbolic level, need to be articulated and addressed. Who are we, what do we do, and why do we elicit such attention and response?

During the December 1988 International Conference on the Empowerment of Jewish Women in Jerusalem, some of the participants convened a prayer group at the Kotel, the Western Wall. The service included a reading from the Torah scroll, as is customary on Thursday mornings. By many who prayed, it was perceived to be a profoundly moving, even historic event. In opposition to our own feelings, there were particular responses that prompted me to further this initiative. One was expressed by some of the irate women present at the Kotel: "The Torah belongs to men" they screamed, as they tried to interrupt our prayers. The Rabbi of the Kotel, Meir Yehudah Getz, made a statement that we had done nothing against *halacha* (religious law); what we had done is simply not accepted in the community of Israel. Furthermore, there was a sense that the impetus for women's group prayer at the Kotel had been imported from North America, that women in Israel were "not ready."

As an Israeli woman committed to Torah, to prayer, to learning, and to the celebration and joy of Jewish life, I was deeply hurt and unwilling to allow these views to be perpetuated. I resolved to influence this *minhag*, custom. I invited the women in my Mishna class and the women who gathered monthly to celebrate Rosh Chodesh to meet at the Kotel for morning prayers with a Torah scroll.

Rosh Chodesh is the beginning of the new month marked by the appearance of the tiny sliver of moon. According to traditional commentaries, Rosh Chodesh was given to Jewish women as a holiday because we did not contribute our gold to the building of the golden calf. The validity of Rosh Chodesh as a women's holiday is confirmed in the Jerusalem Talmud in Tractate Taanit. The cycle of the moon echoes the process of the monthly renewal of our own bodies.

On Rosh Chodesh Tevet 5749 (December 1988), a group of twenty-five women of many affiliations gathered at the Kotel to pray and celebrate. During Chanukah, the festival of the rededication of the Temple, we felt a special sense of *kedusha*, holiness, at the Kotel. We were rededicating the site for all Jewish women. Never could we have anticipated the anger and hatred that was given expression in violence against us. Women shouted, cursed, and pushed at us. Men burst through the *mechitzah* (the partition separating the sections for men and women) into the women's section. At first they circled and then they began to tear at us, our prayer shawls, our clothes and bodies. One woman was thrown onto the stone plaza floor. Some overturned the table on which we had laid the Torah scroll, spilling prayer books onto the ground. Neither the police nor soldiers were able to contain the aggression; we were forced to leave. We completed our service outside Dung Gate.

After we had concluded, we discussed our responses. I was personally moved by the overwhelming sensitivity expressed by the women. In spite of having been violated, we wanted to be less threatening, less conspicuous, blend better into the landscape—yet not so much as to disappear. We agreed to gather for prayers weekly on Fridays, to create a sense of community, to connect ourselves to the experience of the Kotel, and to create a regular presence. These prayers have passed relatively uneventfully, except for intermittent hushing of our already quiet song voices and one extremely wild attack the Friday after Rosh Chodesh Nisan. We have indeed experienced prayerful moments, and we are working to improve our *kavannah*, concentration and intention.

Some of the women in our group expressed a desire to learn more about the *halachot* (religious laws) connected with women and Torah, *minyan* (prayer quorum), and *tallit* (prayer shawls). And so we have met weekly to learn texts and responsa dealing with these issues as well as chassidic and kabbalistic approaches to prayer and to male–female relationships. We discuss our attitudes, our criticisms and our own exegesis as it evolves through this process of study and prayer.

Davening at the Kotel

Over the next several months we met to learn, *daven* (pray), and organize. On Rosh Chodesh Adar 1, we again met with the Torah scroll at the Kotel. We had notified the police, as they had instructed us, and told some reporters, hoping that the presence of the cameras would exert a calming influence. This time we arrived earlier, before the crowds. However, when we opened the Torah, men (having been informed by women who were harassing us on the women's side of the *mechitzah*) began to hurl metal chairs and tables over the *mechitzah* in our direction. In a second wave, they burst into the women's section and assaulted us at close range. We called on the police (who were sitting in a van) to intervene. They refused. With the help of some male and female supporters (including rabbis from all denominations who literally caught chairs in midair, shielding us with tables) we completed the Torah reading and left. We marched with dignity in tight formation around the Torah, singing "Barchenu avinu, kulanu k'echad" ("Bless us our God, we are all as one"), amidst curses that we should die in traffic accidents.

These events evoked deep emotional responses from those who witnessed them. Many cried, torn by their outrage at the violence against people engaged in sincere prayer. Others wept tears of joy, seeing women expressing their commitment to Torah and Judaism. But we were all saddened by the divisiveness of our people.

The prayers, for those of us in the middle who were protected, were extraordinary. We had created a sacred moment in the midst of a very profane experience. We embraced the Torah with all our might, affirming that this is a tree of life, shielding it from the attackers adorned in prayer shawls and phylacteries, God's word bound to their arms and heads. The violence had threatened our very physical being. We lodged our complaints against the police inaction both in their own offices and with the ombudsman of the state. We called upon them to perform their duty of ensuring our safety during our prayers.

On *Taanit Esther* (the fast of Esther, which occurs the day prior to Erev Purim) we assembled outside Dung Gate. We were about one hundred women and came without Torah and *tallit*. We also had a group of male supporters with us. As we approached, a black wall of men, cursing and taunting us, formed, blocking our entry into the Kotel plaza. The ushers and border soldiers cleared a passage. Even without the Torah scroll, women harassed us, pushing prayer books in our faces, men violently thrashing at the partition. One wild, black-coated fellow burst through, hurling a chair on our heads. A visiting American university student collapsed under the blow, bleeding from the neck and head and requiring hospital treatment. We began our prayer, but soon saw a cloud of smoke drifting toward us from across the plaza. Tear gas. Police had hurled two shiny canisters to rid the scene of all of us. One black-coated man, tallit across his face, t'fillin on his head, even grabbed one canister to lob it closer to us. We covered our mouths and noses, vacating as swiftly as possible, coughing and gagging. We concluded where we had begun, outside Dung Gate.

The Supreme Court

That afternoon, four of us met with lawyers to file an appeal to the Supreme Court. In it we named the chief rabbis, the rabbi of the Kotel, the minister of religious affairs and the minister of police. We called upon them to justify why they did not protect us and enable us to pray at the Kotel according to our practice: wearing prayer shawls and reading from a Torah scroll. Our appeal was on behalf of all Jewish women. Any woman who values communal prayer is invited to join her voice with ours in prayer and celebration on Rosh Chodesh mornings at 7:00 A.M.

The Supreme Court accepted the state's request for a seven-month wait before hearing our case. This was meant to be a period of mutual acquaintance, paving the way for the settlement of such a "sensitive matter." During this time, we were forbidden from bringing a Torah to the Kotel and wearing prayer shawls. Indeed, from Adar II onward, we have endured a concerted effort on the part of the ultraorthodox community with the complicity and assistance of state officials to wear us down, beat us up, and throw us out. Meetings transpired, solely on our initiative, with then Minister of Religious Affairs Zevulun Hammer, with chief Rabbi Shapira, and between our lawyers and police officials. On none of these occasions has there been substantive discussion in an effort to achieve any resolution. Indeed, we have not even managed to exact from a single government official a condemnation of the violence against us. The experience of Rosh Chodesh Av is told through an excerpt from my journal:

Av, Rosh Chodesh, Wednesday August 2, 1989:
   Thirty women assembled outside Dung Gate at 6:45 A.M. We trickled into the women's section. When we opened our mouths to pray, 15 female hired security guards, this time wearing skirts, swooped in on us to order us to stop and leave if we so much as muttered a prayer. We assembled in tight formation, by now fifty-five women. We positioned ourselves close to the wall farthest from the partition, in the back third of the section, continuing to pray amidst loud shouting from haredi women, pushing and shoving by the "guards." They were attempting to remove us as a group, and tug at each one of us. We had locked arms to withstand the force and hold our ground. As the *shlichat ha-tzibur*, prayer leader, I was in the middle. I felt the full power of the thrust from all sides, barely able to stay on my feet. Finally we were pushed to the ground. (We had decided that as a last resort, in order not to be removed, we were prepared to sit, passively resisting. This had been a difficult decision which a few of us did not want to implement. We respected these people; they stood alongside us. Some of our considerations: the special connection of sitting on Rosh Chodesh Av, the beginning of the intense period of mourning for the Temple; sensitivity to the holiness of the site; not wanting to appear political. . . .) The guards, taking instructions from the haredi women,

dragged out many of us. They wrenched us apart, two guards using their full force on each one of us. At least one male guard dragged out a woman, though they purport not to touch women. They taunted and laughed at us, snatched our head coverings and prayer books, tearing and shredding them! Meanwhile, some haredi women were drenching us with bottles full of water and spraying us with dirt. The guards were vicious. In the face of all this brutality, twenty of us managed to complete Hallel on the ground! We joined the others outside the women's section. There, even after I had left, one of the guards assaulted me, scratching and bruising my arms. We completed our Torah reading and *musaf* prayers in the archaeological garden protected by our hired guards. Media coverage was full and for the first time sensitive to our struggle.

Following this event, we submitted an urgent request to the Supreme Court to issue an interim injunction ordering the State to protect us while praying. It was denied.

In the Archaeological Garden

On Rosh Chodesh Elul we read Torah in the archaeological garden, above the Kotel plaza, and alongside the steps leading up to the Jewish Quarter of the old city. There we enjoyed a full and beautiful *tefillah*, prayer service, wrapped in our prayer shawls. Each section of the Torah reading was blessed and chanted by a woman who had never before had the opportunity. We danced and sang together, marking the passage of these women into the realm of public ritual, an intense material connection with the central symbolic object of our tradition, the Torah.

I notice that we hold the Torah longer than a traditional men's quorum. We lift it off the stone slab that we use as our *bima* earlier, and hold it until after singing "Eitz Chaim He," "She Is a Tree of Life," before returning it, wrapped in our shawls, our garments to the *bima*. We carry the Torah in a bag of colorful hand-woven Guatemalan fabric, a backpack. Once we Jews carried the tabernacle in the desert draped with beautiful cloths.

Between the Torah reading and *musaf*, we have a *d'var Torah*, a learning session. We begin with a few comments about the Torah reading of the week, about the month, the festivals. People add their responses, sharing their personal feelings, ideas, insights. Usually someone teaches a song at the end from the repertoire of new Jewish women's music, a desire to linger before we disperse. Until next month.

Why do we continue to subject ourselves to this violent, ongoing hateful abuse of our bodies and souls? The impetus for our actions comes from a form-

Rosh Chodesh Elul, September 1989.

ing spiritual consciousness among a new generation of Jewish women. We are women committed to Torah, no longer willing to restrict our intellectual, moral, and creative sensibilities and competence to secular fields. In secular society, we are contributing to the fabric of human life in every facet, but we are still not considered by many to be eligible, counted members of our own religious communities.

Many of the Nashot HaKotel, Women of the Wall, are engaged in the study, teaching, interpretation, and application of Torah. Our intellectual, moral, and creative energy is now being directed toward our own tradition. For more than a decade, women from all segments of the spectrum of Jewish observance have been creating both formal and informal prayer and learning contexts. We have organized groups and communities to celebrate rituals of birth, bat mitzvah, Rosh Chodesh, and *mikvah*, ritual immersion. Yet we need to work overtime to infuse Israeli society—in our homes and workplaces, in the courts, in education, in government and legislation—with a consciousness of women's ability.

Carrying On

Although there has been an effort to devalue us and our prayer, we have expressed a sensitivity and integrity through our words and actions. And we will not be forced to disappear. Our modes of religious expression are sincere, halachic, legitimate. We deserve to be recognized as integral to the community of Israel.

One of the unique contributions we make to the divided people of Israel is that our group is composed of women from many backgrounds, affiliations, and shades of religious observance. Our commitments to each other and to our project of public women's prayer enable us to reach beyond the boundaries and classifications: reform, reconstructionist, conservative, orthodox, and un-affiliated. We strive to build a community that realizes a vision of a more united people of Israel.

The Kotel has been an object of our collective longing for thousands of years. There we are connected to the ebb and flow of the prayers of Jews. When a man comes to the Kotel, he has the option of joining with others in prayer and song, in a community of worship and celebration at virtually every hour; or to meditate and pray alone, in silence or aloud, without interference.

But when a woman comes to the Kotel, she has (until now) only the option of praying alone. We offer every Jewish woman, from all corners of the world, the possibility of connecting with a praying, celebrating community on every Friday morning, and on Rosh Chodesh, at the most powerful symbol of our religious tradition.

At the Kotel we conduct our prayers according to the halachic guidelines established for women's prayer groups over a decade ago. We read from the

Torah scroll when there is a Torah reading, although we omit parts of the service requiring a men's quorum. These practices have been authorized by Rabbi Moshe Feinstein of blessed memory in a personal written communication from his grandson, and by Rabbi Shlomo Goren, on his letterhead as the Chief Rabbi of Israel. Women are indeed permitted, according to halachic authorities, to hold, read from, and dance with the Torah, regardless of their status of ritual purity.

According to the Talmud in Hagigah 16b, women in the Temple performed the ritual of laying their hands on the sacrificial animal, though they were not obligated to do so. Women performed this ritual for *nachat-ruah*, spiritual joy. So, too, we read from the Torah scroll and pray at the Kotel. Indeed, no one is *obligated* to pray at the Kotel. Men, like women, pray there for spiritual joy.

Offering Gifts

Once the Jewish people built a tabernacle from all of the unique gifts offered freely and openly. We knew not only what to contribute. We also knew how to build from those gifts a solid and meaningful structure, rituals and symbols that unified us and expressed our spirit and our Peoplehood. Today, we have a dream and a prayer for a Judaism to which each brings a gift, without fear, anger, or judgment, from her and his own heart and soul.

I believe that every human being has a prayer. But few have the opportunity to express and experience it in an atmosphere of a caring community. We are reaching out to secular and religiously observant Israeli and Diaspora Jews, to empower them in our tradition, to expose them to versions of Jewish practice that are compelling and attractive. The image of a black-coated, hatted man, wrapped in a prayer shawl, rocking to and fro, absorbed in prayer is *one* image of a Jew; it is not the *only* image.

We, the Women at the Wall, are here to offer our daughters and granddaughters an opportunity to claim our portion in the Torah and the destiny of the people of Israel. So the demand made by the daughters of Tzelofchad in the Torah was answered by God through Moses for the sake of our continued participation in the Jewish people. To the children of Israel, we offer not only our nurturing, but also our learning, our interpretation, our prayers, and our songs. We invite all women and men to uphold our right as Jews to pray and celebrate at the Kotel.

Over the past few years, we have been to the Kotel hundreds of times. The scene now is very different from what it was. We know one another. Changes have transpired both within our group and between us and the Kotel praying community. We recognize ourselves and are recognized by others as "regulars." The women beggars who once antagonized and taunted, greet us, and ask about our children's well-being. It is a normalization of relationships. There is no violence. Women praying as a community (without prayer shawls and the Torah) on Rosh Chodesh has become an accepted part of the status quo.

Unfortunately, because of the latent violence and the court order, we have not yet been able to wear prayer shawls or read from the Torah at the Kotel itself. We do sing, yet with sensitivity, quietly, lest we arouse the anger of certain women whom we know to be our opponents or the men who loom on the other side of the partition. And so, we are at the Kotel itself for only the shacharit prayers. For the singing of Hallel, the Torah reading and musaf, the additional prayer on Rosh Chodesh, we regroup in the archaeological garden above the Kotel plaza. There, among the less old stones, we savor our prayers.

Current Status

The Supreme Court rendered a judgment on the case of Women of the Wall in January 1994. Each of the three justices on the bench articulated a different view. In such circumstances, where there is no agreement, the Chief Justice has the prerogative to render the decision. The Chief Justice concluded that this is a case that ought to be worked out through a sociopolitical process, rather than a judicial one. He recommended that a governmental committee be formed that will seek a balance between the claim for freedom of access to the holy site and the sensitivities of different worshippers who might be offended by the beliefs and customs of others. If this committee is not successful, then Women of the Wall are welcome back to the Court to repetition. Therefore, the verdict rendered was not final. It recognizes that the status quo is unsatisfactory. According to the Court, there are different legitimate forms of religious expression, which need to co-exist.

In the light of the verdict, the task of the government is to find ways to formally incorporate the voices and practices of women into Jewish public holy space while interfering minimally with the sensitivities of all of the worshippers. This has become the mandate of the committee appointed in May 1994, with a six-month deadline during which time a recommendation is to be filed. In the letter appointing the committee, the principles of freedom of religious practice and access to the holy site were emphasized. If the recommendation is not satisfactory, Women of the Wall reserves the option to request that the Court reconsider the case. We are looking for a clear affirmation of pluralism as a constitutive part of religious practice in Israel, which includes women. For Women of the Wall, the January verdict is one milestone in a long process of educating the political, judicial, religious, and social sectors, both in Israel and abroad, about women's religious and spiritual activism.

Bonna Devora Haberman (r.) leads service for Sunny's (l.) historic bat mitzvah at the Kotel. Torah reading was held with Women of the Wall on plaza overlooking the Kotel, June 1990. (Photo by Barbara Gingold. © all rights reserved.)

Once, an old bent women, with a cotton kerchief pulled tightly over her hair and across her forehead, approached us. Her eyes were from a distant land. Perhaps born in Iraq, she had never seen women like us. I invited her to have an aliyah. She told me that she did not know the words and could not read. I understood. We gave her the honor of lifting the Torah scroll. She clutched the Torah, eyes crunched closed on her leather face. She held it against her breast as if at the moment of reunion with a child she had nursed, then lost. She said the prayer to thank God for having brought her to this moment. It sounded like Arabic to us. All her life she has been watching, waiting to hold the Torah. We were there on this earth at that moment only to pray with her. It was a union with the past. Distance and borders were melted by the immediacy of sharing in the holiness of the place and our prayers. Tears rolled down; prayers went up.

Women of the Wall chose a legal path because we believed that the Supreme Court is a powerful tool for social change, and that the existing legislation would be interpreted to uphold our claim to exercise our freedom to pray according to our custom. Against the backdrop of a peace process stricken with outbursts of terror, women's prayer is far from center stage. Women's issues are rarely a high priority. Nevertheless, we are committed to both the vision and the praxis that is symbolized by women's communal prayer on Rosh Chodesh at the Kotel. With time, perseverance, and support, we are writing ourselves into the script.

Note

1. All Jewish women are welcome to join Rosh Chodesh prayers at the Kotel at 7:00 A.M. When there are two days of Rosh Chodesh, we convene on the second day, except when it falls on Shabbat. For information, please contact Bonna Devora Haberman, Jerusalem (02) 610 785. There is also an International Committee for Women of the Kotel (ICWK), a support organization of Diaspora women. Please contact Rivka Haut, Brooklyn, New York (718) 252–6250.

8
Rosh Chodesh Observances among Older Sefardic Women

Susan Starr Sered

Rosh Chodesh was a part of the traditional calendrical consciousness of Jewish women in the Middle East. Kurdish and other Middle Eastern women, the vast majority of whom were never taught to read and most certainly could not decipher a written calendar, knew when to expect the new moon, observed a number of prohibitions upon its appearance, and carried out certain rituals on that day.

The first day of particular months merited special ceremonies. For example, Rosh Chodesh Adar (the month in which Purim falls) was known in Kurdistan as "Girls' Rosh Chodesh." On the morning of that day, fathers would invite all of their married daughters, with their husbands and children, for a festive meal. During the day, girls' ears and noses would be pierced, and fathers would give their daughters gifts of jewelry.[1] Girls in Kurdistan went to live with their husbands' families at marriage, which typically took place at a young age. Women remember resenting having to leave their parental homes, and feeling unhappy and forsaken at their in-laws' houses. Rosh Chodesh Adar afforded women the opportunity to return to their parental homes, celebrate with their siblings, and receive gifts, which not only demonstrated their parents' affection, but which also served to remind (or warn) in-laws that the girls' parents continued to take an interest in their well-being.

Today, in contemporary Israel, Middle Eastern Jewish women continue to acknowledge and sometimes honor Rosh Chodesh.[2] Unlike for the Sabbath and most holidays, there are few laws governing behavior on Rosh Chodesh. The only special prohibitions observed by the women concern laundry and sewing (i.e., work that can be postponed). I stress that whereas for middle-class Westerners these prohibitions may seem minor, for poor Middle Eastern women, who traditionally washed clothes in buckets filled with water that they lugged from the river or communal tap, and who often sewed for a living, the benefits of these prohibitions were tangible.

On the day preceding Rosh Chodesh, Middle Eastern women endeavor to visit cemeteries, both family graves and historical shrines such as Rachel's Tomb in Bethlehem.[3] The one ritual commonly enacted by almost all Middle Eastern women today is that of lighting candles on Rosh Chodesh Eve. Younger women typically light one candle, "for the New Moon." Older women light numerous candles, aspiring to light a separate candle for each dead relative. One of my informants explained that on Rosh Chodesh Eve, "we [Iraqi women] light candles for family members, wise men and scholars, and saints who have died. . . . We don't say a real [formal, Hebrew] blessing—just that the soul of the dead one should be in *Gan Eden* [Heaven]." Women light a variety of kinds of candles: Sabbath candles, Chanukah candles, big and small candles, oil and wax, even birthday candles. Candles serve to signal divine attention and to elicit divine assistance. A separate candle should be lit for each individual because the women believe that the flame of the candle represents the individual soul.[4]

Although the constellation of rituals practiced nowadays by Middle Eastern women on Rosh Chodesh is small, these rituals well represent the major themes in their religious world. Women's religion serves, above all, to safeguard family members and family relationships. On Rosh Chodesh Eve, women light candles and visit tombs in an effort to preserve relationships between the living and the dead. Perhaps the most remarkable attribute of these rituals is the casual way in which the women unite their own particular family members who have died with the wider category of Jewish saints and ancestors. A woman might visit her own mother's tomb one month, and Rachel's Tomb the next. She will place a candle on behalf of her dead child next to a candle for Elijah the Prophet. It is through juxtapositions like these that Middle Eastern Jewish women personalize Jewish tradition and sanctify their own lives.

Notes

1. A. Brauer, *Jews of Kurdistan* (Jerusalem: Maarav Press, 1947), pp. 276–279 (in Hebrew).

2. My comments about contemporary Rosh Chodesh practices are a product of fieldwork that I conducted among elderly Middle Eastern women in Jerusalem in 1984 and 1985. For more about these women, see *Women as Ritual Experts: The Religious Lives of Elderly Jewish Women in Jerusalem* (New York: Oxford University Press, 1992).

3. The day before Rosh Chodesh and Rosh Chodesh have been associated with Rachel's Tomb at least since the nineteenth century, when large numbers of Jerusalem Jews would walk or ride on donkeys to the shrine, and spend the day praying and feasting. See Menahem Mendel Reischer, *Shaarei Yerushalayim* (Lemberg: S. L. Kugel, Lewin and Company, 1870), chap. 8.

4. Middle Eastern women light candles at many ritual occasions and whenever family members are in particular danger (for example, traveling in an airplane, giving birth, taking an important exam at school). For more on candle-lighting rituals, see my paper, "Gender, Immanence, and Transcendence: The Candle Lighting Repertoire of Middle-Eastern Jews," *Metaphor and Symbolic Activity* 6:4 (1991): 293–304.

9
Hallel: Praises of God

Roselyn Bell

Hallel is the joy marker in the liturgical calendar of the Jewish year. For a Jew who *davens* (prays) the traditional prayers daily, there are a number of such mood signs or frame-of-mind indicators within the daily service: for example, the inclusion or absence of *Tahanun*, Psalm 27, "LeDavid, Hashem Uri V'Yishi," from the month of Elul through Shemini Atzeret, and Psalm 49, said in a house of mourning. Hallel's inclusion adds a short, intense dose of joyful praise, usually accompanied by bright, upbeat melodies.

Hallel consists of six consecutive psalms from the Book of Psalms, 113 through 118, plus an opening and closing *bracha* (blessing). The thrust of these psalms can be summed up in their last line: "This is the day that the Lord has made; let us rejoice and be glad on it." These particular psalms were chosen, the traditional commentators suggest, because they refer to five redemptive events in the Jewish view of the sweep of history: the Exodus, the splitting of the Red Sea, the giving of the Torah, the resurrection of the dead, and the coming of the Messiah.

The full Hallel sequence is recited on the major festivals and to commemorate times of deliverance from national peril. Thus, it is said on Pesach, Shavuot,

Sukkot, Shemini Atzeret, Chanukah, and, according to the ruling of the Israeli Chief Rabbinate in our day, on Yom Ha'atzmaut and Yom Yerushalayim. It is omitted from the prayers of Rosh Hashanah and Yom Kippur because too much rejoicing would not be seemly on these days of judgment. And Purim, while a celebration of deliverance, does not rate a Hallel since, according to the sages, redemption was incomplete because the Jews remained in exile.

The rabbis were divided about the appropriateness of saying Hallel on Rosh Chodesh. Arachin 10b states that the requirement does not apply to Rosh Chodesh because it is neither a holiday that involves the cessation of work nor a day of deliverance. But the custom nevertheless took root among the people. Rav, a third-century Amora coming from the Land of Israel to Babylon, noted that the practice of saying Hallel on Rosh Chodesh had become accepted among the Babylonian community,[1] but not among the Jews of the Land of Israel. A compromise developed to recite an abridged form of the Hallel—excising the first 11 verses of both Psalm 115 and Psalm 116. This shortened version is called, rather inexactly, *hetzi Hallel* (half Hallel).

The Levush, a law code compiled by Mordecai ben Avraham Jaffe, notes that the abridgment reflects the dual nature of the day, half a holiday and half a mini-day of atonement. Rabbi Samson Raphael Hirsch, the nineteenth-century German commentator, observes that the verses omitted are outcries of distress and should not be said on a day when souls stand in judgment. Others see the reason for omission to be economy of expression: the themes of these verses are repeated elsewhere, according to Eliah Rabbah. Their omission makes the tone even more upbeat, the emphasis more on rejoicing. As in all abridgments, shortening focuses the meaning.

Women and Hallel

The association of Rosh Chodesh as a women's holiday, in which women are exempt from work while men are not, is attributed to the refusal of Israelite women to give up their jewelry for the Golden Calf.[2] Despite this association, there is question regarding women chanting Hallel with a bracha. The Rambam (Moses ben Maimon, 1135–1206) opposes women saying Hallel because he sees it as a positive, time-bound commandment, a category of mitzvah from which women are exempt. [3] This remains the dominant Sephardic view, with authorities such as Rabbi Ovadiah Yosef, a contemporary Sephardic chief rabbi of Israel, claiming that women should not recite the *bracha* before and after Hallel since they are not directly commanded. The dominant Ashkenazic view, however, is that women may say these prayers on Rosh Chodesh, since Hallel on Rosh Chodesh has the status of custom and not *halacha* (law) in any case.

Having established that precedent exists for Ashkenazi women to recite Hallel on Rosh Chodesh, we may ask, "But how well does Hallel serve as an expression of rejoicing for women?" Most of the Hallel verses are genderless—equally suitable as an offer of thanksgiving by either a man or a woman: for example, Psalm 116, "I am filled with love, for God has heard my voice; for God has inclined God's ear to me, so in my days I will call," could be said by either a male or a female worshipper.

An instance of explicit female imagery appears in the last verse of Psalm 113, "God lets the barren woman dwell in her house as a joyful mother of children." Surely these words have a poignancy for women—especially those who have experienced infertility and then overcome it—that may be greater than for a man. Yet many other verses speak to themes of dominance and triumph over adversity, "He lifts the needy out of the dunghill to seat them with princes, with the princes of His people," which are more traditionally male. But on the whole, the verses address the experiences of both men and women: "Out of distress I called upon the Lord; He answered me and set me free." The themes of deliverance, thankfulness, and rejoicing are universally applicable to both men and women.

One verse of the Hallel, however, has always stuck in my throat. As a woman, I find it difficult to recite Psalm 116:14. I am struck and disturbed by the maleness of the expression, "Answer, O God, for I am Thy servant, the son of Thy handmaid." I am always tempted to change the gender of both words for servant, to make the verse read, "Ani amatkha bat avdekha," instead of "Ani avdekha ben amatekha," meaning "I am your maidservant, daughter of your male-servant" instead of vice versa. Such a reading, however, violates the set form of worship (*matbeah tefilla*) and misquotes Scripture, from which this verse is taken. Since Torah is, on some level, the word of God, emending it to make it fit my circumstance is problematic.

The question of whether one can emend a prayer to match the gender of the person praying is one that interests me a great deal. It troubles me more than the more frequently raised issue of changing the names of address to God to more feminine equivalents, such as the *Shechinah*. I have no doubt that the prayee is without and beyond gender; God contains both masculine and feminine qualities.

The author of Psalm 116, however, was clearly a man, who used masculine gender nouns to describe himself as a "manservant." When I pray, should I use his self-identification or my own? Is it more important that I pray in my own, female voice, or that I use the supposedly neutral, but male, forms in the *sidur* (prayer book) so as to be part of the community?

In the case of Hallel, changing words in order to reflect a different gender is not a simple matter of personalizing a prayer. The verses of Hallel are taken from the Book of Psalms, a part of the *Tanakh*. To change them constitutes, depending on one's beliefs, either emending the word of God or misquoting a source more venerated than Shakespeare. I might, however, alter gender in the morning prayer, Modeh Ani (feminizing it to Modah Ani), since this verse is not taken from the *Tanakh*.

After much thought, I have come to a personal decision regarding this matter. I daven the words as they appear in the text when I am in any public setting, such as singing along with a group or leading a women's *tefillah* (prayer service). But when I daven silently, I think to myself, "I am the maidservant, daughter of Your male servant."

The linguistic problem that I have with this verse in some way typifies the difficulty with using Hallel as *the* prime expression of joy in the celebration of Rosh Chodesh among women. Hallel, as the public, communal expression of joy on the dawn of a new month, is for everyone. But because Hebrew always chooses the masculine gender as the "neutral" grammatical construction, the traditional female davener is forced to adapt to a male form of speech.

If we, as traditional women, wish to express a more private, personal, and feminine prayer, we should explore the world of *tkhines*, the popular, personal prayers written for, and occasionally by, religious women of the sixteenth to early nineteenth centuries (see Tracy G. Klirs' chapter in this book, "Tkhines for Rosh Chodesh"). Using old tkhines as well as new prayers being composed today, we can, hopefully, find appropriate ways to express our private joy on the birth of a new month.

Nevertheless, there is beauty, sublimity, and timeless poetry in the words of Hallel. The melodies stir us; the memories—both communal ones, such as those that refer to the splitting of the Red Sea, and personal ones, such as those moments of triumph over adversity—sweep over us. The verses lead us to affirm God's goodness and beneficence. Hallel not only marks joy but makes us feel joyful, as we come together with (in the words from the final paragraph of Hallel) "Your entire people, the House of Israel, to thank, bless, praise, glorify, exalt, extol, sanctify and proclaim the sovereignty of Your Name."

Notes

1. Taanit 28b.
2. Pirke DeRabbi Eliezer, chap. 45.
3. See Kiddushin 34A.

10
Starting and Growing a Rosh Chodesh Group

Ruth Berger Goldston and Merle Feld

In the early 1970s, as Jewish feminism was being born in the United States, a group of American and Israeli women living in Jerusalem began gathering monthly to explore and create new rituals based on the celebration of the new moon, Rosh Chodesh, which had traditionally been observed as a minor festival, particularly by women.[1]

Over the last twenty years, Rosh Chodesh groups have become more widespread in North America. Some have been started by members of the original group who had moved to other locations. The publication of Peninah Adelman's *Miriam's Well: Rituals for Jewish Women Around the Year* in 1986 made the experiences of that original group available to a wider audience and provided program ideas and rituals that could be used by groups that were just beginning. More recently, groups have been started by women whose Jewish backgrounds range from Orthodox upbringing and yeshiva education to liberal, if not assimilated, upbringing and Jewish knowledge that has been acquired in adulthood. Women rabbis have started groups in their synagogues. Other groups have flourished under the aegis of Jewish communal organizations, and many have simply begun spontaneously in the community and have thrived as independent groups.

In addition, the scope of Rosh Chodesh groups has widened: some confine themselves to celebration of the new moon, while others have branched out into Jewish study, personal spiritual exploration, and what we used to call "consciousness-raising." Some groups meet on Rosh Chodesh, others meet on a day close to Rosh Chodesh, and still others content themselves with simply meeting monthly, whenever it's possible for busy members to attend.

Unlike other Jewish women's organizations, Rosh Chodesh groups do not have any kind of central agenda imposed on them by local or national policy or leadership. Instead, the unifying theme of the groups is the exploration of Jewish women's issues, with particular emphasis on personal spirituality, ritual, and celebration. Each group that forms develops its own *minhag* (customs) and procedures to deal with the myriad of issues that all groups face, such as membership, program, leadership, and continuity. Most groups are relatively small[2] and at least somewhat autonomous, a setting that provides women with an opportunity to feel more empowered to take charge of their Jewish lives than they might feel in a larger, more institutionalized setting. For some women, this can be a very liberating experience. Others may hesitate, either because they don't yet trust themselves to participate in a group whose structure and purpose are not explicitly known in advance, or because their needs for Jewish women's community are being met in established organizations. We think it's helpful to think of Rosh Chodesh groups as growing "from the inside out," that is, developing group agendas, styles, and customs based on the concerns, issues, strengths, and interests that particular members bring to the group.

To speak of "starting" a Rosh Chodesh group without considering how groups grow and maintain themselves is a little like using a seed package that instructs you to put the seeds in holes in the ground without mentioning how deep, how far apart, and how and when to water and cultivate the seedlings. So, while we will focus on issues that arise in getting a group started—that is, how to bring women together for an initial meeting—we will also try to address what kinds of "growing pains" a group might experience in its early months, as well as some longer-term "maintenance" issues.

In our small, informal survey of Rosh Chodesh groups around the United States,[3] we found that groups most often "start" in the minds and imaginations of one or two women who feel a need for an intimate setting in which to celebrate, study, and explore Jewish women's issues and their own experiences. A surprising number of groups have developed and been catalyzed by the migrations of women from one community to another. Often, it is the new person in a community who has previously been in a Rosh Chodesh group who provides the impetus for a group's birth, who acts as an important resource for a group's early development, or who may bring fresh ideas and enthusiasm to a group that is running out of steam. It can be helpful to have a person available who has "done it before" to help guide the way, *though it is by no means necessary.* We hope that this chapter, as well as the book of which it is a part, will enable women of all Jewish backgrounds and experiences to feel the confidence that is needed to transform the "spark" in their minds and imaginations into reality.

First Steps in Getting Started

Let's say you're a woman who's got that "spark." You've heard about Rosh Chodesh groups and you wonder what it would be like to be in such a group. Or, you feel you'd like to talk to other Jewish women on a regular basis. Or, perhaps Jewish life in your community is not very satisfying to you and you are looking for an outlet for your spiritual needs. Or, you grew up, as so many of us did, in a Jewish environment where women's participation was minimal, and you've always yearned to find out more and do more, but it's terribly intimidating to take your first steps in a congregation that includes men who seem to know so much more than you.

Share your feelings and thoughts with others. Some will likely "resonate" to your concerns and share an interest in initiating a Rosh Chodesh group.

Obstacles

Probably the two most frequently encountered obstacles at this stage are: (1) feelings of intimidation because you believe you're not smart enough, Jewishly educated enough, a real "leader," or "entitled" in some other more amorphous way to start a group, and/or (2) doubts about anyone else out there who feels the same needs you do. Let's consider both these impediments.

First, we'd like to point out that *it's those of you who feel most intimidated who probably stand to gain the most from participating in a Rosh Chodesh group.* But even women who feel relatively secure and act confidently in other areas of their lives seem to get cold feet about starting something Jewish that isn't a part of synagogue or other communal activities. Perhaps the biggest hurdle to overcome is the feeling that you couldn't possibly know enough Jewishly to take responsibility for planning a meeting or designing a ritual. The first response to that feeling is, of course, you're right: no one ever knows enough Jewishly and there's always more to learn! The trick is to stop focusing on what you *don't* know, to start looking at what you *do* know, and to turn your ignorance into curiosity and the opportunity for learning. It's also true that no one person in the group needs to know everything (we'll get back to that later when we talk about leadership), and *each person in a Rosh Chodesh group can contribute from her own unique skills, talents, and experience for the good of the group as whole.* Some people are whizzes at creating a comfortable atmosphere or are skilled with Hebrew texts; others know group dynamics skills or play the guitar. Some are writers, while others are accountants, artists, teachers, nurses, craftswomen, mothers, or all of the above. What is exciting is having a wide range of skills and talents in the group; what is crucial is promoting an openness to, and a respect for, what each woman has to offer the whole.

A Rosh Chodesh group can provide a unique opportunity for women to share experiences. After all, we *are* experts at our own lives. Talking about our upbringing, relationships with parents and siblings, experiences with death and mourning, the need for a spiritual dimension in our day-to-day lives, the joys and pains of relationships with significant others, how it felt to have an aliyah for the first time—all are potential themes to explore. Sharing the tales of these experiences will broaden your own knowledge while creating a bond between group members.

Second, perhaps you feel that there are no other women who share your concerns. You may simply need to speak up and let people know that you're thinking about trying to get a group started. The "old girl" network—one person tells another, who tells another—could circulate the message. You may choose, as some women have, to advertise through a synagogue newsletter, in the Jewish press, or even via the personals column of your local paper. Perhaps ask others in your Hadassah chapter, at your local day care center, or at the seniors' center where you take Elderhostel classes. Sometimes a specific event, such as a women's Seder, or an occasion when women gather together around a common concern serve as the impetus to form a group.

The Initial Meeting: Establishing an Agenda

A group of women gathers, either in someone's living room, in the shul library, or at the Jewish Community Center. A leader or facilitator—often a woman who's been involved in organizing this first meeting—has planned an introductory program. The format of this program will vary, depending on the interests, expertise, and experience of the leader-facilitator. Some groups will observe a ritual or celebration that is tied to a theme associated with the Jewish month, while other groups may begin and end with a brief song, poem, or activity, but focus mainly on a semistructured discussion or study session.

Regardless of the format, this first meeting should ideally allow people to introduce themselves and begin to get to know one another in the context of a Rosh Chodesh group: that is, as Jewish women. One way of doing this is to have each woman introduce herself by her Hebrew or Yiddish name, and by the names of her mother and grandmothers (for example, "I am Malkah, daughter of Rivkah, granddaughter of Gittel and Sarah"). Sharing a brief Jewish autobiography, as well as one's hopes for, and interests in, the group, is another tool to becoming a group. These activities will hopefully highlight common experiences and themes which can become the basis for future programs and for the group's identity. The leader can facilitate this process by drawing out those who are reticent, containing those who go on at length, and emphasizing commonalties rather than differences among those present (for this reason, we don't encourage highly charged political issues to be the focus of an initial meeting).

By the close of the first meeting, one or several directions toward which the group could proceed have probably emerged. The focus of the group should remain somewhat fluid throughout the first several months, as members come and go and as people get to know one another better. Keeping open at this stage, in regard to people and format, may feel disorienting at times but is well worth the effort in the long run. At this stage, the group needs to establish some structure, to deal with logistics and to ensure continuity.

Program

The range of program ideas is virtually limitless. Programs can include life cycle celebrations, observance of Jewish holidays, traditional and creative prayer, study of Jewish texts, artistic pursuits, learning new Jewish skills, and discussion about a variety of shared experiences. While connecting to the themes of the Jewish month can help the group focus, some groups may prefer to branch out into nonthematic areas.

Adapting ideas from the contents of this book, or other resources, to fit the needs and interests of your own group will provide useful seeds for growing hearty programs.

As we mentioned above, many groups use opening and closing rituals, recognizing that it's important to create a "sacred space" for the group's activities. A song, a poem, a prayer, or a *D'var Torah* can serve this purpose. In some cases, the same ritual is used at every meeting to create a sense of continuity; in others, the form remains the same but the content changes as different members participate. In groups where membership is open, a brief introduction activity may need to be part of the opening ritual, so that all present know each other's names and feel included. A closing ritual could provide a response to the just-completed event and include singing, speaking, or even movement.

How can you make your program participatory? Some very simple techniques, such as breaking into groups of two, three, or four for a discussion or an activity, will ensure that everyone has a chance to participate within a limited period of time. After these more intimate sessions, the entire group can gather again and share the themes and the process of the smaller groups. *Beit midrash* style study, in which people pair up to wrestle with a text, is a time-honored and most appropriately traditional approach, which can easily be adapted to the needs of a Rosh Chodesh group. Whatever the format and content of the program, the leader or facilitator can help people become involved by creating an atmosphere that welcomes and values the participation of each group member.

Membership: Who's In and Who's Out—And How Do We Decide?

The question of membership is one that faces all groups. You became part of the Jewish people either by being born that way or through the process of conversion; you join other groups by applying for membership and/or by paying dues. In order for a group to function, people need to know if they are "in" or "out" of it. Rosh Chodesh groups deal with membership in a number of ways, and no one way is "right" or "wrong." Also, in the course of a group's development, a membership policy that worked well initially may become ineffective as the group matures. Because a Rosh Chodesh group is typically small and at least semiautonomous, it ought to have the flexibility to modify its membership policies and procedures as its circumstances change.

One way to think about group membership is to consider its *boundaries*. Are the boundaries wide *open*, so that people come and go at will? Are they *selective*, letting in some people but not others, or at some times but not other times? Or is the group *closed*, with a fixed set of members that does not change?

Initially, many groups are *open*. Women respond to a public invitation or hear about an initial meeting from friends. Some groups remain open, often with a core of regular attendees and a smaller number of newcomers. The advantage of this format is that the group is constantly being infused with new blood, new enthusiasm, and new ideas. People "self-select," staying with the group if it meets their needs and dropping out if it does not. No one is excluded from membership, which is an appealing egalitarian ideal. The founder of one group that has continued to be open throughout its three-year life noted: "This has been a successful approach. There's a core group who comes nearly all the time, people on the 'fringes' who attend occasionally, and new people. We have a photo album and an orientation pamphlet that have helped people feel involved."

There can, however, be problems with the open group. It may be more difficult for people to experience intimacy and be willing to take personal risks when new members are always appearing. Programming may be more hit-or-miss when the participant group is a "moving target," and the group may have trouble forming an identity or coherent sense of itself. Finally, the group is always vulnerable to "invasion" by someone who can alter its chemistry in a destructive way. Whether or not this actually happens, the group may feel helpless to control who its members are.

Another membership model has *selective* boundaries. This can occur in several ways. Initially, one or two organizers may just invite women who, they believe, have a common vision and who will be compatible with one another. In later stages, if a group is to add members, they must be approved by the existing membership. People are either "invited" to participate, or they "apply" to the group to be admitted. While this gives the group more control than a completely open membership, it can result in hurt feelings on the part of those who are excluded, passionate disagreements within the group as these decisions are being made, and awkwardness between people who are "in" and people who are "out" who may know one another in other community settings. Another type of selective boundary is opening the group occasionally (perhaps once a year) to new members who are interested in joining. This permits the group to rejuvenate itself on a regular basis, while still being able to create a stable environment for its members.

Finally, a group can be *closed*. Initial membership is by invitation from the organizers, and no new members are admitted. The advantage of such a group is that it permits an extraordinary degree of intimacy and risk taking within it. However, it can become vulnerable to the development of rifts, as well as to losses through attrition, and this group model demands a high degree of commitment.

Leadership: "If You Don't Lead, You Don't Become Involved!"

When a new Rosh Chodesh group begins, the leader is usually the woman who has sparked the group to get together. As we mentioned, this person may be a newcomer to the community who has participated in other Rosh Chodesh groups or was perceived by others to have the skills and experience necessary to facilitate the formation of a new group. One woman expressed her reasons for starting a group: "I wanted to make a community for myself here—I guess that was very selfish! But I feel blessed that there were lots of women who wanted to try it."

In other instances, a leader or leaders emerge as the group is forming. The leader serves a crucial purpose in the group, particularly in its initial stages, for without her a group can very easily feel directionless and unable to function. However, despite our conviction that just about any Jewish woman has the capability to start and lead a Rosh Chodesh group, we recognize that many women do not feel that they can be leaders, at least at the beginning. For some it's a matter of personality, and for others it's an issue of not having what are perceived to be the "qualifications" for the job. Whatever the reason, at least initially, it's likely that the leader or leaders of the group will be those who did the initial organizing, those who have the strongest Jewish backgrounds and thus feel confident and secure, and/or those who are skilled in group processes.

Explicit, centralized leadership may be essential to get a group off the ground, but unfortunately, it seems to bring with it some inevitable problems. Hierarchies can develop within the group, when some people feel closer and more connected to the leader, and therefore more empowered, and others feel farther away and more ineffectual. Two leaders can vie for control, fragmenting the group into factions. But, most critical for a Rosh Chodesh group, strong centralized leadership may prevent the members of the group from realizing their own potential within it. Instead of stretching themselves, taking chances at trying new skills, members may find it easier to let the leader run the show, grumbling when they're not satisfied and, perhaps, eventually losing interest in participating.

Many of us have been frustrated by our participation in groups, both in the workplace and in the community, because of these leadership problems. The women's movement has taught us that we can question some of the basic assumptions that seem to be the legacy of centuries of patriarchy. One of these assumptions is that of hierarchy, in which someone is at the "top" and therefore, inevitably, someone is also at the "bottom." Women, having been an underclass for so long, are particularly sensitive to the problems of those at the "bottom." We have learned that one solution is to create a more egalitarian group, where leadership functions are shared among group members.

We favor a shared leadership model for Rosh Chodesh groups, realizing that there are many ways that leadership can be shared. It's important to have a person, or a small committee of people, who will handle logistics—keeping track of a calendar and a membership list, notifying people of meetings, making sure there are events scheduled and places for meetings to take place. These functions could rotate from year to year, and they can provide opportunities for some people to make a valuable contribution to the group.

Programmatic leadership is best rotated so that, depending on the size of the group, each member has the opportunity to plan or help plan a program at least once yearly. A method that works well for one group is to have two members plan each session, bouncing ideas off each other in the planning stages and giving each other courage to take center stage at the session. Teaming up members who have more Jewish background and/or leadership experience with those who perceive themselves to have less is one way of encouraging everyone to "try their wings."

Our small survey of groups around the continent suggests that the transition from one leader to shared leadership can be tricky, though by no means impossible, to accomplish. The original leaders may have been eager to involve others and step back themselves, but, as one woman put it: "When no one signed up to do a program, I struggled with how to deal with it. Should I ask someone, or let it flounder?" Initially, this woman chose to intervene by asking another person to lead the program. Later, she was able to "let go" by putting all the materials, including a guide to planning and facilitating, in a box that each program leader, in turn, used. Another leader had a harder time establishing shared leadership for the group she founded, because the women who attended were reluctant to take those roles. Ultimately, this group wasn't able to maintain itself without her. In some groups, a leader will need to work to develop and empower others by offering support as needed, helping members team up to take new responsibilities, and knowing when and how to let go, even if it means gritting one's teeth as a woman does things in her own, different way.

Many of the women with whom we spoke felt frustrated by the difficulty around relinquishing leadership. They also felt that their spiritual needs, which they hoped would be met by the group, were not being satisfied because they were always playing the role of leader. One woman said: "I felt that leadership was expected of me. I wanted to get something from the group as well as give to it." A rabbi commented: "I wanted to be a resource person for the group, but I knew I wouldn't have the time to prepare each session myself. I felt that I could get more spiritual satisfaction from the group if I wasn't always the one who was worrying about choreography, cake, and constancy."

Maintenance: How to Keep the Group Going

Once the Rosh Chodesh group has passed through the initial stages, you and other group members may experience some well-earned euphoria as the group acquires its own life and direction. Often, a tremendous sense of excitement surrounds events, as people get to know and trust one another, as issues that are deeply significant are discussed, and as the group experiences the cycle of the Jewish year in new and creative ways. Everyone is eager to participate, ideas abound, and energy seems limitless. However, at some later time, perhaps years down the road, the group may lose some of its initial enthusiasm due to a decline in membership, ideas growing stale, or an insurmountable crisis within the group. It's a moment when many groups flounder and when some don't survive.

How can a group manage these pivotal moments? The first step is to get the issues out in the open. Perhaps the group has simply become too small to function, and a new infusion of members is needed. Or, the format of the group, which was so exciting at the beginning, is no longer stimulating, and a new direction is needed. Sometimes, crises involve difficult issues to address: there may be "personality conflicts" or a history of hurt feelings and misunderstandings that have gone unspoken and unresolved. Whatever the circumstances, group members should be given the opportunity to share their feelings and perceptions.

Sometimes everyone agrees that the solution is fairly straightforward: look for new members; try a different type of program; get more people involved in leading sessions. In other instances, the group may be working well for some members, but not for others. Can the group accommodate itself to a variety of needs without sacrificing its integrity? Or does it make more sense for some members to leave the group and look for another, more appropriate setting (or another Rosh Chodesh group)? There is no single right answer, of course, but we believe that everyone benefits from an honest, open, and respectful discussion of the issues, regardless of the outcome.

Some practical suggestions: Many groups try to reserve one meeting a year for planning and accessing the "state of the group." These meetings may be more administrative than ideological, a sign that the group is functioning smoothly. In other years, a "core" conflict or issue emerges, and the group may need several sessions to explore it and reorient itself. A moderator (a group member who is comfortable in that role or an outsider) may be asked to assist with group process. Practicing empathic listening as well as straightforward, sensitive expression of thoughts and feelings will lead to a more satisfactory outcome.

Groups, like individuals, have a natural life cycle, as well as times of growth, times of crisis, and times of stability. The sad truth is that many Rosh Chodesh groups don't survive past the first few years. A multitude of explanations, including each group's own unique circumstances, can be brought forth to help us understand why this is so. We hope, however, that some of the tools we've provided here will help you and your group deal with some of the more common problems that Rosh Chodesh groups face.

Conclusion

Starting, and growing, a Rosh Chodesh group can seem a daunting task. Yet, with a bit of knowledge and resourcefulness, many women have been able to help groups get off the ground, and many groups have not only been born, but have thrived. We have found that being part of a Rosh Chodesh group has been a very special experience of community that we didn't find in other parts of our Jewish lives—a unique opportunity to lead and be led, to grow and to experiment, to learn and to teach, to struggle and to celebrate with our sisters.

Notes

1. For more information on the original group, see *Miriam's Well*, by Peninah Adelman (New York: Biblio Press, 1990).

2. Groups that dwindle to a *minyan* (ten people) or less may just run out of energy; groups of thirty or more may provide such limited opportunity for intimacy as to become emotionally frustrating.

3. In order to formulate our ideas for this chapter, we drew on the knowledge of about a half dozen women who had been involved in starting twelve to fifteen groups in the last two decades. Nearly all of them had moved to new communities at some point and had chosen to become involved in starting new groups.

11
Rosh Chodesh for Children: Learning about and Experiencing the Jewish Lunar Calendar

Ellen Brosbe

Young children are fascinated by magic and the mystery of nature, as the world around them instills both fear and fascination. The young child's awe of and relationship to nature is rooted in animism—the belief that natural objects possess a soul or consciousness.

Children easily understand why we cover the challah on Shabbat (so we won't hurt the challah's feelings when we first say the blessing over wine) because the explanation fits well amid the beliefs of a young child. Three- and four-year-olds love collecting "treasures" such as leaves, little stones, or pebbles. Quartz rocks in the courtyard of the synagogue become "diamonds." And children will often move a rock from a path to change the rock's view.[1]

Children often believe that the moon and the sun follow them. They delight when they look out the car window and watch the moon traveling with them to

Grandma's house. They become astronomers when the sun and moon are both visible during the day.

In the early years, children think of time as something to which they will eventually catch up: taller is older. And although they may be able to recite numbers, the alphabet, days and months, their understanding of time as cyclical remains illusive. The concept of time being linear as on a page in the calendar or cyclical as in the repetition of yearly holidays is often not comprehended until the middle years (ages 9 to 11).

Rosh Chodesh is an important holiday to teach children. It gives them an understanding of the cyclical nature of our calendar and a psychological base of hope: even the difficult moments (of which there can be many in the growing-up years) will pass—the moon will reappear again. Moon-watching provides children with an introduction to the moon's changes and has a way of attuning children to the cycle of the year, teaching them about the lunar–solar base of our calendar and holidays.

When we introduce young children to special Jewish times such as Rosh Chodesh, the educational method should be experiential. A successful model for learning about the Jewish holidays at a young age is exploring the Jewish world through the various senses, which creates Jewish, emotional focal points.

The world around the young child is rich with what Vivian Paley[2] calls "teachable moments." While we may be calling the preschool celebration on noon at Friday "Shabbat," it will not be until a later age that the child realizes that Shabbat really occurs at Sundown on Friday and Havdalah ends Shabbat on Saturday, when three stars appear in the sky.

It is easier for the child to understand these special school times if they become special family times as well. Both formal and informal programming, school and home based experiences, will help the child reconnect with those early, emotional markers. Teaching through the senses allows the teacher to reach all types of learning styles. Learning about Rosh Chodesh via the senses gives us an opportunity to unite our appreciation of God's miracles in nature and the miracles of our bodies. The renewal of the moon's cycle is paralleled for children with the healing of a cut finger, the loss and growth of a tooth, or the physical changes they observe on the growth chart kept at home.

Experiencing Jewish holidays in the classroom is difficult. Trying to *teach* about Shabbat or Havdallah is very different than *experiencing* these times. In the Jewish school, we fit the child with Jewish glasses with which to view the world outside of the school. The young child watching the lighting of Shabbat candles on Erev Shabbat may generalize that candles mean "Shabbat." Eventually, the child will learn to discern the specifics of candle lighting. As children are introduced to more formal education about the Jewish calendar, they will draw on these early experiences and sensori-emotional focal points.

Formal Curricular Materials on the Calendar

A variety of curricular materials are available for Jewish educational programs about Rosh Chodesh. In the preschool setting authentic, child-centered activities emerge from the interests of the children rather than from the teacher. Interest in the solar system, moon, and space travel in general are ways to connect secular interests with Jewish calendar and Rosh Chodesh observance. In Jewish children's literature some quality stories are available. Other than holiday books that mention the calendar and may briefly note Rosh Chodesh, there is nothing specifically for Rosh Chodesh (check your nearest Jewish or public library or book store). Two classics include the Helm story, "The Helmites Capture the Moon" in *The Wise Men of Helm* by Solomon Simon and *What the Moon Brought* by Sadie R. Weilerstein. *Salmon Moon* by Mark Karlins is a beautiful, original story with positive and imaginative images of elders.

Following are a few of the curricula ideas available for both formal and informal instruction.

The *Melton Graded Curriculum* is suggested for the six-hour supplementary school setting. The Alef (first-year, eight-year-olds) curriculum includes Holidays/Mitzvot/Prayer. This five-lesson curriculum contains material on the Jewish calendar, including excellent background material for the teacher. The Dalet (fourth-year, age eleven) curriculum teaches more about the Jewish calendar. These two lessons, written by Gail Dorph, add the intricacies of the calendar in the explanation about the lunar/solar cycles. The 1986 *Milwaukee Curriculum Resource: The Jewish Calendar* by Vicky Kelman (grades 2–3) is a complete resource notebook. The curriculum attempts to link home and community with fifteen lessons to be used throughout the school year in the supplementary school setting. Including the information about the calendar at this stage in the holiday curriculum is developmentally appropriate as many eight-year-olds enjoy the routine of keeping a calendar and keeping track of important events.

Shomrei Adamah is a Jewish ecological organization based in Philadelphia, Pennsylvania. The mission of Shomrei Adamah/Keepers of the Earth is "to cultivate an awareness of nature, a practice of stewardship and a sense of Jewish identity by engaging traditional Jewish wisdom and spirituality." A curriculum book, *Let the Earth Teach You Torah*, by Ellen Bernstein and Dan Fink, is oriented toward "a broad adult and teen audience." It includes eleven chapters including activities and text study, and it can be applied to retreat or havurah settings. One chapter, "Time," includes directions for making a circular calendar, which would be a wonderful Rosh Chodesh learning activity. Shomrei Adamah publishes a newsletter, *Voice of the Trees*, three times a year.

Family Education attempts to connect home and school via programs that educate, support, and enhance Jewish life and a sense of community among families. Jewish Family Education can be multigenerational, including singles, couples, parents, children, and grandparents. Programs about the Jewish calendar are part of a growing number of family programs engaging families in a variety of experiences ranging from one time events to Shabbat retreats. Many schools offer schoolwide moon-watch or star-gazing events. Often, parents or older siblings may be enthusiastic amateur astronomers. Astronomical societies will often provide a resource person and quality telescope for the moon-watch. (Note should be taken that young children, five and under, have a difficult time physically looking through the lens of a large telescope.) These programs have worked best for school-age children who may be using related curricular materials on the Jewish calendar in the school setting. Havurot or mishpaha programs offer additional opportunities for family experiences around the Jewish calendar. *Family Room*, a pilot program by Vicky Kelman, is a havurah-type program offering ongoing gatherings, including a program on "Special Family Times."

One More Thing to Do?

Families are often captives of the messy mass of calendars we maintain. Some of us look to our day-planners as the true *Sifrei Kodesh* (holy books.) We may have work, snack, carpool, chore, and soccer schedules posted on one calendar. When I noticed a beautiful heart sticker on a friend's calendar, I assumed it indicated a special time put aside for her spouse—but actually, it was the day her dog, Bernie, received his heart pill.

Rather than becoming "one more thing to do," like environmental awareness, ecological causes, and our Jewish value of *Ba'al Taschit* (not wasting), learning about the rhythms of Jewish life can be fun. Moon watching can be a natural part of taking a drive or a walk, carpool time, or vacation drives. By becoming aware of the Jewish year, families are able to name everyday experiences in Jewish language: giving the ordinary a special, Jewish name.

One successful parenting technique is a weekly family meeting that includes a calendar session. In addition to listing the activities of the week, make note of the moon's travels through the sky. Discuss the path the moon takes and its phases throughout the month. If your family wants to become more attuned with the rhythm of each Jewish day, family educator Vicky Kelman suggests remembering something special you learned that day before saying the bedtime *Sh'ma*.

For the shul-going family, talking about the cycles of the moon is a great reinforcement to the *Birkat HaChodesh* (blessing) heard in the synagogue on

Shabbat prior to Rosh Chodesh. A reminder to young children to watch and listen for the blessing of the new month is one way to familiarize them with that particular part of the prayer service. If your synagogue has a junior congregation or a Shabbat morning program for young children, an activity of making moon stick-puppets to hold up during the blessing of the new moon would be fun and instructive.

Many secular calendars today mark the Jewish holidays. If your child has a calendar with popular themes from sports, movies, television, or literature, parents can make the calendar Jewish by adding special stickers to mark Shabbat, Rosh Chodesh, and other Jewish holidays. A wonderful addition to a Jewish home are the Kar-Ben Copies Jewish calendars, including "My Very Own Jewish Calendar," pocket or jumbo size. An exciting moon phase poster is available from the Astronomical Society of the Pacific and a large postcard size is available through Johnson Books in Boulder, Colorado.

Rosh Chodesh is an opportunity for families to connect with each other, with "Jewish time" and with the calendar through moon watching and schoolwide, family Rosh Chodesh celebrations. Some synagogues, such as the Sonoma County Synagogue Center, sponsor a family Rosh Chodesh observance. It is a children-oriented, Rosh Chodesh celebration incorporating many of the components of an adult Rosh Chodesh observance, such as song, stories about the month, candle lighting, hand washing, and various new month prayers.

Families with young children might start observing Rosh Chodesh by having a "Tonight is the Moon's Birthday" party. Pointing out how the moon is full at Pesach and Sukkot is a way to connect the two holidays, six months apart. Tu B'Shevat, the Jewish arbor day, is also observed at the full moon and gives us both the ecological and Israel connection.

The mitzvah, or commandment, of Rosh Chodesh is to observe the new moon. And yet, many families don't take time to go outdoors and look at the new moon. Time has become the family's most precious possession. Creating special family times during and around the Jewish calendar can add both a spiritual and renewing dimension to the life of the family in very simple ways. In a recent marketing survey, a large group of families was asked, "What does your family like to do together?" The resounding answer was, "I don't know." By becoming aware of special moments in the course of the day, week, month, or year, it becomes possible to create a "special family times" photo album. Embracing the natural world via the changes of the moon is a wonderful way to acknowledge, celebrate, and share Jewish life. Teaching our children about the moon's cycles and observing Rosh Chodesh with them allows the Jewish family a simple, ongoing, forever recurring moment of awe and wonder, the touchstones of developing Jewish spirituality.

Notes

1. For a discussion about children's development and learning, see Jean Piaget, *The Child's Conception of the World* (London: Paladin Publications, 1973), p. 236.

2. See discussion about teaching in Vivian Paley, *Wally's Stories, Conversations in the Kindergarten* (Cambridge, MA: Harvard University Press, 1981).

12
New Moon–First Moon Celebration: Welcoming Daughters into the Circle of Women

Shonna Husbands-Hankin

Talya's journey to womanhood began with her dream. The dream was scary, intense, and explosive. Graphic and powerful, her deepest inner wisdom was speaking:

> My friend's Bar Mitzvah party was at my house. All of my friends were there. Outside I could see the moon. There was an eclipse. Black blobs of sky were forming around the moon. I was scared. Red splashes were going around the moon. I went into the kitchen to the sink where mom and her friend were washing dishes, and said: "I'm scared—tell me the truth. What is happening?" Mom said, "Eugene [our hometown] is going to blow up and there is no time to escape." I remember that my friend's velvet, satin tefillin bag was on display. Then I woke up from the dream.

At school that day it happened: Talya's moon time began. Talya, the oldest of our two daughters, is eleven and a half years old. Excited and gleeful, she bounded up to her dad in the afternoon to proudly share her news. And I began to think of creating a sacred ceremony to usher her gracefully into this next level of being.

Rosh Chodesh was approaching in a few days, and it seemed the perfect time for gathering together to share and celebrate Talya's womanness in a Jewish ritual. The waxing and waning of the moon has long been regarded as a symbol of women's changing bodies: as the moon and the oceans flow, so, too, do women's bodies.

Tenderly, I broached the idea with Talya, fearing that her natural shyness might inhibit her. However, to my pleasant surprise, she agreed to the idea of a welcoming ritual and drew up a list of friends to invite—three close, lifelong girlfriends, their mothers, and a few other women with whom she would feel safe. Each person was asked to bring a flower and an offering of their own choice.

I quickly scanned all of my books on Jewish ritual and found only one which included a model ritual appropriate for this occasion: "Birkat HaNeetzan— Blessing the Blossom." It is a girl's initiation ritual described in Elizabeth Resnick Levine's, *A Ceremonies Sampler: New Rites, Celebrations and Observances for Jewish Women*, published by the Women's Institute for Continuing Jewish Education. Using this ceremony as a reference, I created a ritual for my daughter.

In the ceremony, I wanted to capture qualities of empowerment, pride, spiritual development, Jewish teachings, feminist teachings, and a sense of love and womanly wisdom. I hoped we could bestow a sense of awe and specialness, as well as connectedness to the flow of the universe. The mystery of creation is forever made new as the silver sliver of the Rosh Chodesh moon miraculously reappears each month. Each woman's cycle brings forth the potential fruit of creation as an offering of life's possibilities. It is a special honor that we carry as women, bearers of creation. Yet our everyday, modern life often jettisons us past recognizing this profundity.

On Rosh Chodesh evening, a few days after her first period began, we gathered around our table. Candles were lit, and the Shehechianu blessing was recited in the feminine form. We each took turns, ushering into our circle the names of mothers, grandmothers, and other women friends. Each person offered a flower, one by one interweaving it into a braided fabric "crown" I had made, which was then placed on Talya's head.

A special kiddush cup was filled with deep, red raspberry and grape juice, fruits of the vine. Around the circle the "simcha cup" was passed, a sacred goblet that has been used at over a hundred Jewish life-cycle ceremonies among our community of extended friends. As each girl or woman held the cup, they offered their own unique blessing for Talya's blossoming. And together we chanted the Hebrew blessing over the fruit of the vine.

A ritual pouch was filled with individual offerings for the newly menstruating young woman, including gifts of seashells, crystals, earrings with moons, and angel cards. Songs and drums filled the air, and stories were shared by those who had gone before on this path of womanhood.

A sweet glow of happiness was reflected on my daughter's face, and the girls all seemed to cherish the specialness of the event, although bringing a bit of nervous giggling energy. As her mother, I said a few words and offered a special prayer. I also, at that time, gave her a new (middle) name to pass on the female lineage in our family through the connection of names that had been worn before her in variations of the name "Star." We closed with a silent prayer and a song. Finally, we shared ritual treats to eat: many seeded fruits as fertility symbols, crescent moon cookies, lush dates and figs, and deep red juices.

It was a beautiful and simple ceremony, weaving together a strand of holiness through a web of women. Embellishments and variations could be made to shape and create such ceremonies honoring and blessing the "blossoms" unfolding in our garden of women. Rosh Chodesh, the celebration of the inner dark cycles rhythmically manifesting into light and life, is a beautiful holiday and poignant moment in which to make sacred a young woman's journey into womanhood.

May each young woman, in her own way, come to know the sacredness of her body as a vessel for holiness. It is the continuity of the life essence, as we all seek to connect to the infinite wisdom of the Great Mother who births and re-births us. May each young woman come to know the sacredness of the recurring moon, birthing a new month before us.

And to this day, the dried flower crown hangs there in the corner of Talya's room, in a place of reverence, a cherished memory. May it always be so.

II

Approaches to Rosh Chodesh

13
Echad B'Yachad: Private Acts of Faith

Charlotte Atlung Sutker

This chapter is devoted to the woman who, for any of several reasons, may not want, or has no opportunity, to belong to a Rosh Chodesh group. Most of the focus in the last twenty years, since the revival of Rosh Chodesh, has been on group observance, stemming in part from three roots: the woman's movement, the havurah movement, and orthodox women's *tefillah*/prayer groups. From the woman's movement, the concept of group consciousness and group support arose. From the havurah movement came the concept of egalitarian participation, and from the women's *tefillah* groups came the idea that women could constitute a davening quorum if certain *minyan*-necessary prayers were not included. It is from this base that Jewish feminists took a look at the holiday that is specifically devoted to women and decided to breath new life into an old tradition. It is only natural that when they did so they would approach it from a group perspective.

However, Jewish tradition also offers another perspective to view Rosh Chodesh. The three traditional *mitzvot* (commandments) of women are all private, home-based acts: challah, *niddah*/observing the laws of family purity,

107

and *hadlikat* haneirot/lighting Shabbat candles. A *midrash* (story) connects these three *mitzvot* to Chana by taking the *chet* ח of challah, the *nun* נ of niddah, and the *hey* ה of haneirot Shabbat to spell her name חנה. Chana is often viewed as a spiritual woman who held on to her inner belief in God in the face of being called a drunk by the priests as she muttered prayers. She is a good role model for women who are seeking a spiritual life.

It was while I was quietly, on my own, lighting Shabbat candles that I realized that there were probably other women like myself who did not belong to a Rosh Chodesh group. I live in a small, isolated community, and the women in our community have tried now and then over the years to gather to celebrate Rosh Chodesh, but it has been hard to sustain a group and often there are periods of months and years when there is no group with which to mark the holiday. Other women, who live in a more urban setting, might still find no organized group for them to join (and not all of us are able to start a new group). Still others may not feel like being part of a group. They are just not "group people."

Most of the published Rosh Chodesh resources assume group observance. I am offering suggestions for a woman alone: how to individually celebrate Rosh Chodesh. Women belonging to a group could also adopt some of these suggestions if they have to miss a group due to scheduling or illness.

I offer several suggestions for observing Rosh Chodesh alone. More than anything, these suggestions serve to increase awareness of Rosh Chodesh and in so doing keep a God consciousness for the day. It is easy for me in my day-to-day activities to lose sight of God. Rosh Chodesh is an opportunity to be reminded of my connection to God, and I welcome the holiday for just this reason. Shabbat has been described as an island of time by Rabbi Abraham Joshua Heschel. In a similar vein, Rosh Chodesh can be thought of as pockets of activities that can be interspersed throughout the day with each activity an opportunity to affirm one's Judaism and connection to God.

I have experimented with various activities and, over time, return to my favorites. I haven't worried if my observance has varied. The important thing is to keep alive the *kavanah*/heartfelt connection for Rosh Chodesh.

Although all observances of Rosh Chodesh are spiritual because they connect me to Hashem, I divide them into two categories: daily activities and religious activities.

Daily Activities

1. Perhaps the simplest thing I do is mark into my calendar Rosh Chodesh for each month. I don't use a Jewish calendar daily, as it doesn't fit my appointment schedule. I only use a Jewish calendar as a reference and, if I rely only on it, Rosh Chodesh surprises me by coming and going, and I miss it. I need to mark it *big* in my daily appointment book.

2. Another easy thing I do is to phone one or two friends who are aware of Rosh Chodesh and wish them a *"Chodesh tov*/a good month."

3. I have a small pottery dish, made by a Jewish potter, with the phases of the moon painted on it. I fill it with water for Miriam who led the Hebrews in the desert to water as they wandered for forty years. She also led the women in singing and dancing after crossing the Red Sea. For me she is a symbol of early women celebrating together. I stand and sing Aryeh Hirschfield's song, "Wings Of Peace."

U'fros aleinu, sukkat shalom,
Spread over us, Wings of peace, shalom,
Draw water in joy, from the living well,
Draw water in joy, from the living well,
Mayim chaim, waters of life, shalom.

4. As the moon is round, I try to serve round food or food in round dishes. This reminds me of the moon, and although the Rosh Chodesh moon is a thin crescent, I am more aware of the moon's phase while I am cooking. A cake in a round pan, a round loaf of bread, a fresh dish of blueberries, and melon balls in a fruit salad are a few ideas.

5. Since Rosh Chodesh is celebrated on the *new* moon, I save *new* things for that occasion. I wait until Rosh Chodesh to start a new project or wear a new article of clothing. Again, in making the decision to wait I am remembering that God is part of my life and that I am a Jew. Although a simple, private act, of which only I am perhaps aware, it will nonetheless contribute to the intentionality of my spiritual life.

6. Like the special Shabbat bread, so, too, on Rosh Chodesh I have tried to make a round bread. Many times I have fantasized a special Rosh Chodesh bread cover like a challah cover, portraying Rosh Chodesh themes; such as the moon, women, and water.

7. On Shabbat I try to restrict my reading to Jewish material, such as an analysis of women and Judaism or simply a novel with a Jewish theme or characters. Because Shabbat is not a workday and my activities are restricted, I have more time to read. When I have the opportunity to read on Rosh Chodesh, I also choose Jewish material.

Religious Activities

1. Lighting a candle Erev Rosh Chodesh/the evening of Rosh Chodesh helps me separate the day from the rest of the month, just as lighting Shabbat candles helps me separate Shabbat from the rest of the week. A friend has a special candlestick that she uses just for Rosh Chodesh. It is ceramic and adorned with

moons. The moon is associated with a special type of light that is soft and feminine. I say the following blessing:

ברוך אתה יהוה מחדש חדשים

Baruch atah Adonai, m'chadesh hachadashim.
Blessed are You, who renews the months.

2. Although I generally do not daven on a daily basis, I do sometimes on Rosh Chodesh.

3. I intentionally use Rosh Chodesh as a time to study and increase my liturgical skills. Sometimes I spend additional time preparing a Torah reading.

4. One of my most rewarding Rosh Chodesh activities, was to form a chevrusah/two-person study partnership. We met each Rosh Chodesh evening for three hours over a period of four years. As "homework," we each read a *Parshat haShavuah*/weekly Torah portion for the upcoming month and independently selected one topic or theme to research. We would share our Torah-related questions and concerns with each other. This could be done as a solo activity, but the exciting exchange of ideas would be missed.

In closing, Rosh Chodesh does not *need* to be a group experience. Our heritage shows us that although a minyan for creating community is necessary for some observances, as individuals we can also observe solo activities to strengthen our involvement with Judaism and God.

14
Reflections on Observing Rosh Chodesh with My Women's Tefillah Group

Norma Baumel Joseph

We are twelve years old; bat mitzvah age. We have come of age according to the traditions of our ancestors. Today we should be able to stand up before the community and announce our admission to the world of halachic responsibility—proudly and publicly. Instead, the accustomed silence of many years greets us. No matter, it does not effect or diminish the quality of our prayer experience nor our deep commitment to Judaism. We have survived these many years only on the basis of prayer; not recognition.

Our Tefillah Group

In the spring of 1982 the Montreal Women's Tefillah group began meeting. Since then, excluding summers, the group has met regularly on Rosh Chodesh to celebrate this traditional women's holiday in prayer. There are many such groups in the United States, England, Canada, and Israel. Some are study groups, many are prayer groups. Few meet as we do on Rosh Chodesh itself. When we started meeting it seemed appropriate to mark the day of the new moon with prayer, study, and Torah reading—a forgotten women's holiday retrieved. We have been fortunate to have always been able to meet in a synagogue, with use of its Torah and guidance from the rabbi.

The idea for the prayer group was sparked at a weekend Shabbat retreat. After heated discussions with friends about women's participation—or lack thereof—in Orthodox synagogue ritual, some of us decided to try a separate women's prayer group. A few months later, with a list of eager volunteers, I called our first meeting. Since that time our membership has changed and grown. Finding our way slowly, we have come to recognize and appreciate our different goals and skills. Over the years, we have welcomed new babies, mourned the loss of friends and relatives, greeted girls as they become bat mitzvah, Jewishly celebrated significant moments in our lives, and learned a great deal about prayer. We learned about the characteristics and tempo of prayer, the necessity for participation and criteria of leadership, and the distinctiveness of public prayer. Mostly, we have learned that prayer sustains its own significance.

Our prayer format has always been quite traditional. We generally follow the morning liturgy, singing Hallel and including the traditional Rosh Chodesh Torah service. Our enthusiasm radiates from hearing our own voices led by our soprano *hazanit*; our inspiration is located in our own ability to read from the covenant that God established with us. Initially, we used a variety of prayer books. Some of us were used to a Sephardic pattern, others Ashkenazic. Some were unused to prayer in any form. Eventually, we were blessed with a gift from one of our members. Barbara Nirenberg decided to create a prayer book just for us. Not only does it eliminate flipping through pages, it uses feminine pronouns in all the instructions. In memory of her father, she edited and printed a wonderful *siddur*, designated *Siftei Hannah*, the lips of Hannah.

Those of us who participate in this *tefillah* (prayer) group do so out of a deep concern for the laws of Judaism and with a profound sense of obligation to pray. We are not attempting to leave our community nor have we turned our backs on its traditional way of life. Rather, we are seeking a vehicle of deeper involvement, an expression of greater commitment, within an Orthodox framework.

Although the synagogue is not the only locus of Jewish activity and ritual, prayer and synagogue are a significant anchor of the ceremonial cycle. What Jews do in the synagogue, the public arena, symbolizes attitudes and norms for the entire community. In that context, the absence or presence of women signifies a range of attitudes and identifications for both individual women and the community at large.

Women Are Obligated to Pray

Women in traditional communities have in the past and continue to pray. Despite common misconceptions, women are not exempt from prayer. According to talmudic precedent, women are obligated to tefillah but are exempt from the recitation of the *Sh'ma*.[1] There are many permutations and combinations of this basic mishnaic statement. The full impact is that women must pray at least once a day. The *Shulhan Aruch* further elaborates that despite the exemption, women should say the *Sh'ma*.[2] However, they are exempt from public, time-constrained prayer. What are the consequences?

Exemption clearly does not mean exclusion. Women do attend services, especially on the Sabbath and High Holidays. But a distortion developed—women were not obligated, and hence not expected. Women were invisible publicly, and so many assumed that they did not have to pray or worse still that their prayers did not count. Moreover, they could not lead the services and were not counted in the official quorum, the minyan. Thus, the simple exemption shifted from a release to an exclusion, and even a banishment.

Ironically, the model of proper prayer is the silent prayer offered by Chana in the sanctuary.[3] There are many instances in biblical narrative of women praying effectively, at times for personal reasons and in other instances for communal welfare. Leah is recorded as having offered the first prayer of thanksgiving to God[4] and Miriam led the women in song and dance as a form of worship.[5] Through her actions, Esther taught us about community fasting as a form of shared prayer, and Rachel weeps for the return of her exiled children. These women's deeds prevail as our paradigms, even today.

Our concern today is with the location and format of women's prayers. The need is for positive communal religious rituals in which women stand at the center. The challenge is to find ways to be more inclusive and to create opportunities for women's spiritual expression in the context of our Jewish heritage.

Contemporary feminist scholarship has uncovered the history of women's personal petitional prayers and regular attendance in synagogue. They prayed in a separate area, removed from the male-centered service. At their own pace, in their own words, and frequently following their own female leader, they uttered devotional prayers that reflected their own religious experiences. These *tkhinot* were communally sanctioned prayers that expressed private and public concerns, usually tendered by women in a public place (see Tracy G. Klirs's chapter in this book, "*Tkhines* for Rosh Chodesh"). The *firzogerin* (women leaders) often led them as a cantor might today and explained or translated the weekly biblical portion as a rabbi does in sermonic description.

The talmudic tractate Soferim states that women were great synagogue goers and that it is a duty to translate the Torah portion for them.[6] At some point in the medieval period, the rabbis encouraged translating the Hebrew prayers into Yiddish for the benefit of the women. Changes in structure and form were made to accommodate women praying in a group.[7]

Instead of relying completely on translations, our generation has learned and taught our daughters how to pray in Hebrew. Every girls' *yeshiva* (religious high school) has set times for group prayer. Is this so different from our tefillah group's Rosh Chodesh services? What is the public domain, and when does a group of females constitute a community? The only consistent difference is our location and our use of the Torah. We who, because of our good Jewish education, know we can touch the Torah, read it, and study from it, are merely establishing that the permissible be permitted. Our Rosh Chodesh services continue the traditions of our female ancestors, in regard to both celebrating the day and joining in prayer.

Women's Centrality in Prayer

Our tefillah group has combined an old path with a radically new one. When we began, I worried that we were merely copying male traditional styles and that by doing so, we were being co-opted into the established system. Yet we have been creative by focusing on women's spiritual expression and centrality. We have been very conventional in our manner while being radical in our female-centered locus. Cynthia Ozick once wrote that the only place she was not a Jew was in her synagogue.

Obviously, there are many outstanding problems associated with a separate women's service. Although segregation has frequently disempowered women, integration has sometimes left us invisible. How can we maintain women's distinctive spiritual quest while asserting our role in shaping the past, present, and future of our people? Some of our responses arose impulsively, while others were carefully thought out. On Purim, we remain in our various congregational settings for the evening. In the morning, we gather for our special women's reading of Megillat Esther. It is one of the spiritual highlights of the year, as many different women participate, each according to her ability. At that moment, we fully qualify as a congregation. We know that in order to develop our spiritual quest, we need serious study and must concentrate on female-centered issues.

There are other theoretical dilemmas. How much do we imitate and how much do we create? How do we establish feelings of continuity with the tradition? Restoring prayer to women and the resultant growth of women's prayer and Rosh Chodesh groups raises both fascinating and unsettling questions. We have chosen to retain the feeling of tradition by preserving the liturgical style of regular services. Our creative moments enter through our presence and celebration of female life-cycle rituals. In that vein, we decided that our charity fund would only go toward helping the *agunot* (women seeking divorce who are denied it).

Rosh Chodesh with Women

Fundamentally, praying with women has been a wholly different experience for me. It is not simply that we pray; women do that regularly. It is not even the experience of public prayer; many of us pray frequently at home or in our own synagogues. Rather, it is inextricably linked with the fact that this is our only opportunity for active participation. To assume a responsibility is to demand of oneself involvement. To be a passive observer or minimal participant is to run the risk of detachment or even alienation.

The first time I took the Torah out of the ark, I was overwhelmed. There is an indescribable difference between standing behind a *mechitzah* (partition) and taking hold of the Torah. I knew that I was acting out of religious fervor, for the sake of heaven and well within halachic (legal) standards.[8]

While everyone cannot always lead, to know the possibility and to sometimes have that experience changes the entire understanding of prayer. There is greater intimacy that develops when one is actively participating; awareness and concentration become a regular part of the prayer service. Combined with greater knowledge—a direct result of having to learn how to do things properly—we are enriched in all our prayer moments.

There have been months when our group numbered very few. I would begin the tefillah thinking: "This is it. We are finished. No one is interested." But even then, there was a sense of accomplishment. No matter our numbers, our prayers counted. Praying instilled in us a purpose, a meaning all its own.

There have been times of exquisite singing and other moments truly off key. Not all our members knew how to pray. We learned and are still learning. We have had classes in prayer and Jewish law; we have celebrated.

I remember a special Rosh Chodesh. Four girls, all day school graduates, stepped forward to lead us. This was their bat mitzvah celebration. With their mothers, they conducted the entire service. Some fathers sat behind the *mechitza* and observed their families in action. One father came late. His wife casually strolled over to him with the sidur and showed him the place. It seemed so appropriate—yet so odd. The role reversal was more than symbolic. The girls were at ease in their roles, at home in prayer. Mothers were taking an active role in the religious celebration with their children, not simply organizing caterers but active at the heart of the religious ceremony.

We are taught to mark moments of Jewish significance with ritual. Women, too, require avenues for expressing commitment and commandment. The girls on that day celebrated not their alienation or their invisibility. They declared their shared destiny with the people Israel through knowledge, action, and worship. And they did it as women and with women.

None of us intends to give up our regular attendance at synagogues where our families attend. None of us wishes to separate from our communities. Yet we have experienced something special together, and we intend to sustain that new-found part of our lives as Jews.

In this notable twelfth year, I trust we will expand our horizons. As we met for Elul and heard an exhilarating blast from the shofar, that ancient rallying call of the Jews, sounded for us by a female Jew, I knew we would continue and flourish. We have publicly proclaimed our part in the covenantal commitment to our people, God, and Torah. Ultimately, that is what happens every Rosh Chodesh.

Notes

1. Talmud Babylonian, B'rachot 20b.
2. Orech Hayim 106.
3. 1 Samuel 1:9–17.
4. Genesis 29:35.
5. Exodus 15:20.
6. Tractate Soferim 18:4.
7. Chava Weissler, "Prayers in Yiddish and the Religious World of Ashkenazic Women," in Judith Baskin, ed. *Jewish Women in Historical Perspective* (Detroit: Wayne State University Press, 1991), pp. 159–181. Also see Emily Taitz, "Kol Isha—The Voice of Women: Where Was it Heard in Medieval Europe?" in *Conservative Judaism* 38 (1986): 46–61.
8. The *Shulhan Arukh, Yoreh Deah* 282, states most explicitly that women, even those who are menstruating, can hold and read/study from the Torah.

15
Bat Kol: Jewish Women in Brazil Observe Rosh Chodesh

Celia Szterenfeld

Chanukah in the middle of the summer . . . Pesach cleaning in the beginning of autumn: it is hard to be a Jew in the Southern Hemisphere when you want to incorporate the Jewish habits and calendar into your daily experience! We can use North American books as resources, but we have to create our own ways; to your experience, we add ours; to your scholarship, we add our intuition; to your formula, we add our own spice.

Chanukah here is in the middle of the summer, when Rio de Janeiro is at its best: most splendorous, lavish, and illuminated. The custom of putting the *chanukiah* (menorah) next to the window—to brighten up the winter's darkness—is useless to *cariocas* (those born in Rio). Welcome to Judaism in the Southern Hemisphere!

Our Rosh Chodesh group in Rio has the task of helping Jewish women integrate apparently fragmented identities. We ask: What is it to be a Jewish Brazilian woman or, better yet, a Jewish *carioca* woman? How do these three identities, Jewish, woman, and *carioca* click together? How do we define them separately? What does this mother say to her child while lighting Chanukah candles near the window?

The Rosh Chodesh group in Rio was created in Iyar 5759/May 1989, when new possibilities were opening up for Jewish women. Rio's first egalitarian synagogue[1] invited women to participate in all realms of synagogue life. Our group was born out of the need for dialogue and learning among women participating for the first time in an egalitarian synagogue experience. Three years later, we named our Rosh Chodesh group Bat Kol.

In the beginning, the group's profile was extremely diverse: women of all ages and life experiences were eager to talk about their Jewish experiences as women. They shared, however, a few points. Most women were professionals whose last contact with Judaism had been some years ago. The women felt Jewish but were not sure of what that meant. Most women were not accustomed to thinking about life as related to woman's experience or women's limitations: as good humanists they thought of themselves as "people." And most of the women were well integrated into Rio's culture, its tolerance for diversity (including other religious practices and the intuitive arts), easy-going manners, and good-humored approaches to daily hardships.

This profile of the group has changed significantly over the years: from dependence on leadership to a more autonomous structure; from less to more homogeneous; from less to more involvement with the synagogue; from a noncommitted, transient group to one of more consistence and commitment.

The group's style was influenced by Penina Adelman's book, *Miriam's Well*, as well as individual group members' talents and creativity. Over eighty women are affiliated with the group, and the average monthly attendance is about twenty women.

Each meeting will typically have three components: We start with a Jewish meditation through creative visualization (*kavanah*), proceed to study of some chosen topic (Talmud Torah), and end with a celebration of song and dance, commemorating special moments in the lives of our members (spiritual *mikvah*).

Two or three women prepare each meeting and "set the tone," mindful of both the Jewish and *carioca* cues for any given month. For example, on Rosh Chodesh Adar, which falls close to both Purim and Brazilian Carnival, we will focus on themes of beauty and *tsinut* (modesty) in both cultures. The influence of Brazilian culture in our group is also represented by the acceptance and adaptation of non-Jewish cultural traditions, such as the study of Tarot and Astrology. Each year, the group selects a program of study.

Program of Study

During our first year (5759/1989), we examined relationships between women in the Torah. We first read or tell the original story. We then study what our history (male rabbis) teaches about it, as well as new interpretations by women scholars and rabbis. We also weave into our discussions the participants' personal experiences with sisters, mothers-in-law, and other women in our lives. This format has proven to be an interesting way for learning root-Judaism while reconstructing participants' links to their families and ancestors.

Our second year was devoted to reading and discussing the book *Written Out of History: Our Jewish Foremothers* by Sondra Henry and Emily Teitz. It was chosen in order to give continuity to our two goals: to teach and refresh our knowledge about general Jewish history/culture and to bond Brazilian Jewish women to a continuum of women's history. Women gathered in groups of two and made presentations based on the chapters of this book.

While the first two years worked as an introduction to Jewish feminist thinking, our third year focused on what Jewish law had to say about women. Taking as a basis Rachel Biale's book, *Women and Jewish Law*, we began to understand rabbinical thinking and language. For many, this was their first contact with original texts and interpretations. It clearly indicated a higher level of interest and a greater capacity to "think" Jewishly for those remaining with the group.

As a result of the Rosh Chodesh group, some women became more involved with the synagogue, finding themselves drawn to its new openness. The group's fourth year was dedicated to the preparation of a collective adult bat mitzvah. This occurred in May 1994, when the morning services were conducted completely by women. The group was challenged with the task of conducting a service that was "proper" and yet imbued with a feminine flavor. We were seeking to create a warmer and more informal climate without compromising the solemnity of prayer. The bat mitzvah service was quite successful, and some of the innovations were incorporated into the regular synagogue prayers.

Our group decided that the next year's program of study would focus on *halacha* and how it affects women's positions in Judaism. This course of study will provide women with a knowledge base and allow them to speak in synagogue forums from a place of maturity and commitment.

Interreligious Activities

Our Rosh Chodesh group has also been involved in various activities that foster interreligious dialogue among women. A memorable experience occurred during the United Nations Ecology Conference in Rio, at the Interreligious vigil at the Non-Governmental Organizations' (NGOs') Forum site.

Imagine a beautiful park, next to the ocean. It faces a powerful mountain where white tents of varied dimensions are mounted to shelter the celebration of a new perception of the world order. The tents are the temporary shelters of the many religious/spiritual traditions participating in this vigil.

Thousands of people of all nationalities spent the night praying and chanting and dancing, not only at the tent of their own tradition, but at the tents of many other cultural and religious traditions. It created an opportunity to learn, in the deepest sense, *echad*, oneness.

Over twenty-five traditions were represented, including Catholics, Afro-Brazilians, and the Sai Baba Movement. Our Rosh Chodesh group gathered women from all traditions to join our celebration of women's spirituality and its role in the world. We met just outside of the Jewish tent, in a circle with a tree in its middle. At first we led the celebration, chanting *niggunim* (tunes, many of our own creation) and songs to the *Shechinah*, asking for a speedy *tikkun olam* (repair of the world). Soon women from other traditions began to lead in ever-changing melodies, rhythms, and dances. Men joined us, young and old, letting all envision a possible future world of harmony.

The night ended at dawn with a collective celebration. The Dalai Lama and representatives of all traditions (Rabbi Zalman Schachter-Shalomi represented the Jewish tradition) prayed for peace and the healing of the world.

Conclusion

What do I say to my child about the chanukiah? It's easy: I say the candle lights are analogous to summer light itself burning in all its possibilities and hopes! As for Pesach "Spring" cleaning in the fall, well, one should clean the house before coming indoors again, after a long summer spent mostly outdoors.

When living by both solar and lunar calendars, living Jewishly and noting the moon, fresh interpretations arise from observance, wherever that happens to be.

The Bat Kol Rosh Chodesh group is preparing resource materials for Brazilian Jewish women in other cities who are interested in forming groups. We are developing materials describing our own experiences as well as translating Rosh Chodesh materials from various Jewish women's resource centers.

We believe that Jewish women in Brazil have much to contribute to Judaism, specifically in the area of reinterpreting Jewish customs and opening dialogues with other religious traditions. The involvement of the Bat Kol Rosh Chodesh group in interreligious campaigns such as antihunger and discrimination efforts, may prove to be a valuable alliance-building tool. It fosters a worldview leading to global democracy and inclusiveness and guides our search for meaning and actualization in Judaism.

Note

1. The Jewish Congregation of Brazil (JCB) is affiliated with the Conservative and Havurah movements. It has, for the first time, a young, non-Orthodox Brazilian rabbi, Rabbi R. Nitton Bonder.

III

The Cycle
of the Month

16
The Dark Rays of the Moon: Yom Kippur Katan as Preparation for Rosh Chodesh

Shefa Gold

In any spiritual practice, preparation and intention make all the difference. When the preparation for Rosh Chodesh can occur in all four realms of my being—physical, emotional, intellectual, and spiritual—then my receptivity to its transformative effects is maximized. The kabbalists of sixteenth-century S'fat understood this essential truth, and they had the creativity and the courage (some might say audacity) to respond by developing a holy day that would address the spiritual challenges of renewal that Rosh Chodesh brings. That holy day came each month on the day preceding Rosh Chodesh and was called Yom Kippur Katan. The custom was to fast from sunrise to sunset and to recite certain prayers, which had the flavor of Yom Kippur and would facilitate the process of self-examination and purification in preparation for receiving the new moon.[1]

Those kabbalists were moon watchers. The lenses through which they gazed were intensely focused on issues of exile and redemption. And so, as the moon waned, the exile of the *Shechinah* (the divine presence) was noted and mourned. With the moon's return came the celebration of the miracle of redemption, a redemption that could be tasted and known but briefly before the cycle of exile continued. They based their custom on a legend that was recorded in the Babylonian Talmud[2] in which God says to Israel, "Bring atonement upon me for making the moon smaller."

They understood "making the moon smaller" as referring to a contraction of divine essence, which in human terms could be experienced as exile. There is another legend that at the time of Messiah, the moon will again be as bright as the sun.[3] The moon's return to glory will mark our redemption. The kabbalists based their reading of these myths on a Lurianic kabbalistic conception of Creation, which says that it was the divine act of *tzimtzum* (God's self-contraction) that made room for the existence of our world. Yet it was this very act of *tzimtzum* that set into play the dramatic cycle of exile and redemption that has become the vehicle for the soul's evolution and the self-realization of every aspect of Creation.

As Gershom Scholem explains it:

> The act of *tzimtzum* itself, in which God limits Himself, requires the establishment of the power of Din (judgment), which is a force of limitation and restriction. Thus the root of evil ultimately lies in the very nature of Creation itself, in which the harmony of the Infinite cannot, by definition persist; because of its nature as Creation—i.e., as other than Godhead—an element of imbalance, defectiveness, and darkness must enter into every restricted existence, however sublime it may be.[4]

With the exile of the *Shechinah*, darkness enters into our existence, and with that darkness comes a longing for her return. Yom Kippur Katan comes at a point in the cycle when that longing is at its peak. Inner reality reflects the absence of moon and manifests as a longing for fullness that claws at the dark empty pause. It is a call to recreate ourselves in God's image.

At the same time, it feels as if God might be doing *t'shuvah* (turning or repentance), taking another look at us and reconsidering the relationship. On Yom Kippur Katan we feel those all-seeing eyes on us and we do what must be done to make ourselves beautiful to God. The dark moon night allows for the visibility of stars and planets that would ordinarily go unnoticed. On Yom Kippur Katan we do an examination of the inward skies as well—the constellations of our being, which, in the busy light of our lives, might remain hidden from view. It is the time for correcting our aim, seeing the ways in which we have been pulled off course. It is the time for paying attention to the subtle details, a time to feel the internal striving after righteousness that is born of love.

The symbol of the moon and its cycles representing our experience of God's presence is significant because it is multilayered. As the moon waxes and wanes, there is a part of me that experiences the shrinking and swelling of light in the night sky. There is another part of me that knows and experiences the moon as a whole sphere, which happens to reflect different amounts of the sun's light. I can often even see the dark part of the moon when there is only a sliver of light. It is the same with the experience of exile. There are times when I feel so very far from God, and yet another part of me knows that it is only a "seeming" distance. God has never left my orbit. Yet I live my life in the drama of these cycles—the waxing and waning of God's presence in my life. Another part of me stands back and understands these cycles as the contractions of labor that birth the soul into wholeness. Though all these layers exist simultaneously, I know that I must give myself fully to the experience of this drama, even to the pain of it.

The challenge of renewal requires us to look hard and honestly at the aspects of our personalities, habits, beliefs, and patterns that need renewing—whatever it is that we have outgrown, whatever it is that holds us back, distorts our vision, prevents our love from flowing freely. If we do this work of examination, purification, and realignment each month, then on Rosh Chodesh we will indeed have something to celebrate.

In a class with Rabbi Zalman Schachter-Shalomi in which we studied the liturgy of Yom Kippur Katan, he said that to really know and celebrate the essence of lunar energy, we must experience the "dark rays of the moon."[5] When we notice and pay attention to the particular power of this time, those "dark rays" will aid us as we meet the challenge of renewal.

As our celebrations of Rosh Chodesh evolve in ways that express our deepest joys and concerns, so must our preparations, both inner and outer, effectively address our present needs. Although I can appreciate the beauty of the liturgy of those sixteenth-century kabbalists, I have also felt a need to express the process of Yom Kippur Katan in a more personal way. And so I offer the following song. The chorus is in Aramaic and comes from the traditional liturgy of Yom Kippur Katan. It says, "Compassionate One, who answers broken hearts, answer us, answer us."

May we all have the courage and strength to let our hearts break, and may the light of renewal, healing, and wisdom stream in to those broken places so that in our wholeness we may shine.

The Dark Rays of the Moon[6]

My flaws are showing all too clear
In the dark rays of the moon.
All my certainties will disappear
In the dark rays of the moon.
I surrender to the shadow's glare
In the dark rays of the moon.
I am strengthened by the truth I bare
In the dark rays of the moon.
Rachamana d'oney litvirey liba, aneyna, aneyna.
[Compassionate One who answers broken hearts, answer us, answer us.]

When the tide is low I search the beach
In the dark rays of the moon.
Broken dreams wash up within my reach
In the dark rays of the moon.
I will hold the shell up to my ear
In the dark rays of the moon.
Till the voice of God is all I hear
In the dark rays of the moon.
Rachamana d'oney litvirey liba, aneyna, aneyna.

In exile I am forced to roam
In the dark rays of the moon.
Till my prayerful longing brings me home
In the dark rays of the moon.
Though I see my life in shades of dark
In the dark rays of the moon.
In the deepest depths there glows a spark
In the dark rays of the moon.
Rachamana d'oney litvirey liba, aneyna, aneyna.

Notes

1. Yom Kippur Katan is not observed for the following months' Rosh Chodesh: Cheshvan, because Yom Kippur has just passed; Tevet, because it would fall during Chanukah, when fasting and penitential prayers are not permitted; Iyar, because it would fall during Nisan, which doesn't allow fasting; and Tishrei, because it would fall on the day of Erev Rosh Hashanah, which doesn't permit penitential prayers. If Rosh Chodesh falls on Shabbat, Yom Kippur Katan is observed on the preceding Thursday. See Isaac Klein, *A Guide to Jewish Religious Practice* (New York: Jewish Theological Seminary, 1979), pp. 262–263.

2. Hullin 60b.

3. Based on Isaiah 30:26.

4. Gershom Scholem, *On the Mystical Shape of the Godhead* (New York: Shocken Books, 1991), p. 83.

5. The phrase, "Dark Rays of the Moon" appears to have been coined during a conversation between Zalman Schachter-Shalomi and Eric Neumann in Jerusalem. Discussing whether the moon gives off its own light or only reflects the sun's light, Eric Neumann said that the moon has its own rays—they are the dark rays of the moon.

6. © Shefa Gold 1989. Available on the audiocassette *Abundance*, P.O. Box 355, Las Vegas, New Mexico 87701. (Notation found on page 293.)

17
Anticipating the New Moon: Birkat HaChodesh

Victor Hillel Reinstein

Birth represents the ultimate hope of renewal and possibility. In the anticipation of birth, hope finds expression and the future is imagined. As the anticipation of the birth of a child provides an unparalleled time for reflection, so, metaphorically, the anticipation of the birth of each new moon provides a time for introspection, for setting priorities, and for giving voice to inner hopes for ourselves and others. As with the birth of a child, anticipating the new moon inextricably links us with past and future; to the generations from which we have come, as individuals and as a people, and to the future toward which the new crescent opens.

Anticipating the new moon and its promise of renewal is formalized in Jewish tradition through *Birkat HaChodesh*, the Blessing of the New Month. The blessing occurs in the synagogue on the Shabbat prior to Rosh Chodesh and that Shabbat is called either *Shabbat Mevorchim*, the Shabbat of Blessing, or

Shabbat HaChodesh, the Shabbat of the Month. The blessing of the month it-self is also called *Mevorchim/Mevorchin HaChodesh*, or in Yiddish, *Rosh Chodesh Bentschen*.[1]

The Blessing of the New Month, which is comprised of four main parts, is a beautiful expression of prayerful yearning. Expression is given to life's universal needs, such as health and sustenance, as well as to the particular needs of Israel. Both explicitly and implicitly, prayer for the unity of Israel courses through the order of the Blessing. The miracle of Israel's redemption in the past is celebrated and supplication made for redemption once again. In this prayerful context, the time and date of the appearance of the new moon is ceremoniously announced with the leader holding a Torah Scroll.

The locus of the Birkat HaChodesh in the order of the Shabbat morning prayers is after the reading of the Torah and Haftarah and before the chanting of Ashrei. The reason for its location here is ascribed to Rabbi Yose in the Talmud Yerushalmi, who said that he would not pray *musaf* on the Shabbat before Rosh Chodesh until he knew when the new moon would be.[2] Elbogen suggests that through the Birkat HaChodesh, we lament our inability to sanctify the month as it was done in the days of the Sanhedrin, and we pray that God "will renew [our] days as of old."[3] Considering the location of Birkat HaChodesh, which is followed shortly by the return of the Torah, echo is given to this theme of renewal in the verse with which the Holy Ark is closed, "Return us to You, God, and we shall return, renew our days as of old."

That the renewal of the moon symbolically represents our own renewal and the renewal of Israel, is learned from the very verse in the Torah that gives us the commandment of Rosh Chodesh, Exodus 12:2. The nineteenth-century German rabbi and commentator, Samson Raphael Hirsch, beautifully translates this seminal verse to reflect the full root meaning of the word Chodesh as new: "This renewal of the moon shall be *for you* a beginning of renewals," and then he comments, "What we are to establish is not an astronomical cycle of months but monthly renewals for ourselves."[4] The Torah commandment specifically requires that the beginning of each month is to be established by a physical viewing of the new moon, *mitzvah l'kadesh al pi r'iyah*.[5] On this illustration of the Jewish emphasis on human interaction with God and creation, Hirsch writes, "The objective astronomical certainty is not sufficient, but the subjective taking note of it is what is desired."[6]

Kiddush HaChodesh: Sanctification of the New Moon by Visual Observation

Prior to the establishment of a fixed calendar in the fourth century, our ancestors would faithfully look to the heavens each month and with the appearance of the moon's new crescent, would sanctify the new month *al pi r'iyah*, through visual observation of the moon. This sanctification of the month, Kiddush HaChodesh marked the official declaration of the start of a new month. The Mishna describes in detail how members of the Sanhedrin would gather on the thirtieth day of each month in a courtyard in Jerusalem called *Bet Ya'azek.*[7] There, a formally constituted *Bet Din* of three, the president of the Sanhedrin and two members, would await the arrival of witnesses who had seen the new moon at its earliest appearance. After carefully questioning the witnesses to determine the veracity of their testimony, in an impressive display of pedagogic pageantry designed to impress upon witnesses the importance of their task, the *Bet Din* would then declare the new month sanctified. When satisfied with the testimony, the head of the *Bet Din* would say, "It is sanctified!" and all the people would answer after him, "It is sanctified! It is sanctified!" The responsive nature of Birkat HaChodesh as it has developed through the ages is reminiscent of this responsive involvement of the people in Kiddush HaChodesh long ago.

The determination of the new moon through visual observation ceased with the end of the Sanhedrin in the latter part of the fourth century. Roman and Christian persecution, directed specifically at public knowledge concerning Rosh Chodesh and other vital calendrical knowledge, threatened the continuity of the Jewish people. In a heroic act of preservation, the last head of the Sanhedrin, Hillel II, established a fixed calendar. He based it upon astronomical calculation and made known the details of calendrical science that hitherto had been the sole province of the Sanhedrin. Without the Sanhedrin, Kiddush HaChodesh through visual observation of the new moon could no longer be done. It is a *mitzvah* that now lies in forced abeyance. Maimonides writes, "In a time when there is a Sanhedrin there [in the Land of Israel]—we fix [the months] according to visual observation; and in a time when there is no Sanhedrin there—we fix [the months] according to this calculation whereby we calculate today."[8]

Birkat HaChodesh: Blessing the New Moon

The custom of announcing and blessing the new month in the synagogue on the Shabbat prior to Rosh Chodesh developed subsequent to the use of a fixed calendar. Unlike the ancient Kiddush HaChodesh, Birkat HaChodesh as the public proclamation of the new month has no astronomical significance in regard to determining the month. Its purpose is to make people aware of when Rosh Chodesh will be. In that, however, even as in ancient times, our proclamation serves to disseminate knowledge of the months among the people and to celebrate the historic and spiritual significance of Rosh Chodesh.

The anticipation of Rosh Chodesh also brings anticipation of the festivals that occur in the coming month. Before the calendar had been fixed, knowing the date for Rosh Chodesh was essential for knowing when the festivals would fall. While the dates of the major festivals were given to us in the Torah, they could only be arrived at by counting from Rosh Chodesh. Precise knowledge of Rosh Chodesh, therefore, was necessary for the timely observance of all festivals. Today, while we can simply use the calendar established by Hillel II some sixteen centuries ago, announcing Rosh Chodesh fosters and enhances an awareness of all that is special in the coming month.

One of the terms for festival in Hebrew is *mo-ed*, from the root *ya'ad*, meaning to appoint or assign in relation to a time or place of meeting. A *mo-ed*, therefore, is a time of gathering, of assembly, of meeting. The *mo-adim*, the festivals that punctuate the Jewish year, are the appointed meeting times of Israel and God. They represent, in effect, times of "conjunction," between God, Torah, and Israel, when God's light, refracted through the Torah, is perceived afresh by Israel in a moment of national and personal renewal.

Rosh Chodesh is the *mo-ed* by which all other *mo-adim* are determined. Of *mo-ed* as "conjunction," Hirsch writes: "The moon, finding itself again in conjunction with the sun is only to be a model for our finding ourselves again with God, the rejuvenation of the moon a picture of, and an incentive to, our own rejuvenation. *Mo-ed* is literally conjunction."[9]

Molad: Birth of the New Moon

The conjunction of the sun, moon, and earth, in that order, provides the symbolic starting point for Israel's renewal. In the framework of a fixed calendar, the old month ends and the new month begins with that conjunction. The moment of conjunction is called in Hebrew the *molad*, meaning literally, "the birth" of the new moon. It is this birth that forms the focus of our anticipation on Shabbat HaChodesh. A fixed calendar provides a different starting point for Rosh Chodesh than when the new moon was determined by visual observation. When the new moon was determined by visual observation the month was sanctified only upon the actual appearance of the new crescent, rather than at the time of the *molad*. With a fixed calendar, the moment of conjunction is known by calculation and the new month begins in that moment, prior to the actual appearance of the new moon. At conjunction, the moon is not visible, because only its dark side is facing the earth. As the moon moves out of conjunction the freshly illumined crescent becomes visible from the earth.

One lunation, or lunar orbit around the earth, is a cycle of approximately 29½ days. More precisely, the lunar cycle is 29 days, 12 hours, 44 minutes, and 3⅓ seconds. When computing a lunation, rather than using minutes and seconds for divisions of time less than 1 hour, Jewish tradition has divided the hour into *chalakim*, meaning parts. There are 1,080 *chalakim* in one hour and 18 *chalakim* in one minute. One *chelek* equals 3 1/3 seconds. In this system, the time from one *molad* to the next, one lunation, is 29 days, 12 hours, and 793 *chalakim*.[10] Using *chalakim* makes calendrical calculation easier by removing fractions.[11] By mathematically calculating the number of lunations from an agreed starting point, a specific *molad* in time, then every other *molad* at any point in the future can be determined by adding cycles of 29 days, 12 hours, and 793 *chalakim*, with little other adjustment. The *molad* of Tishrei for the first year of creation, according to what would become Jerusalem time, is the traditional starting point from which all other *moladot* are calculated. The *Tur* (a fourteenth-century legal compendium of Jacob ben Asher), takes us on a fascinating guided "tour" of calculations back to that first *molad* and instructs us in how to proceed from there to determine any *molad* in the future.[12]

Beyond the practical reasons for using *chalakim,* the division of an hour into such small parts gives beautiful expression to the deep Jewish feeling for the majesty of details. The remarkable scope of our ancestors' knowledge of astronomy and the very fact that the Torah bids us look monthly to the heavens in order to determine our own human cycles of time underscores the importance given to human interaction with the details of creation. In taking note of creation's details, we learn of the Creator: "HaShamayim m'saprim k'vod El, u'ma'aseh yadav magid harakia," "The heavens tell of God's glory, and the sky proclaims the work of God's hands" (Psalm 19).

Even when Rosh Chodesh was determined by visual observation, there were times when calculation was needed. The rabbis in the days of the Sanhedrin were of necessity stargazers. Their astronomical knowledge imbued them with an awe of God. While our ancestors were drawn to a deeper understanding of God and Creation through direct involvement with the details of setting the calendar, Birkat HaChodesh, in approximating the ancient rite by announcing the new moon, and most specifically by announcing the moment of the *molad*, inspires us with a greater awareness of the majesty of creation's details.

As a source of awe, the nature of the *molad* is one of God's "great and marvelous works."[13] At the moment of conjunction, the end and the beginning are as one. It is as harmonious a moment as there can be. This regularly recurring end and beginning in the same moment reflects the continuity of an eternal recurrent cycle. In the harmony of the *molad* is an intimation of God as the One without beginning and without end, the Source of all cycles, the *Ayn Sof*— Infinite One.

A more technical term for the *molad* is *hitkabetz* (from the same root as *kibbutz*), meaning to gather or to assemble. In an astronomical sense it means to "meet" in corresponding orbits. Maimonides describes the lunar cycle of 29 days, 12 hours, and 793 *chalakim* as being marked "from when the moon and the sun are gathered . . . , until they are gathered a second time in their journey," "misheyit*kabetz* hayareyach v'hachamah . . . ad sheyitkabtzu pa'am shniyah b'mahalcham."[14]

The *molad* itself, as a moment of harmony and alignment of one with another, is symbolic of the hope that characterizes the blessing of the new month. The conjunction, as it were, the unity, of all Israel is a prayerful thread that runs through the Birkat HaChodesh. There are various versions of the Birkat HaChodesh, each weaving this common thread, but with some fascinating differences.

Following is the standard Ashkenazic version of the Blessing of the New Month. As though to emphasize the anticipation of a birth, there are nine steps to the prayer, as in the months of gestation.[15] After presenting the order of the Blessing, reflections are offered on some of its themes, with selected themes highlighted.

Blessing of the New Month—Birkat HaChodesh

1. The congregation, standing, recites the paragraph, "Yehi Ratzon."
2. "Yehi Ratzon" is then repeated by the leader who holds a Torah Scroll for the entire blessing, or at least for Mi'She-asah.

Yehi ratzon milfanecha, HaShem Elokeynu velokey avoteynu, she-tichadesh aleynu et HaChodesh Hazeh l'tovah v'livracha. V'titen lanu chaim arukim, chaim shel shalom, chaim shel tovah, chaim shel b'racha, chaim shel parnasa, chaim shel chilutz atzamot, chaim sheyesh bahem yirat shamayim v'yirat chet, chaim she'ayn bahem busha uchlima, chaim shel osher v'chavod, chaim she't'hey vanu ahavat Torah v'yirat shamayim, chaim she'yimalu mi'sh'alot libenu l'tovah. Amen, Selah.

יהי רצון מלפניך יהוה אלהינו ואלהי אבותינו שתחדש עלינו את החדש הבא
לטובה ולברכה. ותתן לנו חיים ארוכים, חיים של שלום, חיים של
טובה, חיים של ברכה, חיים של פרנסה, חיים של חלוץ עצמות,
חיים שיש בהם יראת שמים ויראת חטא, חיים שאין בהם בושה
וכלמה, חיים של עשר וכבוד, חיים שתהא בנו אהבת תורה ויראת
שמים, חיים שימלאו משאלות לבנו לטובה, אמן סלה.

May it be Your will, God, our God and God of our ancestors, that You renew for us this month for good and for blessing. And may You give us long life, a life of peace, a life of good, a life of blessing, a life of suste-

nance, a life of physical health, a life in which there is awe of Heaven
and fear of sin, a life in which there is neither shame nor disgrace, a life
of abundance and honor, a life in which we shall have love of Torah and
awe of Heaven, a life in which the entreaties of our hearts be fulfilled for
good. Amen, Selah.

3. The precise time of the *molad*, according to Jerusalem time, is announced
to the congregation.
  4. The congregation then recites the paragraph, "Mi'she-asah."
  5. The leader, holding a Torah scroll, then repeats, "Mi'she-asah."

Mi'she-asah nisim lavoteynu, v'ga'al otam may'avdut l'cherut, Hu yig'al
otanu b'karov, viykabetz nidacheynu may'arba kanfot ha'aretz, chaverim
kol Yisrael. V'nomar: Amen.

מִי שֶׁעָשָׂה נִסִים לַאֲבוֹתֵינוּ וְגָאַל אוֹתָם מֵעַבְדוּת לְחֵרוּת, הוּא יִגְאַל אוֹתָנוּ
בְּקָרוֹב וִיקַבֵּץ נִדָּחֵינוּ מֵאַרְבַּע כַּנְפוֹת הָאָרֶץ, חֲבֵרִים כָּל-יִשְׂרָאֵל
וְנֹאמַר אָמֵן.

May the One Who wrought miracles for our ancestors, and redeemed them
from slavery to freedom, soon redeem us, and gather our dispersed from
the four corners of the earth, all Israel is bound together. And let us say:
Amen.

6. The leader announces the name of the coming month and then the day
of the week on which Rosh Chodesh will occur.
  7. The congregation then repeats the same announcement concerning Rosh
Chodesh.

Rosh Chodesh [name of month] yihiyeh b'yom [day of the week] haba
aleynu v'al kol Yisrael l'tovah.

רֹאשׁ חֹדֶשׁ____ יִהְיֶה בְּיוֹם ____ הַבָּא עָלֵינוּ וְעַל כָּל-יִשְׂרָאֵל לְטוֹבָה.

Rosh Chodesh [name of month] will be on [day of the week]. May it come
to us and to all Israel for good.

8. The congregation recites "Y'chadshehu."
  9. The leader then repeats "Y'chadshehu."

Y'chadshehu HaKadosh Baruch Hu alenu v'al kol amo beit Yisrael,
l'chaim u'l'shalom, l'sason u'l'simcha, lishua u'l'nechama. V'nomar:
Amen.

יְחַדְּשֵׁהוּ הַקָּדוֹשׁ בָּרוּךְ הוּא עָלֵינוּ וְעַל כָּל־עַמּוֹ בֵּית יִשְׂרָאֵל
לְחַיִּים וּלְשָׁלוֹם לְשָׂשׂוֹן וּלְשִׂמְחָה לִישׁוּעָה וּלְנֶחָמָה וְנֹאמַר אָמֵן

May the Holy One renew the coming month for us and for the entire
people, the House of Israel, for life and for peace, for joy and for gladness, for salvation and for comfort. And let us say: Amen.

Reflections on Selected Themes of Birkat HaChodesh

The opening of Birkat HaChodesh celebrates generational continuity, in relation to our people and in relation to God: "Yehi ratzon milfanecha, *HaShem
Elokeynu velokey avoteynu*," "May it be Your will, God, our God and God of
our ancestors." We begin by considering those from whom we have come, and
God's constant presence throughout time. This becomes a living link between
ourselves and our ancestors. As time turns through the myriad renewals of the
moon the generations are renewed.

"Sheti*chadesh* alenu et HaChodesh hazeh," "that You renew for us this
month": *chodesh*—"month" is formed from *chadash*—"new"; each month is
both new and renewing, bringing renewal to itself and to our lives.

As the opening prayer unfolds through its petitions for a life filled with blessing, there are two different uses of the word *yirah*, which can mean either fear
or awe. *Yirat Shamayim*, therefore can mean either fear of Heaven or Awe of
Heaven: "Chaim sheyesh bahem *yirat shamayim v'yirat chet* . . . , chaim
she't'hey vanu *ahavat Torah v'yirat shamayim*." *Yirat Shamayim*, Awe of
Heaven, appears twice, paired once with *yirat chet*, fear of sin, and thus giving
a parallel sense of fear to *yirat Shamayim*. It is paired the second time with
ahavat Torah, love of Torah, investing *yirat Shamayim* with a parallel sense
of love. There is a commentary that suggests that the first use of *yirah* reflects
fear of punishment and that the second use reflects awe/fear that derives of love
and awe of God's grandeur and majesty.[16] Rosh Chodesh, which celebrates an
awe-inspiring drama, is an ideal moment for inspiring *yirah* as awe, and for
celebrating a relationship with God that is founded on love rather than fear.

While "Yehi Ratzon" is the opening prayer in most Ashkenazic and Sefardic
versions of Birkat HaChodesh (it does not appear in the Lubavitch version),
some *sidurim* add a closing phrase to "Yehi Ratzon" that forms a wonderfully
ironic variant to the usual form of the prayer. Adding a sense of penultimate
closure just before the words, "Amen, Selah," the phrase appears in one of two
forms: "bizchut tefilat Rav," "By the merit of the prayer of Rav," or "bizchut
t'filat [or t'filot] rabim," "By the merit of public prayer."

"Yehi Ratzon," which was a relatively late addition to the Birkat HaChodesh,
originates in the Talmud as the personal prayer of Rav, a third-century Baby-

lonian rabbi, who said it following the *Amidah*. It appears along with the prayers of other rabbis, each providing a window into the soul of the one who "prayed" it. The prayer of Rav, which was slightly emended to fit the context of Rosh Chodesh, is found in Tractate B'rachot 16b. It appears that at some point, a diligent scribe, while copying the handwritten manuscript of the prayer, included its source at the end of the text: *B'rachot, tefilat Rav*, "Tractate B'rachot, the prayer of Rav." Another copyist or printer at a later time somehow changed the letter *resh* in *B'rachot* to a *zayin*, and a simple source note became, *bizchut tefilat Rav*. Yet another copyist or printer now inadvertently (presumably) turned *Rav* into *rabim*, "many," and we had, *bizchut tefilat rabim*, "By the merit of public prayer."[17] While roundly disclaimed as an error, often in a rather scolding tone, it is, nevertheless, a rather providential error whose spirit is entirely in accord with that prayerful thread of hope for the unity of Israel that characterizes the Birkat HaChodesh.

Following the opening prayer, the precise time of the *molad, according to Jerusalem time*, is announced to the congregation. The *molad* is always announced according to Jerusalem time, reminding us of the days when the new month's announcement was sent forth to Jewish communities according to the appearance of the new moon as it was sighted in Jerusalem. Announcing the *molad* on Shabbat M'vorchim according to Jerusalem time creates a bond between all Jews, with each other and with Jerusalem, the heart of the Jewish people.

While serving a practical calendrical function, announcing the *molad* according to Jerusalem time also serves a symbolic and spiritual function. It is one of many focal points in Jewish life that has kept the heart and eye of the Diaspora Jew focused on Jerusalem. Through dark nights of exile, we are ever encouraged by the new moon's emerging light of hope, anticipated as though already in Jerusalem.[18]

Following the announcement of the *molad*, the thread of messianic hope continues with *Mi'she-asah*, linking the miracles of past redemption with the hope of future redemption: "M'ishe-asah nisim lavoteynu, *v'ga'al otam may'avdut l'cherut*," "May the One Who wrought miracles for our ancestors, *and redeemed them from slavery to freedom*." The connection is made between the hope of Rosh Chodesh and "Yitziat Mitzraim," the Exodus from Egypt, the epic journey of redemption. The commandment for Rosh Chodesh is intrinsically linked to the Exodus from Egypt, establishing the relationship between freedom and renewal. The second *mitzvah* derived from our *locus classicus*, Exodus 12:2, is the establishment of the month of Nisan as the first of months: "rishon hu lachem l'chodshey Hashanah," "it [Nisan] shall be for you the first of the renewals [months] of the year." Nisan, the beginning of our renewal as a people, is honored as the month of the Exodus, the beginning of freedom.

"Hu *yig'al otanu* b' karov," "soon *redeem us*": the Exodus from Egypt is the paradigm for the redemption to come. With Nisan as the backdrop, we look forward to the *Pesach l'Atid*, the Pesach of the Future, the final redemption. This is symbolically expressed in the hope for the ingathering of Israel, "v*ikabetz* nidachenu may'arba kanfot ha'aretz," "and *gather* our dispersed from the four corners of the earth." With all Israel gathered together "b'*kibbutz*," "in conjunction with each other," as in the conjunction of sun, moon, and earth at the time of the molad, Mishe'asah ends with the stirring Messianic hope, reminder, and challenge: "chaverim kol Yisrael," "all Israel is bound together—all Israel are friends."

In his classic digest of Jewish laws and customs, J. D. Eisenstein joins the beginning and the end of the "Mi'she-asah," paragraph: "Through miracles we will be redeemed and will merit to sanctify the month by visual observation of the moon confirmed before the Beit Din in Jerusalem, and then all Israel will be bound together/friends in the land of our ancestors."[19] An early liturgical work[20] gives beautiful expression to this theme by adding to the end of "Mi'she-asah": *chaverim kol Yisrael li'Yerushalayim ir hakodesh*, "all Israel is bound together to Jerusalem the Holy City!"

Announcing the name of the coming month and the day of the week on which Rosh Chodesh will occur: All of the months of the year are announced on the Shabbat before their arrival except for Tishrei, the festival-filled month that begins with Rosh HaShanah. Coming on the first of Tishrei, Rosh HaShanah is Rosh Chodesh and the only festival to occur at the time when the new moon is not yet visible. Tishrei is not announced because it is assumed that everyone is aware of the imminent arrival of Rosh Hashanah. At the same time, it is ironic that we don't announce Tishrei, because the entire edifice of the calendar is founded on its *molad* all the way back to the *molad* of the very first Tishrei at the time of Creation, which was Rosh HaShanah, "Yom Harat Olam—The Birthday of the World."

Because Tishrei is not announced, we can make one small symbolic change when announcing the preceding month of Elul, the month of preparation for the "Days of Awe." While every month we ask in the singular, "May *it* come to us and to all Israel for good," "*haba* aleynu v'al kol Yisrael l'tovah," on Rosh Chodesh Elul we can say *haba'im* in the plural, in order to include the two months of Elul and Tishrei.[21]

As we come to the ninth step in anticipating the birth of the new month, "Y'*chadsh*ehu HaKadosh Baruch Hu," "May the Holy One *renew* the coming month," there is a summary of the hopes that have been expressed throughout the Birkat HaChodesh. Completing the cycle from the very beginning with "Yehi ratzon milfanecha . . . , sheyi*chadesh* alenu et HaChodesh hazeh," "May it be Your will . . . that you *renew* for us this month," *Chodesh* once again becomes a word of blessing. As the moon and the month are renewed, so may we be renewed. And let us say: Amen.

Parallels between Birkat HaChodesh and Kiddush HaChodesh

There are a number of parallels between Birkat HaChodesh as we know it and the ancient rite of Kiddush HaChodesh. We stand for the duration of the blessing of the new month as our ancestors stood for Kiddush HaChodesh, when the new month was actually determined and sanctified. There is a deeply responsive nature to today's observance, as we have seen, just as there was then. Through participation, an excellent pedagogic device, people can become more aware of the calendar.

The prayer *Mi'she-asah* is seen to represent the most direct parallel to the ancient observance. Baer suggests that it was instituted in place of Kiddush HaChodesh.[22] The messianic themes running through all versions of the Birkat HaChodesh were also present when the Sanhedrin sanctified the new moon. At that time they were given particular expression in special additions to the Birkat HaMazon following a festive evening meal held in honor of the sanctification of the new month.

In addition to messianic themes, these celebratory blessings added to the Birkat HaMazon also reflect the "majesty of details" that infuses the calendar. Our ancestors in Jerusalem blessed God, "Who hast revealed the secret of the renewal of the moon, Who didst instruct and teach us the [courses of] the seasons, New Moons and Festivals and Who didst appoint men of understanding who determine the times [of the New Moons and Festivals]. Thou, our Rock, hast weighed and calculated the minutest divisions of time whereby those New Moons and Festivals are determined."[23] This excitement and awe finds echo in the Birkat HaChodesh and its choreography.

The placing of Birkat HaChodesh on the Shabbat before Rosh Chodesh is distinctly not parallel with the timing of Kiddush HaChodesh, which, as we have seen, was of necessity done at the time of the actual appearance of the new moon. Observing Birkat HaChodesh on Shabbat, however, gives symbolic expression to the very meaning of renewal and unity that characterizes the rite.

With its origins in a time when virtually all Jews went to shul at least on Shabbat, observing Birkat HaChodesh on Shabbat conveys sensitivity. It suggests a concern to reach out and make an effort to accommodate those Jews who are not regular shul goers during the week, and thereby to maximize the opportunity to include them in the dissemination of Jewish knowledge and awareness of the calendar. This is expressed in a Siddur commentary that reflects a different milieu from that of most North American Jews today; "for on Shabbat all Israel gathers in the Synagogues, even those who are not accustomed to visit the sanctuary of God on week days, and it is made known to them when Rosh Chodesh will fall during the coming week."[24] Knowledge of the calendar is essential for unified Jewish practice.

Enhancing Birkat HaChodesh: Building Anticipation

Shabbat HaChodesh provides an opportunity for *chesbon hanefesh*—stock-taking of the soul, which is an essential first step in any process of change and renewal. Unlike the moon's renewal, change does not simply happen in our lives as part of an unalterable ever-renewing cycle. It takes effort. The prayers of Birkat HaChodesh can help focus that effort. Both in shul and in quiet moments of anticipatory reflection, taking the Siddur and looking at these prayers can help inspire the renewal that Rosh Chodesh offers.

Beyond personal renewal, individuals and communities can reflect on communal renewal, that of their own community and the community of Israel, thus giving meaning to the words, *chaverim kol Yisrael*, "all Israel is bound together—all Israel are friends."

Within the Synagogue many things can be done to maximize the impact of Birkat HaChodesh. Simply highlighting it in the Synagogue bulletin, along with Rosh Chodesh, is a step toward fostering greater awareness of the Jewish calendar and the added specialness of Shabbat Mevorchim. In addition, communities could have a special spot in the bulletin in which to print the verse from Birkat HaChodesh that announces the name of the coming month and the day of Rosh Chodesh.

On Shabbat HaChodesh itself, it is helpful to follow the traditional order of Birkat HaChodesh. Announcing the time of the *molad* in the traditional manner is exciting and creates a bond with Jerusalem and with fascinating details of astronomy. It brings home the "majesty of details" of which I have spoken. The time of the *molad*, given in Yiddish, can be found in a *Luach Bet Ha'K'nesset*, a calendar chart of Synagogue laws and customs generally available in Jewish bookstores. Another very detailed *Luach*, which gives the *molad* for each month in addition to a great deal of other information, is available from Rabbi Hershel Edelstein.[25] Singing "Mi'she-asah Nisim" to a tune associated with an upcoming holiday helps to build anticipation for the new month.

In emphasizing the responsive and educational nature of Birkat HaChodesh, it may be helpful to have the congregation recite the English for some or all of the passages said by the community. According to one commentary on Birkat HaChodesh, the announcing of the new month is for the benefit of children as well as adults.[26] To highlight the completion and beginning of the lunar cycle, it might be fun for a congregation to have children stand at the front or walk around the shul holding up large cardboard cutouts depicting the phases of the moon.

Finally, become "moon watchers"! Go out and see the new moon. The new crescent first becomes visible above the western horizon right after sunset in the evening of the day that follows Rosh Chodesh.[27] The new moon is visible only briefly on that first night, and then, following the sun, it quickly dips beneath the horizon. The beginning of change can be ephemeral and fleeting. Change does not come all at once, but grows little by little toward fullness. Though not for the purpose of setting the calendar, but of celebrating it, going out as witnesses to see the new moon forms a bond with our ancestors who looked to the sky long ago. In that moment of renewal we can become awe-inspired, as they were, and hear "the heavens declare God's glory." By anticipating and celebrating the new moon, may our lives be opened to the hope of its emerging light and to the light of God, Source of all light.

Notes

1. Ismar Elbogin, *HaT'filla B'Yisrael B'Hitpatchutah HaHistorit* (Tel Aviv: D'vir, 1972), p. 94. Elbogin also comments that at one time, the term, *Machrizin HaChodesh*, "Proclaiming the Month," was used, referring specifically to the proclamation of the date of Rosh Chodesh as part of the order of blessing the new month.

2. Talmud Yerushalmi, Sanhedrin 5:3; Aruch HaShulchan, Hilchot Rosh Chodesh 417:8; *Encyclopedia Judaica* 12:1040.

3. Elbogin, *Hat'filla*.

4. Hirsch Chumash, ed. Ephraim Oratz, English translation from the original German by Gertrude Hirschler (New York: The Judaica Press, 1986), p. 250.

5. Rosh HaShanah 25b.

6. Unabridged Hirsch commentary, Samson Raphael Hirsch, *The Pentateuch*, trans. Isaac Levy (Gateshead: Judaica Press, 1989), 2:125.

7. Rosh HaShanah 2:5–7.

8. Mishne Torah, Hilchot Kiddush HaChodesh, 5:2.

9. Unabridged Hirsch commentary, *The Pentateuch*, p. 125.

10. Maimonides tells us "this is the time between each and every *molad*, and this is the renewal of the moon" ("Kiddush HaChodesh" 6:3).

11. Nathan Bushwick, *Understanding the Jewish Calendar* (New York/Jerusalem: Moznaim Publishing, 1989), p. 72.

12. Ibid., p. 76; Tur, Orech Chaim, Hilchot Rosh Chodesh, 427.

13. Maimonides Mishne Torah, "Hilchot Yesodei HaTorah" 2:2.

14. Mishne Torah, "Hilchot Kiddush HaChodesh" 6:3.

15. These nine steps can represent, in effect, a symbolic "birthing" of the new moon, helping us to anticipate it and helping us to look into ourselves, at our hopes, and at our priorities, in preparation for the "birth." "Nine" in this context calls to mind that

wonderful Pesach song, "Echad Mi Yodeah—Who Knows One?" Verse nine, of course, reads or sings, "Tisha mi yodeah? Tisha ani yodeah: Tisha *yarchei* layda," "Who knows nine? I know nine: Nine are the months/moons of pregnancy." The moon and birth are linked, as in *yare'ach* and *molad*. *Yare'ach* is the more common word for moon in Hebrew, from which is derived *yerach*, a less common word meaning "month." The Aramaic reflects the relationship of moon and month most clearly in the term for Rosh Chodesh as "Yoma d'Yarcha," "the Day of the Month/Moon."

16. J. D. Eisenstein, *Otzar Dinim u'Minhagim* (Tel Aviv, 1970), p. 57.

17. Ibid; Sidur Otzar HaT'filot, *Nusach Sefarad* (Jerusalem: N'hora D'Oraytah, 1960), 1:722 ; Elie Munk, *The World of Prayer* (New York: Feldheim Publishers, 1963), 2:49.

18. It is in this same vein that we sing "HaTikva," sustaining hope with *ayin l'Tzion tzofiyah*, an eye to Zion expectantly turned.

19. Eisenstein, *Otzar Dinim*.

20. *Machzor Vitry*, compiled by Simchah son of Samuel of Vitry, France, a student of Rashi, in the eleventh century.

21. Eisenstein, *Otzar Dinim*.

22. Zeligman Baer, *Seder Avodat Yisrael* (Tel Aviv: Schocken, 1937), p. 232.

23. *The Minor Tractates of the Talmud*, ed. Rev. Dr. A. Cohen (London: Soncino Press, 1965), 1:307; "Masechet Soferim 42b, chap. 19, rule 9.

24. *Siddur Otzar HaT'filot* (Jerusalem: Nahora d'Oraita, 1960), 1:722.

25. Rabbi Hershel Edelstein provides information about the *molad* for each month as well as candle lighting times detemined specifically for any given area. This *Luach* can be ordered from Rabbi Edelstein at 4 Albert Drive, Monsey, NY 10952-2948.

26. *She'yihiyu yod'im g'dolim u'k'tanim she'yesh lanu Rosh Hodesh*, "So that adults and children will know that we have Rosh Hodesh" (Elbogin, *HaT'filla*, p. 94); *Siddur Otzar HaT'filot*, p. 722.

27. Bushwick, *Jewish Calendar*, pp. 40–41.

18
Kiddush HaLevana: Sanctifying the New Moon

Geela-Rayzel Raphael

The new moon has become an important celebratory time for women. In addition, there is another little-known ceremony, Kiddush Levana, that actually consecrates the moon and the Cosmic Creator of her light. This service is traditionally held outdoors at least three days after the appearance of the new crescent, but not later than the mid-point of the month. It is generally said following a *ma'ariv* (evening) Shabbat service.

The ceremony of Kiddush Levana serves several purposes. First of all, it reminds us once again, in a concrete way, that Jewish life is tied to a lunar calendar. By taking time to offer prayers and blessings in the light of the moon, we are continually in harmony with the celestial cycles. Second, the Kiddush Levana liturgy serves to bring us directly in contact with natural phenomenon, stirring us to bless the Creator of All. We are witness to the magnificence of creation, and when we become aware of its miracles—are obliged to pronounce a benediction. Third, participation in a Kiddush Levana service provides a framework for meditating on the moon as a symbol of the Jewish people.

The moon, with her cycles of waxing and waning, disappearance and emergence, represented for our sages, Israel's cycle of success and subjugation and also constituted a symbol for blessings and renewed visions. The ritual of Kiddush Levana offers a hope that Israel will return to a time of glory. There is a *midrash*[1] that states that there were fifteen generations from Abraham to Solomon, which waxed mighty, only to degenerate as well. The moon is our metaphor for struggling out of the darkness to the light of truth.

At the beginning of the month we step outside to view the growing light, symbolizing our renewed faith in the Creator. We also view the stars, fixed entities, reminding us that our service and loyalty to God should not waver. As the moon belongs to God, we are subjects as well. We recognize, however, that like the moon, change is constant.

There are two traditional sources for the ritual of Kiddush Levana. In the Talmud, Rabbi Yochanan said that one who blesses the new moon is regarded as one who greets the *Shechinah* (feminine aspects of the Divine).[2] The Talmud also points to the moon and the other heavenly bodies as proof to God's existence.[3] The moon is the most constant reminder of the cosmic cycles, and the Creator who set them in place. Our history and the miracles performed on behalf of Israel provide a certainty to God's existence.

The traditional order for Kiddush Levana consists of several components. As an introduction, Psalm 148 is recited. The content of this psalm refers to the moon and other elements of the heavens. A blessing is then said acknowledging God as the Creator, the One who renews the months. The participants then rise three times on their toes as if to touch the moon, saying "Even as I raise myself up to you but cannot touch you, so may my foes be unable to touch me with evil intent." A curse is then cast on the enemies and David, King of Israel is mentioned—a phrase that signifies messianic vision.

The observance of Kiddush Levana continues with the participants greeting each other and saying, "Shalom Aleichem" (peace be with you) and answering "Aleichem Shalom." The group then sings, or says, "Siman tov u'mazel tov y'hi lanu u-l'chol Yisrael" (may good fortune shine on us and Israel). A section of "Song of Songs" is then recited, including many with allusions to messianic redemption.[4]

Several psalms are then read, including Psalm 121 (one of the psalms of the ascent), which refers to the moon as a benign presence and describes the ways Israel finds strength and protection. Psalm 150, the last psalm in the Book of Psalms, lists a variety of musical instruments for celebrating, reminding us of the various ways each soul celebrates and praises the Holy One. A passage from Sanhedrin 42a is recited, where we learn the custom to say this ceremony while standing. There is a closing prayer asking God to correct the flaw of the moon, referring to the fact that its light was diminished next to the sun. Finally, Psalm 67 is said, appealing for redemption, and the closing prayer is usually Aleynu, serving as a reminder that we are not worshipping the moon, but the Source of Creation who gave us this light.[5]

This short ceremony of Kiddush Levana is a wonderful way to strengthen our connection to nature and her cycles. One may be drawn to the traditional form or an adaptation of it. But setting aside the time to walk in the moonlight, trying to touch what is beyond our grasp will enable us to glimpse and sense the majesty in our universe. In carrying out this ritual, the participants will be inspired and empowered to heal the planet, our people, and ourselves.

The following is a creative rendition of the Kiddush Levana service compiled by Geela-Rayzel Raphael and Margot Stein-Azen. The song, "Sun, Moon, and Stars" and the chant, "Shechinah Moon" were written by Geela-Rayzel Raphael.

The Ceremony

1. Ritual Leader: We gather in a circle to mirror the moon. We know that the moon is a complete circle, even when we can only see a part of her. We know that there is strength, unity, and light even when that is not apparent.

2. Sing "Sun, Moon, and Stars" from Psalm 148 (Musical notation on page 294)

Haleluhu Shemesh v'Yaray-ach, Haleluhu kol kochvay or (2x)
HaleluYah, HaleluYah, (2x) HaleluYah halelu, halelu col kochvay or.

הללוהו שמש וירח הללהו כל כוכבי אור
הללויה הללויה הללו כל כוכבי אור

Verse: The sun she dances up the morning with a light that brightens up our day
Radiant, brilliant, holy shine, Inspiration that makes me want to pray.

Chorus: Sing HaleluYah, HaleluHah (2x),
HaleluYah halelu, halelu Kol kochvay or.

Verse: The moon floats through the evening sky with a glow that spins our spirits right
Luminescent, ghostly, gentle beams, Peaceful rays to guide us through the night.

Chorus:

Verse: The stars they twinkle in the twilight, Sparkle out from under the clouds
Sprinkling us with their friendly light, We hear them singing loud.

3. Prayer:

Brucha At *Shechinah*, Malkat Ha'olam, asher B' amariych, borayt
Shehakim, Uv'ruchan pe- cha kol tz'vaam, sh'hem sassim u-s'maychim
la'asot ritzon konatam.

Hok u-z'man natnah lahem, ad olam. Po-elet Emet she'pe-ulatah emet.
V'lalevana amrah she-teet'hadaysh k'ateret tiferet; v'amusot vaten amrah
she'haym atidot lechitcchadesh k'motah u'lefa-air l'yotzran al shaym
k'vod malchutah. Brucha Yah *Rachamemah*,[6] Mikor Or Hadash,
Michadeshet l'vana bizmana, Amen, Selah.[7]

בְּרוּכָה אַתְּ שְׁכִינָה, מַלְכַּת הָעוֹלָם, אֲשֶׁר בְּמַאֲמָרַיִךְ בּוֹרֵאת שְׁחָקִים

וּבְרוּחַן פִּיךְ כָּל צְבָאָם, שֶׁהֵם שַׂשִׂים וּשְׂמֵחִים לַעֲשׂוֹת רוֹצוֹן קוֹנָתָם,

חוֹק וּזְמַן נָתְנָה לָהֶם עַד עוֹלָם.

פּוֹאֶלֶת אֱמֶת שְׁפְּעוּלָתָה אֱמֶת.

וְלַלְבָנָה אָמְרָה שֶׁתִּתְחָדֵשׁ   כְּעֲטֶרֶת תִּפְאֶרֶת

וַעֲמוּסוֹת בָּטֶן אָמְרָה

שֶׁהֵן עֲתִידוֹת לְהִתְחָדֵשׁ כָּמוֹתָה

וּלְפָאֵר לְיוֹצְרָן עַל שֵׁם כְּבוֹד מַלְכוּתָה.

בְּרוּכָה יָהּ רָחֲמֶמָה מְקוֹר אוֹר חָדָשׁ מְחָדֶשֶׁת לְבָנָה בִּזְמָנָה. אמן סלה

Blessed are You, *Shechinah*, Queen of the World, You whispered the sky
into being with the breath of Your voice. All the celestial hosts delight
and rejoice fulfilling Divine Will. You fixed them in time and space so
they will illuminate everlasting.

She is Truth Worker and Her work is Truth. To the Moon She said,
"May You Renew your crown of Beauty." For those with full bellies she
said, "They renew themselves like her and adorn their Creator for the
sake of Her glory." Blessed be *Rachamemah*, Source of New Light,
Renewer of the Moons in her season.

4. Group reads or chants, together or responsively:

Shechinah Moon

As we rise to greet the moon,
        We welcome *Shechinah*
Our bodies are so tuned
        with our eyes we see your light

We cycle with You
    Flowing with You, *Shechinah*.
You are our symbol
    of life renewed
of changes of feminine energy
    You remind us of our gentle spirit
Growing, shyly showing
    more and more of Yourself each dusk
Until Your brilliance is revealed.
    We love Your crescent
We know Your fullness
    We feel the sadness of Your waning phase.
Then the brightness of Your rays
    fills the sky
Sometimes orange, yellow, gray, or white
    You fill the night
Guarding our way among the stars
    Among the trees, upon the paths of life.
We honor You *Shechinah*, Divine Presence in the Moon
    Who pulls the tides
and shapes our moods
    with Your lunar beams.
Heal us, oh *Shechinah*, empower us
    with the power of Your light
Let us remember the moon as the sign of Your glory.

5. Ritual leader: In our tradition prophesy was often accompanied by a physical act in order to seal the vision. Please feel free to express these chants through movement. **Chant three times**:

Brucha Yotzreych, Brucha Oseyich, Brucha Konech, Brucha Boraych.

ברוכה יוצרך ברוכה עוֹשׂך ברוכה קונך ברוכה בורך

Blessed is your Former, Blessed is your maker, Blessed is the one you belong to, Blessed is your Creator.[8]

6. Say three times while running or leaping toward the moon, trying to touch her: "Just as I dance toward you but cannot touch you, so may none of my enemies touch me for evil."

7. Say each verse three times: Let me learn what I need to learn from my adversaries, and let them be blessed with openness of mind and heart.
Let my spirit rise with fullness as I reach out with love.

8. Sing (to the tune of "David Melech Yisrael"):
Or *Shechinah* l'olam va-ed.

אור שכינה לעולם ועד

The Light of *Shechinah* for ever and ever.

9. Dance "Shalom Aleichem."

10. Sing: Several songs may be sung at this time:

"Siman tov u'mazal tov" (from the Sidur)
"Kol dodi" (from Shir haShirim)
"Esah aynah" (from the Sidur)
"Kol Hanishama" (from Hallel in the Sidur)

11. Share: Share hopes and prayers that Israel will rise again with renewed power and visions for peace.

12. Say to different people in the room (You may add additional blessings of your own.):

May we be inspired to pursue our goals for the sake of each other.
May Israel have the courage to seek peace.
May our actions help heal the planet.

13. Eat Moon cookies and sing other moon songs.

Notes

1. Shemot Rabbah 15:26 is an attempt to explain the verse, "This month shall be for you the beginning of months." (Exodus 12:2). Why is this called the beginning month? Our midrash explains: "Just as the month has thirty days, so your kingdom will last until thirty generations. There were fifteen generations, the first half of the waxing month from Abraham to Solomon, which was considered the time when Israel's moon was full. After Solomon, the kings began to diminish in power until Zedekiah when the light of the moon failed entirely. Since the time of Zedekiah, God makes peace for Israel."
2. Sanhedrin 42a.
3. Rabbeinu Yonah, Berachot 4.
4. Shir Ha-shirim 2:8–9: "The voice of my beloved! Behold he comes leaping over the mountains, bounding over the hills. My beloved is like a hart or young deer. Behold, he stands behind our wall: He sees through the windows, He looks through the lattice."

5. There is a complete commentary to the Kiddush Levana service in the *ArtScroll Sidur*, ed. Rabbi Nosson Scherman (Brooklyn: ArtScroll/Menorah, 1969 [Coney Island Avenue, Brooklyn, New York 11223]).

6. *Rachamema*—a name for God meaning, "Compassionate Womb Mother."

7. This prayer has been "Reconstructed" by Herb Levine, Vivie Mayer, and Jeremy Schwartz based on the blessing according to Rab Judah. It is found in the Talmud Sanhedrin 42a. R. Aha said to R. Ashi: "In the west [Palestine], they pronounce the following benediction: 'Blessed be He who renews the moons.'" Whereupon he retorted: "Such a blessing even our women folk pronounce! Instead one should use the following in accordance with Rab Judah, who gives it thus, 'Praised be the One, Ruler of the Universe, who created the heavens with His word and all his hosts with breath of his mouth. He appointed them fixed laws and times, that they should not change their ordinance. They rejoice and are glad to do the Will of their Creator. They work truthfully, for their action is truth. The moon he ordered that she should renew herself as a crown of beauty for those who He sustains from the womb, and will, like it, be renewed in the future, and magnify their Maker in the name of the glory of His kingdom. Blessed art Thou, O Lord, who renewest the moons.'"

8. This chant is a variation on a traditional kabbalistic chant.

IV

Poetry, Prayers,
Songs, and
Meditations

19
The Origins of Rosh Chodesh: A Midrash[1]

Penina Adelman

The festival of Rosh Chodesh was born in the desert where no shadows existed to hide shapes and colors; neither were there many surfaces to muffle sounds. This was a world of no distinctions between land or sky, wind or air; different from Egypt, which we had just left.

In our wilderness wandering we learned to speak to the heavens and find answers written in the shapes of clouds. The rocks taught us to be patient. The scraggly bushes taught us how to save the rain, embrace the earth. The palm trees clustered together like children around a green pool, showing us how to join them on our knees to drink the blessed water. The desert sustained us all with the same umbilical cord.

Is it any wonder that we who had emerged from the Sea of Reeds together into the wilderness of Sinai all began to live by one rhythm? And is the wonder any greater that the cycles of the moon reverberated in every woman at the same time, in the same way? As soon as the moon was born anew in the sky, each woman began to bleed.

153

Without saying a word to each other, we women knew it was time to separate ourselves from the men. As if the moon were calling us, we left camp and hiked together to a wadi a half-day's distance. We moved at night with her crescent, a white gleaming magnet in the sky.

When we reached the Wadi of the Moon, we lay on the sand, nestling in the rocks still warm from the daytime sun and fell asleep. That night we all had a similar dream.

One woman told it thus: "We were each bathed very carefully in different ways. The moon bathed us with her light. Our mothers soothed us with the lullabies they had sung to us when we were children. We felt purified with a green fragrance which seemed to emanate from the rocks."

When we awoke, rosemary had sprouted overnight beneath us. We rose as in a spell and embraced each other. Then we began to sing.

Our song seemed to make things grow. There were date palms, figs, grapes, olives appearing all at once and in great abundance. From a rock a spring trickled forth.

We remained in that desert garden for a week, receiving strength from the earth by seating ourselves in special postures, bathing in the moonlight by night, and resting in the shelter of the largest rocks by day.

Soon our bleeding ceased. We watched the moon swell to fullness. It was time to return to our camp.

There we found the men were panicking. They shouted about being abandoned, first by Moses who had climbed the mountain to talk to God and then by us women who had disappeared without a word.

The men feared they would die of thirst. They demanded all our gold ornaments, intending to make a god out of metal. We refused and felt pity for them. They turned from us without asking where we had been. With Aaron reluctantly guiding them, they built an idol. Soon there stood a calf of gold high on a pedestal, beaming foolishly at the mountain. We began to doubt if our week apart in the moonlight had ever happened.

However, in time, with the reappearance of the new moon, we understood our reward: because we had refused to give our ornaments to make an idol, we would be "reborn" each month.[2] The moon would teach us about the rhythms of the seasons and the months of the year.

Several women with the best memories became the Keepers of the Months, responsible for remembering which songs were sung, which postures were learned, which stories were told, which ripe fruits were eaten, which type of fragrance the rocks emanated in a particular month so that we could tell our daughters and granddaughters in years to come. We chose the twin sister of the head of each tribe for this task, as it is written, "To each and every [head of the] tribe was born a twin sister."[3]

This sacred knowledge probably remained hidden over the centuries. As the Jewish people traveled beyond their desert existence, women began to menstruate on different days, each in her own unique relationship to the moon.

The women at Sinai had taken this eventuality into account. They had prayed to the Shechinah for guidance. If the sacred knowledge of the months was lost, the Shechinah let them know that in a future time when women sought this monthly wisdom once again, it would be rediscovered as easily as moving aside a rock to uncover the fragrant plant beneath. Then the ritual would be reinstated through a community of women who remember, as in a distant dream, how the moon once called to them at Sinai.

We are that community.

Notes

1. An original midrash by Penina Adelman based on Exodus 32:1–6 and Louis Ginsberg's *Legends of the Jews* (Philadelphia: Jewish Publication Society), 3:121–122.

2. For classical Jewish sources cited on Jewish women being "reborn" each month like the moon, see Arthur Waskow's essay in Susannah Heschel's *On Being a Jewish Feminist* (New York: Schocken Books), pp. 261–272.

3. "Bereshet Rabba" Parshat VaYishlach, 82, in Midrash Rabba.

20
A Rosh Chodesh Bracha

(Song)

Penina Adelman and Suri Levow Krieger

This song uses the words taken from the *Birkat HaChodesh*, the "Announcement of Rosh Chodesh," which occurs during the Shabbat prayer service preceding Rosh Chodesh. The music is a variation of the "Pacabel Canon" arranged by Suri Levow Kreiger and Penina Adelman. The song is recorded on the audiotape *Chodesh Chodesh B'Shir–A Song A Month* and is distributed by SoundsWrite.

Yehi Ratzon Milfanecha, Adonai Eloheynu
Sh'te chadesh aleinu
Et HaChodesh Hazeh
L'tova u-l'vracha.

יחי רצון מלפניך יהוה אלהינו
שתתחדש עלינוּ את החודש הזה לטובה ולברכה

May it be Your will, O God, that You will renew for us this month and grant us happiness and blessings.

156

21
New Moon of the Daughters: Rosh Chodesh Tevet[1]

Matia Rania Angelou

Gather in the darkness of the moon,
  dark as skin of African sisters
  who gently cradle Torah scrolls,
    tenderly kiss and pass them on.

Gather on the New Moon of the Daughters,
  a night to honor women,
  to remember women's lives
    and their courage during hard times.

Light these flames.
  Tiny sparks catch and burn,
  reminding us that in the heart of darkness
    is the greatest light.

Light one flame for Judith
whose wisdom and courage shine through the ages.

Light the second for the Maccabean mother
who kept her faith as her sons were killed for freedom.

The third flame is for all women
expelled from their homes, wandering to settle once more.

Light the fourth for young women, lives unfulfilled,
murdered by Nazi madness.

And the fifth for Ethiopian sisters
whose children were stolen as slaves.

Light the sixth flame for grandmothers
who taught us how to be women.

And the seventh one for all of us
who strive to discover the truth in the darkness.

The eighth, as yet unlit, is for our unborn daughters,
the light and hope of the future.

As the new moon of Tevet waxes from darkness to fullness, let us remember
the women before us who taught the lessons of life. May we find meaning in
the darkness and truth in the light. These tiny sparks, each one alone so small,
burn together with a brightness beautiful to behold. May they burn ever brighter,
increasing our strength and courage. Blessed are You God, Who separates
darkness and light, honoring both.

Note

1. Rosh Chodesh Tevet, depending on the year and whether Kislev has twenty-
nine or thirty days, may fall on the seventh night or eighth night of Chanukah. Rosh
Chodesh Tevet may be a one- or two-day Rosh Chodesh, again depending on the year,
so this candle lighting should be recited for the seventh night of Chanukah. For a fuller
understanding of the holiday, "New Moon for the Daughters," see Leah Novick's chapter, "The History of Rosh Chodesh and Its Evolution as a Woman's Holiday."

22
The Moon as Life's Cycle

Susan Berrin

A crescent kisses
her forehead
as she sucks from a moon breast.
Each morning she sings God's praises.
And then
her toddler legs, stout and solid,
propel her through the afternoon
into evening's diffuse light.

Adolescence waxes
alternating cycles of good night cuddles
and indignant daytime demands.
She blossoms with the spring garden
flowers purple with the chives
bleeds with the moon.

At full moon,
she feeds her round faced children
and beds them down
warmed by a particular, succulent love.
And when shreds of coherency fade into a tomorrow
of weary eyes,
that milky pause of the earth's ceiling says,
"onward."

Waning moon, wandering woman
Blood draining from the moon's face.
Her shadow crosses the wide prairie.
She is, as ever,
a soulful searcher
honoring life's cycles
by the moon's turning.

She lays down with
a full black sky
While a crescent hovers
and kisses her grave.

23
The New Moon
(Pinchas—Numbers 28:1, 11)

Ruth Brin

*And God spoke unto Moses saying: "And in your new moons you shall
present a burnt-offering unto God."*

If God were the sun, then Israel might be
the moon,
her face reflecting His eternal light.

Yes, Israel is like the moon, the moon
who waxes and wanes,
grows old, and then renews herself,
yet never leaves the skies.

Faithfully, she reappears to walk the night
glimmering, silver, in the darkened sky,

161

Faithfully, she spreads her pale and ghostly light
on every room and tree and blade of grass

Until the whole world turns to silver,
transformed from darkness to shimmering beauty.

Yes, Israel, be like the moon
renew your faith each generation.

Even when the earth casts its shadow of
darkness
faithfully reflect the light of God;

Pour over the whole world
the moonlight beauty of holiness.

24
A Woman's Rosh Chodesh Amidah

Diane Cohen

Blessed are You, Holy One, God of our mothers,
God of Sarah, God of Rebecca, God of Rachel, God of Leah,
Who is great and revered above all.
You are gracious, filled with loving kindness,
and generous to Your children,
Forgiving us and showing us Your love.
Because of the devotion of our mothers
You remember us,
Protect us and shelter us.
Blessed are You, Holy One, who remembered Sarah.

You can be gentle.
You can also be strong,
with a power that brings the dead to life.
You send the wind and the rain to nourish the earth.

You sustain us with Your strength
and restore life to the dead,
Support the fallen, heal the sick of mind and weary of spirit,
and free those enslaved to false ideas and false gods.

You are holy and Your name is holy
and holy ones praise You by day, by the sun,
and by night, by the moon.

You have given Your children intelligence to discern
and instinct to feel,
Knowledge and understanding,
Sensitivity and intuition.
We praise You, Holy One, for the gifts of rational knowledge
and the messages of the heart.

Gracious God, bring us back to a knowledge of Your law
and of the traditions of the mothers.
Draw us back to the worship of generations of women who have
Gone before us.
Lead us back to You and we will go.

Redeem us soon, O mighty Redeemer,
Bring us back to the worship of Your holy name
So that our lips may praise You and our hearts rejoice.

Heal our pain, show us Your glory,
and support the ailing among us.

Bless us with a year of blessings and bounty,
O Sustainer of Life,
and send dew and rain for a blessing on the earth.
Bless the year with goodness,
O Nurturer and Sustainer of Life,
that our years may be sweet and good.
We bless You, Holy One, who blesses our years.

Spread forth Your wings over all Your people
and gather in Your exiles from the four corners of the earth.

Restore the wise ones of our people, that they may administer
in truth and justice, O God who loves justice.

Frustrate the hopes of those who malign us
and open the eyes and the hearts of those who do not understand.

Let all evil disappear
and Your enemies be destroyed.
We bless the God who humbles the arrogant.

Return in compassion to Jerusalem, Your holy city,
to the sea swept cities of the coast
and the magical hills of the Galilee.
May Your presence dwell in Your holy city,
A city soon reestablished as the dwelling place of Your glory.
Hasten the advent of the Messiah
and redeem us speedily.

Hear our voices,
Voices long unheard,
Holy One,
Have compassion on us and pity us.
Accept our prayer with loving favor
and do not turn us away unanswered,
You in whom our final hopes lie.
We praise You, Holy One, who listens to the prayers of
Women's voices.

God and God of our mothers, on this day of Rosh Chodesh,
Remember those who went before us.
All Israel stands before You in prayer.
May the waxing of the moon be reflected in the
Waxing strength of women
Seeking in dark places, by the moon's light,
and in the glorious light of day,
the way to You and Your worship.
Grant us life, deliverance, and peace.
Bless us, Holy One, with all that is good,
O source of all Good.

May our eyes witness Your return to Zion.
We are ever grateful to You, O Holy One,
Who defends us, shields and protects us,
and Who will remember us.
Throughout all generations, we have thanked You
and praised You.
We thank You for the miracles that surround us,
and for the miracles of which we are a part.
The earth is truly filled with Your wonders.

You are truly beneficent, with boundless mercy and love,
and our hope has always been with You.

We will ever praise and thank You for all
You have done for us,
and for the strength You give us to do what must be done
to find the voices of our mothers
and to learn to walk the road that leads to You.

Grant full and lasting peace to Your people Israel,
for You are the Creator of peace.
May it please You to bless Your people in this season
and in every season
with peace
and with unpeace,
the unquiet that makes us want to grow.
We bless You, Holy One, the Creator of peace.

My God, let my mouth be opened
and my tongue be sure
Not to hurt
But not to refrain from truth.
Help me to remember my worth
as Your daughter,
that my spine may be straight
and my eye clear.
Open my heart to Your Torah
and my soul to Your light.

Frustrate the designs of those who seek to do me evil.
Make naught of their schemes, for Your sake,
and for the sake of the Mothers.

Answer my prayer for the deliverance of Your daughters.

May the words of my mouth and the meditations of my heart
Find favor before You, Holy One.
May the Creator of peace in heaven bring peace
to us all,
and let us say,
Amen.

25
Meditation and Kiddush for Rosh Chodesh

Marcia Falk

MEDITATION
for the Sanctification over Wine for Rosh Hodesh

The vine is courageous and tenacious, as each of us is called upon to be. Growing toward light, it twists without knowing what may lie beyond. In its journey, the vine intertwines with other vines. We might think of community this way, as an interweaving of the paths of many vines.

Our history, then, is the tapestry of interwoven vines. To it, we continually add new weaving. And tonight we unroll our tapestries, holding them up to the light, where their colors and intricate patterns—each perfect and imperfect stitch—may shine.

From "*Kabbalat P'ney Hahódesh*: Welcoming the New Month," a ceremony for Rosh Hodesh Eve, from Marcia Falk, *The Book of Blessings: New Jewish Prayers for Daily Life, the Sabbath, and the New Moon Festival* (Harper San Francisco, 1996). Copyright © 1996 Marcia Lee Falk. Used by permission.

Kiddush for Rosh Hodesh

Marcia Falk

קִדּוּשׁ לְרֹאשׁ חֹדֶשׁ

וְהָיָה מִדֵּי־חֹדֶשׁ בְּחָדְשׁוֹ
וְשָׂשׂ לִבְּכֶם
וְעַצְמוֹתֵיכֶם כַּדֶּשֶׁא תִפְרַחְנָה.
עַל־פִּי יְשַׁעְיָה סו :כג, יד

נְבָרֵךְ אֶת עֵין הַחַיִּים
מַצְמִיחַת פְּרִי הַגֶּפֶן
וּנְקַדֵּשׁ אֶת רֹאשׁ הַחֹדֶשׁ
בַּאֲרִיגַת פְּתִילֵי חַיֵּינוּ
לְתוֹךְ מַסֶּכֶת הַדּוֹרוֹת.

Kiddush L'rosh Ḥódesh

V'hayah midey-ḥódesh b'ḥod'sho
v'sas lib'khem
v'atzmoteykhem kadéshe tifraḥnah.

N'vareykh et eyn haḥayim
matzmiḥat p'ri hagéfen,
unkadeysh et rosh haḥódesh
ba'arigat p'tiley ḥayénu
l'tokh masékhet hadorot.

Sanctification over Wine for Rosh Hodesh

It shall come to be from one month to the next
that your hearts will rejoice
and your bones will flower like young grass.
                                                                        After Isaiah 66:23,14

Let us bless the source of life
that ripens fruit on the vine,
as we hallow the Rosh Hodesh festival,
weaving new threads
into the tapestry of tradition.

26
Pale Moon

Nancy Lee Gossells

Pale moon
ever coming and going,
lighting and fading
rhythmic flowing
signal of new time and changing seasons,
awaken in us
the mystery of beginnings and endings,
of lives renewed.
Awaken us to the beauty of endless cycles,
visible signs of God's eternal love.

27
Birkat HaChodesh
(Song with Notation)[1]

Linda Hirschhorn

Y'hi ratzon milfanayich shechinat horaynu she-t'chadshi aleinu et HaChodesh hazeh l'tova v'livracha. V'titni lanu chayim aruckim, chayim shel shalom, chayim shel tova, chayim shel b'racha, chayim shel parnasa, chayim shel chilutz atzamot, chayim she'yesh bahem yirat shamayim, v'yirt chait, chayim she-ein bahem busha uch-lima, chayim shel osher v'chavod, chayim shet'hei vanu ahavat torah v'yirat shamayim, chayim she-y'mal'u mishalot libeinu l'tova. Amen. Selah.

יהי רצון מלפניך יהוה אלהינו ואלהי אבותינו שתחדש עלינו את החדש הבא
לטובה ולברכה. ותתן לנו חיים ארוכים, חיים של שלום, חיים של
טובה, חיים של ברכה, חיים של פרנסה, חיים של חלוץ עצמות,
חיים שיש בהם יראת שמים ויראת חטא, חיים שאין בהם בושה
וכלמה, חיים של עשר וכבוד, חיים שתהא בנו אהבת תורה ויראת
שמים, חיים שימלאו משאלות לבנו לטובה, אמן סלה.

And grant us many years to live
seeking peace and justice for the world
sustained by our friendships and not by wealth
renewed with the cycles of the moon

a life that knows no embarrassment or shame
knowing we've lived as fully as we can
a life that's filled with the wonders of the world
renewed with the cycles of the moon

a life that's filled with the love of the Torah
a love of the Torah and wonders of the world
a life that fills the yearnings of our heart
renewed with the cycles of the moon.

Note

1. Notation on page 296.

28
Rosh Chodesh Sh'vat

Vicki Hollander

El-Roe'i
Sh'vat has come.
Your gentle hands
in the depths of the worlds' sleep,
caress earth,
carefully coaxing,
wooing from the deep,
life to emerge.

One who sees,
in this time of gray,
in winters quiet,
enable us to feel inside
the shoots of green.

One who envisions,
open our eyes to know we can come alive.
No matter how dark the world is,
we can renew and blossom.

El-Roe'i,
let us be as the shaked, the almond tree.
Let us blossom in the chill of winter.
Let us lift our branches to the sky defiantly, proudly,
with grace.
Let us kiss the stars and hug the earth.
Let us stand despite wind and storm, heat or drought.

May we change in our seasons,
aging with grace,
growing yet another ring
a circle marking our lives' passages,
etched in our bark.

Watch over us, shokad,
as we celebrate our movement from darkness to light
from seed to tree
from empty branch to blossom
from silence to promise
from sleep to life
from emptiness to Your arms
from ember to flame.
Bless us as we stand.
Root us in the world.

29
Rosh Chodesh Nisan

Vicki Hollander

Hashomer,
You who watch over,
safeguard us,
hold us now.

Pinched between narrow places,
the departure of winter still lingers in our souls.
Like the tree leaves tightly furled,
our souls curl,
not yet trusting light.

The swelling of spring,
rising rainwaters,
not yet realized.
In cloud and fire,
You guide us through the blackness,
through the narrow places,
through the years of pain,
through the places which still hold us captive.

We, shackled, manacled
bear heavy loads.
Our backs burning from life's lashes.
And we follow You,
in Nisan,
from the land of plagues,
from building palaces of death, brick by bloody brick,
to the desert,
to wide, open spaces.

We follow You from the known,
which even in it's painfulness
is at least familiar.
We follow You scared,
fearfilled,
because we've never seen this spot in our souls before,
never felt desert winds,
never smelt desert air,
never experienced our inner wildness.
This spirited thing called freedom.

Watch us,
come with us.
Cloak us as we travel
from night to day,
from narrow to wild and open places,
from the familiar to new terrain.

Let spring break forth inside.
Let us walk in the waves and touch dry land.
Let our tongues know song our eyes, know wonders.
Flood our souls with pulsing life.

Hashomer,
watch us, watch us.
Guide our feet, and catch us.
Wrap us.

In our nighttimes light our way, and
sing to us lullabies
of a land of milk and honey,
of dreams that can be ours
if we but place foot ahead of foot and walk forward.

30
they did not build wings for them

Irena Klepfisz

they did not build wings for them
the unmarried aunts; instead they
crammed them into old maids' rooms
or placed them as nannies with
the younger children; mostly they
ate in the kitchen, but sometimes
were permitted to dine with the family
for which they were grateful and
smiled graciously as the food was passed.
they would eat slowly never filling
their plates and their hearts would
sink at the evening's end when it was
time to retreat into an upstairs corner.

but there were some who did not smile
who never wished to be grafted on
the bursting houses. these few remained

indifferent to the family gatherings
preferring the aloneness of their small rooms
which they decorated with odd objects
found on long walks. they collected
bird feathers and skulls unafraid to clean
them to whiteness; stones which resembled
humped bears or the more common tiger and
wolf; dried leaves whose brilliant colors
never faded; pieces of wood still covered
with fresh moss and earth which retained
their moisture and continued flourishing.
these they placed by their dresser mirrors
in arrangements reminiscent of secret rites
or hung over delicate watercolors of unruly
trees whose branches were about to snap
with the wind.

it happened sometimes that among these
one would venture even further. periodically
would be heard vague tales of a woman
withdrawn and inaccessible suddenly disappearing
one autumn night leaving her room bare
of herself. women gossiped about a man.
but eventually word would come back
she had moved north to the ocean and lived
alone. she was still collecting
but now her house was filled with crab
and lobster shells; discolored claws
which looked like grinning south american
parrots trapped in fish nets decorated
the walls; skulls of unidentifiable
creatures were arranged in geometric patterns
and soft reeds in tall green bottles
lined the window sills. one room
in the back with totally bare walls
was a workshop. here she sorted colored
shells and pasted them on wooden boards
in the shape of common flowers. these she sold
without sentiment.

such a one might also disappear inland.
rumor would claim she had traveled in

men's clothing. two years later it would
be reported she had settled in the woods
on some cleared land. she ran a small farm
mainly for supplying herself with food
and wore strangely patched dresses and shawls
of oddly matched materials. but aloneness
was her real distinction. the house was neat
and the pantry full. seascapes and pastoral
scenes hung on the walls. the garden was
well kept and the flower beds clearly defined
by color: red yellow blue. in the woods
five miles from the house she had an orchard.
here she secretly grafted and crossed varieties
creating singular fruit of shades and scents
never thought possible. her experiments rarely
failed and each spring she waited eagerly to see
what new forms would hang from the trees.
here the world was a passionate place and she
would visit it at night baring her breasts
to the moon.

31
Rosh Chodesh Nisan

Suzanne Kort

Celebrate
the newborn moon:
the first mitzvah
we observed after our Exodus.

A few war filled millennia later
the latest anti-mitzvah
scrawled itself across the world:
Dr. Goldstein of Hebron,
hug your children,
say good-bye,
leave medicine and take gun
into mosque of moon and star
and murder thirty bent in prayer.

A rage of killing fists
turned physician into fuel
for more unholy war,
turned twisted healer into martyr
for a deviant seed

of all Semitic people fallen
breathing gas, grenade,
and countless other kinds of fire
while longing for the time
the human race casts off its curse
to live or die by swords
and celebrates as one instead
the newborn moon,
the star filled sky,
the blue-green earth,
the Holy One
that births us in
our multicolored skin.

32
The Lunar Probe

Maxine Kumin

Long before morning they waked me to say
the moon was undone; had blown out, sky high,
swelled fat as a fat pig's bladder, fit
to burst, and then the underside had split.

I had been dreaming this dream seven nights
before it bore fruit (there is nothing so sweet
to a prophet as forethought come true). They had meant
merely to prick when . . . good-bye, good intent!

Dozing, I saw the sea stopper its flux,
dogs freeze in mid-howl, women wind up their clocks,
lunatics everywhere sane as their keepers.

I have not dreamed since in this nation of sleepers.

33
Meditation for the New Moon

Ruth Lerner

There are as many ways to view the new moon
as there are days in our lives.

to view a moon
a poet's moon
you need only three things:
a silent spot inside you
a willingness to wait in the dark
and a wily nature that refuses to accept the "Man-in-the-Moon"
as the ultimate authority.

here is one way to observe the new moon:
settle upon a path from which to grasp
the handle of white gold waiting above
find a quiet spot inside your sight.

in the darkness, close your eyes
and cover them, as if blessing the shabbos candles

"Praised are You, O Shechinah
who parts the days of the month
calls attention to our covenant and helps us to be
a light upon the earth."

then, slowly open your eyes
and behold the beginning
of time.

34
Rosh Chodesh

Lyn Lifshin

The moon could
be the sea,
washing days
slowly from her
in its waves.
She starts
again even in
the light the
moon's like
clock hands
in a drawer she
can't open,
running, running
out. The month
is water. She
has tried
sea walls, has
tried to root
but feels the

past move from
under her,
the new moon like
a lover's breath
begging her to
start over.

35
Hymn to the Moon

Lesléa Newman

Praised be the moon
as she rises tonight:
a round white pearl
in the velvet earlobe of the world

Praised be her light
that fills my empty teacup and across the jagged city
strokes your sleeping cheek
as you reach through your dreams

for someone who is not there.

36
Red Moon Magic
(Song with Notation)[1]

Geela-Rayzel Raphael

for a flaming, zinging Jewel, 2 Adar, 1992

Spirit flowing alive in me
Music moving into my bones,
Shechinah—Moon—she is calling me
Moon—she waters my soul;
Vanquish the demons, drive out the enemies
Failure and doubt—our inner scars,
With incense and candles—we usher Shechinah
Our sparks charged by the light of the stars.

Chorus:
Shabiri, biri, irri ri
Shall we dance? shall we dance? shall we dance the night away?
A crescent smile hangs over our heads
Celebrating our monthly holy day
Binding us by a red thread.

Once upon a time, a long, long time ago
We drew our power from the red, red moon,
And in the darkness angels guided us
Guarding us from danger and doom;
We called upon the Name, rearranged the letters
Mystical enchantment of fertility,
Womb power birthing—our stories emerging
Weaving a thread through our own tapestry.   Chorus:

Witch of Endor conjures up Samuel
Stirring him from beyond the grave,
Abeyeh's mother uses her formulas
Incantations to protect and save;
Winding, meandering, serpentine through centuries
From mother to daughter—Keepers of the Flame,
Banished, ignored, but never forgetting—
A caldron of blessing for her Divine Name.   Chorus:

The element of air moving us easterly
Southern fire transforming our course,
Western water shaping our destiny
Earth power healing—arrives from the North;
Wound around the ark from synagogue to birthing stool
As the ribbons on braids in Eve's hair,
Red stone necklaces to ward off the evil eye
On the baby's crib to know that She's there.   Chorus:

Note

1. Notation on page 298.

37
Rosh Chodesh Moon

(Song with Notation)[1]

Geela-Rayzel Raphael

It's a moon song
Bubbling up and over me
Darkness, sets my spirit free.
Rosh Chodesh, enchanted time to hallow the month
Lunar spirals, cycle 'round the earth.
   Renew our souls, Reopen up our hearts
   Re-light our internal sparks;
   Mysterious by day, Your wisdom guides our way
   Flowing with the rhythm of the tides.
Brucha Ya Rachamema, Mikor Or Chadash, Michadeshet et Ha-Chodashim,
Amen, Selah!

Its a moon song
Casting our shadows on the ground,
We're humbled by Your ancient glow.
Rosh Chodesh, yearning for your radiant shine
We gather, honoring Divine.
   Your moonbeams catch our eyes
   Releasing heartfelt sighs,

The clouds are blown across our minds;
I can read your face, in the depths of space
Your presence reveals a sacred sign.
Brucha Ya Rachamema, Mikor Or Chadash, Michadeshet et Ha-Z'manin,
AMEN! SELAH!

It's a moon song
Calling through the centuries
Holy tribute to the Queen.
Rosh Chodesh, Mistress of reflected light
Luminescence fills the night.
    Awaken with desire, rekindle inner fire
    Laugh, as we shoot across the sky;
    Circle with the Flame, Dance Your hidden Name
    Sing praises with our voices rising high.
Brucha Ya Rachamema, Mikor Or Chadash, Michadeshet et Ha-
Yerachim, Amen, Selah!

Note

1. Notation found on page 300.

38
Hallel[1]

Carol Rose

dedicated to the Women of the Wall.

the taste
of your
tear soaked
stones stays
on my tongue
not tied
to palate
my right hand
not withered
holds fast
& remembers
Jerusalem
where men
preen their
prayershawls
like peacocks
as women wail

in labor
birthing
songs
of hope
under a new
moon

Note

1. Hallel is a grouping of psalms that are traditional songs of praise. See Roselyn Bell's chapter, "Hallel: Praises of God."

39
A New Moon/Full Moon Meditation

Judith Rose

We come together at the New Moon
To honor our silent energy
To come out of the needed darkness
The silence of Soul gathering

There is a quiet energy beginning with the New Moon
and rising to the Full which
reflects our capacity as women to
become fully developed beings
There is a   current we share with our Selves and
our daughters
and that current is a circle
And that circle has an inner spiral and an outer curve
And this is a meditation
to balance   the inner voice
with the   outer movement.

40
The New Moon Time: A Love Song for the Shechinah

Rosie Rosenzweig

Let the horns be sounded!
Unveil the dance that sways and soothes
In cadence to a Torah trope.
Tonight we stir old spirits for a new rite;
Tonight we bear witness to the new moon,
That round and perfect crown of mystery.

The tides are quiet now within our soul.
The Shofar sings; it is a moonly melody
That ends all mourning and atonement.
The power that it gives is soft
Like moondust that makes mystics out of astronauts,
Like vowels that lift this song of praise.

Sisters in revivals, we will be what we will be—
A new face, a new hope grown strong
Beyond the valley of the shadows.
Pillar by prayer, brick by benediction,
The temple is rebuilt in us tonight
As we wax and wane with feasts and fasts.

At the first kiss of the Morning Star.
By these Aquarian times, we begin again.

41
Grandmother Moon
(Song with Notation)[1]

Sage Medicine Heart

I am wind I am water
I am mother I am daughter
I am grandmother moon.
I am ebbing I am flowing
I am giving I am glowing
I am grandmother moon.

Look to the night and I'll show you my light
Look to the East for my brightness to rise
Look to your heart and I'll show you my part
Look to the West for the woman inside.

Note

1. Notation found on page 301.

42
HaChodesh Hazeh: Rosh Chodesh Song
(Song with Notation)[1]

Hanna Tiferet Siegel

HaChodesh Hazeh lachem rosh Chadashim
Rishon hu lachem l'chodshey hashanah

I give to you the circle of the seasons 'round the sun
And by the cycles of the moon you'll know which month has come.
You can make time sacred when you measure with care
Tell your stories, sing your songs, and gather close in prayer.

Nisan Iyar Sivan Tamuz Av Elul
Tishrei Cheshvan Kislev Tevet Sh'vat Adar

Note

1. Based on Exodus 12:2. Notation found on page 302.

43

Mooning

Louis Sutker

How I envy your birthing without the ripping, tearing, bleeding, groaning, never again protesting.

Starting as if never quite stopping moving from almost nothing to almost something.

Concealing whiteness in blackness for the searchers waiting.

Intimating come again when good-by saying.

Hinting emergence even while disappearing.

Translating faithfulness as fickleness.

Replacing hope with certainty.

Singing novelty in sameness.

Separating and unifying.

Being.

44
Kiddush Levono: Sanctification of the Moon[1]

Chaim Vital

Let us rejoice, let us rejoice, in the blessings of the moon.
Let us rejoice, let us rejoice, in the blessings of the moon.

In the renewal of the moon, by heart rejoices, and sorrow is struck down in the light of the Shechinah.

Let us rejoice . . .

And the worker of truth, his work is true, and it will be completed in the completion of her building.

Let us rejoice . . .

Be renewed Lady, in elevation of adornment, until the crown of glory, in glory of understanding.

Let us rejoice . . .

From the growing of salvation, the oath is annulled, it is clarified, and declared, in the Supernal city.
Let us rejoice . . .

Renewal of the souls, shall be in the worlds, the names shall be illuminated, from the other side.

Let us rejoice . . .

May the supernal light endure, hidden from thought, from its source above, til its lowest measure.

Let us rejoice . . .

Yisrael trusts in the building of house and riches, Yaakov and Rachel please come with us in song.

Let us rejoice . . .

My queen help me, and forgive me any entanglement, and speedily please return the crown of old.

Let us rejoice . . .

May the face of God fall upon us, please send the redeemer now, gather up Yisrael, the people who are your own.

Let us rejoice . . .

Yah hear our plea, send us favor, Please save us, Please bring us success.

Let us rejoice, Let us rejoice in the blessings of the moon
Let us rejoice, Let us rejoice in the blessings of the moon.

Kiddush Levono[2]

שמחו נא, שמחו נא, בברכת הלבנה:

שמחו נא, שמחו נא, בברכת הלבנה:

חדוש הירח, בו לבי שמה, וצר ננגח באור השכינה

שמחו וכו'.

ופועל האמת, פעולתו אמת, ותהי' נשלמת, בשלימות בנינה:

שמחו וכו'.

תתחדש גברת, בעלוי עטרת, עד כתר תפארת, בתפארת בינה:

שמחו וכו'.

ממצמיח ישועה, התר השבועה, בואר והוודעה, בעיר העליונה:
שמחו וכו'.

הדוש הנשמות, יהי' בעולמות, יאירו השמות, מעבר ופינה:
שמחו וכו'.

ימשך אור עליון, הנעלם מרעיון, ממקור נעליון, עד מדה תחתונה:
שמחו וכו'.

ישראל הוא יחל, בנין בית וחיל, יעקב ורחל, בואו נא ברנה:
שמחו וכו'.

מלכי לי תעזור, ולמחלי שום מזור, וחיש נא תחזור עטרה ליושנה:
שמחו וכו'.

חלו נא פני א-ל, ישלח נא הגואל, יקבץ ישראל, עם זו אשר קנה:
שמחו וכו'.

י-ה שמע תחינה, ישלח נא חנינה, אנא הושיעה נא, אנא הצליחה נא:
שמחו וכו'.

שמחו נא, שמחו נא, בברכת הלבנה:
שמחו נא, שמחו נא, בברכת הלבנה:

Notes

1. A song for Kiddush Levono by Rabbi Chaim Vital *ZT"L* of Damascus, from his book *Seder Mishmeret Erev Rosh Chodesh*.

2. The song prepared by the great kabbalist Reb Chaim Vital, the disciple of the Ari HaKadosh.

(שיר קידוש לבנה לרבינו חיים וויטאל זצוק"ל מדמשק מספר סדר משמרת ערב ראש חודש לרבינו חיים וויטאל זי"ע נדפס בעיה"ק צפת"ו ובליוורנו תרל"ט ברכ"ת טו"ב).

Translated by Yehudah Landesman.

Appendix A
A Visual Diagram
of Rosh Chodesh
Textual Sources

Schema on Rosh Chodesh Sources

Chasidic-Musar

Details what women should and should not do on Rosh Chodesh. They should collect tsedakah and they should not do laundry!
Sefer Hemdat Yamim 23b24a

An anthology of chassidic sources, including S'fat Emet, T'helet Mordechai, and many others offering commentary on Exodus 12:2
Eturei Torah

Women are renewed each month like the moon. *Or Zarua*, "Laws of Rosh Chodesh," 454

Midrash

God transmitted to Moshe the laws on how to calculate the months according to the moon. "Sod Ha-Ibur" in *Batei Midrashot*

Rabbi Yehoshua ben Levi teaches that after the exodus from Egypt, the Israelites were mature enough and able to be entrusted with the reckoning of the months; therefore we count the months from Nissan, the month of the Exodus.
Yalkut Shimoni Bo:190

Queen Esther is likened to the moon, as she brought light unto Israel.
Exodus Rabbah 15:6

The primary midrashic source for understanding Rosh Chodesh as a women's holiday.
Pirke deRabbi Eliezer, ch. 45

Halachic-Liturgical

A reason to announce Rosh Chodesh is to know when the holidays will fall and so women will know when they are exempt from work.
Machzor Vitri p. 173

Discussion of laws "Hilchot Rosh Chodesh" in Orech Chayyim, chapter 2,
Aruch HaShulchan

Offers 14th century charts of intercalation following a chapter on the *molad* (birth of the new moon). Each molad of Rosh Chodesh is based on (and can be calculated from) the first molad at the time of creation.
"Hilchot Rosh Chodesh" *Tur Orech Chaim*

Discusses the Rosh Chodesh Seudah (feast) and the details of the molad (birth) of the new moon.
R. Zeven, *Ha Mo-adim B'Halacha*

A majesterial presentation of the astronomical details of the calendar as well as explanation of how during Sanhedrin period and how to calculate the new moon after the Sanhedrin period.
Rambam, *Michna Torah* 2:8–9

Discusses the order of prayers for Rosh Chodesh, "Seder Rosh Chodesh," *Abudahem HaShalem*

Talmud

Provides details and illustration of the conjunction of sun, moon and earth at Rosh Chodesh
R. Adin Steinsaltz
Talmud Bavli Masechet Rosh HaShanah 24a

On the size of the moon in comparison with the sun
B. Talmud Hullin 60b

Discusses the Festival meal on Rosh Chodesh
Talmud Masechet Sofrim 19:9

Discusses Kiddush Levana, the phsical observation of the new moon.
J. Talmud Brachot 9:2

Outlines blessing of thanksgiving on seeing the new moon. "Whoever blesses the new moon in its time welcomes the presence of Schechinah."
B. Talmud Sanhedrin 42a

Explains why there are four aliyot to the Torah on Rosh Chodesh,
B. Talmud Megillah 22b

Details the witnessing of Kiddush HaChodesh
Mishna Rosh HaShanah 2:6

"It is an acceptable custom for women not to work on the new moon."
J. Talmud Ta-anit 1:6

Tanach

"Hear this . . . when will the new moon be gone, that we may sell corn?" from this comes discussion about working on Rosh Chodesh
Amos 8:4–5

"Then Yonatan said to David, tomorrow is the new moon and you shall be missed . . . so David hid himself in the field and when the new moon came, the King sat down to eat the meal. . . . And it came to pass on the day after, the second day of the new moon, that David's place was still empty." From this we learn of the festive meal. Haftarah for Machar haChodesh (when Rosh Chodesh falls on Saturday night/Sunday)
Samuel I 20:18–42

"And on the day of your rejoicing and in your festive seasons, and at the beginning of your months you shall blow with the trumpets over your burnt offerings."
Numbers 10:10

"This renewal of the moon shall be for you a beginning of new moons; it shall be for you the first among the months of the year.
Exodus 12:2

"Blow a *shofar* at the new moon, at the full moon, and on our feast day."
Psalm 81:4–5

"And appointed the moon for seasons: the sun knows when to go down." from the Psalm for Rosh Chodesh,
Psalm 104:19

"And she said I will go to the man of God. And her husband replied, why will you go to him today? It is neither new moon or Sabbath?" From this we learn about visiting on Rosh Chodesh,
2 Kings 4:22–23

"And at the beginnings of your months, you shall bring near to God a burnt offering."
Numbers 28:11

"Moreover the light of the moon shall be as the light of the sun." In messianic days the moon's light shall be as bright as the sun's light.
Isaiah 30:26

"And it shall come to pass, that every new moon and every Shabbat, that all shall come to bow down before Me." from the Shabbat Rosh Chodesh Haftorah,
Isaiah 66:23

Note: This diagram is intended to provide "tastes" of many, but certainly not all, textual sources on Rosh Chodesh.

Appendix B
A Rosh Chodesh
Ceremony

This ceremony is a weaving together of many strands gathered from ceremonies and rituals that have been created and celebrated over the past several years.[1] The ceremonies highlight the many themes of Rosh Chodesh: the crescent moon, water, light, newness, and renewal.

The intent of this ceremony is to provide a skeleton, a framework for Rosh Chodesh observance. Although it is not my intention to create a formula for observing Rosh Chodesh, this ceremony may serve as a base. It is like a tapestry, a weaving of threads; always open to the adding and deleting of threads. It is my hope that Rosh Chodesh groups will use either parts or the entirety of this skeleton ceremony along with specific songs, poems, texts, and midrashim about particular months and holidays, in creating their own rituals and ceremonies. It reminds me of the metamorphosis of a folksong: always finding itself in a new home with slightly different lyrics. Often it is the process of creating the ritual that is as meaningful as participating in it.

My purpose here is not to create a new ritual. What I hope to provide is an amalgamation and reworking, with some new material, of ceremonies sent to me for this book. For some people, ritual is a way of giving voice to inner feelings, and expressing truth in a symbolic way. "It is not an intellectual experience; and the act of the ritual itself is not important, only the inner truth it is expressing. . . . [We] create new rituals to suit the truths of our times."[2]

There is also the question of the durability of new ritual. Similar to the personal nature of women's *tkhines* (petitional prayers of the sixteenth through nineteenth centuries), Chava Weissler wonders whether new rituals will become dated and perceived as irrelevant over time. "The specific, the particular, the personal prayer or ritual, may, at the moment of its composition, utterance, or performance, be *more* powerful than the scholarly work. But its impact may not be as broad or as durable as that of the religious classics."[3] What we seek is ritual that transcends time. While keeping in mind the nature of some newly formed ritual, we might, however, hope that the purpose it serves for the present, that of providing an emotional and physical environment for ongoing Jewish women's observance, judges it worthy of our collective, creative talents and sustains it in our treasury of women's lore.

It should be noted that none of the traditional components of *tefillah* (prayer), such as the *Barechu* or *Sh'ma*, are incorporated into this observance. The following ceremony is not meant to be a formal prayer service, but rather a ceremony for observing Rosh Chodesh. Groups that prefer to observe Rosh Chodesh through traditional *davening* may find this ceremony less relevant. However, the monthly additions and areas for further study could both enhance and augment the core of any Rosh Chodesh gathering.[4]

The Ceremony

Candle Lighting

(Gathering together around the lighting of candles is a meaningful way of beginning the Rosh Chodesh celebration. It is a familiar act for most women, and yet in this Rosh Chodesh context, it takes on a new spiritual dimension. Candle lighting provides an opportunity to center oneself while focusing the group. Any type of candle or candles may be used. Some women prefer to use a wick floating in oil to symbolize the moon in the sky. Others light a twenty-four hour candle, which would continue to give light in the dark sky after the ceremony concludes.)

> Blessed are You, Merciful One, who makes us holy
> by giving us commandments
> and who gives us the New Moon as a sign
> of eternal beginnings.
> Blessed are You, who guides us to renew ourselves like the moon.[5]

Welcome

(This is a general introduction to Rosh Chodesh and the people present.)

בְּרוּכוֹת הַבָּאוֹת

B'ruchot Ha'ba-ot Welcome to all who gather.

בְּרוּכִים הַבָּאִים

B'ruchim Ha'ba-im [if men are present]

(Go around the room, counterclockwise, as the moon travels, naming each person. This may be done in English, Hebrew, Judesmo, Ladino, Yiddish, or any other language. The matrilineal line may extend as far as each woman is able.)
I am _____ daughter of _____ daughter of
_____ daughter of _____ [and on and on].

Together: We welcome Rosh Chodesh _____ [fill in the month].

We welcome our ancestors, the matriarchs Sarah, Rebecca, Leah, and Rachel.

From the East, we call to our sister Sarah, daughter of Mesopotamia, princess and honored one. Sarah, the first matriarch, joins us from the place where the sun rises, the place to which we Jews turn. Mother of beginnings, join us now as we come together to celebrate the cycles of time and change.

From the West, we call to our sister Rebecca, daughter of the well. Rebecca, woman of tenacity and courage, joins us from the land where the sun sets. Mother of contractions and contradictions, join us now as we come together to celebrate the cycles of time and change.

From the North, we call to our sister Leah, tender-eyed and inward-looking. Leah, who learned to live with less, joins us from the fertile north, the land of green and deep running streams. Mother of patience and fortitude, join us now as we come together to celebrate the cycles of time and change.

From the South, we call to our sister Rachel, whose love was stronger than death. Rachel joins us from the place where heat is intense, the light blinding, the truth searing. Mother of pleasure and pain, join us now as we come together to celebrate the cycles of time and change.[6]

Sing (either both or one of the two following songs may be sung):

Hinei Ma Tov U'Mah Nayim   הִנֵּה מַה טוֹב וּמַה נָעִים
Shevat Kulam Gam Yachad   שֶׁבֶת כֻּלָם גַם יַחַד

How good and pleasant it is for us to all sit together.

Sing:

בְּרוּכוֹת הַבָּאוֹת תַּחַת כַּנְפֵי הַשְּׁכִינָה.
בְּרוּכִים הַבָּאִים תַּחַת כַּנְפֵי הַשְּׁכִינָה

B'ru-chot ha-ba-ot ta-chat kan'fei ha Sh'chi'na
B'ru-chim ha-ba-im ta-chat kan'fei ha-Sh'chi-na

May you be blessed beneath the wings of Sh'chi-na
Be blessed with love, be blessed with peace[7]

Rosh Chodesh

Rosh Chodesh, the "head" of the month, is a special holiday for women. It comes
to us as the moon completes and renews its cycle. As the moon courses through
its cycle each month, we as women move through the personal cycles of our
bodies and our lives. Our days, weeks, and months, indeed our lives, are of a
cyclical nature. And as we observe the crescent moon, we again acknowledge
our own renewal.

Rosh Chodesh is discussed as a holiday for women in the Babylonian Talmud (Megillah 22b). Women were given a day of rest each month from the
labors used in building and adorning the *mishkan* (desert sanctuary). The
midrash reveals that women were honored with this holiday for refusing to
participate in the construction of the Golden Calf. When asked to give up their
jewels, they showed perseverance and faith by refusing to participate in an act
of idolatry. Their reward, Rosh Chodesh, is described in Pirke DeRabbi Eliezer,
chapter 45:

> The women heard about the construction of the Golden Calf and refused
> to submit their jewelry to their husbands. Instead they said to them: "You
> want to construct an idol and mask which is an abomination, and has no
> power of redemption? We won't listen to you." And the Holy One, re-
> warded them in this world in that they would observe the New Moons
> more than men, and in the next world in that they would be renewed like
> the New Moons.

Honoring the Month through Study

(In Jewish tradition, there is a blessing for just about everything. The act of
studying is no exception. This blessing, said before we begin to study, provides a way to sanctify and make holy the simple task before us.)

Chochmot banta veita; חוכמות בנתה ביתה

bo-ou sha'areyha b'todah, hatz'rocteha bit'heela.
באו שעריה בתודה חצרותך בתהילה

Wisdom has built her house;
let us enter her gates with thanks, her courts with praise.[8]

Tonight we welcome the new moon of _____ [add the name of the month].

Each month provides a particular focus for observing Rosh Chodesh. Study, or women's pursuit of knowledge through the exchange of ideas, storytelling, scholarly probing, is an important component of ritual, for it not only builds our knowledge base, but it sparks learning in a collective context. The root of the Hebrew word *Chodesh* is חדש. This root, "ש," "ד," "ח," can be built upon to mean month, or *hadash,* which means new; *mechadesh,* which means to renew; *chadshan,* which is an innovator or inventor; or *chidush,* which means creative interpretation. Each month provides us with the opportunity to be innovative and glean insight from our tradition. Use this opportunity of study to find a *chidush* for the *chodesh.*

(The group may wish to study a text or commentary about Rosh Chodesh, Jewish women, or an upcoming holiday. If the group is more interested in experiential participation, you may want to include an experiential ritual focusing on the qualities inherent in the season. Focus ideas for each of the months are included at the conclusion of this ceremony.)

Meditation on the Month

(A poem, song, or meditation particular to this month may be included here. This could also be used as a time for a silent meditation on the moon's crescent and qualities of renewal.)

Prayer for the New Moon

Just as this new moon creates anew the cycle of the month, so too may it inspire us to create anew ourselves and our faith.

Blessed are You, God, who renews Your people with the moon.
ברוך אתה יהוה מחדש את עמך עם הלבנה
Baruch Atah Adonai, M'Chadesh et Amcha Eem HaLevana.

Sing

(While "beholding the beginning," let's sing a song to the new month.
Choose a Rosh Chodesh song from this anthology.)

Memory

(As in many Jewish observances, there is a time to recall and pay tribute to the women who are no longer with us. Some of these women we may know personally, some we have read about. Some have shaped our lives in ways we can only imagine. Now let us recall the lives of women whose *yahrzeit* (the anniversary of a death) dates fall this month.)

Kiddush

(A kiddush, the sanctification of wine, is said. After the blessing, the wine goblet is passed around the circle moonwise, counterclockwise).

Salutations

Chodesh Tov! A good month, a month of health, peace, and fulfillment.

Refreshments

Refreshments for a Rosh Chodesh gathering might include:

Crescent shaped rolls, cookies, or rogelach
Moon cookies–a flat cookie with dark and light icing like a yin/yang symbol
Moon cakes–eaten to celebrate lunar festivals in China–sesame seeds, chopped
    dates, and almonds baked in a sweetened filo dough.
White, round meringues filled with crescent-sliced fruit.

Notes

1. In amalgamating many ceremonies into one, I must acknowledge specifically a few of the people who sent me their ceremonies for this sourcebook. I would like to thank Rabbi Sue Levi Elwell, then of the American Jewish Congress Feminist Center. The center has been organizing Rosh Chodesh celebrations each month for the past several years. Individuals, along with the guidance of the center staff, have created many programs based on original material. The center was very generous in providing me with not only the material but a license to recreate with that material. I would also like to mention Henny Wenkart of the Jewish Women's Resource Center of the National Council of Women, New York chapter, for her interest and support. The JWRC also holds monthly Rosh Chodesh meetings and shared ritual material from their archives. I would also like to acknowledge Sorel Goldberg Loeb and Maxine Fraade of the Monroe, New York, Rosh Chodesh group, for the ceremonies they created for Kislev

and Adar. Their research into tradition and experimentation with the innovative set a perfect backdrop for creating ritual. Penina Adelman's book on Rosh Chodesh ritual, *Miriam's Well: Rituals for Jewish Women Around the Year*, remains an important resource for anyone interested in the experiential observance of Rosh Chodesh.

2. Maxine Fraade letter to Susan Berrin March 10, 1994.

3. Weissler, Chava. "The Tkhines and Women's Prayer" *CCAR Journal*, Fall, 1993 page 84.

4. When using any material, please acknowledge the proper sources. A great deal of the ceremonial material I received was unusable because it lacked any author documentation. In an effort to put together monthly observances, many groups have "cut and pasted" from various sources without including proper references. Unfortunately the authors of these pieces, the women whose inspirations have created these poems, stories, or reflections, then become lost.

5. Used with permission from Rabbi Diane Cohen.

6. Developed by and used with permission from the American Jewish Congress Feminist Center (AJCFC).

7. Used with permission, Debbie Friedman. Audiocassette available from SoundsWrite.

8. Copyright © Rabbi Sue Levi Elwell. Used with permission from the AJCFC.

Appendix C
Focal Points
for Each Month

The following is a resource for programming each month's Rosh Chodesh gathering. A very brief and cursory background is provided for each month. This includes material about the month in general, holidays observed during the month, programming ideas based on themes of the season or themes inherent in the month and the astrological constellation for each month. These focal points are in no way exhaustive of the program ideas available for each month.

Yahrzeit dates for well and less-well known women are also included.[1] You may want to add the names and yahrzeit dates of friends, family, and members of your community who have died. The remembrance of these women could be included in the "Memory" section of the ceremony, or before Kaddish is recited, if observing Rosh Chodesh through a formal prayer service.

These resource materials may be incorporated into any monthly Rosh Chodesh ceremony. Additional creative writing for the various months is included in the section of the Anthology, entitled "Poetry, Prayers, Songs, and Meditations."

Nisan

The *mazal*, or constellation, for Nisan is a lamb. It reminds us of the Pesach lamb, which is symbolized at the Seder by either a shankbone or a roasted beet.

Nisan is the first month of the months. We count the months of the Jewish year beginning with Nisan. It is in reference to Nisan that God announces Rosh Chodesh in Exodus 12:2

"This renewal of the moon shall be for you a beginning of new moons; it shall be for you the first among the months of the year."[2]

החודש הזה לכם ראש חדשים ראשון הוא לכם לחדשי השנה

God chose Nisan as the first of the months, because it was the first new moon after liberation from Egypt. Counting the months from Nisan also reminds us continually of our redemption. It is said that Rosh Chodesh Nisan wears ten crowns, for ten wonderful things happened on that day.[3]

In the northern hemisphere, Nisan comes during the spring. Pesach begins on the full moon of Nisan. But before the Pesach Seder, we ready ourselves for the journey to freedom. It is a time to dust out the closets, search for the *chametz*, the crumbs of leavened food, not only in the house and car, but also within ourselves. What is the *chametz* we carry within our minds and bodies? How do we journey towards freedom? What are our contemporary narrow places (Egypt, Mitzra-im means a narrow place) and how do we gain our freedom? What are we doing for people who are still, today, not free?

There are several important women to remember during the month of Nisan. Miriam, the Prophetess, the keeper of the well of water, sister to Moshe and Aharon, died on the tenth of Nisan. When she died, the well disappeared. Yocheved was the mother of Miriam, Moshe, and Aharon.

Arthur Waskow writes about

the experience of childbirth as a guide to freedom. First there are the midwives—who are the first to resist Pharaoh's decree that all the Israelite newborn boys be murdered. They obey God, not Pharaoh—even though they have never heard God's voice. They do not need to hear the Voice, because they hear it in the cry of each new baby. . . . From giving birth to children, they learn to give birth to freedom. For the newborn carries at the biological level the same message that freedom carries at the historical-political level: it is possible to start over. It is possible for there to be possibility.[4]

Shifra and Pu-ah are the names of the two Egyptian midwives who helped deliver Hebrew babies. Exodus 1:15–20 tells the stories of these heroic women. Study the following passage as many would study texts in Jewish tradition; through the פרדס *PARDES* (orchard). *PARDES* is an acronym for four ways to study and delve into Jewish texts.

פ *P'shat*—the simple way of reading a story—what is written in the text.
ר *Remez*—reading to understand the hinted meaning of the story—what is the story inside of the story, the spaces between the words.
ד *Drash*—pursuing a homiletical meaning from the story—finding connections and patterns within the story.
ס *Sod*—searching for the secret, mystical meaning from the story—understanding the soul of the story, the concealed wisdom and truth.

And the King of Mitzrayim spoke to the Hebrew midwives, of whom the name of one was Shifrah and the name of the other Puah. And he said: "Whenever you deliver Hebrew women, observe the laboring womb: If it is a son, you shall kill him; if it is a daughter, she may live." But the midwives feared God and did not do as the King of Mitzrayim had commanded them, but they kept the male children alive. And the King called for the midwives and said to them: "Why have you done this thing? To have kept the male children alive!" The midwives replied to Pharaoh; "Because the Hebrew women are not like the Egyptian women; they are lively, and they give birth even before the midwife can come to them. And God dealt well with the midwives, and the people multiplied and became exceedingly strong."[5]

ויאמר מלך מצרים למילדת העברית אשר שם האחת שפרה ושם השנית פועה:

ויאמר בילדכן את-העברית וראיתן על-האבנים אם-בן הוא והמתן אתו

ואם-בת הוא וחיה; ותיראן המילדת את-האלהים ולא עשו כאשר דבר

אליהן מלך מצרים ותחיין את-הילדים: ויקרא מלך-מצרים למילדת

ויאמר להן מדוע עשיתן הדבר הזה ותחיין את-הילדים: ותאמרן המילדת אל-פרעה

כי לא כנשים המצרית העברית כי-חיות הנה בטרם תבוא אלהן המילדת

וילדו; וייטב אלהים למילדת וירב העם ויעצמו מאד;

What do the women of the Pesach story teach us about strength, conscience, perseverance? We are told at the Seder to view the exodus from Egypt as though we personally were being liberated. Pesach is the story of liberation, both personally and as a people. What are we doing to help in the liberation of oppressed people? Who are the women today fighting in large and small ways against oppression?

Shir HaShirim, the "Song of Songs," is traditionally chanted on the Shabbat of Pesach. It is the story of love between God and the People, and between man and woman. What are the songs of love that we would write as women to God? What are the songs we would write to our love?

Women's Yahrzeits:

Sarah Bernhardt—9th of Nisan (1845–1923), a French dramatic actress.

Miriam the Prophetess—10th of Nisan

Sadie American—11th of Nisan (1862–1944), the founder of the National Council of Jewish Women and an outspoken social activist.

Rachel Blaustein—29th of Nisan (1840–1931), an early *chalutza* (pioneer) in Palestine and a gifted poet.

Belle Latchman—30th of Nisan (1916–1981) grew up in Toronto and moved to live and work in Phoenix, Arizona, as a wholesale produce broker. She served actively for many years as a leader in the Jewish community and a role model for women both in her voluntary communal work and her business. She had no children but left a legacy of strong spirit and determination to her many nieces and nephews.

Yom HaShoah (Holocaust Memorial Day) is the 26th of Nisan.

Iyar

The *mazal*, or constellation, for Iyar is an ox. The entire month of Iyar is within the journey from Pesach toward Shavuot. It is the month of the Omer. For forty-nine days, beginning on the second night of Pesach until Shavuot, we count the Omer. The Omer calendar, created by the kabbalists, is a calendar of seven weeks of seven days. Each week is associated with one of the *sefirot*, as is each day (Sunday, Monday, etc.). As we go through the forty-nine days, we ready ourselves for receiving the Torah by going through the forty-nine combinations of the sephirotic attributes. Lag B'Omer, the thirty-third day in the counting of the Omer, is on the 18th of Iyar. Lag B'Omer is a day for festivities, picnics, bonfires, and hair cutting, all of the activities forbidden during the Omer counting.

Two recent monumental events are also celebrated during Iyar. On the 5th of Iyar, 5708, the State of Israel was declared. Yom HaAtzma-ut is celebrated each year on Iyar 5. On the 28th of Iyar, 5727, during the six-day war, the Kotel, the Western Wall, came again into Jewish possession. The Prophet Ezekiel's vision of the "valley of the dry bones" is thematically connected to Yom HaAtzma-ut because it tells of life being breathed into dry bones by the four winds, bone to bone, sinew and flesh, and returning to Eretz Yisrael, the Land of Israel (Ezekiel 37:1–14).

Sometimes we are "bone weary"—so overscheduled, overcommitted, tired, worn, and unglued—our body is like a heap of dry bones. How can we use the four winds to blow new breath into our lungs? *Imagine* the *Shechinah* breathing strength into you, breath by slow breath.

This may also be an opportune gathering to learn about women who have helped shaped the modern state of Israel. A few possibilities include:

Golda Meir, who became the Prime Minister of Israel.
Rachel Blaustein, poet of the second aliyah period, buried at Kibbutz Kinneret cemetery.
Naomi Shemer, songwriter, who has composed many of the well known Israeli folk songs.
Shulamit Aloni, member of Knesset and champion of women's rights in Israel.
Leah Shakdiel, activist on behalf of religious women in Israel and the first woman in Israel to sit on a religious council.
Alice Shalvi, founder and director of the Israel Women's Network, and an outspoken supporter of changing the status of the *agunah* (a woman tied to an untenable marriage and unable to obtain a religious divorce).
The Women of the Wall, who are trying to gain equal access to Israel's most significant national religious symbol, the Kotel.

It is a time to sing old folksongs of Israel, and new melodies. To sing of the Land of Milk and Honey, "Eretz Zavat Chalav u'Dvash." To hope for a Land filled with peace. What would some of these women say to us. Think about the possibilities of what might be included in "Sayings of the Mothers." Write one or several verses, meditations, or parables that could be collected into the "Pirke Imahot," "Sayings of the Mothers."

Women's Yahrzeits:
Nellie Sachs—6th of Iyar (1891–1970)—was German-born and a poet who wrote passionately about the Holocaust. She received the 1966 Nobel Prize for Literature.
Louise Weiss—24th of Iyar (1894–1984), a French pacifist and feminist active in the women's suffrage movement.

Sivan

The *mazal*, or constellation, for Sivan is twins. Sivan is known as the month in which we became a People. We received the Torah at *Har Sinai* (Mount Sinai) on the sixth of Sivan, Shavuot, Z'man Matan Torateinu (the Season of the Giving of our Torah). According to *midrash* (legend), everyone at Mount Sinai heard the giving of the Torah according to who they were and their strength. God's voice split into seventy voices and seventy languages in order that all of the nations would understand.[6] Even the unborn generations heard. The act of hearing and receiving the Torah should not be underestimated. As in any relationship, giving is only validated by the receiving; speaking is only worthwhile if it is being heard. Though God gave the Torah, we are active participants in its receiving, understanding, and interpretation.

Shavuot is also known as Chag Hakatzir, the spring harvest; Chag HaBikurim, the holiday of first fruit offering; and Chag HaAtzeret, referring to the conclusion of Pesach with the assembly at Har Sinai.

Shavuot, like Sukkot and Pesach, is one of the *shalosh regalim*, three pilgrimage festivals mentioned in the Torah. At Shavuot, the people would come from all over the Land of Israel to bring their first fruits to the Temple. Today, as the dawn begins to break, people again make their way to the Kotel, the last remnant of the Temple, to pray. After a full night of study (it is a custom to stay up all night studying on the eve of Shavuot), as light begins to break the sky, we wind our way up the rocky paths towards the Old City on the way to the Kotel. The *Tikkun Leil Shavuot,* the all-night study on Shavuot, is a time to recommit ourselves to the ongoing process of learning, seeking, questioning.

The story of friendship is integral to Shavuot. "Megillat Ruth," the story of Ruth and Naomi is chanted or read. It speaks of the love and devotion between Ruth and her mother-in-law, Naomi. Sivan is a time to rededicate ourselves to others, to the deep bonds of friendship that sustain us.

Bring stories and poems of women's friendships to share.

Adrienne Rich wrote a wonderful poem describing the deep friendship between two painters. The poem reads as a letter from Paula Becker to Clara Westhoff. It ends:

"Clara, I feel so full
of work, the life I see ahead, and love
for you, who of all people
however badly I say this
will hear all I say and cannot say."[7]

How do we nurture friendships, and what are the struggles to maintain them? What are the obstacles to developing friendships among women, and how do we overcome these obstacles? How does the relationship between daughter and mother or mother-in-law develop so that it is based on trust, honesty, and love?

Shavuot is the time of receiving the Torah. How do we hear the Torah in our own lives? What are the verses that ring in our ears? Which stories feed our souls?

Women's Yahrzeits:

Fanny Brice—6th of Sivan (1891–1951), a Zigfield follies dancer and singer. She was known as "Baby Shnooks."

Tammuz

The *mazal*, or constellation, for Tammuz is the crab. The seventeenth of Tammuz is a day with many meanings in our history.

It is told that Noach sent out a dove on that day to see if the flood waters had receded, if the mountain peaks were visible. It is a day on which we renew our covenant to protect God's world.

The seventeenth of Tammuz is also the day Moshe returned from the Mountain with the *luchot habrit*, the stone tablets with the ten commandments. As he approached the camp, he found the people dancing around a Golden Calf that they had erected when they lost faith in Moshe's return. In anger and despair, Moshe threw the tablets to the ground, shattering them to bits.

Later in our history (70 C.E.), the seventeenth of Tammuz was a day of destruction, when the Romans broke through the walls of Jerusalem and began their siege of the city.

These three events raise the themes of abandonment and commitment. Noach saw the rainbow as a covenant with God, that God's people would not be abandoned. After Moshe's departure for Mount Sinai, the people felt abandoned, confused, scared. And upon his return, he felt abandoned by the people, angry, hurt. As the Romans approached, the Jews of Jerusalem fought to not abandon their holy city. Then and now, we recommit ourselves through song, Seder, and prayer to never forget Jerusalem. Each of these experiences of abandonment was followed by a recommitment of faith.

The 17th of Tammuz is a semifast day: one fasts only from sunrise to sunset. All other prohibitions regularly found on full fast days are not enforced.

The group may wish to do a textual study of the Prophet Ezekiel Chapter 36 verses 24 through 28. (This is part of the Haftarah reading for Shabbat Parah, one of the four special Shabbatot leading up to Pesach.) These verses discuss moral purification and spiritual renewal, specifically related to the Golden Calf incident.

For I will take you from among the nations, and gather you out of all the countries, and I will bring you into your own land. And I will sprinkle clean water upon you, and you shall be clean; from all your uncleanness and from all your idols, will I clean you. A new heart also will I give you, and a new spirit will I put within you; and I will take away the stony heart out of your flesh, and I will give you a heart of flesh. And I will put My spirit within you, and cause you to walk in My statutes, and you shall keep My ordinances. And you shall dwell in the land that I gave your ancestors; and you shall be my people and I shall be your God.

ולקחתי אתכם מן-הגוים וקבצתי אתכם מכל-הארצות והבאתי אתכם
אל-אדמתכם: וזרקתי עליכם מים טהורים וטהרתם מכל טמאותיכם
ומכל-גלוליכם אטהר אתכם; ונתתי לכם לב חדש ורוח חדשה אתן בקרבכם
והסרתי את-לב האבן מבשרכם חנתתי לכם לב בשר: ואת-רוחי אתן
בקרבכם ועשיתי את אשר-בחקי תלכו ומשפטי תשמרו ועשיתם;
וישבתם בארץ אשר נתתי לאבתיכם והייתם לי לעם ואנכי אהיה לכם לאלהים:

Various commentaries on these verses may be read and discussed, as well as considering the feelings of being sprinkled with clean water and having our hearts refreshed and warmed.

During the month of Tammuz (Parashat Pinchas Numbers 27:1–7), we read about the daughters of Tzelophchad. Tzelophchad had five daughters, Machla, Noa, Chogla, Milka, and Tirtza. He had no sons. When he died, his daughters petitioned Moshe for the right to inherit from their father. They said: "Let not our father's name be lost to his clan just because he had no son. Give us a holding among our father's kinsmen." Moshe brought the case before God and reported back that God said, "The plea of Tzelophchad's daughters is just: You should give them a hereditary holding among their father's kinsmen; transfer their father's share to them." And so set the precedent for women to inherit. These daughters had the courage to speak up and challenge the governing system of inheritance. How do we as Jewish women continue to enrich our communities by questioning authority and advocating just causes?

Learn more about these and lesser known biblical women. Discuss questions of inheritance, both material inheritance and ethical and moral inheritance. Who do we inherit from? How do we use our inheritances? How does our name reflect our inheritance?

Women's Yahrzeits:

Zivia Lubetkin—7th of Tammuz (1914–1978), a member of the Warsaw Ghetto resistance and a founder of Kibbutz Lochamei HaGhetta-ot.

Chaya Ehrenreich—11th of Tammuz (1887–1980), a founding member of Pioneer Women, a labor Zionist organization.

Gertrude Stein—28th of Tammuz (1874–1946), poet, author, critic, and patron of the arts who left the United States for Paris in 1902 and established a salon for art and literature with Alice B. Toklas.

Av

The constellation, or *mazal*, for Av is the lion. When announcing the new moon of Av, we call it Menachem Av, Comforting Av. Av necessitates comfort.

Tisha B'Av, the 9th of Av, is a full fast marking the destruction of both Temples and periods of tragedy in our history. For many Holocaust survivors who have no exact dates to observe the deaths of their family, Tisha B'Av becomes a *yahrzeit* (anniversary of a death) for their family members. Av becomes a time to look at catastrophic destruction, both historically and in our own times. It is a time of collective mourning. It is a time to connect, from a sense of deep mourning, with the tragedies of human destruction.

The Shabbat after Tisha B'Av is Shabbat Nachamu, the Sabbath of Comfort (the Haftarah is Isaiah 40:1–26 and begins, "Nachamu Nachamu Ami," "Comfort, comfort, My people"). Shabbat Nachamu begins seven weeks of consolation, moving us from Tisha B'Av toward the Days of Awe.

Rabbi Vicki Hollander writes:[8]

Av beckons
  Let the tears arise
  for they water
  the garden.
  They prepare the ground
  to receive the seeds.

And from loss we look forward, toward what we have and may grow into. We sing Hashiveinu from Megillat Eicha, the Book of Lamentations, which is read on Tisha B'Av. The song speaks of renewal and return.

Hashiveinu Adonai eilecha V'nashuva
Chadesh, chadesh yameinu k'kedem.

השיבנו יהוה אליך ונשובה חדש ימינו כקדם

The great cycle of the Jewish year is a model, a metaphor, of the great cycle of life—and of the life of the Jewish people. Over and over, we move from birth to maturity to fulfillment, to what seems to be a death—but is really the seed of a new birth, a new life. . . . Tisha B'Av can teach us how to make a new beginning. . . . From the darkness of our mourning comes the night vision, the dream welling up from our unconscious, of new life. From the blankness, empty white space that surrounds the letters of the Torah, from the fluidity and openness, comes new direction. It is not empty blankness, but white fire around the black fire of the letters.[9]

In the Northern Hemisphere, Av comes during the hottest time of the year. How would you correlate each of the four seasons with each of the moon's phases?

Why? How would you describe yourself, in terms of the qualities and moods of a season? How does your body cycle correlate with the moods of the seasons and the phases of the moon?

Women's Yahrzeits:

Rebecca Kohut—8th of Av (1864–1951), a social worker, educator, and philanthropist. She was the president of the World Council of Jewish Women.

Ernestine Potovsky Rose—10th of Av (1810–1892), feminist and antislave activist.

Adah Isaacs Menken—21st of Av (1835–1868), a leader of the 1857 protest against exclusion of Jews from Britain's House of Commons. She was a dancer and appeared in flesh-colored leotard and tights on stage, becoming known as the "naked lady."

Lillian Wald—28th of Av (1867–1940), a pioneer in the fields of social work and public health.

Elul

The constellation, or *mazal*, for Elul is the young child. Elul is the time of preparation before the Days of Awe. On Rosh Chodesh Elul, the shofar is blown for the first time in the season. It is blown each morning of Elul (except Shabbat) until the day before Rosh HaShanah. The trumpeting blast reminds us to awaken ourselves fully and to begin t'shuvah, the turning toward each other and God in anticipation of Rosh HaShanah and Yom Kippur. It is a time to begin to ask for forgiveness.

ELUL אלול, the Hebrew letters that make up this month, are an acronym for the verse from "Song of Songs," "Ani L'Dodi V'Dodi Li":

אני לדודי ודודי לי

I am my beloved's and my beloved is mine. At a time when we are turning towards each other and towards God, at a time of asking forgiveness, it is heartwarming to know that we are loved and can love.

The story of Joseph in Egypt with his brothers is one of the classic tales of t'shuvah. Read the story, beginning with the brothers' second visit to Egypt, chapter 44:20–45:5.

Over the past year, how have we wronged another person?

How have we wronged ourselves?

What are we not yet able to let go of?

To whom do we need to ask forgiveness?

How do we ask forgiveness from ourselves?
What do we ask as a new year blessing for our community?
What do we ask as a new year blessing for ourselves?[10]

Prepare for the New Year by learning to blow the shofar or sending out Shana Tova cards. *Slichot* is the midnight, penitential service on the Saturday evening prior to Rosh Hashanah. Attend or create such a service.

Women's Yahrzeits:
Dorothy Jacobs Bellanca—18th of Elul (1894–1946), a union organizer who founded the American Labor Party.
Rebecca Gratz—19th of Elul (1781–1869), who founded in Philadelphia the Female Hebrew Benevolent Society, the first nonsynagogue Jewish women's organization in the United States.
Lena Himmelstein—26th of Elul (1881–1951), who founded the Lane Bryant retail dress stores specializing in "in-between" sizes. She came upon this idea when designing maternity clothes.
Frieda Warburg—28th of Elul (1876–1958), a philanthropist whose donated home became the Jewish Museum in New York.

Tishrei

The constellation, or *mazal*, for Tishrei is a pair of scales, symbolizing God's judgment of individuals and the world during the High Holy Days. Tishrei is not observed traditionally as Rosh Chodesh. Because Rosh HaShanah, the birthday of the world, falls on the first of Tishrei, observing the New Year takes precedence. Tishrei is a month of beginnings. The new moon of Tishrei is celebrated as the birthday of the world. It is the month that marks the beginning of a new year. It is a time in which we need strength (to get through all of the holidays, especially Yom Kippur, which entails a full day fast) and a time when our strength, especially our spiritual strength, is renewed.

A Rosh Chodesh group may choose to observe Rosh HaShanah together or meet for *tashlich* during the afternoon. *Tashlich* is a short service where we rid ourselves of the year's bad feelings and doings. We meet at a source of water (ocean, river, etc.) and throw crumbs of bread into the water as we recall moments and deeds during the year for which we seek forgiveness. Water songs and dances (such as "U'Shavtem Mayim," "Down by the Riverside,") may culminate this observance.

Another wonderful custom is to gather on Sukkot, which falls on Tishrei's full moon. Meet outdoors in a *sukkah* and ask each woman present to invite (metaphorically) a beloved woman or mentor into the *sukkah*. These guests, known as *Ushpizin*, can be drawn from one's personal history or from our collective Jewish sources. Share the stories of these "invited guests" with the group and the reasons for choosing these *Ushpizin*. Sukkot, the fall harvest, is a time to contemplate our own personal harvest. The *sukkah* is an open and fragile dwelling place. It reminds us of the fragility of our earth home and bids us to open ourselves towards the four directions in which we shake the *lulav*, symbol of Sukkot.

There are four holy days in Tishrei, which correspond to the four phases of the moon.[11] These are: Rosh HaShanah, which is the new moon of Tishrei; Yom Kippur, which falls on the tenth of the month, as the moon swells; Sukkot, which is on the full moon; and Shmini Atzeret, which falls on the twenty-second of Tishrei when the moon is waning.

As Tishrei is the beginning of the new year, *imagine* taking out a road map of life—draw one if you can. Reflecting on last year, name the mountain peaks and valleys, the rivers, bridges, and canyons. For this approaching year, what new directions shall you take? Where might you be going and what motivates you to get there? Where will you travel in your heart and where by foot?

Women's Yahrzeits:

Sarah Aaronsohn—9th of Tishrei (1890–1917), who worked with Nezah Yisrael Lo Yeshakker (NILI), an underground Jewish group in prestate Israel. She was captured, arrested, and tortured by the Turks. She killed herself without disclosing any of the secrets of the NILI.

Cheshvan

The *mazal*, or constellation, for Cheshvan is the scorpion. Cheshvan is often referred to as Mar Cheshvan, bitter Cheshvan, because the month contains no holidays. It is a month that brings quiet after the important holidays of Tishrei. Stay awhile in the empty place that Cheshvan creates. The *Shechinah* is as much in the empty spaces as in the full ones; residing in the pauses between words as much as in the words themselves. If Yaakov was surprised to find God in the place where he slept (Genesis 28:16, "And God was in this place and I did not know"), we, too, may be surprised with what we find when we let ourselves be open to the unknown quiet.

Our foremother Rachel died on the 11th of Cheshvan, so it would be relevant to study her life and the gifts she offered. She is buried in Kever Rachel, a tomb just outside of Bethlehem. It is customary for women to pray at her tomb, especially prayers related to fertility and childbearing (she died during the birth of her son Benjamin).

Rachel and her sister Leah were both wed to Yaakov. The story of their
relationship to each other and to Yaakov provides a fascinating backdrop for
questions about betrayal, family loyalty, envy, and resourcefulness. Read Genesis, chapters 29 and 30, about the lives of these ancestors; then discuss the
tangled web of emotion prevalent in many families.

In the Northern Hemisphere, Cheshvan begins to bring the winter's cold.
We, like the scorpion who burrows into the earth, begin to turn inward, going
back to our origins. This may be a time to work on a family genealogy, a time
to rediscover family legacies. Share stories of outrageous and ordinary women
in your family.

Women's Yahrzeits:
Rachel—11th of Cheshvan, our matriarch.
Emma Lazarus—19th of Cheshvan (1849–1887), a poet, whose sonnet en-
    graved on the Statue of Liberty welcomes new immigrants to the United
    States.
Hannah Senesh—20th of Cheshvan (1921–1944), a Hungarian who made
    aliyah to what was then Palestine and was captured and executed while try-
    ing to aid Hungarian Jews in Nazi Europe. Her poetry and stories are col-
    lected in several books.
Anzia Yezierska—22nd of Cheshvan (1883–1970), a novelist and short story
    writer who wrote descriptively about life for immigrants on the Lower East
    Side of New York.
Rachel Yanit Ben-Tzvi—24th of Cheshvan (1886–1979), the founder of Israel's
    women's labor movement and the wife of Israel's second president, Yitzchak
    Ben-Tzvi.

Kislev

The *mazal,* or constellation, for Kislev is the arching bow, to remind us of the
rainbow and our responsibility to be guardians over the earth. Chanukah begins
on the 25th of Kislev, making the themes of Chanukah relevant to this month.
(Rosh Chodesh Tevet also falls during Chanukah, so some groups prefer to
save Chanukah themes for Tevet.)

The following ritual, which concludes with the paragraph "Tzur Yisrael,"
was written by Sorel Loeb Goldberg for her Rosh Chodesh group. The ritual
recalls biblical heroines, both familiar and less known. Sorel suggests standing around a *chanukiyah* (Chanukah menorah) while naming these Jewish
women. The ritual might be followed by a study discussion focusing on these
or other Jewish heroines.

KISLEV

Darkest month.
Brief days, frosty nights
illumined by the warm glow of candles,
the lights of Chanukah which pierce the darkness
and raise our hearts in pride.
A season to celebrate heroes,
the triumph of hope over despair,
the holy over the mundane,
and the rededication of the spirit.

Not the Macabees alone will we recall on these days of glory,
But the women of our people who themselves illumined lives,
pierced barriers,
and raised the banner of our people.
Their voices shout softly to us across the ages,
Their words mere echoes,
their dances mere shadows among the tales we tell.

Can we be still enough to hear their melodies?
Can we seek deep enough to learn their refrain?

As the smallest flame kindled in the gloom
Can brighten dismal corners,
So the recollection of our mothers
May spark our waking dreams.

As we warm ourselves
in the flickering glow of the Chanukah lights,
Let us dedicate ourselves to reclaiming their stories
and linking them to our own.
Let us light these flames to honor their names,
As we bless ourselves by their memory.

As we greet the chill and dark winter,
We light eight candles to recall our mothers and teachers.
Can we be still enough to hear their melodies?
Can we seek deep enough to learn their refrain?

(Use the *shamash* (helper candle) to light one candle at a time, as you read
the numbered sections.)

1. For our nameless sisters
   known to us only through those
   they birthed or helped to safety,
   or those they cursed in silent rage:
   THE MOTHER OF SAMSON, THE DAUGHTER OF JEPHTAH,
   AND SHE WHO GAVE AID TO ELIJAH
   May we wear our own names with pride,
   As we bless ourselves by their memory.
2. For the strangers among us
   who gave refuge to our people,
   and built up our house
   through noble deeds:
   THE EGYPTIAN MIDWIVES, AND RAHAB OF JERICHO,
   AND YAEL WHO BROUGHT SISERA LOW.
   May we seek and find goodness among all our sisters,
   As we bless ourselves by their memory.
3. For those who bore children
   and gave them proud names,
   who helped them grow deep roots
   and sprout soaring wings:
   SARAH, RACHEL, AND LEAH,
   YOCHEVED AND CHANA.
   May we nurture and support the growth of those we love,
   As we bless ourselves by their memory.
4. For those who were loyal
   and those men despised,
   and those who brought righteous complaint:
   RUTH AND NAOMI, THE DAUGHTERS OF TZELAPHCHAD,
   GOMER THE WHORE, AND THE WITCH OF ENDOR.
   May we never feel shame when we speak our own truths,
   As we bless ourselves by their memory.
5. For those who counseled goodness
   and stood boldly for justice:
   ABIGAIL—INSTRUCTOR, RIZPAH—REBUKER,
   AND THE WISE WOMAN OF TEKOAH—ADVISOR,
   Three who insisted on mercy and prevailed against kings.
   May we be righteous and noble and wise in our judgments,
   As we bless ourselves by their memory.
6. For those who chose action
   to safeguard our future:

REBECCA, TAMAR, AND TZIPORAH,
BATHSHEBA AND ESTHER.
May we actively build for the world of the future,
As we bless ourselves by their memory.
7. For those who sang hymns
   to the Source of Being,
   and those who sought meaning at the Well of Life:
   MIRIAM, DEBORAH, AND HULDAH,
   PROPHETESSES ALL.
   May our lives be songs of praise and dances of joy,
   As we bless ourselves by their memory.
8. For the heroes and teachers each names for herself:
   The mothers who held us,
   the sisters who shared,
   the ones on whose shoulders we stand.
   May we learn from their lives
   and partake of their wisdom and strength,
   As we bless ourselves by their memory.

   Rock of our being, TZUR YISRAEL,
   Source and Sustainer of Life,
   Bless us this season with health of body and spirit,
   With the warmth of love and the lessons of memory.
   Help us be still enough to hear Your melody.
   Help us seek deep enough to learn Your refrain.
   May our hands never falter,
   and our sight never fail,
   as we weave our lives into blessings
   for our loved ones, our people and the world.
   And let us say AMEN.

During the talmudic period, the houses of Hillel and Shammai argued about
how to light the Chanukah candles. Shammai urged that we begin with lighting all eight candles and reduce one candle per night. Hillel argued that we
begin with one candle and move toward more light with more flames, increasing rather than diminishing holiness. Hillel's argument was accepted, and each
night we add another candle to the menorah. We light the newest candle first
and then light from left to right.
    Each of us has an internal flame. May it grow strong and illumine our
thoughts and actions as we move from darkness into light.

Women's Yahrzeits:

Rose Pesotta—12th of Kislev (1896–1965)—and Fannia May Cohn—26th of
Kislev (1885–1962)—both were union organizers among immigrant fac-
tory workers and became vice-presidents of the International Ladies Garment Workers Union.

Sonia Terk Delaunay—15th of Kislev (1885–1979), a Russian-born, French
painter who worked in textile and costume design.

Selma Fraiberg—23rd of Kislev (1918–1981), a psychoanalyst who wrote
widely on child development, including the book, *The Magic Years*.

Tevet

The *mazal*, or constellation, for Tevet is a goat. The tenth of Tevet is a fast day
to remember the attack by the Babylonian King Nebuchadnetzar on Jerusalem. In the Northern Hemisphere, Tevet is a cold, winter month when the days
are short and darkness comes early.

Rosh Chodesh Tevet falls on the sixth or seventh night of Chanukah. (This
depends on the year. See "The Days of the Hebrew Months" for a fuller explanation. Also see Matia Angelou's poem "New Moon for the Daughters," in
this anthology, which incorporates the themes of this holiday into the lighting
of the Chanukah menorah.)

Rabbi Vicki Hollander reflects:

Tevet lies like a blanket upon the earth.
If you look closely you can see her
rise and fall with earth's barely noticeable sleepy breath.

Tevet teaches that,
just as one learns to see at night,
    waits while our eyes empty
    of light, and then adjusts,
only then we can see that which cannot be seen
    at the very first.
Only then can one find one's way through darkness.
Only through the creation of empty spaces
can room be made to receive the new.

This month, with the long dark evenings, is a time to reflect on darkness
and light. What are the dark and light moments in our lives and how do we use
each of them as holy moments of growth? There are two types of exile—spiritual and geographic. How do they intersect with each other? Write a letter to
God describing your exile.

Women's Yahrzeits:

Lina Morgenstern—3rd of Tevet (1830–1909), a German feminist, writer, and peace activist who called for the first International Women's Congress in Berlin in 1896.

Sara Herzog—15th of Tevet (1897–1979), a social welfare advocate and president of Israel's National Women's Religious Organization.

Lily Montague—25th of Tevet (1873–1963), the founder of both the Liberal movement in England and the World Union of Progressive Judaism. She was also the spiritual leader of the West Central Liberal Jewish Congregation in London.

Sh'vat

The *mazal*, or sign, for Sh'vat is a vessel filled with water. Water is a thematic symbol for this month. The Hebrew letter *mem* is the first letter of the word *mayim*, which means water, and *mikvah*, which is the water in which we ritually immerse ourselves. *Mem* is also the first letter in the name Miriam, who was the keeper of water during the desert wandering. A mysterious well followed her throughout her years in the desert. *Mem* has the numerical equivalence of the number forty. It was on Rosh Chodesh Sh'vat, during the wandering in the desert, during the fortieth year, that Moshe began to teach and review the Torah with the people.

Shabbat Shira, the Shabbat of Song, falls during Sh'vat, on the Shabbat of the Torah portion B'Shalach. It is a great time to focus on song and the spiritual import of singing. I sometimes feel that singing is like having an "internal" massage of my lungs, leaving me feeling as refreshed and vital as an outer-body massage. B'Shalach includes the "Shirat HaYam," "Song of the Sea," which Moshe sang in praise of God after crossing over the *Yam Suf.* At its conclusion, we sing Miriam's song, which she sang as she gathered all of the women to sing, play tambourines, and dance to honor their freedom. Geela-Rayzel Raphael, Linda Hirschhorn, and Debbie Friedman have each written wonderful songs about Miriam. (These songs are available on cassettes from Oyster Albums or SoundsWrite.)

It has become my tradition to include an English chanting of Miriam's song, with the same chant as the Hebrew, after the Shirat HaYam aliyah. This draws attention to Miriam's song and her place as a leader of the Jewish people.

Exodus 15:20–21

V'Tikach Miriam HaNevia, Achot Aharon, et Hatof B'yadeha v'Tetzena kol hanashim ahareha b'tupim u'vimcholot. V'ta-an lehem Miriam Shiru L'Adonai ki-ga-oh ga-ah sus v'rochvo ramah v'yam.

וַתִּקַּח מִרְיָם הַנְּבִיאָה אֲחוֹת אַהֲרֹן אֶת־הַתֹּף בְּיָדָהּ וַתֵּצֶאןָ כָל־הַנָּשִׁים
אַחֲרֶיהָ בְּתֻפִּים וּבִמְחֹלֹת; וַתַּעַן לָהֶם מִרְיָם שִׁירוּ לַיהֹוָה כִּי־גָאֹה
גָּאָה סוּס וְרֹכְבוֹ רָמָה בַיָּם;

And Miriam, the Prophetess, sister of Aharon, took the timbrel in her hand and all the women went out after her with timbrels and dances. And Miriam sang unto them: Sing praises to God who is exalted, Who has thrown the horse and rider into the sea.

The Haftarah for Shabbat Shirah is the heroic story of Deborah, the Judge (Judges 4:4–5:31).

Tu B'Sh'vat, the fifteenth of Sh'vat, falls on the full moon. It is the New Year of the Trees, marking an end to winter and the first beginnings of spring (depending on where you live). In Israel, the almond trees are the first to bloom, sending their sweet fragrance over the land. The tree, like woman, moves through cycles. She (the Hebrew word for tree, *aitz*, is feminine) grows towards light. She is the symbol of the Torah, "Aitz Chaim He."

Tu B'Sh'vat is a time to eat of the many fruits mentioned in the Torah. Ask each person coming to Rosh Chodesh to bring a different type of fruit to share, representing three of the four kabbalistic levels of creation:[12]

assiyah (the physical reality)—fruit surrounded by an inedible skin, such as bananas, coconuts, and pomegranates.

yetzirah (formation)—fruit that has an inedible pit, such as olives, nectarines, and dates.

beriah (creation)—fruit that can be eaten without any shell, such as figs and grapes.

atzilut (emanation)—there is no fruit for this category, as it represents the fully spiritual.

Grouping fruits by their edible parts focuses our attention on the symbolic nature of the fruit. "Those parts that can be eaten represent holiness; the inedible parts—that is, the pits—represent the impure; and the shells serve as protection for the fragile holiness inside."[13] According to the kabbalists, eating the fruit helps bring out its holiness and furthers *tikkun olam*, the repair of the world.

Women's Yahrzeits:
Celia Adler Forman—3rd of Sh'vat (1890–1979), an actress of the Yiddish theater.
Else Lasker-Schueler—7th of Sh'vat (1889–1945), a gifted and prize-winning German writer who emigrated to Israel.

Hanna Rovina—16th of Sh'vat (1890–1980), who founded the Habima Theater and became a well-acclaimed Hebrew actress.

Rosa Luxemburg—14th of Sh'vat (1871–1919), a leading figure in the Polish and German socialist and labor movements. Rosa was an economist and edited the Communist daily *Die Rote Fahne*. She was arrested in Berlin in 1919 and murdered en route to prison.

Muriel Rukeyser—24th of Sh'vat (1913–1980), a social activist and a prolific writer and poet, who wrote "To be a Jew in the twentieth century/ is to be offered a gift."[14]

Henrietta Szold—29th of Sh'vat (1860–1945), the founder and first president of the Hadassah Zionist organization, which funds Hadassah Hospital in Israel. She was also an ardent student of Jewish studies, studying at the Jewish Theological Seminary.

Adar

The *mazal*, or constellation, for Adar is two fish. There is a custom to say, "S/He who enters the month of Adar, brings happiness," "MeShe-nichnas Adar, marbim b'simcha," משנכנס אדר מרבים בשמחה.

Purim, the holiday commemorating Queen Esther's bold and clever action to save the Jews in Persia, falls on the full moon of Adar. Purim is a time to dress in costumes and masks, a time to read the Megillah, the story of Esther, her cousin Mordechai, King Ahashverot, and the evil Haman. It is a time to prepare and send mishloach manot, gifts of food to friends, and a time to begin putting aside *tzedakah* for *Ma-ot Chittim*, money to buy Pesach supplies for those unable to do so themselves.

Giving *tzedakah* is a yearlong activity, and it is wonderful to find a specific *tzedakah* project that is drawn from the calendar-holiday cycle. For Rosh Chodesh Adar, reflecting the royal garb of Esther, the beauty pageant that she was subjected to, and the costumes associated with Purim, one suggestion would be to have each person bring clothing to the Rosh Chodesh gathering. The clothing would be assembled and given to a women's shelter. (Discuss this at the Rosh Chodesh Sh'vat meeting, so that women bring clothing that they want to give away.)

Purim is noted for its qualities of the hidden and the revealed. The following ritual was written by Maxine Fraade.

What Is Hidden and What Is Revealed? The Wearing of Masks.

One aspect of the Purim story that deserves our attention is that Esther hid her Jewish identity from King Ahashuarus ("Esther had not made known her people nor her kindred; for Mordechai had charged her that she should not tell it," Megillat Esther 2:10). She only revealed herself later to save her people.

This sounds so familiar. How many times do we as women hide our true nature or opinions to protect ourselves and be acceptable to the world? What do we sacrifice by these deceptions? Sometimes, we feel it is desirable to keep a low profile as Jews as well if we sense we are in a hostile environment. At what cost? Is there any gain?

At this time of year, growth and life are hidden beneath the frozen earth. Just beneath the surface lies vibrant energy and vitality waiting to burst forth when conditions are right and it is safe. Purim is a good time to contemplate what is hidden from view and what and why we hide our true natures. Just as it is a fun aspect of Purim to wear costumes/masks, we need to know when it is safe to take them off.

In this ritual we will go around the circle two times. The first time around the circle we will begin:

> I sometimes have to hide my true nature from the world because . . . [complete the sentence]

The exact words themselves are not important. What is important is that we look inside and see how we often turn ourselves inside out, hide like Esther, and change ourselves, for all kinds of reasons. Within this group we should feel safe to admit our protective secretiveness. If you feel you are that rarity, a totally unmasked person, you can say: "I can be totally myself because . . . " Please keep it simple, short, and spontaneous: one statement is all you need say. You can address this from any viewpoint that you wish. We proceed around the circle moonwise.

The second time around the circle, we proclaim one thing that we would like to tell the world about ourselves. Each participant will begin by saying:

> If I could tell the world one thing about myself, I would say . . . [complete the phrase]

When everyone has had a turn to participate, the ritual is over. The entire group then recites: "So be it."

Women's Yahrzeits:

Anna Ticho—12th of Adar (1894–1980), an Israeli painter whose home in Jerusalem has become part of the Israel Museum. One can visit her home, view her paintings, and enjoy the outdoor garden and cafe just off of Yaffo Road.

Myriam Mendilow—21st of Adar (1909–1989), a lifelong teacher and activist on behalf of the poor and elderly in Jerusalem. She founded *Yad L'Kashish*,

Lifeline to the Elderly, an organization of workshops and programs for the elderly.

Bora Laskin—22nd of Adar (1912–1984), the first Jew to sit on the Canadian Supreme Court.

Marjorie Guthrie—28th of Adar (1918–1983), a dancer and the wife of singer-songwriter Woody Guthrie.

Notes

1. Many of these yahrzeit dates were found in the *Jewish Calendar 5746*, compiled by Michael Strassfeld, Richard Siegel, Sue Levi Elwell, and T. Drorah Setel (New York: Universe Publishers, 1985). I would also like to thank Vicki Hollander for providing some of the dates and suggesting that they be included in the monthly foci.

2. The Rabbi Sampson Raphael Hirsh translation of Shmot/Exodus 12:2.

3. For a description of the ten glories of Rosh Chodesh Nissan, see Eliahu Kitov, *The Book of our Heritage*, trans. from the Hebrew by Nathan Bulman (Jerusalem and New York: Feldheim Publishers, 1978), pp. 135–137.

4. Arthur Waskow, *Seasons of Our Joy* (New York: Bantam Books, 1982), p. 156.

5. Hirsh translation, Exodus 1:15–20.

6. See midrash on Exodus 20:15, "And all of the people perceived thunderings," and Psalm 29:4, "The voice of God was with power."

7. "Adrienne Rich, "Paula Becker to Clara Westhoff," in *The Dream of a Common Language: Poems 1974–1977* (New York: W. W. Norton and Co., 1978), pp. 42–44.

8. "Songs and Teachings of the Spring and Summer Moons," unpublished poem by Vicki Hollander.

9. Waskow, *Seasons of Our Joy*, pp. 219–220.

10. The idea of this questioning came from a Rosh Chodesh Elul 5751/1991ceremony of the American Jewish Congress Feminist Center.

11. See the preface of Waskow's *Seasons of Our Joy* for a fuller description of this. He also, I believe, coins the term "moonth" as a way of showing direct connection between the moon and the monthly cycle.

12. See Waskow's *Seasons of Our Joy,* pp. 107–108, or Michael Strassfeld's *The Jewish Holidays* (New York: Harper and Row, 1985), pp. 180–181, for a fuller description of the kabbalistic understanding of Tu B'Sh'vat and ideas for a Tu B'Sh'vat Seder honoring the fruits and seasons and their spiritual dimensions.

13. Strassfeld, *The Jewish Holidays,* p. 181.

14. From "Letter to the Front VII," in *The Collected Poems of Muriel Rukeyser* (New York: McGraw Hill, 1957).

Appendix D
Specific Notes
Regarding
Rosh Chodesh

Yom Kippur Katan

This is the day before Rosh Chodesh. In kabbalistic tradition, this is a time to prepare for Rosh Chodesh, both intellectually and spiritually.

Shabbat Mevorchim

This is the Shabbat before Rosh Chodesh. We recite Birkat HaChodesh—the announcement and blessing of the New Moon.

Machar HaChodesh

When Rosh Chodesh begins on Saturday evening, a special Haftarah is chanted: Haftarah—1 Samuel 20:18–42.

Shabbat Rosh Chodesh

The following changes in the Shabbat liturgy are made:

Add Ya-aleh v'yavo to Amidah in shacharit, mincha, and ma'ariv prayer
   services.
A special maftir (concluding aliyah) to the Torah reading—Numbers 28:9–15.
A specific Haftarah is chanted—Isaiah 66:1–24.
Hallel (Hallel less two specific paragraphs) is chanted before the Torah reading.
The full Hallel is recited for Rosh Chodesh Tevet because it falls during
   Chanukah.
A special Rosh Chodesh musaf amidah is included.
Psalm 104 is added to the prayer service.
Add Ya-aleh v'yavo to Birkat hamazon (blessing after meals).

Weekday Rosh Chodesh (Sunday through Friday)

Add Ya-aleh v'yavo to Amidah at Shacharit, mincha, and ma'ariv.
Hallel (Hallel less two specific paragraphs) is chanted.
The full Hallel is recited for Rosh Chodesh Tevet because it falls during
   Chanukah.
The Torah reading is Numbers 28:1–15, divided into four aliyot: 1st aliyah,
   28:1–3; 2nd aliyah, 28:3–5; 3rd aliyah, 28:5–10; 4th aliyah, 28:11–15.
Tefillin is removed before a special Rosh Chodesh Musaf.
Psalm 104 is added to the Shacharit service.
Add Ya-aleh v'yavo to Birkat hamazon (blessing after meals)

Kiddush Levana

It is observed at least seventy-two hours after the *molad* (meaning birth; the
molad is the crowning of the Rosh Chodesh moon), but generally on the first
Saturday evening past Rosh Chodesh. Kiddush Levana is done outside where
the moon must be visible. It is a custom to observe and sanctify the moon. This
is not to be confused with the ancient Sanhedrin's observation and announcement of Rosh Chodesh.

Note Regarding Rosh Chodesh and Rosh Hashanah

Rosh Hashanah takes precedence over Rosh Chodesh. For this reason, there is
no observance of Rosh Chodesh for the month of Tishrei. (Rosh Hashanah is
Rosh ChodeshTishrei). There is also no Birkat HaChodesh, Annoucement of
Rosh Chodesh on the Shabbat before Rosh Chodesh Tishrei, as is customary
on Shabbat Mevorchim.

Rosh Chodesh Readings

Shabbat Mevorchim

Birkat HaChodesh (Prayer for the New Month) (Translation from the Sidur Hadesh Yameinu)

This is recited while holding a Torah on the Shabbat before Rosh Chodesh.

May it be your will, Eternal One
our God, and God of our ancestors,
that this coming month renew us with goodness and blessing.
Grant us long life,
a life of peace,
a life of goodness,
a life of blessing,
a life of sustenance,
a life of vigor,
a life free from shame and reproach,
a life marked by love of Torah
and the awe of Heaven,
a life marked by uprightness and intelligence,
wisdom and knowledge,
a life in which the yearnings of our heart
will be fulfilled for good. Amen.
May the One who wrought miracles
for our ancestors
and redeemed them from slavery to freedom
speedily redeem us
and gather our dispersed
from the four corners of the earth,
that all Israel may be united in fellowship,
and let us say, Amen.
The new month of _____ will be on _____. May it come to
us and to all Israel for good.

מִי שֶׁעָשָׂה נִסִּים לַאֲבוֹתֵינוּ וְאִמּוֹתֵינוּ, וְגָאַל אוֹתָם מֵעַבְדוּת לְחֵרוּת, הוּא יִגְאַל אוֹתָנוּ בְּקָרוֹב, וִיקַבֵּץ נְדָחֵינוּ מֵאַרְבַּע כַּנְפוֹת הָאָרֶץ. חֲבֵרִים כָּל יִשְׂרָאֵל, וְנֹאמַר אָמֵן:

רֹאשׁ חֹדֶשׁ (פלוני) יִהְיֶה בְּיוֹם (פלוני) הַבָּא עָלֵינוּ וְעַל כָּל יִשְׂרָאֵל לְטוֹבָה:

יְחַדְּשֵׁהוּ הַקָּדוֹשׁ בָּרוּךְ הוּא, עָלֵינוּ וְעַל כָּל עַמּוֹ בֵּית יִשְׂרָאֵל, לְחַיִּים וּלְשָׁלוֹם, לְשָׂשׂוֹן וּלְשִׂמְחָה, לִישׁוּעָה וּלְנֶחָמָה. וְנֹאמַר אָמֵן:

Shabbat Machar HaChodesh Haftarah

1 Samuel 20:18–42

An English translation of the Machar HaChodesh Haftarah reading is available from several sources, including *The Pentateuch*, translated by Rabbi Samson Raphael Hirsch and published by Judaica Press or *Pentateuch and Haftorahs*, published by the Soncino Press.

שמואל א פרק כ

יח ויאמר לו יהונתן מחר חדש ונפקדת כי יפקד מושבך: יט ושלשת תרד מאד ובאת אל המקום אשר נסתרת שם ביום המעשה וישבת אצל האבן האזל: כ ואני שלשת החצים צדה אורה לשלח לי למטרה: כא והנה אשלח את הנער לך מצא את החצים אם אמר אמר לנער הנה החצים ממך והנה קחנו ובאה כי שלום לך ואין דבר חי יהוה: כב ואם כה אמר לעלם הנה החצים ממך והלאה לך כי שלחך יהוה: כג והדבר אשר דברנו אני ואתה הנה יהוה ביני ובינך עד עולם: כד ויסתר דוד בשדה ויהי החדש וישב המלך על הלחם לאכול (אל) (הלחם): כה וישב המלך על מושבו כפעם בפעם אל מושב הקיר ויקם יהונתן וישב אבנר מצד שאול ויפקד מקום דוד: כו ולא דבר שאול מאומה ביום ההוא כי אמר מקרה הוא בלתי טהור הוא כי לא טהור: כז ויהי ממחרת החדש השני ויפקד מקום דוד ויאמר שאול אל יהונתן בנו מדוע לא בא בן ישי גם תמול גם היום אל הלחם: כח ויען יהונתן את שאול נשאל נשאל דוד מעמדי עד בית לחם: כט ויאמר שלחני נא כי זבח משפחה לנו בעיר והוא צוה לי אחי ועתה אם מצאתי חן בעיניך אמלטה נא ואראה את אחי על כן לא בא אל שלחן המלך: ל ויחר אף שאול ביהונתן ויאמר לו בן נעות המרדות הלוא ידעתי כי בחר אתה לבן ישי לבשתך ולבשת ערות אמך: לא כי כל הימים אשר בן ישי חי על האדמה לא תכון אתה ומלכותך ועתה שלח וקח אתו אלי כי בן מות הוא: לב ויען יהונתן את שאול אביו ויאמר אליו למה יומת מה עשה: לג ויטל שאול את החנית עליו להכתו וידע יהונתן כי כלה היא מעם אביו להמית את דוד: לד ויקם יהונתן מעם השלחן בחרי אף ולא אכל ביום החדש השני לחם כי נעצב אל דוד כי הכלמו אביו: לה ויהי בבקר ויצא יהונתן השדה למועד דוד ונער קטן עמו: לו ויאמר לנערו רץ מצא נא את החצים אשר אנכי מורה הנער רץ והוא ירה החצי להעברו: לז ויבא הנער עד מקום החצי אשר ירה יהונתן ויקרא יהונתן אחרי הנער ויאמר הלוא החצי ממך והלאה: לח ויקרא יהונתן אחרי הנער מהרה חושה אל תעמד וילקט נער יהונתן את החצי ויבא אל אדניו (את) (החצים): לט והנער לא ידע מאומה אך יהונתן ודוד ידעו את הדבר: מ ויתן יהונתן את כליו אל הנער אשר לו ויאמר לו לך הביא העיר: מא הנער בא ודוד קם מאצל הנגב ויפל לאפיו ארצה וישתחו שלש פעמים וישקו איש את רעהו ויבכו איש את

רעהו עד דוד הגדיל: מב ויאמר יהונתן לדוד לך לשלום אשר נשבענו שנינו אנחנו
בשם יהוה לאמר יהוה יהיה ביני ובינך ובין זרעי ובין זרעך עד עולם:

Torah Reading for Rosh Chodesh

Weekdays: Numbers 28:1–15;
Shabbat: Special Maftir Numbers 28:9–15

An English translation of the Rosh Chodesh Torah reading is available from
several sources, including *The Pentateuch*, translated by Rabbi Samson Raphael
Hirsch and published by Judaica Press; *The Torah: A Modern Commentary*,
translated by Rabbi W. Gunther Plaut and published by the Union of American Hebrew Congregations; *The Torah*, published by the Jewish Publication
Society; and *Pentateuch and Haftorahs*, published by the Soncino Press.

וַיְדַבֵּר יְיָ אֶל מֹשֶׁה לֵּאמֹר. צַו אֶת בְּנֵי יִשְׂרָאֵל וְאָמַרְתָּ אֲלֵהֶם, אֶת קָרְבָּנִי לַחְמִי לְאִשַּׁי רֵיחַ
נִיחֹחִי, תִּשְׁמְרוּ לְהַקְרִיב לִי בְּמוֹעֲדוֹ. וְאָמַרְתָּ לָהֶם, זֶה הָאִשֶּׁה אֲשֶׁר תַּקְרִיבוּ לַיְיָ כְּבָשִׂים
בְּנֵי שָׁנָה תְמִימִם, שְׁנַיִם לַיּוֹם, עֹלָה תָמִיד. אֶת הַכֶּבֶשׂ אֶחָד תַּעֲשֶׂה בַבֹּקֶר, וְאֵת הַכֶּבֶשׂ
הַשֵּׁנִי תַּעֲשֶׂה בֵּין הָעַרְבָּיִם. וַעֲשִׂירִית הָאֵיפָה סֹלֶת לְמִנְחָה, בְּלוּלָה בְּשֶׁמֶן כָּתִית רְבִיעִת
הַהִין. עֹלַת תָּמִיד, הָעֲשֻׂיָה בְּהַר סִינַי, לְרֵיחַ נִיחֹחַ אִשֶּׁה לַיְיָ. וְנִסְכּוֹ רְבִיעִת הַהִין לַכֶּבֶשׂ
הָאֶחָד, בַּקֹּדֶשׁ הַסֵּךְ נֶסֶךְ שֵׁכָר לַיְיָ. וְאֵת הַכֶּבֶשׂ הַשֵּׁנִי תַּעֲשֶׂה בֵּין הָעַרְבָּיִם, כְּמִנְחַת הַבֹּקֶר
וּכְנִסְכּוֹ תַּעֲשֶׂה, אִשֵּׁה רֵיחַ נִיחֹחַ לַיְיָ.

בשבת: וּבְיוֹם הַשַּׁבָּת שְׁנֵי כְבָשִׂים בְּנֵי שָׁנָה תְמִימִם, וּשְׁנֵי עֶשְׂרֹנִים סֹלֶת מִנְחָה בְּלוּלָה
בַשֶּׁמֶן, וְנִסְכּוֹ. עֹלַת שַׁבַּת בְּשַׁבַּתּוֹ, עַל עֹלַת הַתָּמִיד וְנִסְכָּהּ.

בראש חודש: וּבְרָאשֵׁי חָדְשֵׁיכֶם תַּקְרִיבוּ עֹלָה לַיְיָ, פָּרִים בְּנֵי בָקָר שְׁנַיִם, וְאַיִל אֶחָד,
כְּבָשִׂים בְּנֵי שָׁנָה שִׁבְעָה, תְּמִימִם. וּשְׁלֹשָׁה עֶשְׂרֹנִים סֹלֶת מִנְחָה בְּלוּלָה בַשֶּׁמֶן לַפָּר הָאֶחָד,
וּשְׁנֵי עֶשְׂרֹנִים סֹלֶת מִנְחָה בְּלוּלָה בַשֶּׁמֶן, לָאַיִל הָאֶחָד. וְעִשָּׂרוֹן עִשָּׂרוֹן, סֹלֶת מִנְחָה
בְּלוּלָה בַשֶּׁמֶן, לַכֶּבֶשׂ הָאֶחָד, עֹלָה רֵיחַ נִיחֹחַ, אִשֶּׁה לַיְיָ. וְנִסְכֵּיהֶם חֲצִי הַהִין יִהְיֶה לַפָּר
וּשְׁלִישִׁת הַהִין לָאַיִל וּרְבִיעִת הַהִין לַכֶּבֶשׂ יָיִן, זֹאת עֹלַת חֹדֶשׁ בְּחָדְשׁוֹ לְחָדְשֵׁי הַשָּׁנָה.
וּשְׂעִיר עִזִּים אֶחָד לְחַטָּאת לַיְיָ, עַל עֹלַת הַתָּמִיד יֵעָשֶׂה, וְנִסְכּוֹ.

Haftarah for Shabbat Rosh Chodesh

Isaiah 66:1–24

An English translation of the Shabbat Rosh Chodesh Haftarah reading is avail-
able from several sources, including *The Pentateuch*, translated by Rabbi
Samson Raphael Hirsch and published by Judaica Press or *Pentateuch and
Haftorahs*, published by the Soncino Press.

ספר ישעיהו פרק סו

א כה אמר יהוה השמים כסאי והארץ הדם רגלי אי זה בית אשר תבנו לי ואי זה מקום
מנוחתי: ב ואת כל אלה ידי עשתה ויהיו כל אלה נאם יהוה ואל זה אביט אל עני ונכה
רוח וחרד על דברי: ג שוחט השור מכה איש זובח השה ערף כלב מעלה מנחה דם חזיר
מזכיר לבנה מברך און גם המה בחרו בדרכיהם ובשקוציהם נפשם חפצה: ד גם אני
אבחר בתעלליהם ומגורתם אביא להם יען קראתי ואין עונה דברתי ולא שמעו ויעשו
הרע בעיני ובאשר לא חפצתי בחרו: ה שמעו דבר יהוה החרדים אל דברו אמרו אחיכם
שנאיכם מנדיכם למען שמי יכבד יהוה ונראה בשמחתכם והם יבשו: ו קול שאון מעיר
קול מהיכל קול יהוה משלם גמול לאיביו: ז בטרם תחיל ילדה בטרם יבוא חבל לה
והמליטה זכר: ח מי שמע כזאת מי ראה כאלה היוחל ארץ ביום אחד אם יולד גוי פעם
אחת כי חלה גם ילדה ציון את בניה: ט האני אשביר ולא אוליד יאמר יהוה אם אני
המוליד ועצרתי אמר אלהיך: י שמחו את ירושלם וגילו בה כל אהביה שישו אתה
משוש כל המתאבלים עליה: יא למען תינקו ושבעתם משד תנחמיה למען תמצו
והתענגתם מזיז כבודה: יב כי כה אמר יהוה הנני נטה אליה כנהר שלום וכנחל שוטף
כבוד גוים וינקתם על צד תנשאו ועל ברכים תשעשעו: יג כאיש אשר אמו תנחמנו כן
אנכי אנחמכם ובירושלם תנחמו: יד וראיתם ושש לבכם ועצמותיכם כדשא תפרחנה
ונודעה יד יהוה את עבדיו וזעם את איביו: טו כי הנה יהוה באש יבוא וכסופה
מרכבתיו להשיב בחמה אפו וגערתו בלהבי אש: טז כי באש יהוה נשפט ובחרבו את
כל בשר ורבו חללי יהוה: יז המתקדשים והמטהרים אל הגנות אחר אחד בתוך אכלי
בשר החזיר והשקץ והעכבר יחדו יספו נאם יהוה (אחת): יח ואנכי מעשיהם
ומחשבתיהם באה לקבץ את כל הגוים והלשנות ובאו וראו את כבודי: יט ושמתי בהם
אות ושלחתי מהם פליטים אל הגוים תרשיש פול ולוד משכי קשת תבל ויון האיים
הרחקים אשר לא שמעו את שמעי ולא ראו את כבודי והגידו את כבודי בגוים: כ
והביאו את כל אחיכם מכל הגוים מנחה ליהוה בסוסים וברכב ובצבים ובפרדים
ובכרכרות על הר קדשי ירושלם אמר יהוה כאשר יביאו בני ישראל את המנחה בכלי
טהור בית יהוה: כא וגם מהם אקח לכהנים ללוים אמר יהוה: כב כי כאשר השמים
החדשים והארץ החדשה אשר אני עשה עמדים לפני נאם יהוה כן יעמד זרעכם
ושמכם: כג והיה מדי חדש בחדשו ומדי שבת בשבתו יבוא כל בשר להשתחות לפני
אמר יהוה: כד ויצאו וראו בפגרי האנשים הפשעים בי כי תולעתם לא תמות ואשם לא
תכבה והיו דראון לכל בשר:

Hallel (Translation from Sidur *Hadesh Yameinu*)

You abound in blessings, Eternal One, our God, Sovereign of all time and space,
who brings holiness to our lives through the mitzvah of reciting the Hallel.

PSALM 113
Hallelujah—Sing God's praise.
Give praise, you servants of the Eternal,
praise the name of the Everpresent.
Blessed be the name of the Eternal,
now and forever.

From the rising of the sun to its setting,
praised is the name of the Everpresent.
The Eternal One is above all nations,
God's presence transcends the heavens.

Who is like the Eternal our God,
dwelling in the heights;
who scrutinizes
both heaven and earth;
who raises up the poor from the dust
and lifts the needy from the ash heap;
who sets them among the noble,
among the noble of God's people.
God makes the barren woman, alone in her house,
as a mother rejoicing in her children.
Hallelujah.

PSALM 114
When Israel went out from Egypt,
the House of Jacob from a people of strange speech;
Judah became the Holy One's own,
Israel, God's dominion.

The sea beheld and fled,
the Jordan turned back.
The mountains skipped like rams,
the hills like flocks of sheep.

What ails you, sea, that you flee,
Jordan, that you turn back?
You mountains, that you skip like rams,
you hills, like flocks of sheep?

Tremble, O earth, before the Noble One,
before the God of Jacob,
who turns the rock into a pool of water,
the flint into a fountain.

(The following is omitted on Rosh Chodesh, unless Rosh Chodesh falls during Chanukah.)

PSALM 115:1–11
Not for us, Eternal One, not for us,
but for your own namesake grant dignity,
affirming your devotion and your truth.

Why should the nations say,
"Where, now, is their God?"
when our God is in the heavens,
having done whatever is desirable.
Their idols are gold and silver,
the work of human hands.
They have mouths, but speak not,
eyes, but see not.

They have ears, but hear not,
noses, but smell not.
They have hands, but do not feel;
feet, but do not walk;
they make no sound in their throats.

Like them will be those who make them,
all those who trust in them.
Israel, trust in the Eternal One!
God is their help and their shield.

House of Aaron, trust in the Eternal One!
God is their help and their shield.
All God-fearing people, trust in the Eternal One!
God is their help and their shield.

PSALM 115:12–18
The Eternal, mindful of us, will bring blessing,
blessing to the House of Israel
blessing to the House of Aaron,
blessing to the God-fearing,
the small and the great alike.

May the Life-giver grant you increase,
you and your children.
You are blessed of the Eternal,
maker of heaven and earth.

The heavens belong to the Eternal One,
but the earth was given over to mortals.
The dead do not praise God,
nor all who go down into silence.

But we, we shall bless God
now and forever, Hallelujah.

(The following is omitted on Rosh Chodesh, unless Rosh Chodesh falls during Chanukah.)

PSALM 116:1–11
I am joyous when the Everpresent hears
my voice, my plea;
who turns an ear to me
whenever I call.

Pangs of death overwhelmed me,
the grave closed round about,
grief and suffering were my lot.
Then I invoked the name of the Eternal One,
"Please, God, let me escape."

Gracious and righteous is the Eternal One
our God is compassionate.
The Eternal One protects the simple;
I was brought low and God saved me.

Return to your tranquillity, O my soul,
for the Life-giver has dealt kindly with you.
For you have delivered my very being from death,
my eyes from tears,
my feet from stumbling.

I shall walk before the Eternal One
in the land of the living.
I remained faithful even when I said,
"I am greatly afflicted."
I spoke rashly when I said,
"all human beings are deceitful."

PSALM 116:12–19
How can I repay the Life-giver
for all the bounties bestowed upon me?

I raise the cup of deliverance
and call upon the name of the Eternal One.

I will fulfill my vows to the Everpresent
in the presence of all God's people.
Grievous in God's sight
is the death of those devoted to the Eternal.

Eternal One, I am your servant
I, your servant, child of your handmaid;
you have untied my bonds.
To you will I offer thanksgiving
and invoke the name of the Eternal One.

I will fulfill my vows to the Everpresent
in the presence of all God's people,
in the courts of the Eternal One's temple,
in your midst, Jerusalem.
Hallelujah.

PSALM 117
Praise the Eternal One, all you nations,
Sing God's praise, all you peoples.
For God's steadfast love strengthens us;
The Eternal One's truth endures forever.
Hallelujah.

PSALM 118:1–4
Give thanks to the Eternal who is good,
for God's steadfast love is eternal.

Let Israel say,
God's steadfast love is eternal.

Let the House of Aaron say,
God's steadfast love is eternal.

Let the God-fearing say,
God's steadfast love is eternal.

PSALM 118:5–24
From the narrowest confines I called out to God
and was answered with God's boundless space.

The Eternal is with me, I shall not fear,
what can human beings do to me?

When the Eternal One helps me
I shall see to my enemy.

It is better to trust in the Eternal
than to rely on human beings.
It is better to trust in the Eternal
than to rely on nobles.

All nations encircled me;
by the name of the Eternal, I cut them down.
They surrounded me, they encircled me;
by the name of the Eternal, I cut them down.

They surrounded me like bees,
they went out like a feeble fire;
by the name of the Eternal, I cut them down.

I had been pushed, about to fall,
when the Eternal One helped me.
God is my strength and my song
and has become my deliverance.

The voice of joyous deliverance
fills the tents of the righteous:
"The right hand of the Eternal does valiantly.
The right hand of the Eternal is exalted;
the right hand of the Eternal does valiantly."

I shall not die but live
to declare the works of God.
God has sorely tested me
but has not given me over to death.

Open for me the gates of righteousness
that I may enter them and thank God.
This is the gate of the Eternal One,
the righteous shall enter it.

(Each of the following verses is chanted twice.)

I give thanks, for you have answered me and have become my deliverance.
The stone that the builders rejected has become the new cornerstone.
This has been the Eternal One's doing; to us, it is a wondrous thing.
This is the day the Eternal has made; let us be glad and rejoice in it.

(*Each of the following verses is chanted first by the reader, then by the congregation.*)

Eternal One, we pray, deliver us.
Eternal One, we pray, deliver us.
Eternal One, we pray, let us prosper.
Eternal One, we pray, let us prosper.

PSALM 118:26–29
You are my God and I thank you;
my God whom I extol.
Give thanks to the Eternal who is good,
for God steadfast love is eternal.

May you be praised, Eternal our God,
by all your works,
May your devoted righteous ones,
those who do what is pleasing to you,
and all your people, the House of Israel,
acclaim you in joyous song.
May they bless, praise, beautify,
extol, revere,
sanctify and enthrone you,
our sovereign, always.
For to you it is good to give thanks;
to your name it is pleasant to sing praises.
From everlasting to everlasting you are God.
Praised are you, Eternal One,
sovereign, celebrated in praise.

בָּרוּךְ אַתָּה יְיָ אֱלֹהֵינוּ מֶלֶךְ הָעוֹלָם, אֲשֶׁר קִדְּשָׁנוּ בְּמִצְוֹתָיו וְצִוָּנוּ לִקְרֹא אֶת הַהַלֵּל.

הַלְלוּיָהּ הַלְלוּ עַבְדֵי יְיָ, הַלְלוּ אֶת שֵׁם יְיָ: יְהִי שֵׁם יְיָ מְבֹרָךְ מֵעַתָּה וְעַד עוֹלָם: מִמִּזְרַח שֶׁמֶשׁ עַד מְבוֹאוֹ, מְהֻלָּל שֵׁם יְיָ: רָם עַל כָּל גּוֹיִם יְיָ, עַל הַשָּׁמַיִם כְּבוֹדוֹ. מִי כַּיְיָ אֱלֹהֵינוּ הַמַּגְבִּיהִי לָשָׁבֶת: הַמַּשְׁפִּילִי לִרְאוֹת, בַּשָּׁמַיִם וּבָאָרֶץ. מְקִימִי מֵעָפָר דָּל, מֵאַשְׁפֹּת יָרִים אֶבְיוֹן: לְהוֹשִׁיבִי עִם נְדִיבִים, עִם נְדִיבֵי עַמּוֹ. מוֹשִׁיבִי עֲקֶרֶת הַבַּיִת, אֵם הַבָּנִים שְׂמֵחָה הַלְלוּיָהּ:

בְּצֵאת יִשְׂרָאֵל מִמִּצְרָיִם, בֵּית יַעֲקֹב מֵעַם לֹעֵז. הָיְתָה יְהוּדָה לְקָדְשׁוֹ, יִשְׂרָאֵל מַמְשְׁלוֹתָיו. הַיָּם רָאָה וַיָּנֹס, הַיַּרְדֵּן יִסֹּב לְאָחוֹר: הֶהָרִים רָקְדוּ כְאֵילִים, גְּבָעוֹת כִּבְנֵי צֹאן. מַה לְּךָ הַיָּם כִּי תָנוּס הַיַּרְדֵּן תִּסֹּב לְאָחוֹר. הֶהָרִים תִּרְקְדוּ כְאֵילִים, גְּבָעוֹת כִּבְנֵי צֹאן. מִלִּפְנֵי אָדוֹן חוּלִי אָרֶץ, מִלִּפְנֵי אֱלוֹהַּ יַעֲקֹב. הַהֹפְכִי הַצּוּר אֲגַם מָיִם, חַלָּמִישׁ לְמַעְיְנוֹ מָיִם:

כשקוראים הלל בדילוג מתחילים ה׳ זכרנו

לֹא לָנוּ יְיָ לֹא לָנוּ כִּי לְשִׁמְךָ תֵּן כָּבוֹד, עַל חַסְדְּךָ עַל אֲמִתֶּךָ. לָמָּה יֹאמְרוּ הַגּוֹיִם, אַיֵּה נָא
אֱלֹהֵיהֶם. וֵאלֹהֵינוּ בַשָּׁמָיִם כֹּל אֲשֶׁר חָפֵץ עָשָׂה. עֲצַבֵּיהֶם כֶּסֶף וְזָהָב, מַעֲשֵׂה יְדֵי אָדָם. פֶּה
לָהֶם וְלֹא יְדַבֵּרוּ, עֵינַיִם לָהֶם וְלֹא יִרְאוּ. אָזְנַיִם לָהֶם וְלֹא יִשְׁמָעוּ, אַף לָהֶם וְלֹא יְרִיחוּן.
יְדֵיהֶם וְלֹא יְמִישׁוּן, רַגְלֵיהֶם וְלֹא יְהַלֵּכוּ, לֹא יֶהְגּוּ בִּגְרוֹנָם. כְּמוֹהֶם יִהְיוּ עֹשֵׂיהֶם, כֹּל
אֲשֶׁר בֹּטֵחַ בָּהֶם: יִשְׂרָאֵל בְּטַח בַּיְיָ, עֶזְרָם וּמָגִנָּם הוּא. בֵּית אַהֲרֹן בִּטְחוּ בַּיְיָ, עֶזְרָם וּמָגִנָּם
הוּא. יִרְאֵי יְיָ בִּטְחוּ בַיְיָ, עֶזְרָם וּמָגִנָּם הוּא:

יְיָ זְכָרָנוּ יְבָרֵךְ, יְבָרֵךְ אֶת בֵּית יִשְׂרָאֵל, יְבָרֵךְ אֶת בֵּית אַהֲרֹן. יְבָרֵךְ יִרְאֵי יְיָ, הַקְּטַנִּים עִם
הַגְּדֹלִים. יֹסֵף יְיָ עֲלֵיכֶם, עֲלֵיכֶם וְעַל בְּנֵיכֶם. בְּרוּכִים אַתֶּם לַיְיָ, עֹשֵׂה שָׁמַיִם וָאָרֶץ.
הַשָּׁמַיִם שָׁמַיִם לַיְיָ, וְהָאָרֶץ נָתַן לִבְנֵי אָדָם. לֹא הַמֵּתִים יְהַלְלוּ יָהּ, וְלֹא כָּל יֹרְדֵי דוּמָה.
וַאֲנַחְנוּ נְבָרֵךְ יָהּ, מֵעַתָּה וְעַד עוֹלָם, הַלְלוּיָהּ:

כשקוראים הלל בדילוג מתחילים מה אשיב

אָהַבְתִּי כִּי יִשְׁמַע יְיָ, אֶת קוֹלִי תַּחֲנוּנָי. כִּי הִטָּה אָזְנוֹ לִי וּבְיָמַי אֶקְרָא: אֲפָפוּנִי חֶבְלֵי
מָוֶת, וּמְצָרֵי שְׁאוֹל מְצָאוּנִי צָרָה וְיָגוֹן אֶמְצָא. וּבְשֵׁם יְיָ אֶקְרָא, אָנָּה יְיָ מַלְּטָה נַפְשִׁי. חַנּוּן
יְיָ וְצַדִּיק, וֵאלֹהֵינוּ מְרַחֵם. שֹׁמֵר פְּתָאיִם יְיָ דַּלּוֹתִי וְלִי יְהוֹשִׁיעַ. שׁוּבִי נַפְשִׁי לִמְנוּחָיְכִי, כִּי
יְיָ גָּמַל עָלָיְכִי. כִּי חִלַּצְתָּ נַפְשִׁי מִמָּוֶת אֶת עֵינִי מִן דִּמְעָה, אֶת רַגְלִי מִדֶּחִי. אֶתְהַלֵּךְ לִפְנֵי
יְיָ, בְּאַרְצוֹת הַחַיִּים. הֶאֱמַנְתִּי כִּי אֲדַבֵּר, אֲנִי עָנִיתִי מְאֹד. אֲנִי אָמַרְתִּי בְחָפְזִי כָּל הָאָדָם
כֹּזֵב.

מָה אָשִׁיב לַיְיָ, כָּל תַּגְמוּלוֹהִי עָלָי. כּוֹס יְשׁוּעוֹת אֶשָּׂא, וּבְשֵׁם יְיָ אֶקְרָא. נְדָרַי לַיְיָ אֲשַׁלֵּם,
נֶגְדָה נָּא לְכָל עַמּוֹ. יָקָר בְּעֵינֵי יְיָ הַמָּוְתָה לַחֲסִידָיו. אָנָּה יְיָ כִּי אֲנִי עַבְדֶּךָ אֲנִי עַבְדְּךָ, בֶּן
אֲמָתֶךָ פִּתַּחְתָּ לְמוֹסֵרָי. לְךָ אֶזְבַּח זֶבַח תּוֹדָה וּבְשֵׁם יְיָ אֶקְרָא. נְדָרַי לַיְיָ אֲשַׁלֵּם נֶגְדָה נָּא
לְכָל עַמּוֹ. בְּחַצְרוֹת בֵּית יְיָ בְּתוֹכֵכִי יְרוּשָׁלָיִם הַלְלוּיָהּ.

הַלְלוּ אֶת יְיָ, כָּל גּוֹיִם, שַׁבְּחוּהוּ כָּל הָאֻמִּים.
כִּי גָבַר עָלֵינוּ חַסְדּוֹ, וֶאֱמֶת יְיָ לְעוֹלָם הַלְלוּיָהּ:

הוֹדוּ לַיְיָ כִּי טוֹב, כִּי לְעוֹלָם חַסְדּוֹ:
יֹאמַר נָא יִשְׂרָאֵל, כִּי לְעוֹלָם חַסְדּוֹ:
יֹאמְרוּ נָא בֵית אַהֲרֹן, כִּי לְעוֹלָם חַסְדּוֹ:
יֹאמְרוּ נָא יִרְאֵי יְיָ, כִּי לְעוֹלָם חַסְדּוֹ:

מִן הַמֵּצַר קָרָאתִי יָּהּ, עָנָנִי בַמֶּרְחָב יָהּ. יְיָ לִי לֹא אִירָא, מַה יַּעֲשֶׂה לִי אָדָם. יְיָ לִי בְּעֹזְרָי,
וַאֲנִי אֶרְאֶה בְשֹׂנְאָי. טוֹב לַחֲסוֹת בַּיְיָ, מִבְּטֹחַ בָּאָדָם. טוֹב לַחֲסוֹת בַּיְיָ מִבְּטֹחַ בִּנְדִיבִים. כָּל
גּוֹיִם סְבָבוּנִי בְּשֵׁם יְיָ כִּי אֲמִילַם. סַבּוּנִי גַם סְבָבוּנִי בְּשֵׁם יְיָ כִּי אֲמִילַם. סַבּוּנִי כִדְבוֹרִים
דֹּעֲכוּ כְּאֵשׁ קוֹצִים, בְּשֵׁם יְיָ כִּי אֲמִילַם. דָּחֹה דְחִיתַנִי לִנְפֹּל, וַיְיָ עֲזָרָנִי. עָזִּי וְזִמְרָת יָהּ,
וַיְהִי לִי לִישׁוּעָה. קוֹל רִנָּה וִישׁוּעָה בְּאָהֳלֵי צַדִּיקִים, יְמִין יְיָ עֹשָׂה חָיִל. יְמִין יְיָ רוֹמֵמָה,
יְמִין יְיָ עֹשָׂה חָיִל. לֹא אָמוּת כִּי אֶחְיֶה, וַאֲסַפֵּר מַעֲשֵׂי יָהּ. יַסֹּר יִסְּרַנִּי יָּהּ, וְלַמָּוֶת לֹא
נְתָנָנִי. פִּתְחוּ לִי שַׁעֲרֵי צֶדֶק, אָבֹא בָם אוֹדֶה יָהּ. זֶה הַשַּׁעַר לַיְיָ, צַדִּיקִים יָבֹאוּ בוֹ.

אוֹדְךָ כִּי עֲנִיתָנִי, וַתְּהִי לִי לִישׁוּעָה.

אוֹדְךָ כִּי עֲנִיתָנִי, וַתְּהִי לִי לִישׁוּעָה.

אֶבֶן מָאֲסוּ הַבּוֹנִים, הָיְתָה לְרֹאשׁ פִּנָּה.

אֶבֶן מָאֲסוּ הַבּוֹנִים, הָיְתָה לְרֹאשׁ פִּנָּה.

מֵאֵת יְיָ הָיְתָה זֹּאת, הִיא נִפְלָאת בְּעֵינֵינוּ.

מֵאֵת יְיָ הָיְתָה זֹּאת, הִיא נִפְלָאת בְּעֵינֵינוּ.

זֶה הַיּוֹם עָשָׂה יְיָ, נָגִילָה וְנִשְׂמְחָה בוֹ.

זֶה הַיּוֹם עָשָׂה יְיָ, נָגִילָה וְנִשְׂמְחָה בוֹ.

אָנָּא יְיָ הוֹשִׁיעָה נָּא:

אָנָּא יְיָ הוֹשִׁיעָה נָּא:

אָנָּא יְיָ הַצְלִיחָה נָא:

אָנָּא יְיָ הַצְלִיחָה נָא:

בָּרוּךְ הַבָּא בְּשֵׁם יְיָ, בֵּרַכְנוּכֶם מִבֵּית יְיָ.

בָּרוּךְ הַבָּא בְּשֵׁם יְיָ, בֵּרַכְנוּכֶם מִבֵּית יְיָ.

אֵל יְיָ וַיָּאֶר לָנוּ, אִסְרוּ חַג בַּעֲבֹתִים, עַד קַרְנוֹת הַמִּזְבֵּחַ.

אֵל יְיָ וַיָּאֶר לָנוּ, אִסְרוּ חַג בַּעֲבֹתִים, עַד קַרְנוֹת הַמִּזְבֵּחַ.

אֵלִי אַתָּה וְאוֹדֶךָּ, אֱלֹהַי אֲרוֹמְמֶךָּ.

אֵלִי אַתָּה וְאוֹדֶךָּ, אֱלֹהַי אֲרוֹמְמֶךָּ.

הוֹדוּ לַייָ כִּי טוֹב, כִּי לְעוֹלָם חַסְדּוֹ.

הוֹדוּ לַייָ כִּי טוֹב, כִּי לְעוֹלָם חַסְדּוֹ.

יְהַלְלוּךָ יְיָ אֱלֹהֵינוּ כָּל מַעֲשֶׂיךָ, וַחֲסִידֶיךָ צַדִּיקִים עוֹשֵׂי רְצוֹנֶךָ, וְכָל עַמְּךָ בֵּית יִשְׂרָאֵל בְּרִנָּה יוֹדוּ וִיבָרְכוּ וִישַׁבְּחוּ וִיפָאֲרוּ וִירוֹמְמוּ וְיַעֲרִיצוּ וְיַקְדִּישׁוּ וְיַמְלִיכוּ אֶת שִׁמְךָ מַלְכֵּנוּ, כִּי לְךָ טוֹב לְהוֹדוֹת וּלְשִׁמְךָ נָאֶה לְזַמֵּר, כִּי מֵעוֹלָם וְעַד עוֹלָם אַתָּה אֵל. בָּרוּךְ אַתָּה יְיָ, מֶלֶךְ מְהֻלָּל בַּתִּשְׁבָּחוֹת.

Psalm 104, said on Rosh Chodesh

(Translation of the first two verses of Psalm 104 from Sidur *Hadesh Yameinu*)

Let all my being praise the Everpresent.
Eternal One, my God, you exceed all measure;
garbed in radiance and splendor,
enfolded in light as in a garment,
unfolding the heavens as a curtain.

בָּרְכִי נַפְשִׁי אֶת יְיָ, יְיָ אֱלֹהַי גָּדַלְתָּ מְּאֹד הוֹד וְהָדָר לָבָשְׁתָּ: עֹטֶה אוֹר כַּשַּׂלְמָה נוֹטֶה שָׁמַיִם כַּיְרִיעָה: הַמְקָרֶה בַמַּיִם עֲלִיּוֹתָיו הַשָּׂם עָבִים רְכוּבוֹ הַמְהַלֵּךְ עַל כַּנְפֵי רוּחַ: עֹשֶׂה מַלְאָכָיו רוּחוֹת מְשָׁרְתָיו אֵשׁ לֹהֵט: יָסַד אֶרֶץ עַל מְכוֹנֶיהָ בַּל תִּמּוֹט עוֹלָם וָעֶד: תְּהוֹם כַּלְּבוּשׁ כִּסִּיתוֹ, עַל הָרִים יַעַמְדוּ מָיִם: מִן גַּעֲרָתְךָ יְנוּסוּן מִן קוֹל רַעַמְךָ יֵחָפֵזוּן: יַעֲלוּ הָרִים יֵרְדוּ בְקָעוֹת, אֶל מְקוֹם זֶה יָסַדְתָּ לָהֶם: גְּבוּל שַׂמְתָּ בַּל יַעֲבֹרוּן בַּל יְשׁוּבוּן לְכַסּוֹת הָאָרֶץ: הַמְשַׁלֵּחַ מַעְיָנִים בַּנְּחָלִים בֵּין הָרִים יְהַלֵּכוּן: יַשְׁקוּ כָּל חַיְתוֹ שָׂדָי יִשְׁבְּרוּ פְרָאִים צְמָאָם: עֲלֵיהֶם עוֹף הַשָּׁמַיִם יִשְׁכּוֹן מִבֵּין עֳפָאיִם יִתְּנוּ קוֹל: מַשְׁקֶה הָרִים מֵעֲלִיּוֹתָיו מִפְּרִי מַעֲשֶׂיךָ תִּשְׂבַּע הָאָרֶץ: מַצְמִיחַ חָצִיר לַבְּהֵמָה וְעֵשֶׂב לַעֲבֹדַת הָאָדָם לְהוֹצִיא לֶחֶם מִן הָאָרֶץ: וְיַיִן יְשַׂמַּח לְבַב אֱנוֹשׁ לְהַצְהִיל פָּנִים מִשָּׁמֶן וְלֶחֶם לְבַב אֱנוֹשׁ יִסְעָד: יִשְׂבְּעוּ עֲצֵי יְיָ אַרְזֵי לְבָנוֹן אֲשֶׁר נָטָע: אֲשֶׁר שָׁם צִפֳּרִים יְקַנֵּנוּ חֲסִידָה בְּרוֹשִׁים בֵּיתָהּ: הָרִים הַגְּבֹהִים לַיְּעֵלִים סְלָעִים מַחְסֶה לַשְׁפַנִּים: עָשָׂה יָרֵחַ לְמוֹעֲדִים שֶׁמֶשׁ יָדַע מְבוֹאוֹ: תָּשֶׁת חֹשֶׁךְ וִיהִי לָיְלָה בּוֹ תִרְמֹשׂ כָּל חַיְתוֹ יָעַר: הַכְּפִירִים שֹׁאֲגִים לַטָּרֶף וּלְבַקֵּשׁ מֵאֵל אָכְלָם: תִּזְרַח הַשֶּׁמֶשׁ יֵאָסֵפוּן וְאֶל מְעוֹנֹתָם יִרְבָּצוּן: יֵצֵא אָדָם לְפָעֳלוֹ וְלַעֲבֹדָתוֹ עֲדֵי עָרֶב: מָה רַבּוּ מַעֲשֶׂיךָ יְיָ כֻּלָּם בְּחָכְמָה עָשִׂיתָ מָלְאָה הָאָרֶץ קִנְיָנֶךָ: זֶה הַיָּם גָּדוֹל וּרְחַב יָדָיִם, שָׁם רֶמֶשׂ וְאֵין מִסְפָּר חַיּוֹת קְטַנּוֹת עִם גְּדֹלוֹת: שָׁם אֳנִיּוֹת יְהַלֵּכוּן לִוְיָתָן זֶה יָצַרְתָּ לְשַׂחֶק בּוֹ: כֻּלָּם אֵלֶיךָ יְשַׂבֵּרוּן לָתֵת אָכְלָם בְּעִתּוֹ: תִּתֵּן לָהֶם יִלְקֹטוּן תִּפְתַּח יָדְךָ יִשְׂבְּעוּן טוֹב: תַּסְתִּיר פָּנֶיךָ יִבָּהֵלוּן תֹּסֵף רוּחָם יִגְוָעוּן וְאֶל עֲפָרָם יְשׁוּבוּן: תְּשַׁלַּח רוּחֲךָ יִבָּרֵאוּן וּתְחַדֵּשׁ פְּנֵי אֲדָמָה: יְהִי כְבוֹד יְיָ לְעוֹלָם יִשְׂמַח יְיָ בְּמַעֲשָׂיו: הַמַּבִּיט לָאָרֶץ וַתִּרְעָד יִגַּע בֶּהָרִים וְיֶעֱשָׁנוּ: אָשִׁירָה לַיְיָ בְּחַיָּי אֲזַמְּרָה לֵאלֹהַי בְּעוֹדִי: יֶעֱרַב עָלָיו שִׂיחִי אָנֹכִי אֶשְׂמַח בַּיְיָ: יִתַּמּוּ חַטָּאִים מִן הָאָרֶץ וּרְשָׁעִים עוֹד אֵינָם בָּרְכִי נַפְשִׁי אֶת יְיָ הַלְלוּיָהּ:

Additions to Birkat Hamazon (Blessings after the Meal) (Ya-aleh v'yavo is translated from Rabbi Daniel Siegel)

Our God and the God of our fathers and mothers, may our prayer arise and come to you, and be beheld, and be acceptable. Let it be heard, acted upon, remembered—the memory of us and our needs, of our ancestors and of the days of our future redemption, the memory of Jerusalem your holy city, and the memory of all your kin, the house of Israel, all surviving in your presence. Act for goodness and grace, for love and care; for life, well-being, and peace on this day of the new moon.

Remember us this day, Adonai our God, for goodness. Favor us this day with blessing. Preserve us this day for life. With your redeeming and nurturing word,

be kind and generous. Act tenderly on our behalf, and grant us victory over all
our trials. Truly, our eyes turn toward you, for you are a providing God; gracious and merciful are you.

אֱלֹהֵינוּ וֵאלֹהֵי אֲבוֹתֵינוּ וְאִמּוֹתֵינוּ
יַעֲלֶה וְיָבוֹא וְיַגִּיעַ וְיֵרָאֶה וְיֵרָצֶה וְיִשָּׁמַע וְיִפָּקֵד וְיִזָּכֵר זִכְרוֹנֵנוּ וּפִקְדוֹנֵנוּ
וְזִכְרוֹן אֲבוֹתֵינוּ וְאִמּוֹתֵינוּ וְזִכְרוֹן יְמוֹת מָשִׁיחַ צִדְקֶךָ
וְזִכְרוֹן יְרוּשָׁלַיִם עִיר קָדְשֶׁךָ וְזִכְרוֹן כָּל־עַמְּךָ בֵּית יִשְׂרָאֵל לְפָנֶיךָ
לִפְלֵיטָה וּלְטוֹבָה לְחֵן וּלְחֶסֶד וּלְרַחֲמִים לְחַיִּים וּלְשָׁלוֹם בְּיוֹם
רֹאשׁ הַחֹדֶשׁ הַזֶּה
זָכְרֵנוּ יהוה אֱלֹהֵינוּ בּוֹ לְטוֹבָה וּפָקְדֵנוּ בוֹ לִבְרָכָה וְהוֹשִׁיעֵנוּ בוֹ לְחַיִּים
וּבִדְבַר יְשׁוּעָה וְרַחֲמִים חוּס וְחָנֵּנוּ וְרַחֵם עָלֵינוּ וְהוֹשִׁיעֵנוּ
כִּי אֵלֶיךָ עֵינֵינוּ כִּי אֵל חַנּוּן וְרַחוּם אָתָּה.

*(Also add to the Birkat haMazon the following verse, within the section
HaRachaman.)*

May Adonai renew this month for goodness and for blessing.

הרחמן, הוא יחדש עלינו את־החדש הזה לטובה ולברכה

Additions to Rosh Chodesh Shacharit and Minchah Amidah
(Ya-aleh v'yavo is translated from Rabbi Daniel Siegel)

Our God and the God of our fathers and mothers, may our prayer arise and
come to you, and be beheld, and be acceptable. Let it be heard, acted upon,
remembered—the memory of us and our needs, of our ancestors and of the
days of our future redemption, the memory of Jerusalem your holy city, and
the memory of all your kin, the house of Israel, all surviving in your presence.
Act for goodness and grace, for love and care; for life, well-being, and peace
on this day of the new moon.
Remember us this day, Adonai our God, for goodness. Favor us this day with
blessing. Preserve us this day for life. With your redeeming and nurturing word,
be kind and generous. Act tenderly on our behalf, and grant us victory over all
our trials. Truly, our eyes turn toward you, for you are a providing God; gracious and merciful are you.

אֱלֹהֵינוּ וֵאלֹהֵי אֲבוֹתֵינוּ וְאִמּוֹתֵינוּ
יַעֲלֶה וְיָבוֹא וְיַגִּיעַ וְיֵרָאֶה וְיֵרָצֶה וְיִשָּׁמַע וְיִפָּקֵד וְיִזָּכֵר זִכְרוֹנֵנוּ וּפִקְדוֹנֵנוּ
וְזִכְרוֹן אֲבוֹתֵינוּ וְאִמּוֹתֵינוּ וְזִכְרוֹן יְמוֹת מָשִׁיחַ צִדְקֶךָ
וְזִכְרוֹן יְרוּשָׁלַיִם עִיר קָדְשֶׁךָ וְזִכְרוֹן כָּל־עַמְּךָ בֵּית יִשְׂרָאֵל לְפָנֶיךָ
לִפְלֵיטָה וּלְטוֹבָה לְחֵן וּלְחֶסֶד וּלְרַחֲמִים לְחַיִּים וּלְשָׁלוֹם בְּיוֹם

רֹאשׁ הַחֹדֶשׁ הַזֶּה

זָכְרֵנוּ יהוה אֱלֹהֵינוּ בּוֹ לְטוֹבָה וּפָקְדֵנוּ בוֹ לִבְרָכָה וְהוֹשִׁיעֵנוּ בוֹ לְחַיִּים
וּבִדְבַר יְשׁוּעָה וְרַחֲמִים חוּס וְחָנֵּנוּ וְרַחֵם עָלֵינוּ וְהוֹשִׁיעֵנוּ
כִּי אֵלֶיךָ עֵינֵינוּ כִּי אֵל חַנּוּן וְרַחוּם אָתָּה.

Additions to Rosh Chodesh Musaf Amidah

Additions to the Weekday Rosh Chodesh Musaf Amidah

(Tefillin is removed before Musaf)
(Translation adapted from *The Complete ArtScroll/Mesorah Siddur*)
"Roshei Chodshim/New Moons" follows "Atah Kadosh/You are Holy" and is
followed by the "Kedushah."

רָאשֵׁי New Moons have You given Your people, a time of atonement for all
their offspring, when they would bring before You offerings for favor and goats
of sin-offering to atone on their behalf. They would serve as a remembrance
for them all and a salvation for their soul from the hand of the enemy. May
You establish a new Altar in Zion, and may we bring up upon it the elevation-
offering of the new moon, and prepare he-goats with favor. In the service of
the Holy Temple may we all rejoice and in the songs of Your servant David
that are heard in Your City, when they are recited before Your Altar. May You
bring them an eternal love and the covenant of the ancestors may You recall
upon the children.

רָאשֵׁי חֲדָשִׁים לְעַמְּךָ נָתָתָּ, זְמַן כַּפָּרָה לְכָל תּוֹלְדוֹתָם. בִּהְיוֹתָם מַקְרִיבִים לְפָנֶיךָ זִבְחֵי
רָצוֹן, וּשְׂעִירֵי חַטָּאת לְכַפֵּר בַּעֲדָם. זִכָּרוֹן לְכֻלָּם יִהְיוּ, וּתְשׁוּעַת נַפְשָׁם מִיַּד שׂוֹנֵא. מִזְבֵּחַ
חָדָשׁ בְּצִיּוֹן תָּכִין, וּבַעֲבוֹדַת בֵּית הַמִּקְדָּשׁ נִשְׂמַח כֻּלָּנוּ, וּבְשִׁירֵי דָוִד עַבְדֶּךָ הַנִּשְׁמָעִים
בְּעִירֶךָ, הָאֲמוּרִים לִפְנֵי מִזְבְּחֶךָ, אַהֲבַת עוֹלָם תָּבִיא לָהֶם, וּבְרִית אָבוֹת וְאִמָּהוֹת לַבָּנִים
תִּזְכּוֹר. וַהֲבִיאֵנוּ לְצִיּוֹן עִירְךָ בְּרִנָּה, וְלִירוּשָׁלַיִם בֵּית מִקְדָּשְׁךָ בְּשִׂמְחַת עוֹלָם וְשָׁם נַעֲשֶׂה
לְפָנֶיךָ אֶת קָרְבְּנוֹת חוֹבוֹתֵינוּ תְּמִידִים כְּסִדְרָם, וּמוּסָפִים כְּהִלְכָתָם. וְאֶת מוּסַף יוֹם רֹאשׁ
הַחֹדֶשׁ הַזֶּה, עָשׂוּ וְהִקְרִיבוּ לְפָנֶיךָ בְּאַהֲבָה, כְּמִצְוַת רְצוֹנֶךָ, כְּמוֹ שֶׁכָּתַבְתָּ עָלֵינוּ בְּתוֹרָתֶךָ,
עַל יְדֵי מֹשֶׁה עַבְדֶּךָ מִפִּי כְבוֹדֶךָ, כָּאָמוּר:

"U'vRoshei/And your New Moons" and "Eloheynu v'Elohey/Our God"
follow "V'havi-einu/May You bring." (*Add words in brackets during leap year.*)
וּבְרָאשֵׁי And on your New Moons you are to bring an elevation-offering to
HASHEM: two young bulls; one ram; seven yearling rams—unblemished. And
their meal-offerings and their drink-offerings as specified: three-tenth-ephah
for each bull; two-tenth-ephah for the ram; one-tenth-ephah for atonement, and
two continual daily offerings according to their law.

אֱלֹהֵינוּ Our God and the God of our ancestors, inaugurate for us this month
for good and for blessing (Amen), for joy and for gladness (Amen), for salva-

tion and for consolation (Amen), for pardon of sin and forgiveness of iniquity (Amen), [*during a leap year add: and for atonement of willful sin (Amen)*], for You have chosen Your people Israel from all the nations, and You have set forth the decrees of the New Moons for them. Blessed are You HASHEM, Who sanctifies Israel and the New Moons.

וּבְרָאשֵׁי חָדְשֵׁיכֶם תַּקְרִיבוּ עוֹלָה לַיְיָ, פָּרִים בְּנֵי בָקָר שְׁנַיִם, וְאַיִל אֶחָד, כְּבָשִׂים בְּנֵי שָׁנָה שִׁבְעָה תְמִימִם: וּמִנְחָתָם וְנִסְכֵּיהֶם כִּמְדֻבָּר, שְׁלֹשָׁה עֶשְׂרֹנִים לַפָּר, וּשְׁנֵי עֶשְׂרֹנִים לָאַיִל, וְעִשָּׂרוֹן לַכֶּבֶשׂ, וְיַיִן כְּנִסְכּוֹ, וְשָׂעִיר לְכַפֵּר, וּשְׁנֵי תְמִידִים כְּהִלְכָתָם:

אֱלֹהֵינוּ וֵאלֹהֵי אֲבוֹתֵינוּ וְאִמּוֹתֵינוּ. חַדֵּשׁ עָלֵינוּ אֶת הַחֹדֶשׁ הַזֶּה, לְטוֹבָה וְלִבְרָכָה, לְשָׂשׂוֹן וּלְשִׂמְחָה. לִישׁוּעָה וּלְנֶחָמָה. לְפַרְנָסָה וּלְכַלְכָּלָה. לְחַיִּים וּלְשָׁלוֹם. לִמְחִילַת חֵטְא וְלִסְלִיחַת עָוֹן (בשנת העבור וּלְכַפָּרַת פָּשַׁע). כִּי בְעַמְּךָ יִשְׂרָאֵל בָּחַרְתָּ מִכָּל הָאֻמּוֹת. וְחֻקֵּי רָאשֵׁי חֲדָשִׁים לָהֶם קָבָעְתָּ: בָּרוּךְ אַתָּה יְיָ, מְקַדֵּשׁ יִשְׂרָאֵל וְרָאשֵׁי חֲדָשִׁים:

Additions to the Shabbat Rosh Chodesh Musaf Amidah

(Translations adapted from The Complete ArtScroll/Mesorah Siddur)
The "Atah Y'Tzarta/You fashioned Your World" addition follows the regular Shabbat Kedushah and is included rather than Tikanta Shabbat/You established Shabbat.

אַתָּה יָצְרְתָּ You fashioned Your world from of old; You completed Your work on the Seventh Day. You loved us, found favor in us, and raised us above all tongues, sanctified us through Your commandments and drew us near to Your service, our Ruler and Your great and holy Name You proclaimed upon us. And You gave us, HASHEM, our God, with love, Sabbaths for contentment and New Moons for atonement. But because we sinned before You—we and our ancestors—our City was destroyed and our Holy Temple was made desolate, our honor was exiled and glory was taken from the House of our life. So we cannot fulfill our responsibilities in Your chosen House, in the great and holy House upon which Your Name was called, because of the hand that was sent against Your Sanctuary. May it be Your will, HASHEM, our God and the God of our ancestors, that You bring us up in gladness to our land and plant us within our boundaries. There we will perform before You the rite of our required offerings, the continual offerings in their order and the musaf offerings according to their laws. And the musaf offerings of this Sabbath day and this day of the New Moon we will perform and bring near to You with love according to the commandment of Your will, as You have written for us in Your Torah, through Moses, Your servant, from Your glorious expression, as is said.

אַתָּה יָצַרְתָּ עוֹלָמְךָ מִקֶּדֶם, כִּלִּיתָ מְלַאכְתְּךָ בַּיּוֹם הַשְּׁבִיעִי. אָהַבְתָּ אוֹתָנוּ וְרָצִיתָ בָּנוּ, וְרוֹמַמְתָּנוּ מִכָּל הַלְּשׁוֹנוֹת, וְקִדַּשְׁתָּנוּ בְּמִצְוֹתֶיךָ, וְקֵרַבְתָּנוּ מַלְכֵּנוּ לַעֲבוֹדָתֶךָ, וְשִׁמְךָ

הַגָּדוֹל וְהַקָּדוֹשׁ עָלֵינוּ קָרֵאתָ. וַתִּתֶּן לָנוּ יְיָ אֱלֹהֵינוּ בְּאַהֲבָה שַׁבָּתוֹת לִמְנוּחָה, וְרָאשֵׁי
חֳדָשִׁים לְכַפָּרָה. וּלְפִי שֶׁחָטָאנוּ לְפָנֶיךָ אֲנַחְנוּ וַאֲבוֹתֵינוּ, חָרְבָה עִירֵנוּ, וְשָׁמֵם בֵּית
מִקְדָּשֵׁנוּ, וְגָלָה יְקָרֵנוּ, וְנִטַּל כָּבוֹד מִבֵּית חַיֵּינוּ. וְאֵין אֲנַחְנוּ יְכוֹלִים לַעֲשׂוֹת חוֹבוֹתֵינוּ
בְּבֵית בְּחִירָתֶךָ, בַּבַּיִת הַגָּדוֹל וְהַקָּדוֹשׁ שֶׁנִּקְרָא שִׁמְךָ עָלָיו, מִפְּנֵי הַיָּד שֶׁנִּשְׁתַּלְּחָה
בְּמִקְדָּשֶׁךָ: יְהִי רָצוֹן מִלְּפָנֶיךָ יְיָ אֱלֹהֵינוּ וֵאלֹהֵי אֲבוֹתֵינוּ, שֶׁתַּעֲלֵנוּ בְשִׂמְחָה לְאַרְצֵנוּ,
וְתִטָּעֵנוּ בִּגְבוּלֵנוּ. וְשָׁם נַעֲשֶׂה לְפָנֶיךָ אֶת קָרְבְּנוֹת חוֹבוֹתֵינוּ, תְּמִידִים כְּסִדְרָם וּמוּסָפִים
כְּהִלְכָתָם. וְאֶת מוּסְפֵי יוֹם הַשַּׁבָּת הַזֶּה, וְיוֹם רֹאשׁ הַחֹדֶשׁ הַזֶּה, עָשׂוּ וְהִקְרִיבוּ לְפָנֶיךָ
בְּאַהֲבָה כְּמִצְוַת רְצוֹנֶךָ, כְּמוֹ שֶׁכָּתַבְתָּ עָלֵינוּ בְּתוֹרָתֶךָ, עַל יְדֵי מֹשֶׁה עַבְדֶּךָ. מִפִּי כְבוֹדֶךָ,
כָּאָמוּר:

אֱלֹהֵינוּ וֵאלֹהֵי אֲבוֹתֵינוּ וְאִמּוֹתֵינוּ, רְצֵה בִמְנוּחָתֵנוּ וְחַדֵּשׁ עָלֵינוּ בְּיוֹם הַשַּׁבָּת הַזֶּה, אֶת
הַחֹדֶשׁ הַזֶּה, לְטוֹבָה וְלִבְרָכָה, לְשָׂשׂוֹן וּלְשִׂמְחָה. לִישׁוּעָה וּלְנֶחָמָה. לְפַרְנָסָה וּלְכַלְכָּלָה.
לְחַיִּים וּלְשָׁלוֹם. לִמְחִילַת חֵטְא וְלִסְלִיחַת עָוֹן. (בשנת העבור וּלְכַפָּרַת פָּשַׁע). כִּי בְעַמְּךָ
יִשְׂרָאֵל בָּחַרְתָּ מִכָּל הָאֻמּוֹת, וְשַׁבַּת קָדְשְׁךָ לָהֶם הוֹדָעְתָּ, וְחֻקֵּי רָאשֵׁי חֳדָשִׁים לָהֶם קָבָעְתָּ:
בָּרוּךְ אַתָּה יְיָ, מְקַדֵּשׁ הַשַּׁבָּת וְיִשְׂרָאֵל וְרָאשֵׁי חֳדָשִׁים:

Kiddush Levana/Sanctification of the Moon

(Translation adapted from *The Complete ArtScroll/Mesorah Siddur*)
Psalm 148:1–6

הַלְלוּיָהּ Halleluyah! Praise HASHEM from the heavens; praise God the heights.
Praise God all God's angels; praise God, all God's legions. Praise God, sun
and moon; praise God, all bright stars. Praise God the most exalted of the heavens and the waters that are above the heavens. Let them praise the Name of
HASHEM, for God commanded and they were created. And God established
them forever and ever; God issued a decree that will not change.

One should look at the moon before reciting this blessing:

בָּרוּךְ Blessed are You, HASHEM, our God, God of the Universe. What with
God's utterance created the heavens, and with the breath of God's mouth all
their legion. A decree and a schedule did God give them that they not alter their
assigned task. They are joyous and glad to perform the will of their Owner—
the Worker of truth Whose work is truth. To the moon God said that it should
renew itself as a crown of splendor for those borne [by God] from the womb,
those who are destined to renew themselves like it and to glorify their Molder
for the name of God's glorious kingdom. Blessed are You, HASHEM, who
renews the months.

Recite three times—Blessed is your Molder; blessed is your Maker; blessed
is your Owner; blessed is your Creator.

Upon reciting the next verse, rise on the toes as if in dance:

Recite three times—Just as I dance toward You but cannot touch You, so
may none of my enemies be able to touch me for evil.

Recite three times—Let fall upon them fear and terror; at the greatness of Your arm, let them be still as stone.

Recite three times—As stone let them be still, at Your arm's greatness; terror and fear, upon them let fall.

Recite three times—David, King of Israel, is alive and enduring.

Extend greetings to three different people—Peace upon you—who, in turn, respond—Upon you, peace.

Recite three times—May there be a good sign and a good fortune for us and for all Israel. Amen.

קוֹל The voice of my beloved—Behold! It came suddenly, leaping over mountains, skipping over hills. My beloved is like a gazelle or a young hart. Behold! He was standing behind our wall, observing through the windows, peering through the lattices.

Psalm 121

שִׁיר לַמַּעֲלוֹת A song to the ascents. I raise my eyes to the mountains; whence will come my help? My help is from HASHEM, Maker of heaven and earth. God will not allow your foot to falter; your Guardian will not slumber. Behold, God neither slumbers nor sleeps–the Guardian of Israel. HASHEM is your Guardian; HASHEM is your Shade at your right hand. By day the sun will not harm you, nor the moon by night. HASHEM will protect you from every evil; God will guard your soul. HASHEM will guard your departure and your arrival, from this time and forever.

Psalm 150

הַלְלוּיָהּ Halleluyah! Praise God in God's Sanctuary; praise God in the firmament of God's power. Praise God for God's mighty acts; praise God as befits God's abundant greatness. Praise God with the blast of the shofar; praise God with lyre and harp. Praise God with drum and dance; praise God with organ and flute. Praise God with clanging cymbals; praise God with resonant trumpets. Let all souls praise God, Halleluyah!

תְּנָא The Academy of Rabbi Yishmael taught: Had Israel not been privileged to greet the countenance of their Creator in Heaven except for once a month—it would have sufficed them. Abaye said: Therefore one must recite it while standing.

Who is this who rises from the desert clinging to her Beloved!

וִיהִי May it be Your will, HASHEM, my God and the God of my ancestors, to fill the flaw of the moon that there be no diminution in it. May the light of the moon be like the light of the sun and like the light of the seven days of creation, as it was before it was diminished, as it is said: "The two great luminaries." And may there be fulfilled upon us the verse that is written: They shall seek HASHEM, their God, and David, their king. Amen.

Psalm 67

לַמְנַצֵּחַ For the Conductor, upon Neginos, a psalm, a song. May God favor us and bless us, may God illuminate God's countenance with us, Selah. To make known Your way on earth, among all the nations Your salvation. The peoples will acknowledge You, O God, the peoples will acknowledge You, all of them. Nations will be glad and sing for joy, because You will judge the peoples fairly and guide the nations on earth, Selah. Then peoples will acknowledge You, O God, the peoples will acknowledge You, all of them. The earth has yielded its produce; may God, our own God, bless us. May God bless us and may all the ends of the earth fear God.

סדר קדוש לבנה

הַלְלוּיָהּ, הַלְלוּ אֶת יְיָ מִן הַשָּׁמַיִם, הַלְלוּהוּ בַּמְּרוֹמִים: הַלְלוּהוּ כָל מַלְאָכָיו, הַלְלוּהוּ כָּל צְבָאָיו: הַלְלוּהוּ שֶׁמֶשׁ וְיָרֵחַ, הַלְלוּהוּ כָּל כּוֹכְבֵי אוֹר: הַלְלוּהוּ שְׁמֵי הַשָּׁמַיִם וְהַמַּיִם אֲשֶׁר מֵעַל הַשָּׁמָיִם: יְהַלְלוּ אֶת שֵׁם יְיָ, כִּי הוּא צִוָּה וְנִבְרָאוּ: וַיַּעֲמִידֵם לָעַד לְעוֹלָם, חָק נָתַן וְלֹא יַעֲבוֹר:

ברכת הלבנה

בָּרוּךְ אַתָּה יְיָ אֱלֹהֵינוּ מֶלֶךְ הָעוֹלָם, אֲשֶׁר בְּמַאֲמָרוֹ בָּרָא שְׁחָקִים, וּבְרוּחַ פִּיו כָּל צְבָאָם, חֹק וּזְמַן נָתַן לָהֶם שֶׁלֹּא יְשַׁנּוּ אֶת תַּפְקִידָם. שָׂשִׂים וּשְׂמֵחִים לַעֲשׂוֹת רְצוֹן קוֹנָם, פּוֹעֵל אֱמֶת שֶׁפְּעֻלָּתוֹ אֱמֶת, וְלַלְּבָנָה אָמַר שֶׁתִּתְחַדֵּשׁ עֲטֶרֶת תִּפְאֶרֶת לַעֲמוּסֵי בָטֶן, שֶׁהֵם עֲתִידִים לְהִתְחַדֵּשׁ כְּמוֹתָהּ וּלְפָאֵר לְיוֹצְרָם עַל שֵׁם כְּבוֹד מַלְכוּתוֹ. בָּרוּךְ אַתָּה יְיָ, מְחַדֵּשׁ חֲדָשִׁים.

שלש פעמים בָּרוּךְ יוֹצְרֵךְ, בָּרוּךְ עוֹשֵׂךְ, בָּרוּךְ קוֹנֵךְ, בָּרוּךְ בּוֹרְאֵךְ.
שלש פעמים כְּשֵׁם שֶׁאֲנִי רוֹקֵד כְּנֶגְדֵּךְ וְאֵינִי יָכוֹל לִנְגֹּעַ בָּךְ, כַּךְ לֹא יוּכְלוּ כָל אוֹיְבַי לִנְגֹּעַ בִּי לְרָעָה.
שלש פעמים תִּפֹּל עֲלֵיהֶם אֵימָתָה וָפַחַד, בִּגְדֹל זְרוֹעֲךָ יִדְּמוּ כָּאָבֶן.
שלש פעמים כָּאָבֶן יִדְּמוּ זְרוֹעֲךָ בִּגְדֹל וָפַחַד אֵימָתָה עֲלֵיהֶם תִּפֹּל.

שלש פעמים דָּוִד מֶלֶךְ יִשְׂרָאֵל חַי וְקַיָּם.
ויאמר לחברו שלש פעמים: שָׁלוֹם עֲלֵיכֶם. והחברו משיב: עֲלֵיכֶם שָׁלוֹם.
שלש פעמים סִמָּן טוֹב וּמַזָּל טוֹב יְהֵא לָנוּ וּלְכָל יִשְׂרָאֵל, אָמֵן.

קוֹל דּוֹדִי הִנֵּה זֶה בָּא, מְדַלֵּג עַל הֶהָרִים, מְקַפֵּץ עַל הַגְּבָעוֹת: דּוֹמֶה דוֹדִי לִצְבִי אוֹ לְעֹפֶר הָאַיָּלִים, הִנֵּה זֶה עוֹמֵד אַחַר כָּתְלֵנוּ, מַשְׁגִּיחַ מִן הַחַלּוֹנוֹת מֵצִיץ מִן הַחֲרַכִּים.

שִׁיר לַמַּעֲלוֹת, אֶשָּׂא עֵינַי אֶל הֶהָרִים, מֵאַיִן יָבוֹא עֶזְרִי: עֶזְרִי מֵעִם יְיָ, עֹשֵׂה שָׁמַיִם וָאָרֶץ: אַל יִתֵּן לַמּוֹט רַגְלֶךָ, אַל יָנוּם שֹׁמְרֶךָ: הִנֵּה לֹא יָנוּם וְלֹא יִישָׁן שׁוֹמֵר יִשְׂרָאֵל: יְיָ שֹׁמְרֶךָ, יְיָ צִלְּךָ עַל יַד יְמִינֶךָ: יוֹמָם הַשֶּׁמֶשׁ לֹא יַכֶּכָּה, וְיָרֵחַ בַּלָּיְלָה: יְיָ יִשְׁמָרְךָ מִכָּל רָע יִשְׁמֹר אֶת נַפְשֶׁךָ: יְיָ יִשְׁמָר צֵאתְךָ וּבוֹאֶךָ מֵעַתָּה וְעַד עוֹלָם:

הַלְלוּיָהּ, הַלְלוּ אֵל בְּקָדְשׁוֹ, הַלְלוּהוּ בִּרְקִיעַ עֻזּוֹ: הַלְלוּהוּ בִּגְבוּרֹתָיו, הַלְלוּהוּ כְּרֹב גֻּדְלוֹ: הַלְלוּהוּ בְּתֵקַע שׁוֹפָר, הַלְלוּהוּ בְּנֵבֶל וְכִנּוֹר: הַלְלוּהוּ בְּתֹף וּמָחוֹל, הַלְלוּהוּ בְּמִנִּים וְעֻגָב: הַלְלוּהוּ בְּצִלְצְלֵי שָׁמַע, הַלְלוּהוּ בְּצִלְצְלֵי תְרוּעָה: כֹּל הַנְּשָׁמָה תְּהַלֵּל יָהּ, הַלְלוּיָהּ:

תָּנָא דְּבֵי רַבִּי יִשְׁמָעֵאל: אִלְמָלֵי לֹא זָכוּ יִשְׂרָאֵל אֶלָּא לְהַקְבִּיל פְּנֵי אֲבִיהֶם שֶׁבַּשָּׁמַיִם פַּעַם אַחַת בַּחֹדֶשׁ, דַּיָּם. אָמַר אַבַּיֵּי: הִלְכָךְ צָרִיךְ לְמֵימְרָא מְעֻמָּד. מִי זֹאת עֹלָה מִן הַמִּדְבָּר מִתְרַפֶּקֶת עַל דּוֹדָהּ.

וִיהִי רָצוֹן מִלְּפָנֶיךָ יְיָ אֱלֹהַי וֵאלֹהֵי אֲבוֹתַי וְאִמּוֹתַי, לְמַלֹּאת פְּגִימַת הַלְּבָנָה וְלֹא יִהְיֶה בָּהּ שׁוּם מְעוּט, וִיהִי אוֹר הַלְּבָנָה כְּאוֹר הַחַמָּה וּכְאוֹר שִׁבְעַת יְמֵי בְרֵאשִׁית, כְּמוֹ שֶׁהָיְתָה קֹדֶם מִעוּטָהּ, שֶׁנֶּאֱמַר: אֶת שְׁנֵי הַמְּאוֹרוֹת הַגְּדוֹלִים. וְיִתְקַיֵּם בָּנוּ מִקְרָא שֶׁכָּתוּב: וּבִקְּשׁוּ אֶת יְיָ אֱלֹהֵיהֶם וְאֵת דָּוִיד מַלְכָּם, אָמֵן.

לַמְנַצֵּחַ בִּנְגִינוֹת מִזְמוֹר שִׁיר: אֱלֹהִים יְחָנֵּנוּ וִיבָרְכֵנוּ, יָאֵר פָּנָיו אִתָּנוּ סֶלָה: לָדַעַת בָּאָרֶץ דַּרְכֶּךָ, בְּכָל גּוֹיִם יְשׁוּעָתֶךָ: יוֹדוּךָ עַמִּים אֱלֹהִים, יוֹדוּךָ עַמִּים כֻּלָּם: יִשְׂמְחוּ וִירַנְּנוּ לְאֻמִּים, כִּי תִשְׁפֹּט עַמִּים מִישֹׁר, וּלְאֻמִּים בָּאָרֶץ תַּנְחֵם סֶלָה: יוֹדוּךָ עַמִּים אֱלֹהִים, יוֹדוּךָ עַמִּים כֻּלָּם.אֶרֶץ נָתְנָה יְבוּלָהּ, יְבָרְכֵנוּ אֱלֹהִים אֱלֹהֵינוּ: יְבָרְכֵנוּ אֱלֹהִים, וְיִירְאוּ אֹתוֹ כָּל אַפְסֵי אָרֶץ:

Appendix E
Moon Musings

Although this is not a book on astronomy, I offer a few interesting pieces of information about the moon.[1]

The moon has one-sixth the gravity of the earth.

Its highest mountain rises 25,000 feet, and its deepest crater dips 10,000 feet.

The moon has no atmosphere—there is no air to breathe.

Each moon day and moon night is fourteen earth days long.

The dark side of the moon is the side we do not ever see because the moon turns in the same amount of time as it orbits the earth.

The moon is approximately 238,857 miles from the earth.

A moon beam is the light that shines off the moon towards earth. It takes that light 1.2 seconds to reach the earth from the moon.

The moon has no seasons. (The seasons of the earth are due to the 23-degree tip of the earth's axis.)

Because of the moon's gravitational force on the earth, it is responsible for the oceans' tides. (With one side of the earth farther from the moon than the other, the moon's gravitational force is stronger on the earth's nearer side, which causes the tides.) Spring tides (not based on the season, but referring to the larger size of the tide) occur twice monthly, at new and full moon when the sun, moon, and earth are lined up in conjunction.

No matter where we are on the earth, we see the same fraction of the moon. Jews around the world celebrate Rosh Chodesh at the same time.

Someone familiar with the phases of the moon could tell time by the place of the moon in the sky. The moon rises in the sky according to its phases.

Note

1. Much of this information about the moon is taken from Kathleen Cain, *Luna: Myth and Mystery* (Boulder: Johnson Books, 1991).

Appendix F
Diagram of Conjunction: The Sun, The Moon, and The Earth at Rosh Chodesh

The moon takes twenty-nine and a half days to complete its cycle from one new moon to another. That is why some months are twenty-nine days long and others are thirty days long. This also accounts for the number of Rosh Chodesh days per month.

When the moon is exactly between the earth and the sun, we do not see it because the earth is facing the moon's dark side. At the moment that the earth passes between the moon and the sun, it is completely invisible to us. This moment is called the *molad*, birth, of the moon. It marks the beginning of Rosh Chodesh, the new moon.

As the moon moves around the earth, we begin to see a sliver of moon that is being lit from the sun. This is the crescent waxing moon. The moon continues its cycle and each night we see a bit more of the moon until it is full, and then begins to wane.

The following illustration, which is viewed from right to left as the moon travels, shows the seven phases of the moon. I have included the returning new moon to illustrate the cyclical nature of the moon's travel through *seven* phases. The light areas reflect what we see of the moon.

new   waning crescent   waning gibbous   full   waxing gibbous   waxing crescent   new

The chart below[1] explains when, during a twenty-four hour period, we could see the moon according to its phase (on a four-phase cycle).

	new moon	first quarter	full	last quarter
rising:	at dawn	at noon	at sunset	at midnight
setting:	at sunset	at midnight	at dawn	at noon
visibility:	invisible	late afternoon	all night	late night/early morning

The following diagram illustrates how the sun, moon, and earth are positioned at Rosh Chodesh.

Note

1. Diana Brueton, *Many Moons* (New York: Prentice Hall, 1991), p. 218.

Appendix G
The Days
of the Hebrew Months

Month	Number of Days	Days of R.C.	Focus	Calendar Month	Letter	Tribe	Quality
Nisan	30 days	1	Pesach, Spring, Liberation	March/April	Hey	Judah	Speech
Iyar	29 days	2	Journeying, Omer, bow/rainbow/covenant	April/May	Vav	Issachar	Thought
Sivan	30 days	1	Torah, Shavuot, Peoplehood	May/June	Zayin	Zevulun	Action
Tammuz	29 days	2	Abandonment and connection, inheritance	June/July	Chet	Reuven	Sight
Av	30 days	1	Mourning, destruction, comfort	July/Aug.	Tet	Simion	Hearing
Elul	29 days	2	Searching, preparing oneself for The Days of Awe	Aug./Sept.	Yud	Gad	Action
Tishrei	30 days	1	New Year, renewal of Torah cycle, Fall	Sept./Oct.	Lamed	Ephraim	Coition
Cheshvan	29 or 30 days	2	Quiet, without Holidays, our matriarch Rachel	Oct./Nov.	Nun	Menasseh	Smell
Kislev	29 or 30 days	1 or 2	Rededication, Chanukah	Nov./Dec.	Samech	Benjamin	Sleep
Tevet	29 days	1 or 2	Light in darkness, fullness from emptiness	Dec./Jan.	Ayin	Dan	Anger
Sh'vat	30 days	1	Trees and fruit, Miriam's song and timbrels	Jan./Feb.	Tzadey	Asher	Taste
Adar[1]	29 days	2	Hidden and revealed, Purim/Queen Esther	Feb./March	Kuf	Naftali	Laughter

The months with 29 days have a two-day Rosh Chodesh, and months with 30 days have one day of Rosh Chodesh.

Each month of the year is joined to a Hebrew letter, tribe of Israel, quality, and permutation of the letters of the *Shem HaM'forash*, Tetragrammaton, the ineffable Name. Based on the *Sefer Yitzirah*, the Dynover Rebbe presented these "associations" with each month based on verses and personalities significant to the month.

Note

1.   There is a second month of Adar inserted into the calendar in a Jewish leap year. When this occurs, Adar I has thirty days and one day of Rosh Chodesh, and Adar II has twenty-nine days and two days of Rosh Chodesh. The Jewish calendar is based on an intercalation of solar and lunar cycles.

Appendix H
Five-Year Calendar
of Rosh Chodesh
Observances

Month	1999-2000 5759-5760	2000-1 5760-1	2001-2 5761-2	2002-3 5762-3	2003-4 5763-4
Nisan	March 18	April 6	March 25	March 14	April 3
Iyar	April 16-17	May 5-6	April 23-24	April 12-13	May 2-3
Sivan	May 16	June 4	May 23	May 12	June 1
Tammuz	June 14-15	July 3-4	June 21-22	June 10-11	June 30-July 1
Av	July 14	Aug. 2	July 21	July 10	July 30
Elul	Aug. 12-13	Aug. 31-Sept. 1	Aug. 19-20	Aug. 8-9	Aug. 28-29
Tishrei	Sept. 11	Sept. 30	Sept. 18	Sept. 7	Sept. 27
Cheshvan	Oct. 10-11	Oct. 29-30	Oct. 17-18	Oct. 6-7	Oct. 26-27
Kislev	Nov. 8-9	Nov. 28	Nov. 16	Nov. 5-6	Nov. 25-26
Tevet	Dec. 9-10	Dec. 27	Dec. 15-16	Dec. 5-6	Dec. 25-26
Sh'vat	Jan. 8	Jan. 25	Jan. 14	Jan. 4	Jan. 24
Adar	Feb. 6-7	Feb. 23-24	Feb. 12-13	Feb. 2-3	Feb. 22-23
Adar II	March 7-8			March 4-5	

Appendix I
Annotated Directory of
Rosh Chodesh Groups

The 1994 edition of this Directory was compiled by Susan Berrin, based on a 1992 listing by Beth Edberg for the Jewish Women's Resource Center of the National Council of Jewish Women, New York branch.

This directory has been organized for the benefit of those who would like to connect with other members of Rosh Chodesh groups. Some may wish to share ideas, creative rituals, or just learn from the experiences of other Rosh Chodesh observers. When traveling on Rosh Chodesh, you may want to visit a group in another area. If you are a member of a Rosh Chodesh group that was not included in this directory, please send a brief description of your group with a contact name, address, and phone number to Susan Berrin (address listed under British Columbia).

Brazil

Bat Kol Rosh Chodesh Group of the Jewish Congregation of Brazil
Av. Rui Barbosa 702/1201 Flamengo
Rio de Janeiro RJ, Brazil
contact: Esther Bin Szterenfeld 011–55–21– 551–1617 (from out of the country) or (021) 551–1617 (from within Brazil)
or contact: Celia Szterenfeld (021) 246–0695

We meet on the Wednesday closest to the day of Rosh Chodesh at 8:30 P.M. The Jewish Congregation of Brazil is a Conservative and egalitarian synagogue. The Bat Kol Rosh Chodesh group has been meeting for four years now to explore Jewish women's spirituality. Meetings follow a course of study determined by the group in the beginning of each Jewish year. We also include healing meditation techniques and new rituals designed for women living in the South. Some of our programs have been: The relationships between women in Torah, studying books such as *Written Out of History,* and women and halacha. We also prepare adult women for bat mitzvah. The group emphasizes interreligious dialogue and meets regularly with women from other traditions, mostly Catholic, Protestant, and Afro-Brazilian.

Canada

British Columbia

Or Shalom Rosh Chodesh Group
contact: Naomi Fenson
710 East 10th Street
Vancouver, British Columbia, Canada V5T 2A7
(604) 872–1614

Our group meets on the Tuesday evening closest to Rosh Chodesh at the Or Shalom building. Each woman brings a vegetarian snack to share. We have been meeting, in one form or another, since the early 1980s. Our rituals and gatherings vary. If you come to a Rosh Chodesh evening, this is an example of what you might experience. When you arrive you may be greeted by someone wanting to wash your hands or feet. You will find an altar in the center of the room, which may have candles, flowers, and sacred or symbolic objects on a beautiful cloth or scarf. The celebration itself will usually begin with a song, which may include dancing and drumming followed by an invocation over the candles. Then everyone will introduce themselves. One particularly nice custom is to give your name and the name of your mother and her mother as far back as you know.

Next there will be an exploration of a theme. This may be the month itself, the holiday it contains, or the theme of a Torah portion of that month. Other themes might honor a biblical or historic woman, or include a ritual for an important life-cycle event. Themes may be explored through a presentation followed by discussion, story, poem or midrash writing, song, dance, arts and crafts, and so forth. This is the focal point of the Rosh Chodesh gathering. Following this will be a healing ceremony and more music. The celebration will then close with final prayers and refreshments.

contact: Susan Berrin
903 Linden Avenue
Victoria, B.C., Canada, V8V 4G8
(604) 388–5498

We are a diverse group of women who meet on Rosh Chodesh to daven Schacharit together. We begin with a matrilineal welcome and include Hallel and a Torah reading in our service. We share refreshments and a time to visit and enjoy each other at the conclusion of the *tefillah* (service). Our group encourages women with varying skill levels to come forward and try out new davening skills. We also sponsor an annual women's seder and hopefully a women's learning retreat.

Manitoba

contact: Carol Rose
349 Matheson Avenue
Winnipeg, Manitoba Canada R2W 0C9
(204) 589–2026
or contact: Sharon Siegel
539 Waverly St.
Winnipeg R3M 3K7
(204) 488–6131

We have fifteen members and have been meeting for two years. We meet monthly on or close to Rosh Chodesh. We recently conducted a feminist seder for members and women in the community at large. We do rituals for healing and for members' life transitions (for example, after a *get*–divorce). We incorporate art, candle lighting, and movement into our monthly "renewal of creativity rite."

Quebec

Montreal Women's Tefillah Group
contact: Norma Joseph
5107 Lacombe
Montreal, Quebec Canada H3W 1S1
(514) 342–5931

We meet on Rosh Chodesh, usually at 8:00 A.M. We daven a traditional service using a siddur that we created (but do not distribute). We began thirteen years ago and have always met in a synagogue. We have access to a Sefer Torah and include a Torah reading in our service. We have special sessions for study, read Megillah on Purim, and study on Simchat Torah.

Israel

Jerusalem

contact: Debbie Weissman
P.O.Box10668
Jerusalem, Israel 91104
Telephone: (02) 721–247

Our group meets on Rosh Chodesh, or near to it. We are a closed group of ten to twelve women, with occasional, invited guests. We generally have a topic, related to the month, to discuss, such as "growth" for Sh'vat, "light" for Kislev, or "grief" for Av. Each woman who attends the meeting is free to bring a text or some creative writing to share. Someone will teach a song, another person will lead a discussion. We always have lots of food, soda, juice, and hot drinks to share.

Yeruham

contact: Leah Shakdiel
P.O. Box 285
Yeruham, Israel 80552
Telephone: (07) 580387

The group grew in the Afikim BaNegev (formerly Mashmi'a Shalom) Synagogue, the only synagogue in town (8,000 residents) where women vote and take office and say a D'Var Torah outside of services (during Kiddush, or Tikkun Leil Shavu'ot). At first we met for study on Rosh Chodesh. Ten years ago we started reading the Megillah on Purim. Four years ago we added Talmud study every Shabbat (Baba Matzi'a, with help from the English Steinsaltz edition). Last year, after our second encounter with the WUJS Kol Isha project, we started reading the Torah on Rosh Chodesh, and one Bat Mitzvah girl celebrated with us by reading. For the time being, we avoid saying D'var Shebi'k'dusha, and do not constitute a minyan. We develop together, read, write, talk, and keep up with similar developments across the Jewish world. Additional members and guests are welcome.

Netherlands

contact: Marcella Levie
Prinseneiland 291
Amsterdam, 1013 LP Netherlands
Telephone: (020) 624–1523
from outside of Holland, phone 00–31–20–6241523
or contact: Henny Esther van Dijk
De Lairessestraat 54/1
1071 PC Amsterdam Netherlands
Telephone: (020) 673–5470

Our group was formed in 1990 at the initiation of our friend, Leah Soeterdorp. We have about twenty women in the group. We generally begin our meeting with a candle lighting. Every woman lights their own candle and says a prayer, a wish, or anything she wants to share at that moment. Each month, the Rosh Chodesh evening is held in a different woman's home. One woman is the logistic hostess and another prepares the spiritual content of the evening.

Apart from sharing on an intellectual level (someone gives a short lecture on a Jewish subject or a teaching on a deeper meaning of a minhag), we have worked regularly with meditation, singing, more intimate sharing, and evaluating the goals and hopes for this group.

For the past few years, we have organized a beautiful seder, where lots of women showed up. We have also done special rituals for Yom Kippur and other holidays. We are always searching for new rituals. Every woman brings something to eat at our gatherings. The sharing of food is very important to us. We would like to see an international Rosh Chodesh event—bringing women together from all over the world—maybe next year in Israel!

United Kingdom

There are many Rosh Chodesh groups throughout the United Kingdom. Sharon Lee has been instrumental in creating a network of Rosh Chodesh groups and activities, as well as a newsletter, *The Jewish Women's Network*. For a listing of the groups, or to contact a specific group, please write:

Sharon Lee
41 Dorset Drive
Edgware, HA8 7NT, MIDDX, England
Telephone: 081–952–5308

United States of America

Arizona

Temple Beth Sholom
contact: Rabbi Bonnie Koppell
316 S. LeSueur
Mesa, AZ 85204
(602) 964–1981

Our group has taken several forms. We have had evening meetings featuring a combination of ritual, study, and sharing and lunchtime discussion groups. We are evolving into a synagogue-based women's group.

The Southwest Women's Rosh Chodesh Group
contact: Rabbi Ayla Grafstein (602) 759–7066
1501 E. Fairfield Street
Mesa, AZ 85203

Feminist, egalitarian, Jewish renewal orientation–including Orthodox, Conservative, Reform, Reconstructionist, and nonaffiliated. A sensitive, joyous group that shares on a deep personal level and creates special rituals monthly that reflect the particular energy of each month. Blends the traditional with the new. We hope to sing and dance more and meet outdoors in sacred places. Arizona has a lot to offer when it comes to beauty and nature.

California

Nishei Chabad Rosh Chodesh Group—East Bay San Francisco area
contact: Mitzi Cahn
1439 Bonita Avenue
Berkeley, CA 94709
(510) 848–3436

Meets in homes in Oakland, Berkeley, Albany, and El Cerrito. Speakers are invited to discuss topics related to holidays, Torah learning, family life, and so forth. Attendance is open to all. There are usually ten to twenty participants, and refreshments are served.

South Bay Rosh Chodesh
contact: Renee T. Sokolski
601 Via Monte D'Oro
Redondo Beach, CA 90277
(310) 540–5631

We have been in existence for five years and meet monthly as close to Rosh Chodesh as possible. Meetings are eclectic with two women presenting Jewish themes (Jewish art, political, etc.). Our group was an outgrowth of a women's retreat sponsored by the Jewish Federation. We have created a beautiful chupa that has all our Hebrew names in felt embroidered thereon, and at the close of each meeting we gather under this chupa, say the blessings over wine and bread, and sing a closing song.

Temple Isaiah Rosh Chodesh Group
contact: Rabbi Judy Shanks
3800 Mount Diablo Boulevard
Lafayette, CA 94549
(510) 283–8575

Our group meets each month on the Monday night closest to Rosh Chodesh in the synagogue. We are supported by the Temple Sisterhood and membership is open to all women, even if they are not Temple members. Each month we explore a different theme of Jewish women's spirituality, history, literature, festivals, and so forth. For the most part, members of the group take responsibility for planning the sessions, in consultation with the Rabbi. There is usually an opening ritual and/or songs, a "check-in" time where members can share news, updates, problems, and so forth; a programming time; and a closing ritual. We always have refreshments, provided by members and seasonally and/or ritually appropriate to the month.

The group has been meeting regularly for two years, with a core group of about thirty women.

Kehillath Israel
contact: Rabbi Alexis Roberts
Kehillath Israel 16019 Sunset Boulevard
Pacific Palisades, CA 90210
(310) 459–2328

We meet on a monthly Tuesday close to Rosh Chodesh. We open with poetry and prayer and close with a circle outdoors with candles and poetry. In between, we have a discussion or presentation related to the Torah portion or some women's issue. Basically, it is a discussion and support with a feminist group and spiritual basis.

Praise the 13th Moon
contact: Judith Rose
638 Hill Street no. 3
Santa Monica, CA 90405

I share Rosh Chodesh poetry and prayer with Jewish women on the telephone who are house-bound or who cannot get to a Rosh Chodesh circle that month. Traveling women are welcome to call. I have been doing this for the last few years with pleasure. My belief is: "When women are listened to they will be healed and the world will be healed."

contact: Rabbi Patricia Philo
P.O. Box 1066
Rohnert Park, CA 94931
(707) 664–8622

Our group is informally connected to our synagogue. The Rosh Chodesh service we use is designed for families to use and can be self-led. We incorporate candles, water, songs and prayers, and a story. One song is in sign language. Children and adults participate equally.

Rosh Chodesh Celebration
contact: Carol Lewis
759 E. Casad Street
Covina, CA 91723
(818) 966–3994

We meet on Rosh Chodesh except if it falls on a Friday or Saturday night. We base our celebrations on "Miriam's Well" and make our own contributions and modifications as we and the group unfold. We began meeting and celebrating in 1992 as a monthly study group of Dor Hadash Hadassah and we welcome all women in the Los Angeles vicinity, especially the San Gabriel and Pomona Valleys.

Temple Mishkan Tephilo's Women's Rosh Chodesh Group
contact: Rabbi Naomi Levy
201 Hampton Drive
Venice, CA 90291
(310) 392–3029

A group of women have been meeting at our synagogue to welcome the new moon for five years. We used to meet on a Sunday afternoon prior to Rosh Chodesh and share learning, creativity, ritual, music, and prayer. Now we meet on Rosh Chodesh with a women's minyan (Schacharit, Hallel, Torah reading, etc.), study, meditation, and lunch. We have, over the years, created many poems, prayers, works of art, tallitot, and rituals.

Jewish Feminist Center of the American Jewish Congress
contact: Director
6505 Wilshire Boulevard Suite 417
Los Angeles, CA 90048
(213) 651–4601

The center has sponsored innovative rituals to welcome each Rosh Chodesh over the past several years. Currently the center is working with local synagogues throughout Los Angeles to provide Rosh Chodesh celebrations. You may contact the center to find out about current programs.

Colorado

Jewish Women's Resource Center
contact: Marilyn Bogan
Jewish Community Center
P.O. Box 6196
Denver, CO 80206
(303) 322–9837 (home)

Monthly meetings are held at individuals' homes. Each month a member of the group leads a presentation/discussion on a relevant topic of interest to Jewish women. Topics have included God, prayer, women in Israel, holidays, lifecycle events, aging, intermarriage, and Jews in prison.

Nashei Hareh Shalom—Peaceful Women of the Mountains
contact: Cindy Gabriel
1701 W. Stuart Street
Fort Collins, CO 80526–1530
(303) 482–0710

We have been meeting on the Sunday evening closest to the new moon since Cheshvan 5751 (October 1991). Our membership is open to "all Jewishly connected women" and ten to twenty-five women gather each month as we study traditional texts, contemporary texts and our lives as text. We always study from the perspective of women. We have an annual women's Seder (seventh night) and a three-day summer retreat. We support each other in creating rituals, writing liturgy, and in exploring (wrestling with) our evolving relationships with Judaism and the Divine.

Connecticut

contact: Elana Ponet
35 High Street
New Haven, CT 06511
(203) 624–7158

Often we begin with candle lighting and some words of introduction by members of the group. The content of the celebration varies from shared study, discussion of a theme, a videotape, singing, poetry, and so forth. There is not a particular orientation and new members are always welcome.

Georgia

contact: Sherry Frank
140 Abernathy Road
Atlanta, GA 30328
(404) 255–1878 home
(404) 233–5501 work

We have been meeting since 1991 under the auspices of the Ahavat Achim Synagogue in Atlanta. Each month we meet, study about the new month, and discuss a chosen text we've read. We read books, articles, etc. about and by Jewish women. We have held three women's seders and a Tu B'Sh'vat seder, and for each new year we have begun a tradition of welcoming babies born into the group during the year at Succot. We've written creative verses to Dayenu for our seders, and we are going to write liturgy for the babies we welcome in our sukkah.

Kentucky

Judy Goldsmith
325 McDowell Road
Lexington, KY 40502
(606) 269–7218

We are still trying to form our group.

Illinois

The Rosh Chodesh group
contact: Susan P. Siebers
3949 Foster Road
Evanston, IL 60203
(708) 674–8999 or (312) 902–5675

We meet in members' homes in Chicago and its near north suburbs on Rosh Chodesh or, on occasion, on an intermediate day, when the service component is based on Kiddush HaLevanah, rather than Rosh Chodesh.

Our group has been meeting since 1980 and represents a wide range of personal observance. A typical Rosh Chodesh begins with a short service led by one of our members. Certain features have evolved over the years and are always included, such as everyone blowing the shofar, lighting a Rosh Chodesh candle, blessing a new fruit, and concluding with the Shehecheyanu.

There is always a topic for discussion, usually led by a different member. Some years we have had a unifying theme, such as life-cycle events, women from the Bible, or Jewish women from U.S. or world history. We may also discuss a short story, poetry, or a book that we have all read. Past topics have been ritual, God language, names, Midrash, and tkhines. We have visited art exhibits as a group and shared pot luck dinners in a sukkah. Each month there is some type of refreshment shared. Members provide postcards to one of our members who sends them back with the location, topic, and leader for the next celebration.

Massachusetts

Women of Temple Israel, Natick
contact: Shiela Wolfs
5 Gannon Terrace
Framingham, MA 01701
(508) 875–3735

Our group formed in March, 1993, and meets on the first Shabbat after Rosh Chodesh, immediately following Shabbat services at Temple Israel, a Conservative synagogue in Natick. We have a "lite" lunch together. Responsibility for the program varies from member to member, each month. Topics are holidays, life-cycle events, prayer, women's issues, and so forth. We generally have between ten and fifteen women at each session.

Haverot Hashkediya/Friends of the Almond Trees
contact: Judith Spiegel-Markson
11 Playstead Road
Newton, MA 02158–2124
(617) 244–4707

We began on Rosh Chodesh Sh'vat, February 1991. Our group combines study, art making—such as drawing or collage—creative movement, singing, and networking. We open our group with a candle welcome ceremony. Each member introduces herself through her matrilineal descent and then "checks in" about how the month has been. We close with a healing/strengthening circle.

Rosh Chodesh Bet of Temple Shalom
contact: Linda Grosser
(617) 965–6121
61 Collins Road
Newton, MA 02168

We formed in December 1991 and meet monthly. Our meetings often follow Penina Adelman's *Miriam's Well*, or we choose topics focused on spirituality, women, traditions of our mothers. We include prayers and meditations. Each year we do a women's seder for Passover, using a homegrown haggadah.

B'nai Or Women's Rosh Chodesh Group
contact: Carol Goldman
86 Carey Avenue
Watertown, MA 02172
(617) 926–1126

Carol has coordinated an open Rosh Chodesh group in the Boston area for six years. She would be happy to share rituals, stories, and ideas used by the group.

Temple Shalom of Newton
contact: Linda Krouner
54 Sheffield Road
Newton, MA 02160
(617) 964–1916

Temple Shalom sponsors several Rosh Chodesh groups, but any may be contacted through Linda Krouner. The groups meet individually each month and twice a year meet together. While the groups started out using Penina Adelman's *Miriam's Well* as a resource, they now choose to study topics such as women in the Torah, midrash, mitzvot, Jewish immigration and family trees, and so forth. The groups create rituals for each other and always spend tashlich as one large group.

contact: Janet Freedman
66 Stone Ledge Road
South Dartmouth, MA 02748
(508) 997–5481 home or
(508) 999–8663 work

Our bimonthly meetings open with a brief ritual, followed by a discussion on a topic determined at the previous meeting. We try to have facilitators or co-facilitators of the discussions, but they are often quite unstructured. The overall feeling is almost always one of warmth and sisterhood. Our sense of community is special, despite our diversity. We have had some very wonderful celebrations, including a baby-naming ceremony for a single mother in our group, dancing on the beach in the summer moonlight, hearing the stories from the mother of one of our members about the Yiddish community that nourished her spiritual and political life, learning how the daughter of another expresses herself as a young Jewish woman with a strong social conscience, celebrating holidays, and much more. Each summer we have a luncheon, often including a speaker from the annual Judaic Institute at Southeastern Massachusetts University.

South Shore Rosh Chodesh Group
contact: Sarah de Ris
363 Massapoag Avenue
Sharon, MA 02067
(617) 784–2032

Meets in participants homes in several towns south of Boston—Jamaica Plain, Weymouth, Sharon, Easton, Randolph, and Holbrook. This group of approximately thirteen women has been going for several years and is open by invitation only, both because of space considerations and for confidentiality reasons. We are a diverse group, observant and nonobservant, lesbian and straight, but we are all committed to feminist, egalitarian expressions of Judaism. We experiment with new rituals and prayers keyed to the Jewish calendar, share laughter and tears, have an annual group mikvah, cook, dance, and create. We made a beautiful Kaddish panel for the Names Project AIDS quilt.

Kesher Nashim of Temple Shalom
contact: Mona Yaguda Ross
38 Locksley Road
Newton Center, MA 02159
(617) 332–0095

We have been together over two years. We meet monthly on the Monday night closest to the new moon. We do introductory prayers and then study a topic (holiday, biblical woman, mitzvah). We always have food to close the evening.

contact: Penina Adelman
243 Upland Road
Newtonville, MA 02160
(617) 965–8309

Our group has recently started. Most of the members belong to the same conservative synagogue in Worcester. The members are looking for a chance to explore feminist spirituality through study, meditation, and ritual.

Cape Ann/Gloucester Rosh Chodesh group
contact: Ellen Solomon
179 Concord Street
Gloucester, MA 01930
(508) 281–2376

We began observing as a group on Rosh Chodesh Shevat, 1991. As we drove to our first meeting, we heard that the Gulf War had begun. We are a strong group with an age range from twenty-eight to fifty-six and a wide range of experience and comfort with traditional Judaism. We use Penina Adelman's *Miriam's Well* and Arthur Waskow's *Seasons of Our Joy* as our main resources. We are searching for a balance between creating each Rosh Chodesh anew every year, and feeling that we can repeat rituals that worked well in the past. We keep relearning the difference between ritual and discussion. We reach out to women from all over and beyond the Cape Ann area.

contact: Matia Angelou
P.O. Box 132
Wayland, MA 01778
(508) 358–7237
or contact:
Janet Zimmern
78 Kirkland Street
Cambridge, MA 01238
(617) 661–3157

Our group has been meeting in different members' homes around the Boston area for about fourteen years. We have a spiritual orientation with a feminist, egalitarian perspective. We are involved in group co-creation of new ceremonies—with singing, movement, meditation, discussion, personal sharing, some textual study—blending traditional themes with personal growth. We have about a dozen members of this long-standing Rosh Chodesh Group whose members are storytellers, singers, dancers, Jewish educators, and artists. To protect the intimacy of the group we do not have visitors, but would be happy to share resources and ideas. Some of our members contributed to Penina Adelman's book, *Miriam's Well,* and a photograph of our group appears in the book.

Temple Sha'aray Shalom Rosh Chodesh Group
contact: Anne Tolbert
367 Beach Avenue
Hull, MA 02045
(617) 925–1749

We have had an active Rosh Chodesh group at the Temple in Hingham, MA, for over three years. We use material from Penina Adelman's *Miriam's Well* as a starting point, but we go in many different directions. We create rituals to honor and celebrate events in the lives of the women in our group. We usually begin with a candle lighting, a blessing for the new month, new moon, a "kos Miriam," and a meditation. We also use Vicki Hollander's poem, "An Opening Ceremony," as printed in *Four Centuries of Jewish Women's Spirituality,* edited by Ellen M. Umansky and Diane Ashton. We have developed specific ceremonies for (1) coming of age, welcoming a young girl after her first period into the company of women, (2) a bride-to-be, (3) a *simchat,* or *brit, bat* (a welcoming ceremony for new babies) and (4) celebrating "being sixty" (as inspired by Phyllis Ocean Berman's article, "Recreating Menopause," in *Moment Magazine,* February 1994).

Temple Bnai Brith
contact: Rona Fischman
Temple Bnai Brith
201 Central Street
Somerville, MA 02145

Our group began Tishrei 5752 (October 1991). We do cycles of study (the life cycle, the holiday cycle, etc.) for a few months at a time. We made a tallit for ourselves (or our children). We sometimes read and discuss together books and articles.

Michigan

Chabad House
contact: Esther Goldstein
715 Hill Street
Ann Arbor, MI 48104
(313) 955–3276

Meets in different homes and at the Ann Arbor Chabad House. Our Rosh
Chodesh Women's group is scheduled at the beginning of every Jewish month.
Our gatherings are informal and include discussions about the new month. From
time to time we feature a special speaker or special entertainment by a Jewish
woman.

New Jersey

Women's Rosh Chodesh Group of Highland Park
contact: Judy Petsonk
149 N. 5th Avenue
Highland Park, NJ 08904
(908) 985–7513

We meet in different homes on the first Sunday evening after Rosh Chodesh
from 8:00 to 10:00 P.M. There is a wide range of observance in our group,
including a number of women who have been involved in the feminist and
havurah movements. We range in age from college students to grandmothers.
We rotate the planning and hosting of the group each month. Our group uses
Rosh Chodesh to share, search and grow together spiritually, learn about and
respond to the stories of women in the Jewish tradition, explore how the holidays and themes of Judaism are relevant to our lives as women, and develop
new rituals for transitions in our lives as women that are not traditionally recognized (e.g., postpartum, menopause). We use movenient, meditation, song,
and discussion in creative ways that are not generally possible in the context
of a traditional service. There is a $5 per year donation to cover the cost of
mailings.

Chabad of Edison, New Jersey
contact: Sarah Goodman
317 Harper Place
Highland Park, NJ 08904
(908) 846–6064

Chabad House has been running a monthly Rosh Chodesh women's group for the past five years. We celebrate Rosh Chodesh by gathering area women for an evening with a speaker and food and socializing. Discussions are a major part of those gatherings, investigating the vital power and influence the Jewish women of today possess and use.

contact: Rabbi Stephanie Dickstein
830 Hudson Street
Hoboken, NJ 07032
(201)–659–2614

Our group meets in the homes of participants on a weekday evening during the week of Rosh Chodesh. The group is now five years old. We generally choose a new topic for each session, with a theme inspired by the month. The topics range from poetry by and about women, biblical role models, and historical issues. Recently, we have begun experimenting with rituals at the beginning of the evening. Our group is organized through the United Synagogue of Hoboken, which is part of the Conservative movement. We are open to new members and we send study material out in advance of our meetings.

New York

Sharsheret
contact: Risa Shulman
P.O. Box 2276
Stuyvesant Station
New York, NY 10009
(212) 874–4621

We are a grass-roots organization connecting young (twenties and thirties) Jewish feminists with each other. We meet on Rosh Chodesh, and our service generally includes ritual and text study.

Agudat Achim Women's Network (sponsor)
contact: Jenny Frank
2117 Union Street
Schenectady, NY 12309
(518) 374–0434

Meets at different women's homes at 8:00 P.M. between the new moon and the full moon. The hostess decides on the topic for the evening. Past topics have ranged from women in the Bible, Judith, Women at the Wall, to Honoring Difference: Women who work outside the home and those who don't.

We light round floating candles with hopes for the month and extinguish them with what we want to let go of. We recite the Kiddush Levanah outside and say Marcia Falk's blessing for Rosh Chodesh. Our members have a conservative orientation and some have strong feminist feelings while others do not. Most members are mothers with young children, though not all are. We have a strong sense of community.

The Amy Gerstein Rosh Chodesh Study Group of the
 Sisterhood of Congregation Shearith Israel
contact: Dr. Janice E. Ovadiah
8 West 70th Street
New York, NY 10023
(212) 873–0300

Meets in the homes of members on a rotating basis. The Rosh Chodesh Study Group, organized under the auspices of the Sisterhood of the Spanish and Portuguese Synagogue, was created by Dr. Janice E. Ovadiah in the month of Shevat in 1986. The group has an orthodox orientation and meets on the Sunday closest to Rosh Chodesh. The group has methodically been studying Jewish women in the Tanach. One year was also devoted to studying and discussing the mitzvot of women. We are currently studying *Pirke Avot* (*The Sayings of Our Fathers*).

Each meeting begins with a presentation and discussion of the holidays, if any, that are occurring in that particular month. Then a presentation is made by one of the members on the specific theme that had been designated for that session. There is always a lively discussion following the presentation. Approximately ten to twenty women of all ages attend on a regular basis. We are open to all women of the congregation. The specialness of this group can be attributed to the fact that the women who participate have all been learning and growing together and sharing experiences. The sessions end with coffee, tea, and cookies served by the hostess.

Hadassah
contact: Amy Erani
50 West 58th Street, 8th floor
New York, NY 10019
(212) 303–8263

Meets September through May at 8:30 A.M. every Rosh Chodesh at the address above. Hadassah's Rosh Chodesh service is egalitarian. Both men and women count for the quorum. The attendees are women, but we encourage men to come as well. Non-Hadassah members are welcome. The morning Kaddish is recited.

The service is rich and full. On Mondays and Thursdays we read the entire Rosh Chodesh Torah portion. Thoughtful commentaries on the sedra, the Jewish life cycle, and Jewish holidays are presented by participants. Passages in the siddur are explained so that beginners, too, can feel comfortable. Light breakfast refreshments and coffee are served after prayer.

Jewish Women's Resource Center–National Council of Jewish Women, NY Section
contact: Emily Milner
9 E. 69th Street
New York, NY 10021
(212) 535–5900

Meets usually on the first day of the new month at 6:30 P.M. at the address above, but this may vary slightly depending on scheduling. The group is generally made up of about six women of all ages and backgrounds. A different moderator each month leads the participants through an exploration of Jewish spirituality using sources such as *Miriam's Well*. Included in the celebration is a discussion about any number of Jewish feminist topics, symbolic food, singing, dancing, as well as the sharing of aspirations and goals. The group is open to all Jewish women.

Ma'yan: The Jewish Women's Project
contact: Rabbi Sue Levi Elwell
180 West 80th Street
New York, NY 10024
(212) 580–0099

Located at the JCC on the Upper West Side of New York, Ma'yan is an innovative, educational, training, and resource center for women concerned with the future of Jewish life, the Jewish community, and women's place in that community. In addition to several other women's programs, Ma'yan offers a monthly Rosh Chodesh gathering, generally featuring a prominent Jewish woman scholar or artist.

Rosh Chodesh Breakfast Shiur for Women
Gustave Hartman YM-YWCA, Educational Center
contact: Rachel Pill
257 Beach 17th Street
Far Rockaway, NY 11691
(718) 868–2900

Meets on the Monday before each Rosh Chodesh from 9:30 A.M. to 11:00 A.M. We offer an opportunity for women to meet and enjoy a bagel breakfast and an inspiring lecture on topics of interest to Jewish women. This year's lectures will highlight a different woman in Jewish history each month. Everyone is welcome to come and bring friends.

Woodstock Women's Rosh Chodesh group
contact: Ellen Weaver
120 Chestnut Hill Road
Woodstock, NY 12498
(914) 679–9706

Our group is fairly new and is open to new members. We begin with songs and introductions. We use material in our celebrations from many sources. A particular focus of each meeting is journeying into the time and/or place with the ancestral mother we are working with.

contact: Laurie Hoffman
308 Front Street
Upper Nyack, NY 10960
(914) 353–0719

Meets occasionally on Rosh Chodesh. Our group grew out of a Conservative synagogue. We have studied women's issues: prayer, mikvah, tallit, and texts. We have studied the holidays in depth and learned zemirot. The group would like to refocus on an "arts" perspective.

Temple Beth El Rosh Chodesh Group
contact: Sorel Goldberg Loeb
22 Cambridge Circle
Monroe, NY 10950
(914) 782–0835

Our group usually begins its ritual celebration of Rosh Chodesh with a group welcome, and we conclude with an oneg of sweet fruit juices and cakes or cookies (usually round or crescent-shaped). Members of the group often develop specific rituals for months focusing on holidays. For example, for Kislev, Sorel wrote a special meditation for lighting the *chanukiah* (Chanukah menorah). It names and honors women in our tradition. For Adar, the month of Purim, when costumes and masks are worn, Maxine Fraade created a ritual about "what is hidden and what is revealed." Written material may be obtained from the above address.

Ma'ayan Miriam Rosh Chodesh Group
contact: Nancy Schmitz
33 Peel Street
Selkirk, NY 12158
(508) 475–9424

We meet at members' homes for a pot-luck dinner between the new moon and the full moon. Our group is diverse in terms of our Jewish upbringing and our current theologies and levels of observance. We are trying to create and affirm a Jewish feminist perspective on ritual, Torah, midrash, and holiday observance. We light floating candles and honor our mothers and grandmothers. We are eclectic in our liturgy, mixing traditional and new prayers. We also make use of songs, meditative exercises, and innovative ritual. Currently we are focusing on creating midrash to enhance our exploration of Torah and the yearly cycle. We celebrate holidays together, often including our families and have begun tzedakah projects. We do not have a leader, and while we share responsibility for generating topics and readings, we do sometimes invite guests to focus and stimulate discussion. We are not currently recruiting new members but would be pleased to correspond and exchange ideas with other Rosh Chodesh groups.

New Rochelle
contact: Wendy Goulsten
24 Gramercy Place
New Rochelle, NY 10804

Our nine-person group has been meeting for one year on the Sunday evening closest to Rosh Chodesh. The book, by Penina Adelman, *Miriam's Well*, has provided some ideas for our monthly focus and activities. In our three-hour meetings, we move to and from structured ritual and woman talk. We begin by lighting a candle with the blessing "Schechechianu," each invoking our foremothers, then each sharing introspection about the past month and hopes for the coming month. We discuss the month's astrological symbol and our feelings about the Jewish festivals and Parsha themes of the coming month. Sometimes we sing, meditate, draw. We share ideas, laughter, and tears as we discuss the significance of any text we study to our personal lives as Jewish mothers, wives, worshipers, lovers, professionals, and daughters.

Pennsylvania

Tiferet Bet Israel Synagogue
contact: Morris Cohen
Place 1 Apt. 327
777 West Germantown Pike
Plymouth Meeting, PA 19462

If Rosh Chodesh falls on a Sunday, our synagogue Men's club conducts services including the special Torah reading. If Rosh Chodesh is on a weekday, we try to implement a specially organized minyan.

Mishkan Shalom Rosh Chodesh Group
contact: Michelle Friedman
246 W. Upsal Street #G404
Philadelphia, PA 19119
(215) 844-6071

Started just over two years ago, Mishkan Shalom's Rosh Chodesh group just celebrated its anniversary with our congregation's feminist scholar weekend. Our connection to the larger Mishkan Shalom community reflects the openness of our small and fluid group, in which different women lead the rituals every month. Generally, the leader establishes our kavonot (intentions) for our service based on the month's holiday. These usually include candle lighting, water blessings, Jewish angel cards, and matrilineal introductions, which reflect our group's commitment to welcoming the community of Mishkan women.

Contact: Gwen Borowsky
208 Farwood Road
Wynnewood, PA 19096
(215) 649–5118

We try to meet monthly nine times a year. We have some holiday-related rituals (feminist seder), discuss books, go to interesting, Jewish women-related theater and films, bake challah, and talk about being daughters/mothers.

Lehigh Valley Rosh Chodesh Group
contact: Nehira Hoffman
6277 Glenn Avenue
Coopersburg, PA 18036
(610) 967–2722

We hold monthly meetings on the Sunday night closest to Rosh Chodesh. We meet at a member's home and every meeting has a theme. We begin with a circle of candles (one for each woman present) and light them one at a time as we hum a niggun. We recite "A New Kiddush for Rosh Chodesh" by Marcia Falk. (We keep a binder that holds tefillot, brachot, and songs.) We then begin the evening program, which generally focuses on the seasonal holiday. We have used art to explore our differences and similarities and take guided meditations to help us explore our Jewish roots and identities. We laugh, cry, talk, and sing. We end the evening singing Debbie Friedman's version of "Mi Shebeirach." We have forty-five women in our group, spanning the ages of twenty to eighty. We are a creative group of women who support and challenge each other.

contact: Lisa Hostein
2751 Pennsylvania Avenue, no. B104
Philadelphia, PA 19130
(215) 232–5729

Our group is a diverse one, ranging from secular to Orthodox, but with a decidedly feminist perspective. Each session includes short rituals, a pot-luck meal, and discussion focusing on a specific text, book, or creative endeavor.

contact: Lisa Hostein
657 W. Kingsley Street
Philadelphia, PA 10144
(215) 843–1953

We meet at members' homes on the Sunday evening closest to Rosh Chodesh at 7:30 P.M. We are a group of eleven Jewish women who have been meeting since 1990. We have been looking for a balance in celebrating Jewish ritual and exploring our personal lives. We help support and guide each other through life passages. In the time we have been meeting, we have shared joy and great sadness—the births of eight babies, a bat mitzvah and a high school graduation, and college matriculation; four of us have celebrated our fortieth birthdays; three of us have had therapy with our mothers, and one of us lost her mother.

We do have a few constants: we generally start our meetings by putting out snacks on a tablecloth. After everyone has arrived, we sit in a circle around the cloth (and food) and each light a candle in our own candlestick and recite our matrilineage—in Hebrew, English, Yiddish, or some combination. We invoke the names of Berthe, Temma, Frumma Sheina, Basha, Peshie, Zelda, Sophie, Chaya D'vaida, and Gittel. We usually sing at least one song during the course of the meeting. Sometimes we perform or create rituals to mark life events (welcoming a newborn) or Jewish holidays (such as tashlich). For several months in our third year we took turns telling each other our life stories. Lately we have been going around the circle, checking in on the last month's happenings. And for the last two years we have planned weekend outings to give ourselves more time to enjoy each other and deepen our connections.

We have decided not to accept new members.

University of Pennsylvania Hillel
contact: Rabbi Sharon Stiefel
202 S. 36th Street
Philadelphia, PA 19104
(215) 898–7391

Meets at the address above on the evening of Rosh Chodesh. The group is redefined each year by the women in the group. As the group is by and for students, it changes along with the participants.

Bryn Mawr College
contact: Mindy Shapiro
Bryn Mawr, PA 19010
(610) 526–5538

Our group is redefined each year by the women students in the group.

Rhode Island

Temple Am David Sisterhood
    contact: Alice Goldstein
    95 Kiwanee Road
    Warwick, RI 02888

The sisterhood on occasion sponsors and conducts a Rosh Chodesh Shabbat service.

Texas

Temple Emanu-El Rosh Chodesh group
contact: Rabbi Debra Robbins
Temple Emanu-El
8500 Hillcrest
Dallas, TX 75225
(214) 368–3613

Utah

Salt Lake City Havurah Rosh Chodesh
contact: Lisa Goldstein Kieda
386 "F" Street
Salt Lake City, UT 84103
(801) 359–7447

We have been meeting since 1992 and have a mailing list of 37 women. Our monthly attendance is between twelve and fifteen women spanning the ages of late twenties to sixty, with the majority of women of childbearing age. We have become an important resource for women in the Jewish community. We have generally followed rituals and suggestions in Penina Adelman's *Miriam's Well*. We have had two mountain retreats, which have solidified friendships and helped us to unify around births and a death in our group.

Vermont

contact: Judith Chalmer
18 Summer Street
Montpelier, VT 05602
(802) 229–0432

Our Rosh Chodesh celebrations almost always begin by ushering out the old month and ushering in the new with the lighting of a candle. We almost always eat at the end. The format varies depending on who is leading. We all take turns leading and some prefer experiential activities such as meditation and the arts, while others prefer discussion and personal sharing. We are not affiliated with any of the congregational movements and cherish our independence.

Washington

contact: Rabbi Vicki Hollander
7509 39th NE, no. 3
Seattle, WA 98115
(206) 524–0141

We are not currently meeting, but hopefully, our Rosh Chodesh group will resume soon.

Washington, DC

Beth Shekinah
contact: Sarah Buxbaum and Robin Margolis
c/o BiCentrist Alliance
P.O. Box 2254
Washington, DC 20013–2254
(202) 828–3071

We are a Jewish Feminist Women's Spirituality Study Group that holds gatherings for study and Rosh Chodesh.

Appendix J
Musical Notation

In The Dark Rays Of The Moon

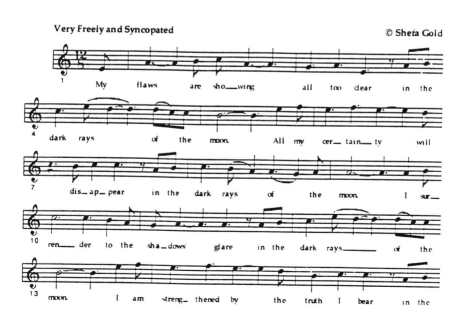

Very Freely and Syncopated

© Sheia Gold

My flaws are sho__wing all too dear in the

dark rays of the moon. All my cer__tain__ty will

dis__ap__pear in the dark rays of the moon. I sur__

ren__der to the sha__dows glare in the dark rays____ of the

moon. I am streng__thened by the truth I bear in the

Sun, Moon and Stars

Birkat HaChodesh

Slowly with devotion

Hassidic
© English words by Linda Hirschhorn

cha__yim she__yesh ba__hem yir__at sha__ma__yim yir__at sha__ma__yim y__

yir____at____chet cha__yim she__en ba__hem bu__sha uch__li__ma

cha____yim shel__o__sher v'__cha____vod cha__yim shet'__he va__nu

a__ha__vat to____ra a__ha__vat to__ra v'__yir__at sha__ma__yim

cha__yim she__y__ma, l'__u mish__a__lot li be____nu l'__to__va a__men se____la

Red Moon Magic

© Geela Rayzel Raphael

31 we drew our pow — er from the red, red moon and in the dark — ness an —

34 gels gui ded us, guard — ing us from dan — — ger and doom. We

37 called up on the name and re — — ar — ranged the let — ters. Mys — ti cal en — chant — ment of fer —

40 ti — li — ty womb pow — er bir — thing our sto — ries e — mer — — ging

43 wea — — ving a thread thru our own ta — pes — try Sha

D.S. al Fine

Rosh Chodesh Moon

© Geela Rayzel Raphael

Grandmother Moon

© Sage Medicine Heart

HaChodesh Hazeh - Rosh Chadesh Song

© Hanna Tiferet
Exodus 12:2

With spirit

A
Ha__ cho. desh ha__ zeh la_chem   rosh cha. da__ shim Ri__

shon hu la__ chem l' chod__ shey ha__ sha_____ nah

B
I give to you the cir. cle of the sea_sons round the sun. And

by the cy__cles of the moon you'll know which month has come. You can make time

sa_ cred when you mea__ sure it with care.

Tell your sto_ ries, sing your songs and ga_ ther close in prayer

C
Ni__ san I__yar Si_van Ta__muz Av E__lul Tis__ hri Hesh-

van Kis__ lev Te_____ vet Sh'vat A____ dar

Glossary

Aliyah means "going up" and refers to the person called to bless the Torah reading. There are four aliyot (pl.) on Rosh Chodesh.

Amidah silent prayer that is part of the three daily services.

Birkat HaChodesh the blessing of the new month.

Birkat hamazon the blessings after the meal.

Bracha blessing.

Bruchim ha'ba-im welcome men.

Bruchot ha'ba-ot welcome women.

Chadesh new.

Chag holiday.

Chalakim a way of measuring time; 1,080 chalakim in each hour.

Chanukiah Chanukah menorah.

Chodesh month.

Chodesh tov a greeting meaning, "Have a good month."

Daven to pray (Yiddish).

Haftarah the readings from the Prophets that are included on Shabbat and holidays.

Haggadah the text read during the Passover seder.

Hallel Praises of God. Hallel are psalms included in the prayer service for Rosh Chodesh and other holidays.

Kabbalah the mystical tradition within Judaism.

Kavanah heartfelt intention.

303

Kiddush   the blessing over the wine for Shabbat and holidays.

Kiddush levana   the physical observance and sanctification of the new moon.

Kotel   the Western Wall, Israel's foremost national religious symbol.

Levana   moon

Maftir   the last aliyah of the Torah reading.

Ma-ot chittim   tzedakah for Pesach.

Mazal   celestial constellation.

Megillah   scroll—generally refers to the Scroll of Esther read at Purim.

Midrash   stories and interpretations of a text.

Mikvah   ritual waters for immersion.

Mishkan   the desert sanctuary.

Mishna   part of the Talmud.

Mitzvah   commandment from God.

Mo-ed   time of gathering, used to describe the Jewish festivals.

Molad   birth. It refers to the moment that the new moon is born.

Musaf   additional part of the prayer service, which replaces sacrificial offerings.

Omer   period of seven weeks between Passover and Shavuot.

Parasha   the weekly Torah portion.

Pardes   orchard. It is an acronym for the four ways of studying a text: a simple reading, what is hinted, the analytic, and the secret meaning.

Pesach   holiday of Passover.

Rechem   womb—the acronym of *R*oshei *Ch*odshi*m* spells *rechem.*

Rosh Chodesh   a holiday marking the beginning of the Hebrew month.

Roshei Chodshim   new months.

Sanhedrin   the high court of seventy judges that heard testimony about the new moon's appearance.

Seder   the Passover ritual and meal that falls on the first two nights of Passover.

Sefirah   mystical attributes of God.

Seudah   a meal. On Rosh Chodesh a festive meal is traditional.

Shabbat   the sabbath.

Shabbat Mevorchim   The Shabbat prior to Rosh Chodesh when Birkat HaChodesh, the announcement of the new moon, occurs during the prayer service.

Shana   year.

Shechinah   God's feminine attributes.

Sh'mot   Exodus, the second book of the Torah.

Shofar   ram's horn blown on Rosh Chodesh Elul and each day until the day before Rosh HaShanah, and then as part of the Rosh HaShanah and Yom Kippur services.

Shul   synagogue.

Sidur   prayer book.

Sukkah   the outdoor structure that is used during the holiday of Sukkot.

Tallit   prayer shawl.

Talmud   an enormous collection of rabbinic and legal discussion from the period 200 B.C.E. to 500 C.E.

Tanach   the *T*orah, *N*evi-im (Prophets), and *K*etuvim (writings).

Tashlich   a service during the afternoon of Rosh HaShanah at waterside. One symbolically casts bread crumbs into the water as a way of acknowledging one's wrongdoings during the previous year.

Tefillah   prayer.

Tikkun   repair of the world.

Tkhine   women's devotional prayers of the sixteenth to early nineteenth centuries.

Torah   the five books given to Moses on Mount Sinai, which include the teachings of Judaism.

Tshuvah   repentence. The word actually means turning, as we turn one to another in seeking forgiveness.

Tu B'Sh'vat   holiday marking the new year of the trees. It is customary to eat the many types of fruit mentioned in the Torah.

Tzedakah   rightousness. The giving of charity.

Tzit-tzit   the fringes on a tallit or *tallit katan* (undergarment tallit), which remind us of God's commandments.

Ushpizin   guests welcomed into the sukkah.

Yare-ach   moon.

Yirah   awe, fear.

Yom Kippur Katan   day preceeding Rosh Chodesh.

Yuntev   a holiday (Yiddish).

Zohar   kabbalistic mystical text of the thirteenth century.

Bibliography
and Resources

Secondary Sources in English

Adelman, Penina V. *Miriam's Well: Rituals for Jewish Women Around the Year.* New York: Biblio Press, 1990.

Alpert, Rebecca. "Our Lives Are the Text: Exploring Jewish Women's Rituals." *Bridges* 2:1 (Spring 1991/5751): 66–80.

Bayerlin, Walter. *Near Eastern Religious Texts Relating to the Old Testament.* London: SCM Press, n.d.

Blumenthal, H. Elchanan. "New Moon, Announcement of." *Encyclopaedia Judaica.* Vol. 12, pp. 1040–1041.

Bridges: A Journal for Jewish Feminists and Our Friends. Available at P.O. Box 18437, Seattle, WA 98118.

Broner, E. M. *The Telling: The Story of a Group of Jewish Women Who Journey to Spirituality through Community and Ceremony.* San Francisco: Harper, 1993.

Brueton, Diana. *Many Moons: The Myth and Magic, Fact and Fantasy of Our Nearest Heavenly Body.* New York: Prentice Hall Press, 1991.

Bushwick, Nathan. *Understanding the Jewish Calendar.* New York: Moznaim Publishing, 1989.

Cain, Kathleen. *Luna: Myth and Mystery.* Boulder: Johnson Books, 1991.

Carnay, Janet, Magder, Ruth, Paster, Laura Wine, Spiegel, Marcia Cohn, and Weinberg, Abigail. *The Jewish Women's Awareness Guide.* New York: Biblio Press, 1992.

Cooper, J. C. *An Illustrated Encyclopedia of Traditional Symbols.* London: Thames and Hudson Publishing, 1978.

————, ed. *Brewer's Book of Myth and Legend.* Oxford: Helicon Publishers, 1993.

Delaney, Janice, Lupton, Mary Jane, and Toth, Emily. *The Curse: A Cultural History of Menstruation.* New York: Dutton and Company, 1976.

Eisenstein, J. D. "New Moon, Blessing Of." *The Jewish Encyclopedia.* Vol. 9, pp. 244–245.

Eliade, Mircea. *The Sacred and the Profane: The Nature of Religion.* New York: Harcourt Brace and World, 1957.

————. "The Moon and Its Mystique." In *Patterns of Comparative Religion,* ed. Mircea Eliade. London and New York: Sheed and Ward, 1958.

Falk, Marcia. *The Book of Blessings: A Re-Creation of Jewish Prayer for the Weekdays, The Sabbath and The New Moon Festival.* San Francisco: Harper, 1995.

Ginsberg, Louis. *Legends of the Jews.* Philadelphia: Jewish Publication Society.

Goelman, Hillel. "The B'nai Yissasschar: A Thematic Translation and Commentary." In *Worlds of Jewish Prayer: A Festschrift in Honor of Rabbi Zalman M. Schacter-Shalomi,* ed. Shoshana Harris Wiener and Jonathan Omer-Man. Northvale, NJ: Jason Aronson Inc., 1994.

Goldman-Wartell, Barbara. "The Development of Rosh Chodesh Liturgy." Unpublished rabbinic thesis, Hebrew Union College, 1985. [Available at the Hebrew Union College Library.]

Graetz, Naomi. *S/He Created Them: Feminist Retellings of Biblical Stories.* Chapel Hill, NC: Professional Press, 1993.

Grahn, Judy. *Blood, Bread and Roses: How Menstruation Created the World.* Boston: Beacon Press, 1993.

Gray, John. *Near Eastern Mythology.* London: Hamlyn Publishing Group, 1969.

Green, Arthur, ed. *Jewish Spirituality.* Vols. 1, 2. New York: Crossroad Publishing, 1987.

Greenberg, Blu. *On Women and Judaism: A View from Tradition.* Philadelphia: Jewish Publication Society, 1981.

Greenberg, Irving. *The Jewish Way: Living the Holidays.* New York: Summit Books, 1988.

Grossman, Susan, and Haut, Rivka. *Daughters of the King: Women and the Synagogue.* Philadelphia: Jewish Publication Society, 1992.

Hacohen, Dvora, and Hacohen, Menachem. *One People: The Story of the East-*

ern Jews. New York: Adama Books, 1986. (Includes descriptions of Rosh Chodesh customs among Mizrachi Jews.)

Hall, Nor. *The Moon and the Virgin: Reflections on the Archetypal Feminine.* San Francisco: Harper and Row, 1981.

Harding, M. Esther. *Woman's Mysteries: Ancient and Modern.* New York: Harper Colophon Books, 1976.

Hayden, Paul. *Queen of the Night: Exploring the Astrological Moon.* Shaftsbury: Element Books, 1990.

Henry, Sondra, and Teitz, Emily. *Written Out of History: Our Jewish Foremothers.* Fresh Meadows, NY: Biblio Press, 1983.

Heschel, Susannah, ed. *On Being a Jewish Feminist.* New York: Schocken Books, 1983.

Hirsh, Samson Raphael. *The Pentateuch.* New York: Judaica Press, 1986. (See Rabbi Hirsh's translation of and commentary on Sh'mot 12:2, pp. 249–250.)

Kaye/Kantrowitz, Melanie, and Klepfisz, Irena, eds. *The Tribe of Dina: A Jewish Woman's Anthology.* Montpelier, VT: Sinister Wisdom, 1986.

Klein, Isaac. *A Guide to Jewish Religious Practice.* New York: Jewish Theological Seminary Press, 1979.

Klirs, Tracy Guren. *The Merit of Our Mothers.* Cincinnati, OH: Hebrew Union College Press, 1992.

Kohler, Kaufman. "New Moon." In the *Jewish Encyclopedia,* ed. Isidore Singer. Vol. 9. New York: Funk and Wagnalls Co., 1912, pp. 243–244.

Koltun, Elizabeth. *The Jewish Woman.* New York: Schocken Books, 1976.

Levi Elwell, Sue. "Reclaiming Jewish Women's Oral Tradition? An Analysis of Rosh Chodesh." In *Women at Worship: Interpretations of North American Diversity,* ed. Marjorie Procter-Smith and Janet R. Walton, pp. 111–126. Louisville, KY: Westminster/John Knox Press, 1993.

Levine, Elizabeth Reznick, ed. *A Ceremonies Sampler: New Rites, Celebrations, and Observance of Jewish Women.* San Diego: Woman's Institute for Continuing Jewish Education, 1991.

Lilith: The Jewish Women's Magazine. 250 West 57th Street, no. 1326, New York, NY, 10019.

Munk, Elie. *The World of Prayer.* New York: Feldheim Publishers, 1963.

Neshama: Encouraging the Exploration of Women's Spirituality in Judaism. P.O. Box 545 Brookline, MA 02146.

Orenstein, Debra. *Life Cycle: Jewish Women on Life Passages and Personal Milestones.* Woodstock, VT: Jewish Lights Publishing, 1994.

Patai, Raphael. *The Hebrew Goddess.* Detroit, MI: Wayne State University Press, 1967. Reprint, 1978.

Phillips, Robert, ed. *Moonstruck: An Anthology of Lunar Poetry*. New York: Vanguard Press, 1974.

Piercy, Marge. *The Moon Is Always Female*. New York: Alfred Knopf, 1981.

———. "At the new moon: Rosh Hodesh." In *Mars and Her Children*. New York: Alfred Knopf, 1992.

Plaskow, Judith. *Standing Again at Sinai: Judaism from a Feminist Perspective*. San Francisco: Harper Collins, 1990.

Plaskow, Judith, and Christ, Carol P. *Weaving the Visions: New Patterns in Feminist Spirituality*. San Francisco: Harper, 1989.

Pogrebin, Letty Cottin. *Debra, Golda and Me: Being Female and Jewish in America*. New York: Crown Publishers, 1991.

Robbins, Debra. " . . . They Shall Serve as Signs for the Set Times. . . . " Unpublished rabbinic thesis on the Hebrew calendar, Hebrew Union College, 1991. [Available at the Hebrew Union College Library.]

Rothkoff, Aaron. "New Moon." *Encyclopaedia Judaica*, Vol. 12, pp. 1039–1040.

Rupp, Joyce. *May I Have This Dance?* Notre Dame, IN: Ava Maria Press, 1992. (This book, written by a member of the Servants of Mary community, looks at prayer on a month-to-month basis. Although it is a Catholic book, some of the discussion and exercises are not Catholic-specific.)

Rush, Ann Kent. *Moon Moon*. New York: Random House, 1976.

Schauss, Hayyim. *The Jewish Festivals*. New York: Schocken Books, 1938.

Schneider, Susan Weidman. *Jewish and Female*. New York: Simon and Schuster, 1984.

Seeds, Michael A. *Foundations of Astronomy*. Belmont, WA: Wadsworth Publishing Company, 1992.

Sered, Susan Starr. *Women as Ritual Experts: The Religious Lives of Elderly Jewish Women in Jerusalem*. New York: Oxford University Press, 1992.

Shelmay, Kay. *Music, Ritual and Falasha History*. Detroit: Michigan State University Press, 1989.

Solomon, Judith. *The Rosh Hodesh Table: Foods at the New Moon*. New York: Biblio Press, 1995.

Spiegel, Marcia C., and Kremsdorf, Deborah Lipton. *Women Speak to God: The Prayers and Poems of Jewish Women*. San Diego: Woman's Institute for Continuing Jewish Education, 1987.

Stone, Merlin. *Ancient Mirrors of Womanhood*. Boston: Beacon Press, 1979.

Strassfeld, Michael. *The Jewish Holidays: A Guide and Commentary*. New York: Harper and Row, 1985.

Trachtenberg, Joshua. *Jewish Magic and Superstition*. New York: Atheneum, 1974.

Umansky, Ellen M., and Ashton, Dianne. *Four Centuries of Jewish Women's Spirituality*. Boston: Beacon Press, 1992.

Walker, Barbara G. *The Woman's Encyclopedia of Myths and Secrets*. San Francisco: Harper and Row, 1983.

———. *The Woman's Dictionary of Symbols and Sacred Objects*. San Francisco: Harper and Row, 1988.

Waskow, Arthur. *Seasons of Our Joy: A Celebration of Modern Jewish Renewal*. New York: Bantam Books, 1982.

———. "Feminist Judaism: Restoration of the Moon." In *On Being a Jewish Feminist*, ed. Susannah Heschel, pp. 261–272. New York: Schocken Books, 1983.

Weissler, Chava. "The Tkhines and Women's Prayer." *CCAR Journal*, Fall 1993, pp. 75–88.

Wenkart, Henny. *Sarah's Daughters Sing: A Sampler of Poems by Jewish Women*. Hoboken, NJ: Ktav Publishing, 1990.

World Union of Jewish Students. *HERitage and HIStory: Visions for an Equal Future*. Jerusalem: World Union of Jewish Students Press, 1993.

Children's Books and Resources

Bernstein, Ellen, and Fink, Dan. *Let the Earth Teach You Torah*. Wyncote, PA: Shomrei Adamah Publications, 1992.

Brown, Margaret Wise. *Goodnight Moon*. San Francisco: Harper and Row, 1947. Translated into Hebrew by Yehuda Meltzer as *Laila Tov Yareach*. Jerusalem: Motzeim L'Or, 1983.

Burns, Marilyn. *This Book Is about Time*. Boston: Little Brown, 1978.

Burstein, Chaya. *The Jewish Kids Catalogue*. Philadelphia: Jewish Publication Society, 1984.

Cornell, Joseph Bharat. *Sharing Nature With Children*. Nevada City, CA: Ananda Publications, 1979.

Dorph, Gail Zaiman, and Holtz, Barry W. *Prayer: A Teacher's Guide to Rosh Chodesh*. In Melton Research Center Graded Curriculum Series, ed. Barry W. Holtz. New York: Jewish Theological Seminary Publications, 1979.

Dorph, Gail Zaiman and Kelman, Victoria Koltun. "Holidays Mitzvot and Prayer: A Teacher's Guide to the Jewish Calendar." In Melton Research Center Graded Curriculum Series, ed. Barry W. Holtz. New York: Jewish Theological Seminary Publications, 1979.

Elkington, John. *Going Green: A Kid's Handbook to Saving the Planet*. New York: Viking Press, 1990.

Ganz, Yaffa. *Follow the Moon: A Journey through the Jewish Year*. Jerusalem and New York: Feldheim Publishers, 1984.

Gregory, Nan, and Ray, Melanie. *Moon Tales*. Audiocassette of Chinese folk-tales performed by Gregory and Ray. Music by Huang Ji Rong. Vancouver, B.C., Canada: First Avenue Studios, 1989.

Grover, Judy, and Wikler, Madeline. *My Very Own Jewish Calendar*. Rockville, MD: Kar-ben Copies, 1993.

Karlin, Mark. *Salmon Moon*. New York: Simon and Schuster, 1993.

Kelman, Vicki. *The Jewish Calendar*. Curriculum material developed for the Milwaukee Association for Jewish Education. 6401 N. Santa Monica St., Milwaukee, WI 53217, 1986.

Sheehan, Kathryn, and Waldner, Mary. *Earth Child Games, Stories, Activities, Experiments and Ideas About Living Lightly on Planet Earth*. Tulsa, OK: Counsel Oaks Books, 1991.

Simon, Solomon. "The Chelmites Capture the Moon." In *The Wise Men of Chelm*. New York: Behrman House, 1973.

Van Cleave, Janice. *Astronomy for Every Kid: 101 Easy Experiments that Really Work*. New York: John Wiley and Sons, 1991.

Weilerstein, Sadie R. *What the Moon Brought*. Philadelphia: Jewish Publication Society, 1945. Reprint, 1970.

Willard, Nancy. *Nightgown of the Sullen Moon*. New York: Harcourt, Brace Jovanovich, 1983.

Additional Resources

American Jewish Congress Feminist Center
    6505 Wilshire Boulevard, Suite 417
    Los Angeles, CA 90048
    213–651–4601

Jewish Women's Resource Center
    9 East 69th Street
    New York, NY 10021
    212–535–5900

Johnson Books—carries a variety of books, posters, calendars, and other paraphernalia associated with the moon.
    1880 So. 57th Court
    Boulder, CO 80301

"Kos Miriam"—"The Cup of Miriam"
    For more information on uses for Jewish rituals, please contact:
    Nishmat HaNashim
    P.O. Box 132
    Wayland, MA 01778

Ma'yan: The Jewish Women's Project
   180 W. 80th Street
   New York, NY 10024
   212-580-0099
Rosh Chodesh Exchange Newsletter
   Adina Levin
   20 Banks Street
   Somerville, MA 02144
SoundsWrite—a clearinghouse for Jewish music.
   Randy Friedman
   6685 Norman Lane
   San Diego, CA 92120
VOCOLOT: Songs of Renewal, Voices of Joy
   A women's a capella group that performs Hebrew and Jewish music.
   c/o Oyster Albums
   P.O. Box 3929
   Berkeley, CA 94703
Women's Institute for Continuing Jewish Education
   4126 Executive Drive
   La Jolla, CA 92037
   619-442-2666

Sources in Hebrew

(Please see Appendix A for additional primary Hebrew sources.)

Abudahem, "Seder Rosh Chodesh," discusses the order of prayers for Rosh Chodesh.

Amos 8:4–5 on working on Rosh Chodesh.

Babylonian Talmud, Hullin 60b, re size of the moon in comparison with sun.

Babylonian Talmud, Megillah 22b, explanation of four aliyot for Rosh Chodesh Torah reading.

Babylonian Talmud, Sanhedrin 42a, blessing of thanksgiving on seeing the new moon.

Baer, Zeligman. *Seder Avodat Yisrael.* Jerusalem: Schocken, 1937.

B'nai Yissasschar.

Brauer, A. *Jews of Kurdistan.* Jerusalem: Maarav Press, 1947.

Eisenstein, J. D. *Otzar Dinim U'Minchagim.* Tel Aviv: Divr, 1970.

Elbogin, Ismar. *HaT'fillah B'Yisrel B'Hitpatchutah HaHistorit.* Tel Aviv: Divr, 1972.

Exodus 12:2.

Exodus Rabbah 15:6—Queen Esther likened to the moon.

Exodus Rabbah 15:24 on Kiddush Levana sanctification of new moon.

Isaiah 66:23—last verse is repeated about new moon as a time for prayer to God.

Jerusalem Talmud, Brachot 9:2, Kiddush Levana.

Jerusalem Talmud, Sanhedrin 5:3, Aruch HaShulhan, Hilchot Rosh Chodesh.

Jerusalem Talmud, Taanit 1:6.

Lipschitz, Chaim U. *Kiddush L'Vono* (text, commentary, law and customs). New York: Maznaim Publishers, 1987.

Mekore Haminchagim no. 38.

Midrash HaGadol, Pinchas 15, on Torah reading.

Minor Tractates of Talmud, Masechet Sofrim 19:9—discussion of the festive *seudah* (meal) on Rosh Chodesh and the additional blessings for the Birkat haMazon.

Mishna Rosh Hashanah 2:5–7.

Mishne Torah, "Hilchot Kiddush HaChodesh."

Moses Maimonides. Mishna Torah 2:8–9, "Sanctification of the Moon."

———. Sefer Z'manim, "Hilchot Kiddush HaChodesh"—how Kiddush HaChodesh was done during the Sanhedrin times.

———. "Hilchot Yesoder HaTorah."

Numbers 10:10, 28:11

Pirke DeRabbi Eliezer, ch. 45

Reischer, Menahem Mendel. *Shaarei Yerushalayim.* Lomberg: S. L. Kugel, Lewin and Company, 1870.

1 Samuel 20:18–42, haftarah for Machar HaChodesh—story of Jonathan and David on new moon

Sefer Hemdat Yamim, Vol. 1, pp. 23b–24a.

Shulchan Aruch/Mishnah Berurah.

Zeven. "HaMu-adim B'Halacha"—Material on the Seudah Rosh Chodesh and on the sighting of the molad.

Notes on
the Contributors

Penina Adelman, author of *Miriam's Well: Rituals for Jewish Women Around the Year*, lives in the Boston area. She has an M.S.W. from Boston University and an M.A. in folklore from the University of Pennsylvania. She has also attended Pardes Institute in Jerusalem. She has a private practice in social work and leads workshops in Jewish ritual.

Arlene Agus, founding executive director of the Poretsky Foundation, was an original member of Ezrat Nashim, the first Jewish feminist organization in the United States. Her 1976 article on Rosh Chodesh is credited with reviving international awareness of this day as a traditional women's holiday.

Matia Rania Angelou is a poet and singer who uses her voice as part of a Jewish women's healing group. Matia is an educational consultant, giving workshops on Jewish values and prayer, writing, and women's spirituality. Dedicated to exploring the various forms of women's spiritual expression, she has helped create life-cycle ceremonies for Jewish women using Kos Miriam, the Cup of Miriam. Matia has been an active member of a Rosh Chodesh group for many years. Because of her interest in creating a safe space for women to learn and grow spiritually, she founded Nishmat haNashim and has also helped birth many Rosh Chodesh and meditation groups.

Roselyn Bell is the publications coordinator of the Coalition for the Advancement of Jewish Education (CAJE) and managing editor of its journal, *Jew-*

ish Educational News. She is former senior editor of *Hadassah* magazine
and a member of its editorial board. She is a member of a women's tefilla
group and the Central Jersey Rosh Chodesh Group. She lives in Edison, New
Jersey, and is the mother of Daniel, Elisheva, and Alexander.

Susan Berrin lives in Victoria, British Columbia, Canada, with her husband,
Victor Reinstein, and their three children, Noa, Yosef, and Tzvia. She is an
avid gardener and active member of her community. Susan is a trained social
worker in gerontology and has produced an audiovisual program for the
Jewish elderly entitled *Jewish Memories.* She is currently collecting materials for a sourcebook on Jewish aging titled *Wisdom from the Heart: Growing Older as a Jew.*

Ruth Brin has written four books of poetry and liturgy, five children's books,
and five libretti for Jewish composers. Reconstructionist, Reform, Conservative, and Jewish Renewal prayer books include her work.

Ellen Brosbe is a Jewish educator in Santa Rosa, California. She is a devoted
reader of James Thurber's *Many Moons* and mourns the fact that one of her
four children no longer wants to be a refrigerator when she grows up. Ellen
finds glow-in-the-dark solar system stickers very helpful when her children
can't fall asleep.

Diane Cohen is the spiritual leader of Temple Bnai Israel, Willimantic, Connecticut. She was ordained by the Jewish Theological Seminary of America
and holds a master's degree in education from the University of Judaism.
Rabbi Cohen's interests include the writing of new Jewish ritual, and she
has been published in *Conservative Judaism* and the *Jewish Bible Quarterly.*

Marcia Falk's recent books include *The Song of Songs: A New Translation
and Interpretation* (Harper San Francisco, 1990), *With Teeth in the Earth:
Selected Poems of Malka Heifetz Tussman* (Wayne State University Press,
1992), and *The Book of Blessings: New Jewish Prayers and Rituals for Daily
Life, the Sabbath, and the New Moon Festival* (Harper San Francisco, 1995).
She is currently working on further volumes of liturgy; the next to appear
in the series will be *The Book of Blessings for the Turning of the Year: A
Re-Creation of Jewish Prayer for the High Holiday Season.*

Merle Feld is an award-winning playwright, poet, social activist, and long-
time Jewish feminist. She has had her poetry published in, among other
places, *Tikkun* and *Sarah's Daughters Sing.* She has helped to start Rosh
Chodesh groups in New Jersey and New York.

Maxine Fraade lives in upstate New York. She writes rituals for her Rosh
Chodesh group.

Barbara Gingold (photographs accompanying the chapter, "Nashot HaKotel")
is a photographer living in Jerusalem. She currently works at the David Yellin
Teachers College in public relations.

Judith Glass (B.A., Barnard College; Ph.D., University of California at Los Angeles) has held a number of teaching and administrative positions in higher education including director of the M.B.A. program at the University of Judaism and acting director of the Institute for the Study of Women and Men at the University of Southern California. A labor economist by training, she has just completed a project that has been published by the Institute of Industrial Relations at the University of California at Los Angeles in two volumes: *Working in the 21st Century: Gender and Beyond* and *Encountering the Glass Ceiling: Gender, Values and the Structure of Work.* Judith is a member of the board of commissioners for the American Jewish Congress Feminist Center and a founding member of Shabbat Shenit, a feminist minyan in Los Angeles, and of Bat Kol, an annual feminist spiritual retreat.

Hillel Goelman received s'micha from Rabbis Zalman Schachter-Shalomi, Shlomo Carlbach, and Akiva Mann. A member of the Or Shalom community in Vancouver, Hillel is also a teacher in the faculty of education at the University of British Columbia. He is married to Sheryl Sorokin, is the father of Zach and Nadav, and thinks a lot about time.

Shefa Gold is a senior rabbinical student at the Reconstructionist Rabbinic College and an active participant in the Pnai Or Religious Fellowship. She is also on the faculty of the Jewish Renewal Life Center in Philadelphia. Shefa is a composer and performer of spiritually oriented music and has just produced her sixth album. Her liturgy has been published in several prayer books.

Ruth Berger Goldston is a psychologist and a former chair of the National Havurah Committee. She has been an occasional contributor to *Lilith*. With others, she was involved in starting a Rosh Chodesh group in Princeton, New Jersey.

Nancy Lee Gossels is a writer living near Sudbury, Massachusetts.

Blu Greenberg writes and lectures on issues of contemporary Jewish interest. She lives with her husband, Irving Greenberg, in Riverdale, New York. She is the author of *On Women and Judaism: A View from Tradition* and most recently, *Black Bread: Poems After the Holocaust.*

Bonna Devora Haberman is a philosopher, Jewish educator, and social activist. She received her Ph.D. in moral philosophy and education from the University of London. Bonna is the founder and director of a Jerusalem experimental educational project, *Tsohar*, a Jerusalem elementary school and teachers' seminar. She is the mother of five children. She is currently a scholar-in-residence in women's studies at Brandeis University.

Linda Hirschhorn is a singer, songwriter, and cantorial soloist. She is a member of VOCOLOT, a women's a capella quintet, which performs Hebrew and English songs. Linda, a graduate of a New York yeshiva, received musical training in Jerusalem, New York, and San Francisco. She currently lives in Berkeley, where she has recorded four albums of original songs.

Vicki Hollander, who was ordained in 1979, was among the first wave of women to enter the rabbinate. She currently guides Congregation Eitz Or in Seattle. Trained as well as a marriage-and-family therapist, she also works as the bereavement coordinator at Hospice of Seattle. Rabbi Hollander weaves the creation of ritual and poetry. Her work can be found in *Four Centuries of Jewish Women's Spirituality, Redefining Sexual Ethics*, and *The World of the High Holidays*.

Shonna Husbands-Hankin is a Judaica artist living in Eugene, Oregon, with her husband and two daughters. She calligraphies ketubot and paints silk sacred garments such as tallitot and chuppot. Her Torah mantles, Ark curtains, and chuppah designs enhance the beauty of several synagogues.

Norma Baumel Joseph is a member of the faculty in the department of religion at Concordia University, Montreal. For the past eighteen years she has been teaching, lecturing, and publishing on women and Judaism, Jewish law and ethics, and women and religion. She founded the Montreal Women's Tefillah group. She has lobbied for Jewish women's rights in a variety of contexts, forming local and international groups to further these goals. Currently, she is president of the International Coalition for Agunah Rights (ICAR). She is also a director of the International Committee for Women of the Kotel (ICWK). Norma appeared in and was consultant to the film, *Half the Kingdom*. Norma lives in Montreal with her husband, where she raised four children.

Irena Klepfisz has been an activist in the lesbian and Jewish communities for the past twenty years. She is the author of *A Few Words in the Mother Tongue: Poems Selected and New* and *Dreams of an Insomniac: Jewish Feminist Essays, Speeches and Diatribes*. Committed to the recovery of Jewish women activists and intellectuals in Yiddish-speaking communities in Eastern Europe and the United States, she serves as editorial consultant on Yiddish language and culture for the Jewish feminist magazine *Bridges*.

Tracy Guren Klirs was born in 1955 in Vancouver. She was raised in Vancouver, San Mateo, and Seattle. She recieved her B.A. in Yiddish literature at the University of Chicago and graduated Phi Beta Kappa in 1977. She was ordained as a rabbi from the Hebrew Union College Jewish Institute of Religion in Cincinnati in 1984. She currently serves as director of education and youth at Agudas Achim Congregation in Alexandria, Virginia. Her book, *The Merit of Our Mothers: A Bilingual Anthology of Jewish Women's Prayers*, was published by HUC Press in 1992. She is married to Elisha Guren Klirs and has three children, Lior, Carniel, and Talya.

Suzanne Kort lives in Victoria, British Columbia, Canada, with her husband and two children. She has worked as a technical writer, an environmentalist, and as a therapist for chronic pain patients. Since becoming a full-time parent, she has coauthored two travel books with her husband, continues to write poetry and fiction, and has discovered a renewed interest in her Jewish heritage. Besides the earth, the moon is her favorite natural phenomenon.

Suri Levow Krieger is a musician and teacher of music at a Solomon Schechter Day School in New Jersey. She lives with her family in Demarest, New Jersey.

Maxine Kumin is the author of ten collections of poetry, most notably *Up Country*, which won the Pulitzer Prize in 1973, and *Looking for Luck*, which was awarded the Poet's Prize in 1994. She served as consultant to the Library of Congress in 1981–1982 and has taught at universities ranging from Princeton to Brandeis. She and her husband live in central New Hampshire, where they raise horses.

Yehudah Landesman (translator of Chaim Vital's poem, "Kiddush Levono") was raised in London, England. He has explored a wide spectrum of religious disciplines within Judaism. He is currently involved with the Jewish Renewal Movement. He lives in the California Bay Area with his wife and daughter.

Ruth Lerner: Listen, she said from her home in Los Angeles, this is who I am—I laugh, I cry, and I like to create poetry that reflects and celebrates the Jewish feminine. Married? Yes. Kids? Yes. Fresh flowers and herbs? Yes. Snorkeling and sun? Yes, Yes, Yes!

Lyn Lifshin is the author of many books of poetry, including *Tangled Vines*, *Upstate Madonna,* and, most recently, *Marilyn Monroe.* She lives in Vienna, Virginia.

Jane Litman is on the faculty of California State University at Northridge and rabbi of Congregation Kol Simcha of Orange County. She is chair of the Southern California Religious Coalition for Abortion Rights and spearheads its "No Need to Hide" campaign, a program to support doctors and other health care workers targeted for harassment by the radical Right.

Sorel Goldberg Loeb is a Jewish educator and author. She is the cofounder of Mentsch Makers Preschool and the coauthor of *Teaching Torah—A Treasury of Insights and Activities* (Alternatives in Religious Education, Denver, 1984). In 1993 she founded the Rosh Chodesh group at Temple Beth El in Monroe, New York, where she lives with her husband and two children.

Sage Medicine Heart is a native healer and writer. She is the only non-Jewish contributor to this anthology.

Lesléa Newman is a fiction writer, poet, and editor, with sixteen books to her credit. Her work frequently explores Jewish themes. Her titles include "A

Letter to Harvey Milk" (short story), *In Every Laugh a Tear* (novel), and
*Bubbe Meisehs by Shayneh Maidelehs: An Anthology of Poetry by Jewish
Granddaughters about Our Grandmothers.*

Leah Novick is an author, ritualist, and spiritual teacher whose work is focused
on restoring the Shechinah to contemporary Jewish practice. She began leading Rosh Chodesh groups in the early 1980s in Berkeley and has continued
to present New Moon ceremonies and workshops around the country. Rabbi
Leah lives in Carmel, on the beautiful central coast of California, where she
often celebrates Rosh Chodesh at the beach. It is rumored that she includes
otters, seals, and dolphins in her davening.

Geela-Rayzel Raphael, rabbi of Center City Reconstructionist Congregation
and director of the graduate student project of Hillel of Greater Philadelphia, is also currently studying at the Reconstructionist Rabbinical College
in Wyncote. She has also studied at Hebrew University, at Brandeis University, and the Pardes Institute. Geela-Rayzel would love to be a Jewish
feminist rock 'n' roll star, transforming Jewish tradition with music. Rosh
Chodesh is one of her primary forms of spiritual practice. She has started
Rosh Chodesh groups in Tennessee, Toronto, and Philadelphia.

Victor Hillel Reinstein is father to Noa, Yosef, and Tzvia; husband to Sue;
and rabbi to the people of Congregation Emanu-El in Victoria, British Columbia.

Carol Rose is a writer, educator, workshop facilitator, counselor, and mother
of five children. She lives in Winnipeg, Manitoba. Her manuscript, "Jerusalem: Another Version of the Story," is nearing completion with the help of
a Manitoba Arts Council grant. She won second prize in the Stephen Leacock
International Poetry competition for 1994. Carol plans to return to Jerusalem soon to study with her mentor, Madame Colette Abulker-Muscat.

Judith Rose has a dream: to share her prayer-poetry with Jewish women of
the world. The dream is being fulfilled in Rosh Chodesh circles around Los
Angeles. She recently sent her prayer-poems to Russia with her daughter.
Her upcoming book, *Prayers for Wholeness*, will be available from Dark
and Light Press.

Rosie Rosenzweig, a Boston-based liturgical poet with an M.A. in American
and British literature, has been published in *Genesis 2*, *Vetaher Libaynu* (the
first nonsexist prayer book), *Sarah's Daughters*, and *Ethical Wills*. She has
been writing a column called "From the Back of the Shul" for the past twenty-
five years for Congregation Beth El of Sudbury. Presently, she designs and
conducts workshops for people of all ages. As founder of the Jewish American Women's Poetry Festival, she has been invited to a University of Ala-
bama Conference on Marge Piercy to talk about "Jewish Feminism: A Paradigm Shift." She is proud to have been born Canadian in Windsor, Ontario.

Susan Starr Sered is a senior lecturer in the Department of Sociology and Anthropology at Bar-Ilan University in Israel. Her publications include *Women as Ritual Experts: The Religious World of Elderly Women in Jerusalem* and *Priestess, Mother, Sacred Sister: Religions Dominated by Women,* both published by Oxford University Press. She and her family are currently conducting fieldwork on the Ryukyu Islands.

Hanna Tiferet Siegel was ordained in 1982 as an *Eshet Hazon* and *Miyoledet Neshama*—"A Woman of Vision and Midwife of the Soul." She writes music, sings songs, and dances in the light of the moon. Hanna lives in the northeastern United States and serves as a teacher and scholar-in-residence for Jewish spiritual retreats.

Charlotte Atlung Sutker is a psychologist who lives in Victoria, British Columbia, Canada. She is a member of Congregation Emanu-El, which is a national historic site and the oldest synagogue in Canada in continuous use. Her community is small and isolated, but she enjoys the emotional and spiritual support of a small group of Jewish women.

Louis Sutker is a jew–poet–psychologist–family man now living in Victoria, British Columbia, Canada.

Celia Szterenfeld was born in 1958. She has an M.A. and M.Ed. in counseling psychology. Celia lives in Rio de Janeiro, where she works at the Institute of Religious Studies, a nonprofit, nongovernmental organization, where she coordinates projects on health, education, and human rights aimed at marginal groups—prostitutes, transvestites, the gay community, and prison inmates. Celia also participates in the Espirito da Coisa group, an interracial, interreligious women's dialogue group at Rio de Janeiro's Council of Jewish Women. She has a private practice for women only and is coeditor of the periodical *Pardes*, which focuses on Jewish spirituality.

Chaim Vital (1542–1620) was born in Eretz Yisrael and became one of the great kabbalists and scribes of his day. He was a principal disciple of Isaac Luria in Safed. He was a prolific writer, mainly of esoteric subjects.

Simone Wallace is cofounder of the Sisterhood Bookstore of Los Angeles, one of the first feminist bookstores in the United States. She cofounded Bat Kol and Shabat Shenit, the Jewish women's spiritual groups. She lives in Venice, California.

Robin Zeigler received her Ph.D. in clinical psychology from the University of Illinois at Chicago in 1985. She works part-time as a consultant to Jewish Family Services of Richmond, Virginia. She is also a free-lance writer and writes a column for the local Jewish newspaper. Her particular interests lie in the areas of psychology, Judaism, spirituality, and women's issues. She and her husband, Dr. Jonathan Ben-Ezra, reside in Richmond with their two children, Eliana Malka and Akiva Dov, and their dog, Holly.

Credits

Permission to reprint the following material is gratefully acknowledged:

An earlier version of the chapter "Examining Rosh Chodesh: An Analysis of the Holiday and Its Textual Sources" appeared as "This Month Is for You" by Arlene Agus in *The Jewish Woman*, ed. Elizabeth Koltun. Published by Schocken Books. Copyright © 1976 Arlene Agus. Used by permission of the author.

"Ancestors' Song" and "Dark Rays of the Moon" by Shefa Gold from the audiocassette *Abundance*. (Available from Shefa Gold at P.O. Box 355, Las Vegas, NM 87701.) Copyright © 1989 Shefa Gold. Used by permission of the author.

"A New Moon/Full Moon Meditation" copyright © Judith Rose. The first stanza of this poem was written in 1988. The remainder of the poem was written in 1979. They were combined as a meditation in 1990. Used by permission of the author.

"A Rosh Chodesh Bracha" by Penina Adelman and Suri Levow Krieger from the audiocassette *Chodesh Chodesh B'Shir*. Copyright © 1984 Penina Adelman and Suri Levow Krieger. Used by permission of Penina Adelman.

"At the new moon: Rosh Hodesh" by Marge Piercy from *Mars and Her Children*. Published by Alfred Knopf. Copyright © 1992 Marge Piercy. Used by permission of the publisher.

"The New Moon" by Ruth Brin from *Harvest Collected Poems and Prayers*. Published by Reconstructionist Press. Copyright © 1986 Ruth Brin. Reprinted by permission of the author.

"The New Moon Time: A Love-Song for the Schechinah" by Rosie Rosenzweig was commissioned by women congregants at Congregation Beth El, Sudbury, MA, and read at one of their ceremonies for the new moon, 1990.

"The Origins of Rosh Chodesh: A Midrash" from *Miriam's Well: Rituals for Jewish Women Around the Year*. Published by Biblio Press. Copyright © 1990 Penina Adelman. Used by permission of the author.

"they did not build wings for them" by Irena Klepfisz from *A Few Words in the Mother Tongue: Poems Selected and New (1971–1990)*. Published in Portland by Eighth Mountain Press. Copyright © 1990 Irena Klepfisz. Reprinted by permission of the author.

"Tkhine texts and translations" from *The Merit of our Mothers: A BiLingual Anthology of Jewish Women's Prayers* by Tracy Guren Klirs. Published in Cincinnati by Hebrew Union College Press. Copyright © 1982 Hebrew Union College Press. Reprinted by permission of the publisher.

Translations of Birkat HaChodesh, Psalm 104, and Hallel are from the siddur *Hadesh Yameinu* by Rabbi Ron Aigen. Used by permission of the author.

Translations of Kiddush Levana and the Rosh Chodesh additions to the weekday and Shabbat musaf adapted from *The Complete ArtScroll Siddur*. Copyright © 1984 ArtScroll/Mesorah. Used by permission of the publisher.

Translation of "Ya-aleh v'yavo in Appendix D is by Rabbi Daniel Siegel.

"Wings of Peace" by Aryeh Hirschfield copyright © 1980. Used by permission of the author.

The lines from "Paula Becker to Clara Westhoff" are reprinted from *The Dream of a Common Language: Poems 1974–1977* by Adrienne Rich. Copyright © 1978 W.W. Norton & Company, Inc. Used by permission of the author and W.W. Norton & Company, Inc.

The poems "Rosh Chodesh Sh'vat" and "Rosh Chodesh Nisan" as well as the lines from the poems "Songs and Teachings of the Spring and Summer Moons" and "Rosh Chodesh Tevet" by Rabbi Vicki Hollander are used by permission of the author.

Woman at Rosh Chodesh is one of a series of watercolors on women and the moon by Phyllis Serota. It was commissioned by Susan Berrin for *Celebrating the New Moon* and is used with permission by the artist. Information regarding other works of painter Phyllis Serota is available through the artist at 128 Montreal Street, Victoria, British Columbia, Canada V8V 1Y8.

Index

teachings of, xxviii–xxix
textual sources, visual diagram of,
    203–205
tkhines (women's prayers) for,
    xxix–xxx, 19–20, 49–65
women and, xvi–xvii, xxiv, xxix–
    xxx

Schachter-Shalomi, Zalman, 44,
    120, 127
Scholem, Gershom, 126
Sefardic women, Rosh Chodesh
    observances of, 78–80
Segal, Seril bas Yankev Halevi, 50,
    52, 53
Sered, Susan Starr, xxix, 78–80
Shapira, Tzvi Elimelech, 40
Shofar, Rosh Chodesh and, xxiii
Shulamay, Kay, 19
Siegel, Hanna Tiferet, 197
Simon, Solomon, 98
Singer, Isaac Bashevis, xiii
Sioux Indians, moon symbol, xxxiii
Soloveitchik, Joseph B., xvii
Sore bas Toyvim, 50, 51
Stein-Azen, Margot, 146
Sutker, Charlotte Atlung, xxx, 107–
    110
Szterenfeld, Celia, xxx

Tefillah Group, Rosh Chodesh, 111–
    116
Teitz, Emily, 119
Time, bridges in time, *B'nai
    Yissasschar*, 47; *see also*
    Chronology

Tkhines (women's prayers), 49–65
    for blessing of new moon, 56–58
    examples of, 58–64
    overview of, 49–55
    for Rosh Chodesh, xxix–xxx,
        19–20, 55–56
Torah, Rosh Chodesh and, xxiii
Tree of life, *B'nai Yissasschar*,
    42

Vital, Chaim, 199–201

Wallace, Simone, 23–32
Werbemacher, Hana Rachel, 20
West, Vita Sackville, xxxiv
Whitman, Walt, xxxiv
Wiccan practices, moon symbol,
    xxxiii
Women
    Hallel and, 83
    moon symbol and, xxvii
    Rosh Chodesh and, xvi–xvii,
        xxiv, xxix–xxx
    work and, 6–8
Women's prayer. *See* Tkhines
    (women's prayers)
Work, women and, 6–8

Yehudah Hanasi, 9
Yom Kippur Katan, Rosh Chodesh
    preparation, 125–129
Yosef, Ovadiah, 82

Zeigler, Robin, xxvii, 33–39
Zeitlin, Hillel, 10
Zot, B'nai Yissasschar, 43–44

About the Editor

Susan Berrin teaches and lectures on Jewish issues, specifically in the areas of Jewish women, aging, and interfaith dialogue. She also teaches Jewish ritual and life skills. She has developed and produced audiovisual materials, including "Jewish Memories," a reminiscence program for Jewish elderly, and is currently working on an anthology, *Wisdom from the Heart: Growing Older as a Jew*. Berrin is a graduate of the University of California, Santa Cruz, and received her master's degree in social work from Boston University. She lives in Victoria, British Columbia, with her husband and three children. She has been involved with Rosh Chodesh groups in Jerusalem and Victoria.